Industrialists in Olive Drab:
The Emergency Operations
of Private Industries During
World War II

Ohly receiving a civilian meritorious service award from Under Secretary of War Robert P. Patterson for a job well done!

Industrialists in Olive Drab

The Emergency Operation
of Private Industries During World War II

by

John H. Ohly

Edited by Clayton D. Laurie

CENTER OF MILITARY HISTORY
UNITED STATES ARMY
WASHINGTON, D.C., 2000

Library of Congress Cataloging-in-Publication Data

Ohly, John H. (John Hallowell), 1911–1990
    Industrialists in olive drab : the emergency operation of private industries
during World War II / by John H. Ohly ; edited by Clayton D. Laurie.
      p. cm.
    Includes bibliographical references and index.
    1. World War. 1939–1945—United States. 2. United States—Armed
Forces—Mobilization. 3. United States. War Dept. 4. Industrial
mobilization—United States—History—20th century. I. Laurie, Clayton D.
(Clayton David), 1954–   . II. Title.
D769.2.038 1999
940.54'1273—dc21   99–28479
                                                                  CIP

First Printed 1999—CMH Pub 70–32–1

For sale by the Superintendent of Documents, U.S. Government Printing Office
Washington, D.C. 20402

Foreword

World War II was a war of production as well as of battles, campaigns, and strategies. As the United States Army faced its greatest challenge abroad in the form of the Axis military threat, soldiers and civilians on the American home front met an equally serious challenge: keeping the fighting men and the Allies supplied with the weapons, munitions, and other materiel needed to achieve victory.

When vital war production was threatened by some of the most serious labor-management disputes in American history, the War Department intervened quickly and decisively, taking physical control of the affected industrial facilities and operating them under federal authority. Although the length and depth of that control varied with the severity of the dispute, the nature of the enterprise, and the importance of the industry to the war effort, the federal government was at least able to continue production without resorting, as in the past, to the use of armed force.

This, then, is the story of a small group of individuals in the War Department who were charged with the mission of guaranteeing that private companies provided the military goods that had been promised. Initially prepared by the individual most closely involved with this effort, John H. Ohly, this history shows how combined military and civilian teams, well-schooled in law and in modern business management, financial, and arbitration practices, settled repeated disputes without significant delays in production or, when necessary, operated war plants in the name of the federal government, peacefully and efficiently.

The development and implementation of procedures for the temporary but direct military supervision of private industries during World War II represented an innovation in the ever-growing role of the U.S. Army and the federal government in the production of war materiel. Although the work of Ohly and his compatriots was part of an expanding partnership of government and private industry, their experiences were in many ways unique. Grappling with difficult civil-military problems during a period of great national stress, they devised highly creative solutions—ones that still speak to us today and ones that will provide guidance in the future. For soldiers and civilians currently in the field of procurement, the following story thus has many lessons, not the least being the resolution of conflicting interests between the needs of the state and those of the private sector within the framework of our constitutional democracy.

Washington, D.C.
1 June 1998

JOHN W. MOUNTCASTLE
Brigadier General, USA
Chief of Military History

The Author

John "Jack" H. Ohly was born in New York City in 1911 and was educated at Brooklyn Friends School, Williams College, and Harvard Law School. After completing his education, he taught briefly at Harvard and then spent four years as a law clerk for Breed, Abbott, and Morgan, a New York City law firm. His career with the federal government began in mid-September 1940, when he moved to Washington, D.C., to take a position with the War Department in the office of newly appointed Assistant (later Under) Secretary of War Robert P. Patterson.

From the fall of 1940 until well after V–J Day (September 1945) John Ohly was deeply involved with manpower, labor relations, and other labor problems affecting the missions of the War Department, first in the Office of the Under Secretary of War and then in the Labor Relations (later Labor) Branch, Civilian (later Industrial) Personnel Division, Headquarters, Services of Supply (later Army Service Forces). His primary responsibility during those years was the development of War Department policies and procedures for the seizure and operation of private industrial, communications, and transportation facilities at which actual or threatened interruption of operations constituted, or would likely constitute, a threat to the prewar national defense buildup or subsequent war effort. His position required that he act as the general overseer of actual seizure operations from the Washington headquarters. As the plant takeover business wound down after V–J Day, Ohly was assigned to write the history of War Department seizure operations. His efforts over a span of four months during the winter of 1945–46 produced a monumental draft history.

In early June 1946, following the Eisenhower reorganization of the War Department, John Ohly, at age thirty-five, became the top civilian special assistant to Patterson, now the secretary of war. In this new position Ohly encountered increased responsibilities unrelated to his wartime plant seizure work, and he later described the first fifteen months in this new job as being tantamount to "going from the frying pan into the fire."[1] Among many other assignments, he was loaned to the White House in December to act as the executive secretary to President Harry S. Truman's newly created blue ribbon advisory commission on Universal Military Training, directed by MIT President Karl T. Compton.

The unification of the U.S. armed forces had a pivotal effect on Ohly's career. By the time the Compton Commission delivered its report to President Truman in May 1947, the National Security Act of 1947 was already working its way through Congress, the culmination of years of discussion and debate. When the act was

---

[1] Ltr, Ohly to Laurie, 22 Aug 89, Ohly files, U.S. Army Center of Military History (USACMH), Washington, D.C.

signed into law by the president on 26 July, thereby creating the National Military Establishment (in August 1949 renamed the Department of Defense), and when James V. Forrestal was sworn in as the first secretary of defense on 17 September, John Ohly became one of Forrestal's three statutory special assistants along with lawyer Marx Leva and budget expert Wilfred J. McNeil. Ohly's past work in the War Department, his knowledge of Army and Air Force affairs and service needs, and his role as a special assistant to the secretary of war were crucial factors in his appointment, which served to mitigate Army and Air Force criticism that Forrestal's new office was overwhelmingly composed of transplanted Navy personnel from his days as secretary of the Navy.

In this new job Ohly carried out an ever-expanding number of functions as the Office of the Secretary of Defense (OSD) grew in importance during the early years of the Cold War. Ohly saw to the needs of the Committee of Secretaries, a civilian counterpart of the Joint Chiefs of Staff consisting of the three civilian military secretaries; he acted as secretary of the War Council, a committee consisting of the secretary of defense, the armed forces' chiefs of staff, and the civilian service secretaries who advised the secretary of defense on broad military policy; and he served as secretary to the group representing the National Military Establishment on the National Security Council. In addition, Ohly did developmental staff work for the National Security Council, for what would become the Department of Defense, and later for the North Atlantic Treaty Organization. One of Ohly's most important functions during these early months, however, was to act as Forrestal's eyes and ears as liaison with the National Security Resources Board, the Munitions Board, the Research and Development Board, and the National Security Council. All of these responsibilities were in addition to Ohly's job as supervisor of the OSD's Office of the Secretariat and the Special Programs Division. He met all challenges and exceeded all expectations. According to one OSD staffer, "Jack Ohly was a secret weapon. He could turn out more good work under great pressure than any man I have ever seen."[2]

Eight months after Forrestal's resignation in late March 1949 Ohly left the Office of the Secretary of Defense for the Department of State, where he became the deputy director of the Mutual Defense Assistance Program. He later became the assistant director and later deputy to the director for policy and program development in the Office of the Director of Mutual Security. During this period Ohly worked with foreign aid programs and was instrumental in coordinating Marshall Plan economic aid with American military aid, thereby creating an international security system.

In late 1953 Ohly became the deputy director for programs and planning with the Foreign Operations Administration of the State Department, a post he held for two years. Joining the International Cooperation Administration (ICA) in 1955, he

---

[2]For a detailed examination of Ohly's postwar career with the Department of Defense, see Steven L. Rearden, *The Formative Years, 1947–1950*, History of the Office of the Secretary of Defense (Washington, D.C.: Historical Office, Office of the Secretary of Defense, 1984). Quotation from page 65.

remained on the staff when the ICA became the independent Agency for International Development in 1961. He retired from government service in 1968.

In private life John Ohly continued research on foreign aid programs and policies before retiring for a second time in 1976. Thereafter he lived in McLean, Virginia, and Williamstown, Massachusetts, where he died in September 1990. He was eulogized by family friend and former Defense Department colleague Najeeb E. Halaby as a man who did not talk about doing things but simply did them. "The wise men of that period," Halaby stated, "had very wise aides, whether it was Stimson, or Patterson, or Forrestal, or Acheson, or Marshall, or Lovett, or McCloy, or Averell Harriman. Behind every one of these wise, effective men was a wise man, Jack Ohly. . . . One of his colleagues in that late 40's period . . . told me Jack was 'the most brilliant man I ever worked with—the most effective and yet the most anonymous.'" Halaby concluded with the words that "World War II was won by U.S. production, which Jack Ohly helped assure through [the] labor management work he did."[3]

[3]Remarks of Najeeb E. Halaby at Memorial Service for John Hallowell Ohly (1911–90), 29 Sep 90, Meeting House of the First Congregational Church of the United Church of Christ, Williamstown, Mass., Ohly files, USACMH.

The Editor

Clayton D. Laurie received a B.A. in history at the University of Northern Iowa in 1977 and taught American history and government in Council Bluffs, Iowa, until 1984. He earned an M.A. in history at the University of Nebraska in 1982 and a Ph.D. in history at the American University in 1990. Since joining the U.S. Army Center of Military History in 1986, he has taught at the American University and the University of Maryland in Baltimore County. He is the author of *The Role of Federal Military Forces in Domestic Disorders, 1877–1945*; *The Propaganda Warriors: America's Crusade Against Nazi Germany*; and, a forthcoming work, *The U.S. Army and Psychological Warfare Operations, 1918–1945*. He is completing several volumes for the Center, including one that describes the medical and disaster relief missions of the U.S. Army. Dr. Laurie was awarded a Secretary of the Army Research and Study Fellowship in 1994, at which time he began writing two World War II histories—one on the War Department's Military Intelligence Division and the other on the Allied Intelligence Bureau in the Southwest Pacific. He also has published over twenty-five articles on various military history topics.

Preface

John Ohly's history, originally entitled "The Emergency Operation of Private Industrial Facilities by the War Department During World War II," recounts the story of the War Department's participation in the nationwide seizure and operation of private industries deemed vital to the Allied war effort. As he states in his Introduction, the concept of having the War Department seize American firms producing goods crucial to Army programs worldwide was a radical innovation, one that had not been attempted on a large scale at any prior time in American history. The technique constituted a milestone in the still evolving doctrine dealing with federal military involvements in civil affairs, especially interventions in labor-management disputes and domestic disturbances. It further represented a new departure for the federal government, which had previously hesitated to intervene in routine labor-industrial conflicts, viewing such disputes as being beyond the purview of a democratic government in a free market economy or as a function better performed by the states except in extraordinary or extreme cases. This attitude changed immediately prior to World War II, and as a result the War Department's seizure of plants idled by or threatened with labor unrest or management noncompliance with federal policies developed into a major U.S. Army domestic function during the course of the conflict. Initial War Department takeovers were fraught with problems and pitfalls as soldiers and civilians in the War Department sought to define legal parameters and acquire the business and labor-management skills essential for such operations. By V–J Day, however, after nearly five years of effort, these skills had been mastered and the process so well refined that most seizure cases were routine.

In the decades since this history was written its value has grown significantly. Because it describes the War Department's initial failures and later accomplishments with wartime plant seizures, its original purpose was to provide federal military and civilian agencies with a how-to guide for implementing and conducting such operations to maintain vital war production. But this study is particularly valuable as a unique first-person account of the war effort on the American home front during World War II from a military perspective. Foremost, it offers a look at the state of wartime labor-industrial relations, an area of American social and economic life that was undergoing major transitions during the 1930s and 1940s. Second, it presents a clear picture of the War Department's domestic role between 1940 and 1945, when small teams of technically skilled Army officers and civilians trained in business management and labor-industrial relations were utilized rather than the combat troops so frequently seen during the previous seventy years of labor dispute interventions. And lastly, it provides the reader with a detailed look at the complex state of wartime civil-military relations in the United States. Ohly contributes much useful insight into the internal workings of the War Department, especially the labor branches of the Office of the Under Secretary of War, of the Army Service Forces, and of the Army Air Forces, and their interactions with other federal agencies and private industries concerned with American war production. Whether his participation in the events he describes has left a residue of organizational or analytical bias is something only the reader can decide.

The production of Ohly's history in its present form involved many individuals over the course of five decades. Kent Roberts Greenfield, the Army's Chief Historian in 1945–46, showed the initial interest while Ohly was still completing the study for the Office of the Under Secretary of War. In late 1947, before a final draft could be given to the Army's Historical Division for future publication as part of the United States Army in World War II series, Ohly was made a special assistant to the secretary of defense and could no longer work full-time on the project. He turned over the relevant documents and the incomplete manuscript to the Historical Division, where Jonathan Grossman began the task of reviewing the volume. But in 1948 work on the project was delayed because several of the cases described (such as those concerning Montgomery Ward) were the subject of possibly renewed litigation. It was the opinion of the U.S. attorney general that publication would prejudice pending government cases. Second, many of the individuals involved in the cases themselves were still living and active in defense matters and private labor-industrial affairs. On this point the Department of Justice ruled that publication of the history, which contained details of delicate negotiations and controversial subjects, would not be in the best interests of the parties involved, especially the federal government and the Department of the Army. Most important, however, was the fact that the cited documents were still classified in the late 1940s for reasons of national security and therefore could not be made public. In consideration of these obstacles, and because Ohly was still in government service, preventing his direct input, the plant seizure manuscript was set aside.

The Office of the Chief of Military History revived interest in Ohly's history in the 1960s and further work was done by Stetson Conn, the Chief Historian. But the growing American military involvement in Vietnam and the quickening production of the U.S. Army in World War II series prevented the manuscript from moving forward. In the late 1970s Stanley F. Falk and Maurice Matloff of the U.S. Army Center of Military History (CMH) again raised the issue, holding that the now declassified Ohly manuscript was suitable for publication. Many of the individuals discussed in its pages had retired from public life or had died, and the legal statute of limitations on all cases had long since expired. During the mid-1980s, as the Center of Military History continued work on its three-volume history of the role of federal military forces in domestic disorders, interest in publishing the Ohly manuscript as a complementary volume was considered by Acting Chief Historian Morris J. MacGregor, Jr. In 1989 I was assigned the somewhat daunting task of editing and revising Ohly's history.

Preparing the manuscript for publication in a form suitable for the general reader presented several editorial challenges. As with other War Department reports of the 1940s, Ohly wrote his monumental history quickly, largely in the passive voice, using a then-standard extended narrative outline format. Unfortunately, even though he participated in the events described, the text was often repetitive and in places unclear, providing little information as to the identity, importance, or background of the primary participants and organizations involved. Ohly also included each cited document in appendixes of over one thousand pages and listed all seven hundred plus endnotes in consecutive order in one comprehensive section at the end of the work. Intended only for internal War Department use, no attempt was made at the time to simplify or consolidate the manuscript's original chapter organization or documentation; to remove repetitious material; to correct misspellings and grammatical errors; or to confirm titles, ranks, company names, union affiliations, or other technical data.

Although significant differences exist between this edited and revised version and Ohly's original work, his research, recounting of events, basic facts, and interpretations remain unaltered. I made only those changes that were necessary to render the text more readable, to clarify events and technical points, and to identify and confirm the accuracy of information concerning organizations and characters unknown to present-day readers. I also made a conscious effort to improve upon Ohly's original organization and to delete repetitious material in the text, appendixes, and documentation.

Specifically, I converted the original manuscript from a narrative outline to narrative prose, removing in the process much of the passive voice while still maintaining Ohly's recounting of events and his interpretations. In chapters that repeated information previously covered I either deleted or substantially edited them, and also combined several extremely short chapters dealing with general events with larger chapters concerning specific seizures. To identify various participants and organizations known to Ohly but probably not familiar to present-day readers, I added explanatory numbered footnotes throughout each chapter where necessary, based on research from both primary and secondary sources. I separated and renumbered Ohly's original endnotes by chapter, retaining the form of chapter endnotes and identifying each number in parentheses in the text. To avoid repetition and improve clarity, I edited and combined the endnotes. Although now in abbreviated form, the pertinent information contained in the endnotes is in this volume. Finally, the list of the copious appendixes found in the original manuscript follows the Conclusion. To facilitate the understanding of present-day readers, I selected eighteen appendixes for inclusion in this volume. Each is identified by the letter and title given in the list. Appendixes D–2, D–3, E–1, E–3, and E–4 are photographic reproductions of the author's original graphs.

With the publication of this volume Ohly's original manuscript and supporting documentation will be retired to CMH's Historical Resources Branch, where it will be made available to future researchers.

In addition to those individuals already mentioned as having been closely connected with this study since it first reached the Army's Historical Division in the late 1940s, I am indebted to my fellow CMH colleagues who provided outstanding assistance in preparing this volume for publication. Joanne M. Brignolo offered excellent editorial services and critical advice to improve the overall narrative, while Roger Wright, John Birmingham, Sherry L. Dowdy, and Beth F. MacKenzie used their respective photographic, design, cartographic, and desktop publishing skills to craft the book. Thanks also go to summer intern Jodi C. Robinson for her proofreading support and to contractor Susan Carroll for her preliminary editorial services and the useful index.

As always, for any errors that may be found, I alone accept responsibility.

Washington, D.C.   CLAYTON D. LAURIE
1 June 1998

Contents

Charts

Map

Illustrations

But for the three illustrations from the Library of Congress that appear on pages 21 and 183, all others are from the National Archives and Records Administration.

Industrialists in Olive Drab

Introduction

This monograph purports to tell the story of the War Department's participation in the emergency operation of private industrial facilities during World War II. It is the story of what is commonly referred to as plant seizures(1)—a dramatic story that constituted an important part of wartime industrial relations.

The War Department was the seizing authority in about half of the plant takeovers of World War II. Even in those in which it played the major part, it cooperated with many other government agencies. This book does not purport to be a complete history of plant seizures in World War II, but rather it is an account of the Army's role in the field.

Seizures were emergency measures generally employed only in situations in which it was of great importance to the government, for any of several reasons, to maintain the production or service involved and in which other less drastic measures had failed or were impractical. The cause of the interruption or threatened interruption varied from case to case—labor disputes, incompetent management, or insolvency, among others. It so happened that the cause of every War Department seizure during World War II was a labor dispute, and as a result this history restricts itself to discussing seizures of that character. The Navy Department was involved in seven takeovers completely unrelated to labor conditions,(2) and three of the War Department's four World War I seizures were likewise of a nonlabor origin.(3)

The importance of the plant seizure technique during World War II should not be underestimated. During the National Emergency Period and for the first two years of the war the ultimate significance of plant seizures as an emergency war measure was not apparent. Until the late fall of 1943 the War Department was engaged in only four of these operations(4) and the entire government in barely a dozen. Moreover, four of these had taken place before the war, three were for nonlabor reasons, and another occurred outside the continental United States.(5) Plant seizure seemed destined to be one of the many curious oddities of wartime. However, in 1944 and 1945 seizing plants developed into a major government business, which by V–J Day in September 1945 included the operation of at least twenty-four enterprises nationwide administered by six different federal agencies, eleven by the War Department alone.(6) In the period from June 1941 to V–J Day the government undertook sixty separate seizures. Moreover, during the remainder of 1945 there were four additional seizures, and the practice continued into early 1946. Many of these seizures were of a multiple character in the sense that either they involved a large number of concerns—such as the cases involving American railroads, coal mines, and midwestern trucking companies and the post-V–J Day

Navy seizure of the facilities of some thirty major oil companies(7)—or they embraced a large number of separate properties of a single company.(8) Almost two million American workers were affected by the twenty-nine War Department seizures, and perhaps three quarters of a million more were employed in facilities seized by other federal agencies. Long before V–J Day plant seizure was the principal technique of the government for restoring or maintaining industrial peace in critical facilities where serious strikes were in progress or were threatened. In the three months before V–J Day the government was taking over approximately one plant a week, and in a score of other situations seizures were averted only at the last minute or because the war ended.(9)

The question of plant seizure was handled on a very informal basis by a small group of persons involved with the problem for the duration. This small group included Brig. Gen. Edward S. Greenbaum, a partner in the New York law firm of Greenbaum, Wolff, and Ernst, who, as a lieutenant colonel, was Under Secretary of War Robert P. Patterson's representative in the North American Aviation case and who later, as executive officer for the under secretary, personally supervised and directed the last twenty-five War Department plant seizures; Edward F. McGrady, vice president of the Radio Corporation of America and a former assistant secretary of labor, who served as a special consultant to the secretary of war on labor matters in each case; Col. Karl R. Bendetsen, JAGD, who, as a major, functioned as judge advocate in the North American Aviation and Air Associates cases; Julius H. Amberg, special assistant to the secretary of war and one of the foremost lawyers in Michigan, who was extremely active at headquarters and contributed much of the important thinking on the subject; Lt. Col. Paul M. Hebert, dean of the University of Louisiana Law School, and Maj. (later Lt. Col.) Victor Sachse, a leading member of the Louisiana bar, who together developed the plant seizure manual, directed the legal aspects of all but the first two seizures, and served as the principal judge advocates in the field; Maj. Joseph W. Bishop, Jr., JAGD, who in a civilian capacity with the Labor Section, Office of the Under Secretary of War, in 1941 and 1942 conducted research into the War Department's experience with plant seizure in World War I and did a great deal of the initial thinking on the subject; and Col. Curtis G. Pratt, vice president of the New York advertising firm of Young and Rubicam, who, as the War Department's representative, initiated many valuable reforms in field organization and operating techniques. Others—such as Maj. (later Lt. Col.) A. H. Raskin, labor reporter for the *New York Times*; Washington attorney Lt. Col. Daniel L. Boland; Lt. Col. John H. Savage, Jr.; and Harold A. Wythes—made important contributions to certain technical phases of the work, respectively public relations, labor, disbursing, and fiscal matters.

● ● ● ● ● ● ● ●

It is fortunate that source materials on plant seizures are extensive and complete. At an early date, both at headquarters and in the field, a system of reporting and recording was adopted that resulted in comprehensive, well-organized files on nearly every seizure and on most technical phases of the subject. With the exception of the first three cases, official daily or weekly reports were made by War Department representatives to headquarters. These took the form of activity summaries telephoned late each evening, or each week when there was little change in the situation, to the Office of the Provost Marshal General and distributed by that office the following morning to all interested headquarters components, including the under secretary of war, the commanding general of the Army Service Forces (or Army Air Forces), the judge advocate general, the fiscal director, the deputy chief of staff for service commands, the commanding general of any service command involved, the directors of the Industrial Personnel and Military Intelligence Divisions of the Army Service Forces, and the chief of any technical service concerned. These reports constitute an excellent, brief summary of most seizures, although they often do not reflect the reasons for action taken or the preliminary discussions that preceded such action. Such matters were ordinarily covered in separate informal reports, in official requests for instructions and subsequent replies, or in telephone conversations recorded in headquarters memoranda that likewise were widely distributed. From the outset the War Department representative also filed comprehensive preliminary, interim, and final reports,(10) each in a more or less standardized form with all significant documents attached, organized, and indexed.(11) Extensive files were maintained in each of the divisions at headquarters concerned with seizures, and particularly by the Industrial Personnel Division and its predecessor organizations. Both sets of records contain memoranda and other unofficial communications that deal with important substantive problems that ordinarily were only mentioned in official communications.

Perhaps the single most valuable general and special source of material on the subject is to be found in the successive editions of the War Department manual entitled "Emergency Operation of Industrial Facilities," prepared by the Judge Advocate General's Department in cooperation with other War Department components, principally the Office of the Fiscal Director, the Industrial Personnel Division, and the Office of the Under Secretary of War.(12) The successive editions clearly show the evolution of plant seizure thinking and practice, even though some statements were not concurred upon by all concerned and the manual could not be revised with sufficient frequency to reflect all developments. It should be noted that this history was written largely relying on the files of the Industrial Personnel Division, which included virtually all headquarters documents, copies of the regular reports to the provost marshal general, and the preliminary, interim, supplemental, and final reports of War Department representatives. Field files were not extensively examined. Three cautions that bear on the historical validity of what is written should be added. First, the history is undoubtedly slanted from the standpoint of the Industrial Personnel Division, where it was prepared. Second, the history was written almost exclusively by referring to documents, and practically no consultation was had with the participants in the various seizures. Finally, much information has been supplied out of the writer's own memory without documentation or acknowledgment of this fact.

Endnotes

(1) The War Department avoided using the term *plant seizure* early in the war for fear that it might give the erroneous impression of an arbitrary commandeering of private property. This accounts for the cumbersome title of the War Department manual on the subject, "Emergency Operation of Industrial Facilities." Nonetheless, the term *plant seizure* persisted and was used universally by the press to describe these operations.

(2) Brewster Aeronautical Corporation, EO 9141, 1942, 7 F.R. 2961; Triumph Explosives, Inc., EO 9254, 1942, 7 F.R. 8333; Howarth Pivoted Bearings Company, EO 9351, 1943, 8 F.R. 8097; Remington Rand, Inc. (Southport, N.Y., properties), EO 9399, 1943, 8 F.R. 16269; Los Angeles Shipbuilding and Drydock Corporation, EO 9400, 1943, 8 F.R. 16641; Lord Manufacturing Company, EO 9493, 1944, 9 F.R. 12860; York Safe and Lock Company, EO 9416, 1944, 9 F.R. 936.

(3) Liberty Ordnance Company, Federal Enameling and Stamping Company, and Mosler Safe Company.

(4) North American Aviation, Inc. (1941); Air Associates, Inc. (1941); S. A. Woods Machine Company (1942); and Fairport, Painesville, and Eastern Railroad (1942).

(5) Of the other agency operations seven were for labor reasons: Federal Shipbuilding and Drydock Company (Navy, 1941), Three Ships (Maritime Commission, 1941), General Cable Corporation (Navy, 1941), Toledo, Peoria, and Western Railroad Company (ODT, 1942), the coal mines (Interior, 1943–45), American Railroad Company of Puerto Rico (ODT, 1943), and Atlantic Basin Iron Works, Inc. (War Shipping Administration, 1943); and three were for nonlabor reasons: Brewster Aeronautical Corporation (Navy, 1942), Triumph Explosives, Inc. (Navy, 1942), and Howarth Pivoted Bearings Company (Navy, 1943).

(6) *War Department*: Montgomery Ward and Company, Inc. (miscellaneous properties in Detroit, Mich., Portland, Oreg., Chicago, Ill., San Rafael, Calif., St. Paul, Minn., Jamaica, N.Y., and Denver, Colo., engaged in civilian retail and mail-order business); S. A. Woods Machine Company, South Boston, Mass. (manufacturing woodworking machinery and shells); Cudahy Brothers Company, Cudahy, Wisc. (meat processing and packing); Farrell-Cheek Steel Corporation, Sandusky, Ohio (steel foundry); Hughes Tool Company, Houston, Tex. (leading manufacturer of oil well drilling equipment); Cocker Machine and Foundry Company, Gastonia, N.C. (textile machinery); Gaffney Manufacturing Company, Gaffney, S.C. (textiles); Mary-Leila Cotton Mills, Inc., Greensboro, Ga. (textiles); U.S. Rubber Company, Detroit, Mich. (tires); Bingham and Garfield Railway Company, Bingham, Utah (spur railroad serving the largest U.S. copper mine); and Springfield Plywood Corporation, Springfield, Oreg. (plywood). *Navy Department*: San Francisco machine shops, San Francisco, Calif. (one hundred shops doing a variety of war work, principally subcontracting for ship repair and construction); United Engineering Company, San Francisco, Calif. (ship repair and construction); Goodyear Tire and Rubber Company, Inc., Akron, Ohio (tires and miscellaneous rubber products); Lord Manufacturing Company, Erie, Pa. (rubber engine and instrument mounts for aircraft); Los Angeles Shipbuilding and Drydock Corporation, Los Angeles, Calif. (shipbuilding); and Howarth Pivoted Bearings Company, Philadelphia, Pa. (bearings). *Petroleum Administration for War*: Cities Service Refining Company, Lake Charles, La.; Humble Oil and Refining Company, Ingleside, Tex.; Pure Oil Company (Cabin Creek Oil Field), Dawes, W.Va.; Texas Company, Port Arthur, Tex.; and Sinclair Rubber, Inc., Houston, Tex. (all oil producing or refining facilities, or closely related thereto). *Interior Department*: Miscellaneous coal mines in Kentucky and West Virginia. *Office of Defense Transportation*: Toledo, Peoria, and Western Railroad Company, Chicago, Ill. (belt railroad); Midwest Motor Carrier Systems (eighty-one trucking companies in the Midwest); Cartage Exchange of Chicago (being a large share of all trucking companies in Chicago, Ill.).

(7) EO 9412, 1943, 8 F.R. 17395, in connection with the American railroads; EOs 9340 (1943, 8 F.R. 5695), 9469 (1944, 9 F.R. 10343), 9474 (1944, 9 F.R. 10815), 9476 (1944, 9 F.R. 10817), 9478 (1944, 9 F.R. 11045), 9481 (1944, 9 F.R. 11387), 9482 (1944, 9 F.R. 11459), 9483 (1944, 9 F.R. 11601), 9536 (1945, 10 F.R. 3939), and 9548 (1945, 10 F.R. 5025), all relating to coal mines; EO 9462, 1944, 9 F.R. 10071, relating to midwestern truckers; and EO 9639, 1945, 10 F.R. 12592, relating to oil companies. Other illustrations include the thirteen leather manufacturing companies in

Salem, Peabody, and Danvers, Mass. (EO 9395B, 1943, 8 F.R. 16957); the seven textile mills in Fall River, Mass. (EO 9420, 1944, 9 F.R. 1563); the one hundred machine shops in San Francisco (EOs 9463 and 9466, both 1944, 9 F.R. 9879 and 9 F.R. 10139), and the Toledo, Ohio, Mechanics Educational Society of America case (plants of eight companies) (EO 9496, 1944, 9 F.R. 13187).

(8) Montgomery Ward and Company, Inc. (properties in seven cities) (EO 9508, 1944, 9 F.R. 15079); Navy oil seizure (see note 7); coal mines (see note 7); and Department of Water and Power of the City of Los Angeles (water and utility system covering a large part of southern California, and with properties in Nevada) (EO 9426, 1944, 9 F.R. 2113).

(9) Some of the major threats that nearly developed into seizures during the closing months of the war were: Kelsey-Hayes Wheel Company, Detroit, Mich. (Apr 45); Dodge plants of the Chrysler Corporation, Detroit, Mich. (Mar 45); LaCrosse Rubber Company, La Crosse, Wis. (May 45); Western Foundry Company, Chicago, Ill. (May 45); Minnesota Railroad and Warehouse Commission, St. Paul, Minn. (Jun 45); Lane Cotton Mills, New Orleans, La. (Mar 45); Pacific Gas and Electric Company, Calif. (Apr 45); Shell Oil Company, Houston, Tex. (May 45); Briggs Manufacturing Company, Detroit, Mich. (Mar 45); Pan-American Refinery, Texas City, Tex. (Jul 45); Solvay Process Company, Syracuse, N.Y. (Jul 45); Firestone Tire and Rubber Company, Akron, Ohio (Jul 45); United Fuel Gas Company, Charleston, W.Va. (Jul 45); Pennsylvania Electric Company (Jul 45); Libby-Owens-Ford Glass Company and Pittsburgh Plate Glass Company (all plants) (Jul 45); Dodge Division of Chrysler, Chicago, Ill. (Jul 45); Wright Aeronautical Products Company, Paterson, N.J. (Jul 45); and Page Steel and Wire Division of American Chain Company (Apr 45). In the three cases first mentioned plant seizure teams had already arrived at the city of the proposed takeover when the need for action was averted. In several other cases personnel had been briefed and a plan of action prepared. Earlier cases in which the War Department had an interest, and where seizure was seriously contemplated, include: American Car and Foundry Company, Berwick, Pa. (recurrently); Centrifugal Fusing Company, Lansing, Mich. (Jul 44); Condensor Corporation, South Plainfield, N.J. (Apr 42); Detroit Edison Company, Detroit, Mich. (Jan 45); Eastern Massachusetts Street Railways (Sep 44, May 45); Little Brothers Foundry, Port Huron, Mich. (Nov 44); Los Angeles Street Railways (Aug 44); Mosher Steel Company, Dallas, Tex. (Spring 45); Dayton, Ohio, to Washington, D.C., regional telephone strike (Nov 44); Detroit foremen strike (May 44); U.S. Rubber Company, New Bedford, Mass. (Dec 44); Steel industry (Dec 43); Aluminum Company of America [Alcoa], Cleveland, Ohio (recurrently during 1941–43); Illinois Ordnance Plant, Carbondale, Ill. (recurrently); Pacific Electric Railway Corporation, Los Angeles, Calif. (Sep 43); Windsor Manufacturing Company, Philadelphia, Pa. (Feb 43); Western Cartridge Company, East Alton, Ill. (May 42); Celanese Corporation, Newark, N.J. (Apr 43); Capital Transit Company, Washington, D.C. (recurrently on issue of discrimination). See Appendix BB–16 for a partial list of key personnel who participated in plant seizures.

(10) While such reports were less formal and complete, in the first three cases they are adequate for most purposes. These reports were usually mimeographed, bound, prepared, and distributed in large numbers, the original going through the commanding general to the adjutant general.

(11) Copies of the more important documents were usually made in at least quintuplicate, and sets were forwarded to each interested division of the War Department at the conclusion of a case. The originals went to the adjutant general.

(12) Earliest drafts were entitled "Military Operation of Industrial Plants." See Memo, Lt Col Hebert, sub: Revision of Plant Seizure Manual, March 1944, which was prepared in the Industrial Personnel Division.

CHAPTER 1

Early Planning for Plant Seizures

The early months of 1941 witnessed an unprecedented outbreak of strikes that was critical from the standpoint of the national defense program. A natural consequence was extensive, though uncoordinated and somewhat superficial, consideration by all agencies, particularly those most directly affected, of all the possible techniques that might be employed by government if any of these situations should become a serious threat to the war effort. This study was given much impetus by the celebrated Allis-Chalmers strike, which began in January 1941 and continued into April. The Minneapolis plant of this company was one of the key facilities in the defense program, and a halt in its production was potentially the most disastrous of the entire war period because of its impact on the destroyer program. The protracted inability of the Office of Production Management[1] or the National Defense Mediation Board (NDMB)[2] to make any progress in effecting a settlement resulted for the first time in serious consideration of a government seizure. Because the Navy had the primary interest and would serve as the seizing agency, and because a return to work occurred shortly after seizure began to be considered, the War Department did little active planning in connection with this case or against the possibility of some similar future contingency.

The Labor Section in the Office of the Under Secretary of War (OUSW)[3] did, however, undertake research into War Department experiences in World War I and

---

[1] The Office of Production Management (OPM) was established within the Office of Emergency Management by Executive Order 8629, 7 January 1941, to formulate and execute measures to increase, coordinate, and regulate production of defense materials and to provide emergency plant facilities. It was abolished by Executive Order 9040, 24 January 1942, when its personnel, records, property, and funds were transferred to the War Production Board. See Richard J. Purcell, *Labor Policies of the National Defense Advisory Commission and the Office of Production Management, May 1940 to April 1942* (Washington, D.C.: Government Printing Office, 1946); and U.S. Civilian Production Administration, *Industrial Mobilization for War: History of the War Production Board and Predecessor Agencies, 1940–1945* (Washington, D.C.: Government Printing Office, 1947). For OPM records, see Record Group 179, National Archives and Records Administration (NARA), Washington, D.C.

[2] The National Defense Mediation Board was established by Executive Order 8716, 19 March 1941, to approve all changes in wage rates; settle all labor disputes affecting the war effort; and provide, by binding order, the terms and conditions governing the relations between parties in any labor dispute. It was abolished after the creation of the National War Labor Board by Executive Order 9017, 12 January 1942. See U.S. Department of Labor, Bureau of Labor Statistics, *Report on the Work of the National Defense Mediation Board* (Washington, D.C.: Government Printing Office, 1942). For NDMB records, see Record Group 202, NARA.

[3] The Labor Section, OUSW, was created on 25 February 1941 to formulate—in coordination with the Navy, Maritime Commission, Department of Labor, Office of Price Administration, Advisory Commission of the Council of National Defense, and Federal Security Administration—War Department labor policies, study labor problems, collect information on labor matters (especially disputes), represent the War Department in dealings with other agencies on labor matters, and advise the secretary of war. For OUSW records, see Record Group 107, NARA.

considered several general aspects of the problem. This study was stimulated by current events and the knowledge that the technique had been used with great success in the famous Smith and Wesson case. The scanty War Department files on World War I seizures were examined, together with articles in legal and other periodicals, by attorney Joseph W. Bishop, Jr., and resulted in several scholarly reports accompanied by important original documents. Bishop's reports on World War I plant seizures were historical and analytical, and they constituted an important influence on the subsequent development of the takeover technique and formed a basis for many parts of the plant seizure manual prepared two years later.(1) Most of the studies, however, were not completed until mid-June 1941, after the War Department had been plunged suddenly into its first case.

The Civil War had seen the federal takeover, pursuant to special legislative authority, of northern railroads and telegraph lines. This action was undertaken because the seized systems were within a theater of operation and were needed for military use and not because of labor difficulties or management failures. In World War I there were four takeovers of this type, as well as simple requisitions for governmental use or convenience of the physical facilities of two other concerns.(2)

The most significant case was that of the Smith and Wesson Company, a small arms manufacturing concern located in Springfield, Massachusetts. It was the sole instance of a plant seizure resulting from labor difficulties. The employees struck after the company had discharged an entire workers committee that had recently requested wage increases and then successively dismissed various individuals who were believed to be union organizers. Because of the importance of the plant the War Department endeavored to mediate the dispute and, upon failing to do so, referred the matter to the National War Labor Board (NWLB),[4] which granted a portion of the employees' wage demands and directed the company to accept the principle of collective bargaining. The company informed Secretary of War Newton D. Baker that it would not recognize the decision. This caused a major crisis because the company's production was vital to the war effort and because this was the first test case of situations involving management defiance of government labor policies. Moreover, it came at the same time as the first serious instance of labor defiance in the so-called Bridgeport case.(3) Baker, acting under the provisions of Section 120 of the National Defense Act of 1916,(4)[5] placed a compulsory order on the company directing it to manufacture forthwith the goods called for

---

[4]The National War Labor Board was established by President Woodrow Wilson on 8 April 1918 following labor-management sessions seeking to adopt procedures for the peaceful, nondisruptive settlement of wartime labor disputes. In addition to creating the NWLB, the agreements included acceptance of closed shops, union organization, and the freezing of hours, wages, and working conditions for the duration. The joint chairmen of the NWLB were William Howard Taft and Frank P. Walsh. Between 30 April 1918 and 31 May 1919 the NWLB heard 1,245 cases. See Valerie J. Connor, *The National War Labor Board: Stability, Social Justice, and the Voluntary State in World War I* (Chapel Hill: University of North Carolina Press, 1983). For NWLB records, see Record Group 2, NARA.

[5]Section 120 of the National Defense Act of 1916 (39 Stat. 166, 213; 50 U.S.C. 80) was approved on 3 June 1916 and authorized the president to place compulsory orders for military supplies during wartime, or when war was imminent, with any firm capable of producing them. The president was further authorized to take possession of any company that did not give the government preference or that failed, or refused, to fill government orders.

under contracts already in effect, but upon the condition that these contracts be performed "under conditions as to labor prescribed by the United States Labor Board." The strength and legal validity of this order was reinforced by the presence in the War Department's contract of a provision that bound the company to accept the terms of any settlement of a labor dispute imposed by the secretary of war.(5) Upon the company's refusal to comply with the order, the War Department, acting under Section 120, took possession of the properties. The company acquiesced in and virtually invited such action and the employees, upon seizure, promptly returned to work.(6) The scope of the requisition is not clear, although it appears that the property seizures were limited to those assets deemed necessary to the actual operation of the facilities and did not include intangibles, such as bank accounts and securities.

The method of operation was unique. Rather than undertaking operation of the plant itself or engaging some outside company, the War Department turned management of the properties over to the National Operating Corporation. This was a company organized by the federal government under the laws of Delaware for the purpose of handling "plants commandeered by the United States in those cases where a competent contractor could not be engaged on a satisfactory basis." All the directors were Army Ordnance officers. This corporation took Smith and Wesson's properties under a contract that provided that it would furnish the materials still undelivered on the basis of cost plus a $1 profit. While the corporation ostensibly operated as a private enterprise, entering into contracts with outside concerns and treating its employees as nongovernmental workers, it was financed entirely with federal funds. The United States held title to all properties, and the corporation was subject by the specific terms of its contract to a high degree of control by the chief of ordnance over outside contracts for materials, methods of operation, costs, and wage increases. It was a dummy corporation in every sense of the word, a device adopted in lieu of direct government operation in order to free the employees from Civil Service restrictions and to avoid the complications of financing a direct government operation.(7)

The government successfully operated the plant until early 1919 when it was returned to the owners. The production rate had been slightly increased (although costs had also risen), primarily because the corporation placed in effect the wage increases directed by the NWLB, which the company had refused to accept. Following termination there were lengthy hearings before the War Department Board of Appraisers on the company's claim against the government for reasonable compensation for the use and occupancy of its properties under the provisions of Section 120 of the National Defense Act. The company was awarded a sum of $673,225.28 as contrasted with its claim for $2,180,349.88. Despite the disparity in amounts, Smith and Wesson never appealed the award.

The three other World War I seizures in which the War Department was involved were not the result of labor disputes. The Federal Enameling and Stamping Company of McKees Rocks, Pennsylvania, was seized late in 1918, when the company, which manufactured booster casings, fuse sockets, and fuse socket holders, informed the Ordnance Department that due to insolvency it would close within days. Its properties were turned over to the National Operating Corporation following a short period of direct government operation, during which the general principles and practices followed in government arsenals were applied. The other two plants, the Liberty Ordnance Company of Bridgeport, Connecticut, and the Mosler Safe Company of Hamilton, Ohio, were commandeered because of the inability or unwillingness of the particular companies to produce vital war materials at reasonable prices. In both of these cases a different approach was taken and the properties were turned over to going concerns for operation, rather than to the National Operating Corporation—Liberty Ordnance to the American Can Company and Mosler Safe to the American Rolling Mill Company. The contract with American Can provided that the contractor receive reimbursement for costs but no compensation for the performance of the contract. The United States was to furnish any capital required and to bear the entire cost, including a fixed sum per month for the contractor's general administrative and overhead expenses in addition to those directly incurred in plant operation. In some respects the operating contract resembles the kind of contract used in the case of government-owned, privately operated plants during World War II.

The experience garnered from studying these cases led to several conclusions concerning the best techniques for seizing and operating properties, how to handle administrative procedures within the War Department, and the best manner of compensating owners for commandeered properties.(8) It was assumed, although with certain reservations, that the government was empowered to seize properties during labor disputes that interfered with vital production. There were doubts, however, about the propriety of doing so under Section 120 of the National Defense Act or under the comparable Section 9 of the Selective Training and Service Act.[6] The assumption rested on the belief that the wartime constitutional powers of the president were sufficient. The study of the Smith and Wesson case indicated that great care should be taken to limit seizure to the property actually required to carry out the war production involved so as to minimize the danger of unnecessary costs, stating "no part of the plant should be seized which is not affected by the cause of the seizure and which is not so inextricably associated with the properties seized that it would be impossible to operate the two under different managements." The report suggested language for inclusion in any executive order to surmount any uncertainties as to what properties could, and should, be seized while at the same time providing for considerable flexibility of action on the part of the secretary of war. It emphasized the desirability of an inventory at the earliest possible moment and suggested a segregation of those properties to which absolute title was taken from those the United States took for only temporary use. This would simplify the problem of computing reasonable compensation for use and occupancy at the termination of government possession.

---

[6]Section 9 of the Selective Training and Service Act of 16 September 1940 (54 Stat. 892; U.S.C. App. 309), known as the "seizure section," repeated the main points of Section 120 of the National Defense Act of 1916.

As to method of operation, Bishop outlined at least three basic types of approach. The first was direct operation by the government of the properties taken in the same manner as a federal arsenal. This procedure necessitated complicated bookkeeping and was aggravated by rules concerning the use of government funds imposed by Congress or the comptroller general. It also required the substitution of Civil Service rules and regulations for the practices of private industry and any collective bargaining arrangements that might exist. These difficulties made this type of operation undesirable where other alternatives were available. A second method was that followed in the Liberty Ordnance Company and the Mosler Safe Company cases. This method too was objectionable, first because the arrangement with the American Can Company did not work out in an entirely satisfactory fashion. Both the company and the government apparently expected the other to take proper steps for the preservation of the physical property of Liberty Ordnance, with the result that upon conclusion of manufacturing operations neither did, and the plant went to rack and ruin at great expense to the United States. The second objection lay in the difficulty of finding a corporation willing to operate the properties of another company, particularly if the seized company was a competitor. This approach was particularly undesirable in cases where labor troubles were the cause of the seizure because the managing corporation might be severely handicapped in any negotiations with employees at the seized properties by the necessity of keeping in mind the effect upon labor relations in its own operations. The third method was that adopted in the Smith and Wesson case—simply turning the properties over to a dummy corporation created for managing seized plants. This method had the advantages, like the second method, of removing the employees from the scope of Civil Service restrictions and of freeing the operating group from the problems associated with direct government operation. It also obviated some of the difficulties encountered under the second approach. This procedure was particularly useful in cases where labor difficulties were the cause of seizure. The report strongly urged that responsibility for any seizures be centralized in a section of the Office of the Under Secretary of War to preclude the kind of red tape and serious confusion that resulted during World War I from division of responsibility and lack of intradepartmental cooperation.

As the spring of 1941 went on, and as strikes continued to plague the defense program, greater attention was given in all quarters of government to the possibility of seizures as a remedy. Discovering a legal basis for such action received the most attention. The attorney general studied the applicability of Section 9 of the Selective Training and Service Act and considered the issuance of regulations for use in case of labor disturbances. However, doubts arose as to the legal propriety of resting a seizure on this provision and about the constitutional powers of the president to requisition private plants in peacetime, or even in time of war, without legislative sanction. Because of the extraordinary nature of the remedy, it was deemed preferable to spell out the government's powers in a specific form. This led to proposals that special legislation be enacted and to the subsequent introduction in both houses of Congress of simple bills designed to vest specific

Secretary of War Henry L. Stimson   *Secretary of the Navy W. Franklin Knox*

authority in the president to take over a plant where a labor disturbance was interfering with vital production. Under the impetus of the North American Aviation case, one of these bills passed the Senate and received strong support from the War Department but not from the Roosevelt administration.

At this time federal executive agencies were giving more consideration to techniques other than seizures that might be employed to reduce the number of strikes. Many believed that some of the worst strikes were Communist-inspired and that if a procedure could be devised to deter Communist activity in key plants the situation would be greatly improved and the necessity for other drastic remedies removed. Many people thought, for example, that the Allis-Chalmers strike was staged by Mr. Christoffel, a local union leader suspected of being a Communist; that the serious stoppage at the Harville Die Casting Company in March(9) and at the Aluminum Company of America—or Alcoa—in Cleveland were the work of Mr. Cheyfitz, another alleged Communist; and that the North American Aviation shutdown was of Communist origin.(10)

There was enough evidence of this possibility to cause Secretary of War Henry L. Stimson[7] to raise the matter in a cabinet meeting and, together with

[7]Henry L. Stimson (1867–1950) was educated at Yale and Harvard Universities and entered private law practice in 1893. He was the U.S. attorney for the Southern District of New York (1906–09), the Republican candidate for New York governor (1907), secretary of war under William Howard Taft (1911–13), governor general of the Philippines (1927–29), secretary of state under Herbert Hoover (1929–33), and again secretary of war under Franklin Roosevelt (1940–45).

Secretary of the Navy W. Franklin "Frank" Knox,[8] to forward a letter to President Franklin D. Roosevelt recommending that the Federal Bureau of Investigation (FBI) look into the matter. This letter stated that "strikes and deliberate slow-downs . . . are having a markedly deterrent effect on our military and naval production" and that "we are morally certain, from a great variety of information reaching our Departments, that strikes and slowdowns are in many cases instigated by Communists and other subversive elements acting in the interest of foreign enemies."(11) President Roosevelt evidently shared these views, for he directed Attorney General Robert H. Jackson[9] to increase the investigative responsibility "of the FBI in the fields of subversive control of labor," and stated in a memorandum to Stimson and Knox that "you are also correct in saying that strikes and slow downs are in many cases instigated by Communists and other subversive elements acting in the interest of foreign enemies."(12) The Office of Production Management and the cabinet both discussed the possibility of legislation, and John Lord O'Brian,[10] OPM's general counsel, prepared several draft amendments to the Sabotage Act[11] intended to make it a felony to induce a slow-down or a strike for subversive purposes. Counterproposals were drafted and considered in the War Department.(13)

Paralleling these efforts were attempts by Secretary of Labor Frances Perkins,[12] in conjunction with other high government officials, including Stimson, to develop antistrike legislation applicable to cases pending before the NDMB. Secretary Perkins first suggested an amendment to the criminal code, making it a felony for any individual to advocate a strike while the NDMB had jurisdiction. She later became convinced that such a procedure was unworkable and drafted another bill, deemed enforceable, giving the NDMB the power to order employees

---

[8]W. Franklin "Frank" Knox (1874–1944) was a Boston-born lawyer, publisher, and statesman educated at the University of Michigan. Knox was a journalist and newspaper owner in Minnesota, New Hampshire, and Massachusetts before becoming the owner of the *Chicago Daily News* in 1931. A former Rough Rider during the Spanish-American War, he ran for the vice presidency on the Republican ticket in 1936. President Roosevelt appointed him secretary of the Navy in July 1940, a post he held until his death in 1944.

[9]Robert H. Jackson (1892–1954) was born in Pennsylvania and practiced law in New York before becoming the general counsel for the Bureau of Internal Revenue (1934). He served as U.S. solicitor general (1938–39), as U.S. attorney general (1940–41), and as an associate justice of the U.S. Supreme Court (1941–54). Jackson was the chief Allied prosecutor at the Nuremberg war crimes trials (1945–46).

[10]John Lord O'Brian (1874–1973) was born in Buffalo, New York, and was educated at Harvard and Buffalo Universities. He practiced law in Buffalo (1898–1945), served in the New York State Assembly, and was the U.S. attorney for the Western District of New York (1909–14). During World War I he was the head of the War Emergency Division of the Justice Department. He returned to private practice in 1921, later served as an assistant to the U.S. attorney general (1929–33), and ran unsuccessfully for the U.S. Senate from New York as a Republican. In 1941 he accepted the post of general counsel to the Office of Production Management and the War Production Board, serving until December 1944.

[11]The Sabotage Act (40 Stat. 533) was passed on 20 April 1918 and provided for punishment of "malicious destruction or injury to property, no matter how essential the property might be to the conduct of the war." It followed passage of the Espionage Act of 15 June 1917, which it strengthened, and preceded the Sedition Acts of 16 May 1918.

[12]Frances Perkins (1882–1965), a Boston-born social worker, served on the New York Council for War Service (1917–19), the New York Industrial Commission (1919–21, 1929–33), the New York Industrial Board (1923–33), and as secretary of labor (1933–45).

Secretary of Labor Frances Perkins   *Philip Murray*

to refrain from striking and employers from changing the status quo for a period of thirty days.(14)

For a short time a real possibility existed that some form of legislation might be proposed by the administration or pushed by Congress as a partial cure for serious labor difficulties. Although strikes continued at a high level, both of the above suggestions were abandoned, undoubtedly because of the effectiveness of the North American Aviation takeover. Any further consideration of legislation to deal with allegedly subversive elements in labor disputes was also affected by the Soviet Union's entry into the war on 22 June 1941 and the concomitant change in the Communist party line and by the results of informal conferences between government officials and top labor representatives, particularly a conference between then Solicitor General Francis Biddle[13] and Congress of Industrial Organizations President Philip Murray[14] in late June. Most of the proposals, including those of Perkins, were pigeonholed until the next serious crisis.

[13]Francis Biddle (1886–1968) was born in Paris and educated at Harvard before entering private law practice in Philadelphia (1915–39). He served as a special assistant to the U.S. attorney general (1922–26), as a judge on the U.S. Circuit Court of Appeals (1939–40), and as U.S. solicitor general and U.S. attorney general (1940–45).

[14]Philip Murray (1886–1952) was a Scottish-born labor leader who emigrated to the United States in 1902. He served as vice president of the United Mine Workers of America (1920–42) and was a co-founder of the CIO and chairman of the Steel Workers Organizing Committee (1936–42). He succeeded John L. Lewis as CIO president in 1940 and became president of the United Steel Workers Association (USWA) in 1942. Due to differences with Lewis, Murray and the USWA were expelled from the CIO in 1942. Supportive of Roosevelt's wartime productivity programs, Murray served on the National Defense Mediation Board and represented labor on the Economic Stabilization Board of the Office of Economic Stabilization, on the Management-Labor Policy Committee of the War Manpower Commission, and on the Advisory Board of the Office of War Mobilization and Reconversion.

Endnotes

(1) Bishop's principal memoranda were: Bishop for Amberg, 8 Jul 41, sub: Operation of Plants Seized by the United States (App. F–3); Bishop for Amberg, 21 Jun 41, sub: Further Data on Smith and Wesson (App. F–2); Bishop for Amberg, 18 Jun 41, sub: The Smith and Wesson Case (App. F–1). The specific memoranda were requested by the under secretary of war in a memorandum for Amberg on 7 June 1941, but the materials had been collected many weeks previously (Memo, Amberg for Bishop, 9 Jun 41, untitled). Subsequent memoranda of Bishop will be referred to at appropriate points. One phase of the subject is discussed in Memo, Tripp for Amberg, 28 Jul 41, sub: Possible Methods of Financing a Corporation Proposed To Be Organized To Enter Into Contracts With the Government for the Operation of Plants for the Production of Defense Needs Which May Be Taken Over by the Government (App. F–4).

(2) For an example of Civil War legislation see 12 Stat. 334 (1862). The plants affected during World War I were: Liberty Ordnance Company, Bridgeport, Conn. (Req. 26 A/C, Ord. No. 27, 5 Jan 18); Smith and Wesson Company, Springfield, Mass. (Req. 709 B/C, Ord. No. 604, 31 Aug 18); Bigelow Hartford Carpet Company, Lowell, Mass. (Req. 20 A/C, Ord. No. 62, 27 Dec 17); Hoboken Land and Improvement Company, Hoboken, N.J. (Req. 37 A/C, Ord. No. 516, 28 Feb 18); Federal Enameling and Stamping Company, McKees Rocks, Pa. (Req. 738 B/C, Ord. No. 609, 11 Sep 18); Mosler Safe Company, Hamilton, Ohio (Req. 781 B/C, Ord. No. 612, 23 Sep 18).

(3) "A Report of the Activities of the War Department in the Field of Industrial Relations During the War" (Washington, D.C.: Government Printing Office, 1919), pp. 34–35, transmitted from Stanley King to the secretary of war on 1 June 1919 (hereafter cited as King Rpt).

(4) 39 Stat. 213, 50 U.S.C. 80.

(5) Such a contract provision was not in general use in World War II. This provision rather than the authority of Section 120 was the real basis for seizure.

(6) Memo, Bishop for Amberg, 18 Jun 41; King Rpt.

(7) Until otherwise noted, the information is from Memos, Bishop for Amberg, 18 and 21 Jun 41.

(8) Memo, Bishop for Amberg, 8 Jul 41.

(9) "Lessons of the Inglewood Strike" by William Z. Foster, *Daily Worker*, 17 Jun 41; Memo, Lt Col Crist, Mil Intel Div, for OUSW, 16 Jan 42, sub: Former Employees of North American Aviation, Inc.; Ltr, Hoover to Under Sec War, 5 Jul 41, and attached report; Memo, McGrady for Asst Sec War, 17 Dec 40.

(10) Ltr, Sec War and Sec Navy to President, 29 May 41 (App. G–1).

(11) Memo, President for Sec War and Sec Navy, 4 Jun 41 (App. G–2).

(12) Several drafts are shown in Appendixes G–3, G–4, and G–5. See also Ltr, Amberg to O'Brian, 11 Jun 41 (App. G–6).

(13) App. G–7.

(14) Ltr, Sec Labor to Sec War, 12 Jun 41, with attached draft of proposed bill (App. G–8). Reference to these and other similar efforts was contained in an article in the *Washington Post*, 12 Jun 41, p. 1.

Chapter 2

The North American Aviation Case, June 1941

Background and Importance of the Dispute

The plants of North American Aviation, Inc., in Inglewood, California, were producing approximately 20 percent of all American military aircraft in June 1941, including trainers and medium bombers for the Army Air Forces (AAF) and Great Britain's Royal Air Force. The company held contracts in the aggregate amount of $200 million. A halt in production could interfere seriously with American defense preparations and do incalculable damage to the British war effort.[1]

Industrial difficulties had threatened production since December 1940 due to a bitter struggle between the United Automobile Workers of America (UAW)[2]—affiliated with the Congress of Industrial Organizations (CIO)—and the International Association of Machinists[3]—affiliated with the American Federation of Labor (AFofL)—for control of the bargaining unit. Only after a runoff election sponsored by the National Labor Relations Board (NLRB)[4] had the CIO won control by the narrow majority of seventy votes out of some six thousand votes cast. Many of these votes were challenged by the AFofL. In late May the CIO sought its first collective bargaining agreement with the company and made certain

---

[1] On the aircraft industry, see Irving Brinton Holley, Jr., *Buying Aircraft: Materiel Procurement for the Army Air Forces* (Washington, D.C.: Office of the Chief of Military History, 1964); idem, "The Management of Technological Change: Aircraft Production in the United States During World War II," *Aerospace Historian* 22 (Winter/December 1975): 161–65; and John B. Rae, *Climb to Greatness: The American Aircraft Industry, 1920–1960* (Cambridge: MIT Press, 1968). For the industry in California, see Allen A. P. and Betty V. H. Schneider, *Industrial Relations in the California Aircraft Industry* (Berkeley: University of California Press, 1956).

[2] The United Automobile Workers was organized in 1935 with an AFofL charter. It subsequently joined the CIO in 1936, following its suspension from the AFofL, and in 1939 split into AFofL- and CIO-affiliated factions. By 1940 the UAW (CIO) was by far the stronger and larger of the two groups, although a rump UAW (AFofL) continued to exist. The UAW (CIO) membership totaled 19,100 in 1940, growing to 53,400 by 1945.

[3] The International Association of Machinists, organized from the United Machinists and Mechanical Engineers of America in 1891, received its AFofL charter in 1895. It had a membership of 206,500 in 1940.

[4] The National Labor Relations Board was created by the National Labor Relations Act on 5 July 1935 (49 Stat.; 29 U.S.C. 151–66). Its three appointed members were to prevent unfair labor practices, decide the appropriate collective bargaining unit in disputed contests, conduct hearings and investigations, issue cease-and-desist orders, and initiate court actions. The NLRB had twenty-two regional offices by 1945. See Fred Witney, *Wartime Experiences of the National Labor Relations Board, 1941–1945* (Urbana: University of Illinois Press, 1949). For wartime records, see Record Group 25, NARA.

demands including the establishment of a 75-cent minimum wage (as contrasted with an average 55-cent minimum in most other southern California aircraft plants) and a 10-cent per hour across-the-board wage increase. The union also sought a closed shop.

Negotiations were unproductive, even with the assistance of a U.S. commissioner of conciliation, and the union threatened to strike. The case was then certified to the National Defense Mediation Board (NDMB) and all parties were summoned to Washington for a conference. Union officials promised not to strike before the board had an opportunity to investigate and make its findings and recommendations. Whether or not this commitment was made in good faith is not entirely clear. In any event, after one postponement the employees struck on 5 June 1941, at the very moment when their leaders were before a panel of the board. Powerful picket lines were formed and, in spite of the repeated urging of the leaders of the defeated but still powerful AFofL group, only a few employees attempted to work.

Preparations for a Takeover

The strike caused a major crisis not only because it crippled essential aircraft production but because it also represented a serious challenge to the government's labor policy. Aggravating factors were the broken promise of the union leaders and the widely held belief that the strike was Communist-inspired.[5] Even Sidney Hillman of the Office of Production Management,[6] who had been minimizing the importance of strikes and urged a course of restraint and government noninterference, felt that a showdown was necessary. The cabinet meeting on 6 June was largely devoted to the dispute, and the decision was reached that the government should seize the facility unless work resumed on 9 June. The plan called for a presidential announcement of the government's intended course of action in the hope that this announcement, coupled with the efforts of the UAW's Richard T. Frankensteen[7] at a scheduled 8 June union meeting, would prompt a return to work. The company would be asked to open the plant under its own auspices with assistance from local civil authorities. If these efforts failed, the War Department would intervene.

---

[5]See James R. Prickett, "Communist Conspiracy or Wage Dispute? The 1941 Strike at North American Aviation," *Pacific Historical Review* 50 (1981): 215–33.

[6]Sidney Hillman (1887–1946) emigrated to the United States from his native Lithuania in 1907. He organized the United Garment Workers of America, was president of the Amalgamated Clothing Workers of America, and was a member of the National Recovery Act Advisory Board (1933) and of the National Industrial Recovery Board (1935). After 1939 he served as vice president of the CIO and chairman of the Executive Council of the Textile Workers Union of America (CIO). During the war years Hillman acted as a labor advisor to Roosevelt and as a member of the National Defense Advisory Committee (1940), the Office of Production Management (1941), the War Production Board (1943), and the CIO's political action committee.

[7]Richard T. Frankensteen (1907–77) was born in Detroit and educated at the University of Dayton. He began working at Dodge Motors in 1932 and by 1936 was the president of the company union that became the Automotive Industrial Workers Association. The association later merged with the UAW. He was the UAW's vice president in 1937 and negotiated the first union contract with Chrysler. During World War II he served as the national director of aircraft organization for the CIO (1941) and served on the WPB and the NWLB. He ran unsuccessfully for mayor of Detroit in 1945.

Sidney Hillman

Richard T. Frankensteen

On 7 June President Roosevelt made his announcement. Simultaneously, the War Department stated it was ready to seize at the president's command. This was, to say the least, a very bold overstatement. Nobody in the War Department or the government had any clear idea about the technique of plant seizure or its feasibility. Individuals assigned to the task were only vaguely familiar with the World War I precedents, and none of those precedents had involved a situation in which labor, as distinguished from management, did not comply. Army organization for such a mission was wholly nonexistent. As a consequence, the entire War Department high command(1) spent most of Friday night and the following weekend developing a program and perfecting an organization. An executive order was drafted in conjunction with the Department of Justice, as were instructions for the War Department representative, Lt. Col. Charles E. Branshaw, the AAF's procurement chief on the West Coast. Lt. Col. Edward S. Greenbaum,[8] accompanied by legal, fiscal, and contractual experts, was sent to the West Coast to aid Branshaw. Troops were alerted; liaison was established between Branshaw

---

[8]Brig. Gen. Edward S. Greenbaum (1890–1970) was born in New York and educated at Williams College and Columbia Law School. He joined the infantry in September 1917 and was commissioned a captain in the Judge Advocate General's Department in January 1918. He was discharged as a major in 1920. After the war Greenbaum returned to private law practice, but reentered the Army in October 1940 as a lieutenant colonel and legal advisor to the Office of the Chief of Ordnance. He held a variety of positions with the Ordnance Department until being named executive officer, with the rank of colonel, to the under secretary of war in July 1942. He was promoted to brigadier general in March 1943 and retired in January 1946.

Brig. Gen. Charles E. Branshaw   *Brig. Gen. Edward S. Greenbaum*
(Photographed in 1942)   (Photographed in 1943)

and corps area troop commanders; and a plant reconnaissance was ordered. There was understandable confusion, doubt, and divergence of opinion as to objectives, techniques, and timing. These were reflected in an all-night conference on 8 June.(2) As the evening progressed, Branshaw reported that the union meeting had repudiated Frankensteen and had voted to continue the strike, to increase the picket lines, and to resist government intervention. His reports also indicated that other labor groups in California were planning to give both physical and moral support to the strikers.(3)

Under Secretary of War Robert P. Patterson[9] and Assistant Secretary of War John J. McCloy[10] were initially of the opinion that there was a strong nucleus of AFofL members who wanted to go back to work and would do so if protected by

---

[9]Robert P. Patterson (1891–1952) was born in New York State and educated at Union College and Harvard. He served with distinction in the American Expeditionary Forces in France, returning to private law practice in 1920. Patterson was appointed U.S. district attorney for the Southern District of New York (1930–39) and served as a judge on the U.S. Circuit Court of Appeals (1939–40), as assistant secretary of war (July–December 1940), as under secretary of war (December 1940–September 1945), and as secretary of war (September 1945–July 1947).

[10]John J. McCloy (1895–1989) was a Philadelphia-born lawyer, banker, and statesman, who was educated at Amherst College and Harvard Law School. He served with the American Expeditionary Forces in France, and entered private law practice in New York City and Paris in 1921. He made a name for himself in legal circles for his skillful litigation of the 1916 "Black Tom" Sabotage case (1930–39) and was asked by Secretary of War Stimson to serve as a consultant at the War Department in October 1940. Soon thereafter McCloy became a special assistant to the secretary of war and, in April 1941, the assistant secretary of war.

local authorities. This view was reinforced by the repeated assertions of the
mayor of Los Angeles that the entire
police department was available and
adequate for this purpose. Secretary of
War Stimson's special consultant,
Edward F. McGrady,[11] however, took
the position that police were notorious-
ly ineffective in strike situations and
that the local political situation was
such that the War Department should
not expect a satisfactory job from the
Los Angeles police. He urged that the
War Department take over at once and
open the plant. As an alternative he
suggested that the Army be prepared to
move in immediately if it became
apparent that the local police were
unable to insure the orderly return of
nonstrikers. Because the company
expressed strong opposition, however,
and because the president was on his
yacht and therefore unavailable to

Edward F. McGrady

approve any change in plans before the following morning, the first alternative
was abandoned. McGrady succeeded, however, in convincing the others that the
second course was imperative. Instructions were immediately given to deploy
some 2,600 federal troops under cover of predawn darkness in and around Los
Angeles so as not to be more than thirty minutes from the plant. Due to the late
hour, inadequate instruction from the G–1 (personnel) officer, the distance of
troops from the scene, the difficulty in using customary military channels, and
confusion over the fact that troop command, as well as plant operation, was to be
placed under Colonel Branshaw rather than under the corps area commander,
strict adherence to the time schedule seemed doubtful.

The Takeover

The plant was scheduled to open at 6:30 A.M. Long before that hour,
Branshaw, who had nine investigators at the scene and who was in radio contact

---

[11]Edward F. McGrady (1872–1960) was a New Jersey born labor official who was educated in Massachusetts.
He had broad experience in union affairs dating back to 1894, when he began work as a newspaper pressman.
McGrady later served as the president of the Newspaper Printing Pressman's Union, the Boston Central Labor
Union, and the Massachusetts State Federation of Labor. He became the first assistant secretary of labor in 1933.
After leaving government service for the first time in 1937, McGrady joined the Radio Corporation of America
as vice president (later director) in charge of labor relations. On 5 December 1940 he was appointed as a special
consultant to the secretary of war.

with a plane observing the progress of the three troop columns to their rendezvous posts, began phoning reports at fifteen-minute intervals regarding the gathering of pickets, the assembly of returning workers, the activities of local police, and the congregation of large numbers of reporters, photographers, and newsreel cameramen. Each successive report showed a large increase in pickets and only a small increase in the number of police. Ten minutes after the start of the shift there were nearly one thousand pickets and less than a hundred policemen. Only five workers had entered the plant, but more than a thousand persons with dinner pails were congregated outside. Sporadic fights began around 7:15. The police were unable to maintain control and failed completely in one effort to open the picket lines at the east gate. A half hour later the police began shooting tear gas into the ranks of the picketers, who quickly threw the gas canisters over the plant fence and forced the police to withdraw under a rain of rocks and bottles.

As it became obvious to Washington officials that the local authorities would never regain control, McCloy hastened to meet the presidential yacht and briefed Roosevelt as they went to the White House. There, after a short conference with Patterson, Attorney General Jackson, and Hillman, and after the receipt of a last-minute report from Branshaw, Roosevelt signed an executive order directing seizure at 7:50 A.M. Patterson instructed Branshaw by phone to proceed at once and "to see that the troops under your command afford adequate protection against any interference whatsoever to workers entering or leaving the plant, and at their homes." By this time the company was closing its gates and an appeal by the chief of police and the mayor to the strikers was falling on deaf ears. At 8:10 Branshaw, having concluded that the situation was out of the control of state and local authorities, called for troops and advised the press that the Army was taking over.

The troops deployed twenty minutes later. Branshaw forcibly drove through the picket line and reached the plant offices shortly before 9:00 A.M. Outside, determined troops with fixed bayonets went methodically about the business of clearing the gates and roads, driving the pickets away from the plant. It was a well-executed operation. There was only one slight injury, the accidental bayoneting of one picket. By 10:30 workers were coming into the plant in large numbers.(4)

Problems Confronting the Government

Although Branshaw was safely established in the plant and some workers were now returning, this was merely the beginning of his job. It was easy enough to notify the company of the fact of possession, to post notices of government occupancy, and to perform other administrative tasks, but the real problems confronting him were numerous, novel, and urgent. First, and of dominating importance, was the problem of restoring production and getting men back to work. Second was the question of how to settle the initial dispute that necessitated government intervention. Upon the answer to this would depend the length of government possession. Third was the problem of determining the status of the company and its stockholders under War Department control. Was the government to supplant the company completely and, if so, under what authority and upon what terms? Finally, and closely related to the last problem, was the practical question of how the War Department was going to operate this huge industrial facility. What funds would be used to finance the enterprise? What steps should be taken, such as the conduct of an inventory and the establishment of purchasing, sales, and accounting records reflecting War Department activities, to protect the government's interest? What individuals would actually run the plant and what would be their relation to company officials?

At the hour of takeover it is improbable that anyone could have stated the issues so clearly, but a certain amount of solid thinking was going on in Washington. For example, Howard Petersen, a special assistant to the secretary of war, had, with unusual foresight, set forth some of the government objectives in a memorandum to Secretary Stimson:(5)

1. The strikers must not gain an advantage while the government is taking over. Otherwise, every plant in the United States on defense work will have a strike shortly to force the government to takeover.

2. The company has in this case had a completely clear record and must not be penalized any more than absolutely necessary by reason of the takeover.

3. If the government becomes the direct employer of labor an infinite number of technical difficulties arise. . . .

4. In order to produce planes, complete management cooperation must be obtained and it seems to me doubtful whether this can be accomplished by making the management individual government employees.

More detailed views on other phases were expressed to Patterson by Stimson's special assistant, Julius H. Amberg, on 7 June.(6) The views of these two individuals, to some extent, became the views of the War Department during the following week.

Obtaining a Full Return to Work

Restoration of production presented major difficulties. While many employees were returning to work, or promised to return if given protection, hundreds of strikers were still out and gave every evidence of resisting the government. They were defiant of their international union leadership and loyal to their local union. Moreover, their position had the support of many other unions throughout California, which threatened sympathy strikes on a wide scale in other equally critical war plants. A flood of rumors unfavorable to the government were widely circulated,(7) and for several days loudspeakers operating in the shadow of the plant were urging the men not to go back to work. Moreover, there were many reported instances of threats against returning workers.(8) As late as 23 June resistance was still evident, even though the strike had ended.(9)

The government proceeded adhering to the theory that a large number of employees wanted to come back to work if assured of protection against violence and if a sufficiently strong appeal were addressed to them. Once the majority of the workers was back on the job, the strike itself would probably collapse. In addition, if the workers were given the impression that they were now employees of the government, rather than of the company, this expected trend might be rapidly accelerated. At the same time, it would have to be made clear that their return to work was a voluntary matter, a moral obligation on their part as American citizens, and that government coercion and intimidation would not be used. While this approach would not bring about a final disposition of the dispute, assure cooperation of the more vehement strikers, or pave the way to a return of the properties, it would, if successful, result in aircraft production at an early date.

The job of maintaining free access to the plant and of protecting workers raised a number of subsidiary questions. Before the seizure it had been hoped that any necessary protection could be furnished by local authorities,(10) but it was now evident that military forces were essential for this purpose.

There was confusion at the outset as to what should be done about the picket lines. The original instructions from Branshaw to Col. Jesse A. Ladd directed the elimination of all picketing, but this order was modified in accordance with word from Washington that orderly pickets should not be molested.(11) By 9:30 A.M. the pickets had been pushed back half a mile in all directions and by midafternoon a full mile; instructions were given that no picketing was permitted within the cleared area, a policy followed for the duration of the War Department's operation.(12) Shortly thereafter the picket lines began to disintegrate for the lack of pickets. With one minor exception, which led to the arrest and temporary detention at Fort MacArthur of fourteen pickets, there was little resistance to the troops carrying out these instructions, and the conduct of the troops themselves was so exemplary that even the strikers appeared to harbor no resentment toward them.(13)

The task of furnishing protection to workers and their families, including their homes, as directed by Under Secretary Patterson,(14) proved more formidable. Arrangements were made for a patrol of twenty-four radio-equipped cars operating from strategic points throughout the city. Despite the aid of police and the implementation of other precautions, numerous reports of intimidation were received. The situation was tense enough that Branshaw felt compelled on three separate occasions to state categorically that specific measures would be taken to protect vulnerable individuals. He went so far as to say, "I guarantee [the employees] absolute safety and protection while they are on the job, while they are proceeding to or from work, and while they are in their homes," and he repeated this guarantee in individual telegrams to each employee requesting his immediate return to work.(15) Nevertheless, intimidation, though decreasing, continued, and the many reported instances of violence, general interference, and efforts of strikers to undermine the morale of working employees prompted Patterson to recommend to the president on 12 June that the Department of Justice proceed with civil and criminal actions.(16) The Federal Bureau of Investigation (FBI) conducted an investigation, but no legal actions were instituted, even though further incidents occurred. The Department of Justice, subsequent to the Army's withdrawal, concluded that exiting federal law offered no basis for prosecution.(17) Nevertheless, the activities of the Army's mounted patrols and the FBI gradually removed fear as a serious obstacle to a return to work.

By emphasizing the importance of the plant's production and government fair treatment and protection to all who returned, the Army persuaded the great mass of employees to resume work. This appeal was keynoted by a statement from Roosevelt that emphasized the workers' role in the country's defense and his confidence that as loyal citizens they would return to work. The statement further pledged that "their fundamental rights as free citizens will be protected by the government and negotiations will be conducted through the process of collective bargaining to reach a settlement fair and reasonable to the workers and to the company."(18) As a further inducement, Roosevelt pointed to the very compelling fact of a prior company statement that any settlement reached would be retroactive to 1 May. The same points were forcefully reemphasized in Branshaw's releases, given wide distribution by the press and radio and in telegrams to the individual workers.(19) Sidney Hillman issued a lengthy statement designed to reassure North American employees of government fairness, to discredit the local strike leaders, and to strengthen the parent international union. He emphasized the allegations that workers were led to strike by an irresponsible group who, contrary to the best interests of their members, had defied the government, the president, and their own international union. He also dwelt on the fact that labor's right to bargain collectively at this plant had been unaffected by the takeover.(20) Hillman was torn between his passionate desire to see defense production go forward and his similarly deep conviction that forcible government intervention in strikes was abhorrent. He faced an emotional and intellectual dilemma that greatly troubled him. His statement was, in part, an attempt to justify his support as a labor leader for government action that he had finally not only endorsed but urged.(21) The press and radio cooperated magnificently in carrying these messages, thus creating the kind of atmosphere favorable to a return to work and counteracting the extremely vocal activities of agitators.

It was made clear to North American employees that they were returning to work for the United States, although throughout the seizure there was disagreement as to whether this was in fact the case. Patterson initially felt that if the United States was to step in it must do so completely in spite of any resulting Civil Service difficulties, as did Branshaw.(22) The latter's concept, however, that the terms of employment should be those that prevailed in a government establishment, was at variance with other views that held that the plant, even under government control, should be operated under the same terms and conditions of employment as were in effect at the time of the seizure—the view that ultimately prevailed. To further the impression that the employees were working for the government, it was suggested that each employee be required to take the oath customarily given to federal workers, but Patterson and others in Washington decided that this was unwise, perhaps from a fear that this might bring these employees under Civil Service, a complicating result that they wished to avoid.(23) A decision was reached, however, that checks in payment of wages, while drawn by the company, would carry the notation "For the Account of the United States" so that it would appear that the federal government rather than the company was the actual employer. It was also hoped that such a procedure would obviate complicated payroll deduction problems relating to Social Security and group insurance.(24)

While urging employees to return to work, the government made it clear that they should harbor no illusions that they had won a victory or that they had obtained any of the concessions previously demanded. Their position in relation to the company was not changed by government intervention. Furthermore, the return to work must be unconditional, with no suggestion that strike leaders were being recognized. This policy was implemented without deviation. Branshaw refused to see or negotiate with strike representatives, although these individuals made repeated efforts, not only directly but also indirectly through the War Department, independent labor officials, and the mayor of Los Angeles, to obtain the removal of all troops and the reinstatement of certain excluded employees as a condition to any agreement to return to work. Branshaw publicly repudiated rumors that any such negotiations were undertaken or any concessions made. It was also decided that while both strikers and nonstrikers would be reinstated without distinction, they would be taken back only as individuals and not in groups. Consequently, an effort of the strikers to march to the plant in a group was broken up at the one-mile limit and the participants were forced to approach and enter the plant individually without demonstration. Refusal to compromise in any way with the holdouts and refusal to permit them to demonstrate in the neighborhood of the plant or to take any other action that they might claim constituted a victory undoubtedly had an effect on the prompt, orderly return to work.

Colonel Branshaw decided at an early point not to have any dealings with the local strike instigators, and he ordered their exclusion from the plant as inimical to full production. His view was strengthened by his knowledge of the very active participation of some of these men in the riots preceding War Department seizure, by his suspicion that they were Communists, and by the fact that they had been suspended as local officials by the international union.(25) The War Department, the National Labor Relations Board, and the Office of Production Management all concluded that exclusion of these individuals from the plant did not violate the National Labor Relations Act.[12] In addition, Judge Advocate General Maj. Gen. Allen W. Gullion[13] reviewed the legal propriety of such action and concluded that the authority for taking such a step existed. As a final precaution, Colonel Branshaw talked with Frankensteen of the international union, who expressed no objection, before instructing the troop commander to that effect.(26) The resulting protests of the nine affected individuals were referred to the U.S. attorney, but because Branshaw's accompanying statement had indicated that the individuals were merely suspended pending investigation, it was felt desirable to hold a hearing on their cases. This hearing took place on 13 June with Frankensteen as the principal witness. At its conclusion the suspensions were confirmed.(27) These men were never again readmitted to the plant, even after War Department withdrawal, although they retained wide influ-

---

[12]The National Labor Relations Act, or the Wagner Act (49 Stat. 449), became law on 5 July 1935. It insured the right of employees to organize unions, to bargain collectively, to choose their own bargaining representatives, and to engage in concerted activities for their mutual aid and protection. It also created an independent National Labor Relations Board to administer and oversee enforcement of the act.

[13]Maj. Gen. Allen W. Gullion (1880–1946) was a West Point graduate (Class of 1905) with experience in military law dating from 1917. On 31 July 1941, just after the North American Aviation seizure, Gullion became the provost marshal general, a position he held until going overseas in April 1944. He retired in December 1944.

Maj. Gen. Allen W. Gullion   Brig. Gen. Lewis B. Hershey

ence within the local union until the international union concluded a favorable contract with the company several weeks later. The position followed was later crystallized in a general policy statement, approved by Acting Secretary McCloy and Attorney General Jackson, that read, "Known Communists, suspended officers of the local union, and all others whose presence the officer in charge deems to be inimical to the object of the Mission, namely the speedy production of aircraft will be excluded by him from the plant."(28)

A final avenue of approach to stimulate a return to work in this and other then-current strikes was the invocation of certain provisions of the Selective Training and Service Act by Brig. Gen. Lewis B. Hershey.[14] This step had the express approval of the president. Hershey ordered all his state directors to reclassify deferred workers who were "impeding the national defense program."(29) Local Selective Service boards in Los Angeles were already in the process of reclassification when this order was announced.

The measure had an effect. By the middle of the afternoon of 9 June Colonel Branshaw reported, perhaps overoptimistically, that three-quarters of the employees

---

[14]Maj. Gen. Lewis B. Hershey (1893–1977) was an Indiana native, who was educated at Tri-State College. He served on the Mexican border in 1916 and with the American Expeditionary Forces in France, entering the Regular Army in 1920 and retiring in 1946. Hershey was the secretary to the War Department General Staff's Joint Army-Navy Selective Service Committee in September 1936 and helped draft the Selective Training and Service Act of 1940. He became the deputy director of the Selective Service in 1940 and director in July 1941, a post he held until his final retirement in 1973.

had returned to work and that production was already at half speed. The failure to obtain greater production was due to the general atmosphere of excitement that prevailed and to the distracting events going on outside. On the evening shift 625 out of 2,000 scheduled to work reported, and on the following morning 5,100 out of 7,300. By the afternoon shift 3,304 out of 3,798 were back at their jobs, and on 11 June employment was normal.(30)

Settling the Basic Dispute

A return to work did not solve the labor dispute or provide the basis for War Department withdrawal. From the outset Roosevelt was of the opinion that it was desirable to withdraw as soon as possible but not until mediation proceedings were again well under way.(31) This presented a problem. Restoration of normal collective bargaining seemed impossible as long as the local leaders had de facto control of the members, even though they had been suspended from office by the international union. Yet if the dispute was to be worked out promptly, someone must represent these workers. Similarly, many thought that any negotiations for a permanent settlement should be conducted by private management rather than by the War Department. On 10 June the president decided that in future negotiations as to labor relations, the company was to represent management and the national and regional heads of the CIO [sic]. Frankensteen would appoint new local representatives.(32)

Because of an apparent latent distrust of the War Department in the field of labor relations, and in an effort to allay any labor fears of military domination, the civilian agencies had insisted, over the War Department's objections, that the executive order contain a provision directing the secretary of war to employ a competent civilian advisor on industrial relations. Eric Nicol, an assistant to Hillman, was selected for this position.(33) Immediately upon his arrival on the West Coast, he conferred with Frankensteen, Branshaw, and company officials and all recommended that the NDMB proceedings be resumed at once.(34) While this had a salutary effect, the influence of the suspended leaders continued and the War Department repeatedly emphasized to the president, to Hillman, and to others the necessity for strong steps by the UAW in reorganizing the local union.(35) Frankensteen assigned several people to this job, and they gradually succeeded in weaning the local membership away from its former leaders. In fact, it was not until a very favorable decision was rendered by the NDMB and incorporated in a proposed contract between the union and the company that the international union had a sufficiently powerful weapon with which to discredit these leaders and gain member support. The contract itself received enthusiastic approval from the employees, and thereafter Frankensteen was in complete control. The local union was reorganized and the substantive dispute disposed of.(36)

Company and Stockholder Status

The attention paid to restoring production obscured the question of what happened to the company and its stockholders after government seizure. War

Department officials had concluded at an early date that there was no reason why the company should be penalized for something for which it was not to blame,(37) but how to avoid this presented a difficult problem. Doubt as to its solution was clearly reflected by Secretary Stimson at a press conference on the afternoon of the seizure, when he stated that the stockholders would discover their status in due time and that "Mr. Kindleberger, president of this company, has a very good reputation with the government for making airplanes and as a square shooter. There are not enough like him. We do not want to do any injury to such a man. You may draw your own inferences from this."(38) This confusion was further evidenced by the fact that Colonel Branshaw was simultaneously issuing the following statement: "North American has no voice in the operation. We are calling upon the company executives for information because they are familiar with the plant but we are calling up machinery for more extensive operation by government men."(39) For several days the company was in a complete quandary, although it seems to have approved generally of the manner in which the War Department was proceeding.(40)

The Manner in Which the Plant Was Operated

The final question that faced the government was the very practical one of how it would actually make the business run. While it seemed plain that company personnel would have to be used in a managerial capacity at first, it was not clear whether such personnel would be employed directly by the War Department or supplanted entirely as soon as qualified government personnel were found. A little thinking convinced everyone that the same people must do the job irrespective of their technical legal status. The possibility of turning the entire operation over to a government corporation was explored by Petersen and Amberg and discussed with representatives of the Defense Plant Corporation.(41)[15] The general question of method of operation was considered at a White House meeting on 10 June. The president laid down the following criteria as reported by Secretary Stimson: "The President's views coincided with the other three to the effect that in these cases of taking possession of plants we should keep the practice fluid so as to be adjustable to the different circumstances of each case. Also, that in this case it was desirable to assume as little of the relationship of direct management to the operations of the company and its labor relations as possible, and that the company should be treated as the agent of the government for that purpose."(42)

Roosevelt's policy proved extremely wise, not only in this but in subsequent cases. Funds and business direction were entirely provided by the company, the

---

[15]The Defense Plant Corporation (DPC) was established to produce, acquire, carry, or sell, or otherwise deal in, strategic and critical materials; to purchase or lease land, plants, and supplies for the manufacture of implements of war and strategic and critical materials; and to engage in such manufacture itself. The DPC also produced, leased, and purchased railroad and aviation equipment for the government. It was transferred from the Federal Loan Agency to the Department of Commerce by Executive Order 9071, 24 February 1942, and was returned to the former by an Act of Congress (59 Stat. 5; 12 U.S.C. 1801) on 24 February 1945. It was dissolved by Public Law 109 (79th Cong., 1st Sess.) on 30 June 1945. For DPC records, see Record Group 234, NARA.

only exception being with respect to matters involving employment or labor poli-cy.(43) This made it possible, when the operation was finally terminated, for the government and the company to bring an end to the entire case by a simple exchange of mutual releases and obviated any need for a complicated financial settlement. Similarly, it eliminated the possibility of any compensatory claims by the company for use of the property.

Early confusion about general operating methods naturally affected a number of subsidiary questions relating to insurance, accounting, the keeping of separate records and books, the handling of incidental labor problems, the taking of an inventory, and the purchase and sale of goods. The original instructions to Branshaw on these and other points, based principally upon suggestions of Amberg,(44) proved satisfactory and adaptable, and with later refinements and modifications they became the standard instructions to War Department repre-sentatives. These instructions, which ran directly from Stimson to Branshaw, included the following: make a complete inventory; employ, without regard to Civil Service rules, any person, agency, association, firm, or company necessary to carry out the operation; fix rates of compensation to correspond as nearly as possible to rates currently in effect; procure, either from the company for the account of the government or directly, by purchase, rental, or any other means, any material, supplies, machinery, equipment, and tools necessary; permit the company to carry on procurement for its own account or for the account of the government; maintain a system of accounting to reflect all transactions embraced in the government's operations; notify insurers of the change in status of the plant; provide protection to the property taken and to employees, resorting first to state and local authorities before requesting aid from the corps area comman-der; avoid assuming any existing obligations of the company, referring all inquiries with respect thereto to the corporation; and furnish reports on all impor-tant matters. These instructions gave Branshaw complete local control over both operations and the use of troops.

As might have been expected, some of the instructions proved difficult to carry out. It appeared, for example, that the taking of a complete inventory would require a considerable number of accountants, consume many weeks, and involve a large expense. A decision was therefore made to undertake a briefer inventory that merely described the plant and its contents as accurately as possible without giving dollar amounts. Such an inventory was completed on 12 June, and the tak-ing of more complete inventory was apparently abandoned as the policy of treat-ing the company as an agent rendered such an undertaking unnecessary.(45) Establishment of a separate accounting system presented comparable difficul-ties,(46) however, but these and similar problems were worked out on a satisfac-tory makeshift basis. Each point in the instructions was discussed at great length by Branshaw and his staff with company officials, including, as early as 12 June, the preparation of proposed mutual releases for use at the end of the operation.(47)

In view of the existing labor situation, it was felt that the handling of daily labor relations, as distinguished from the adjustment of the basic dispute, could not be entirely turned over to the company.(48) This operating problem, insofar as

War Department intervention was required, resolved itself into two principal questions: the handling of grievances, and the demand for government recognition by the previously defeated AFofL union. Needed reforms in the company's general approach to labor problems was a long-range job and not a War Department responsibility.

The AFofL had been quick to see the opportunity of capturing a majority of the plant's workers. CIO officials admitted that until a contract was negotiated, the AFofL could have won a majority in any election held. On 10 June AFofL representatives asked Branshaw to approve a special election to prove their majority.(49) They were informed that, in view of the NLRB's certification, he could not recognize the AFofL in any way and that their remedy, if any, was with the board.(50) An exchange of letters during the following days confirmed this position(51) and in doing so established a policy followed in subsequent seizures.

The grievance issue was acutely raised by the fact that foremen were laying off and discharging persons without reference to Branshaw. Since these actions could have a material bearing on the entire labor situation at the plant, instructions were given that no dismissals were to be taken without the prior approval of Branshaw or his representative. A committee was established with Branshaw's executive officer as chairman to conduct a hearing on all recommendations for discharge.(52) This constituted an abandonment of the normal grievance procedure in effect before War Department intervention, but shortly after Nicol's arrival and a plea from Frankensteen it was decided to reinstate the old procedures subject to several conditions that met the approval of the union's international representatives.(53) Nicol believed this had a beneficial effect, and no apparent difficulties were experienced.(54)

Termination of Government Operation

Roosevelt desired a War Department withdrawal as soon as possible, and the topic was reexamined almost daily by Secretary Stimson and Colonel Branshaw.(55) At first the unstable situation precluded a withdrawal, which would almost certainly have brought about a repetition of the strike.(56) Even as late as 20 June the prospects for a complete withdrawal seemed poor because of the slow progress being made in reorganizing the local union. The conclusion was gradually reached that it would be unsafe to terminate operations until the agreement then being worked out through the NDMB had been ratified.(57) At this time, Branshaw, who had followed the policy of releasing troops as quickly as possible, was hesitant about removing his remaining forces. However, the company's feeling that the final labor agreement should not be acted upon while any troops were still in the plant prevailed, and the soldiers were withdrawn on 24 June, although a few camped in the vicinity for several days, ostensibly for recreational activities. With union ratification of a contract the whole situation changed, and Branshaw immediately recommended complete withdrawal. Stimson and Roosevelt, after consulting Hillman, accepted this recommendation, and on 2 July an executive order directing termination was issued and promptly carried out.

Significance of the Case

The North American takeover was the most significant case of the war because it was the first plant seizure of the World War II period and the first operation of its kind that had ever been undertaken in a situation where labor, as distinguished from management, refused to obey a government order. It was the first instance in many years in which federal troops had been used in any capacity in a labor dispute.(58) It represented a decision by the federal government that it would insist that the parties to a critical labor dispute follow orderly processes without resort to economic weapons and that the government would use force, if necessary, to carry out such policy. In many respects the government went further in this case than in any subsequent takeover involving labor noncompliance, particularly with respect to its discharge of the ringleaders of the strike. With the exception of the 1944 Philadelphia Transportation Company seizure, this takeover was more a straight military operation than any subsequent incident.

The case set the general pattern followed in other plant seizures, although, of course, experience in this case and others showed the desirability of many modifications. Important policies were established, though not wholly recognized as such at the time, including: that the return to work of strikers must be without concession of any kind; that the takeover should in no way benefit the noncompliant; that the seized properties should be operated under the same terms and conditions of employment as existed at the time of seizure—a policy later embodied in Section 4 of the War Labor Disputes Act; and that the dispute that precipitated the seizure must be worked out by the parties themselves in a normal fashion in conjunction with the labor agencies of government and without direct participation of the seizing agency. Furthermore, the method finally adopted of using the company as the War Department's agent to operate the plant, utilizing its own funds and its own personnel and retaining the profits, became the general objective in subsequent cases. There thus had been developed, almost unconsciously, the broad outlines of technique for takeovers that would obviate many of the difficulties inherent in the methods of operation employed in World War I and considered theoretical obstacles during the early days of 1941. Above all, there had been a practicable demonstration of the efficacy of plant seizure in a strike situation.

Endnotes

(1) This included Under Secretary Patterson and Secretary Stimson's special assistants, Amberg and Petersen; Assistant Secretary McCloy; Assistant Secretary for Air Robert A. Lovett; Judge Advocate General Gullion, special assistant to the secretary; and Maj. Karl R. Bendetsen, the judge advocate for the case.

(2) Present at this conference for the first time were Labor Section representatives and special consultant McGrady, Under Secretary Patterson, Assistant Secretary McCloy, Amberg, and representatives of the General Staff, including General Bryden, then assistant chief of staff for personnel (G–1).

(3) Recorded telephone conversations (Telecons) of 8 June 1941 as follows: Lt Col Branshaw, McGrady, and Patterson at 2120 (EST); Branshaw, Patterson, General Bryden, Col Martin, and McCloy at 2235 (EST); Branshaw and Patterson at 2335 (EST). Telecons of 9 June 1941 as follows: Branshaw and Maj Smith at 0050 (EST); Steinmetz and Ohly at 0450 (EST); Steinmetz, Smith, and Ohly at 0830 and 0855 (EST); Branshaw, Smith, and Lt Robinson at 0925 (EST); Steinmetz and Smith at 1005 (EST); Branshaw and McGrady at 1035 and 1145 (EST); Col Ladd, "Report of Activities of U.S. Troops Employed in Opening North American Aviation Plant at Inglewood, Calif., 7–11 June 1941," pars. 1–8d (hereafter cited as Ladd Rpt); chronological report of events attached to Memo, Lt Col Branshaw for Sec War, 2 Jul 41, sub: Military Possession and Operation of North American Aviation, Inc. (App. H–1). For a defense of the activities of the mayor and the Los Angeles police force, see Ltr, Paul Shoup, Pres, Los Angeles Merchants and Manufacturers Association to Merrill Meigs, Chief, Aircraft Sec, OPM, 18 Jun 41. All of the foregoing documents are to be found in the official War Department files on this case. Except where otherwise noted, this is true of all other references in the North American Aviation case.

(4) Memo, Sec War, sub: Conference at White House With President, Jackson, Hillman, and Stimson on June 10, 1941 (hereafter cited as Memo of White House Conference, 10 Jun 41). See App. H–2.

(5) Memo, Petersen for Sec War, 9 Jun 41 (App. H–3). Petersen became assistant secretary of war in 1946.

(6) Memo, Amberg, 7 Jun 41, sub: Some Thoughts With Respect to Directive From the Secretary of War to Colonel Branshaw With Respect to North American Aviation, Inc. (App. H–4).

(7) Telecons between Thom (War Dept) and Wysanski (NDMB), 9 Jun 41, at 2100 (EST), and Col Steinmetz and Ohly, 10 Jun 41, at 2100 (EST).

(8) Memo, Under Sec War for Sec War, 11 Jun 41; Memo, Under Sec War for President, 12 Jun 41; Ltrs, Hoover to Under Sec War, 23 Jun 41 and 5 Jul 41.

(9) Memo, E. K. Merritt for Lt Col Branshaw, 23 Jun 41, sub: Meeting CIO Sunday, June 22, 1941, 8:00 P.M.; Memo, Lt Col Greenbaum for Under Sec War, 23 Jun 41.

(10) Chronological report of events by Lt Col Branshaw, 7 and 8 Jun 41 (App. H–1); Memo, Amberg, 7 Jun 41, pars. 16, 17 (App. H–4); Ltr, Acting Sec War to Lt Col Branshaw, 9 Jun 41 (App. H–5).

(11) Memo, Amberg, 7 Jun 41, par. 19 (App. H–4); Ladd Rpt. The latter is very complete on all troop activities.

(12) Memo, Gen Peek for Col Ladd, 9 Jun 41.

(13) Rpt of CIO Meeting at Centinella Park, Inglewood, Calif., at 0520 on 11 Jun 41.

(14) Ltr, Acting Sec War McCloy to Lt Col Branshaw, sub: Supplementary Instructions, 9 Jun 41.

(15) Branshaw's statements and the telegram are contained in Appendixes H–6, H–7, H–8, H–9, and H–10.

(16) Telecons, Under Sec War and Lt Col Branshaw, 11 Jun 41, at 1450 (EST), and 12 Jun 41, at 1250 (EST); Memo, Under Sec War, 11 Jun 41; Memo, Under Sec War for President, 12 Jun 41.

(17) Ltrs, Hoover to Under Sec War, 21 and 23 Jun 41; Memos, Lt Col Greenbaum for Under Sec War, 18, 20, and 23 Jun 41; Ltr, Hoover to Under Sec War, 9 Jul 41.

(18) Statement by President, 9 Jun 41.

(19) See Apps. H–6 through H–10.

(20) Statement by Sidney Hillman concerning the situation at the plant of North American Aviation, Inc., 9 Jun 41.

(21) Petersen to Sec War, 9 Jun 41.

(22) Statement of Lt Col Branshaw to Press, 9 Jun 41; Telecon, Battley and Greenbaum, 9 Jun 41, at 1645 (EST); Memo, Lt Col Greenbaum for Lt Col Branshaw, 10 Jun 41, sub: Compliance with Order from Sec War, June 9, 1941, par. 8.

(23) Memo of White House Conference, 10 Jun 41 (App. H–2); Memo, Lt Col Greenbaum for Lt Col Branshaw, 10 Jun 41, par. 8; Memo, Lt Col Greenbaum for Lt Col Branshaw, 14 Jun 41, sub: Compliance With Order From the Secretary of War, June 9, 1941, pars. 4 and 8.

(24) Memo, Lt Col Greenbaum for Lt Col Branshaw, 14 Jun 41, par. 12(a); Telecons, Battley and Greenbaum, 9 Jun 41, at 1605 (EST), McGrady, Branshaw, and Greenbaum, 10 Jun 41, at 1545 (EST), and Ohly and Branshaw, 10 Jun 41, at 1640 (EST) and 1650 (EST).

(25) Telecons, Battley and Greenbaum, 9 Jun 41, at 1605 (EST), and Greenbaum and McGrady, 10 Jun 41, at 1400 (EST).

(26) Telecons, Branshaw and McGrady, 10 Jun 41, at 1405 (EST), 1545 (EST), and 1550 (EST), Bendetsen, Greenbaum, and Ohly, 10 Jun 41, at 1620 (EST), Dinsmore and Greenbaum, 10 Jun 41, at 1630 (EST), and McGrady and Branshaw, 10 Jun 41, at 1603 (EST); Memo, Lt Col Branshaw for Col Ladd, 10 Jun 41.

(27) Telecon, Battley and Greenbaum, 13 Jun 41, at 1430 (EST); Memo of hearing on 13 June 1941, sub: Statement of Richard T. Frankensteen; Memo, Lt Col Branshaw, 13 Jun 41, sub: Military Activities, Inglewood Plant, North American Aviation, Inc.

(28) Memo, Lt Col Greenbaum for Lt Col Branshaw, 14 Jun 41.

(29) Statement of [Brig] Gen Hershey, Acting Selective Service Dir, 9 Jun 41.

(30) Telecons, Greenbaum and Battley, 9 Jun 41, at 1605 (EST), Branshaw and Battley, 9 Jun 41, at 2115 (EST); and numerous others during the course of 10 and 11 June 1941.

(31) Memo of White House Conference, 10 Jun 41 (App. H–2).

(32) Ibid.

(33) Telecon, Wyzanski and Thom, 9 Jun 41, at 2100; Memo, Amberg, 7 Jun 41, par. 18 (App. H–4); Memo of White House Conference, 10 Jun 41 (App. H–2).

(34) Eric Nicol, "Report of Industrial Relations Activities, North American Aviation, Inc., During Operation by United States Government," transmitted to the under secretary of war on 17 June 1941 (hereafter cited as Nicol Rpt).

(35) Memo, Under Sec War for President, 12 Jun 41; Memo, Under Sec War for Hillman, 20 Jun 41. The report by Nicol contains a detailed account of this situation and the difficulties experienced.

(36) Nicol Rpt.

(37) Memo, Petersen for Sec War, 9 Jun 41 (App. H–3).

(38) Transcript of Secretary Stimson's Press Conference, 9 Jun 41.

(39) Statement of Lt Col Branshaw to Press, 9 Jun 41.

(40) Telecon, Kindleberger, President of North American Aviation, Inc., and Merrill Meigs of WPB, 10 Jun 41.

(41) Memo, Petersen for Sec War, 9 Jun 41 (App. H–3); Memo, Amberg for Under Sec War, 9 Jun 41, sub: Methods of Operation of Inglewood Plant (App. H–11); Memo, Amberg for Under Sec War, 9 Jun 41, sub: Conference re Defense Plant (App. H–12).

(42) Memo of White House Conference, 10 Jun 41 (App. H–2).

(43) Telecon, Under Sec War and Lt Col Branshaw, 12 Jun 41, at 1250; Memo, Lt Col Greenbaum for Lt Col Branshaw, 14 Jun 41.

(44) Ltr, Acting Sec War to Lt Col Branshaw, 9 Jun 41 (App. H–5); Memo, Amberg, 7 Jun 41 (App. H–4).

(45) Memos, Lt Col Greenbaum for Lt Col Branshaw, 10 and 14 Jun 41.

(46) Memo, Lt Col Greenbaum for Lt Col Branshaw, 10 Jun 41, par. 11; chronological report of events by Branshaw.

(47) The many technical and operating problems are discussed in Branshaw's final report; Greenbaum's various memoranda for Branshaw and for the under secretary of war; and various recorded telephone conversations, including questions as to insurance coverage, maintenance of

records, and procurement. Most of these problems became academic with the decision to treat North American Aviation as an agent. Some are discussed in subsequent chapters.

(48) Telecon, Under Sec War and Lt Col Branshaw, 12 Jun 41, at 1250.

(49) Nicol Rpt.

(50) Ibid.

(51) Ltr, E. L. Lynch, Grand Lodge Representative, International Association of Machinists, to Kindleberger, 10 Jun 41, and reply to Lynch from Lt Col Branshaw, 14 Jun 41.

(52) Memo, Lt Col Greenbaum for Lt Col Branshaw, 14 Jun 41, par. 7; Nicol Rpt; weekly and daily Rpts of Grievance Committee, 2 Jun to 30 Jun 41, being in the form of memoranda from Howe Thayer and Robert McCullock for Kindleberger; Procedure for Handling Grievances (App. H–13).

(53) Memos, Lt Col Greenbaum for Under Sec War, 19 and 20 Jun 41; Nicol Rpt.

(54) Nicol Rpt.

(55) Memo of White House Conference, 10 Jun 41 (App. H–2); successive memoranda, Greenbaum for Branshaw, 10 and 14 June 41, and later for the Under Sec War, 19, 20, 21, 23, and 24 Jun 41.

(56) Telecon, Under Sec War and Lt Col Branshaw, 14 Jun 41, at 1445 (EST); Memo, Under Sec War for Sec War, 11 Jun 41; Memo, Under Sec War for President, 12 Jun 41; Memo, Lt Col Greenbaum for Lt Col Branshaw, 14 Jun 41, par. 13.

(57) Memos, Lt Col Greenbaum for Under Sec War, 20, 21, 23, and 24 Jun 41; Nicol Rpt.

(58) The last preceding case had been in 1921, when federal troops intervened in West Virginia mine disturbances. See "Use of Federal Troops in Labor Disputes," *Monthly Labor Review* (Sep 1941).

CHAPTER 3

General Developments During the Summer of 1941 and the Seizure of Air Associates, Inc., in October

General Developments

From a headquarters standpoint the North American Aviation operation had been handled in a somewhat haphazard and disorganized fashion because no single well-defined channel of communication and command existed between Washington and the field. While this was perhaps inevitable in an unprecedented situation where policy questions required War Department and government leaders to participate directly in supervising the operation, it was a condition that merited correction. An effort had been made by the Labor Section, OUSW, to pull the various aspects of the operation together and to channel all communications through its office, an effort aided by the fact that most of the important nontechnical questions were of a labor character. In any event, this experience demonstrated the desirability of centralizing responsibility for handling subsequent operations of this kind. Since it was felt that the North American Aviation case may have been atypical and that legal, fiscal, procurement, production, and other technical problems, rather than labor issues, might predominate in future cases where management cooperation was not present, the Labor Section concluded that this responsibility should be placed in a newly formed unit that might also undertake War Department duties under the requisition law then in the process of congressional enactment. The Labor Section presented its views to Under Secretary Patterson, and, at his request, prepared several studies on the subject.(1) The matter was pushed vigorously because after the North American Aviation case two other situations developed where the possibility of government seizure appeared real. In one of these situations management cooperation appeared unlikely.(2) In addition, in August 1941 the Navy Department suddenly found itself operating the Federal Shipbuilding and Drydock Company as a result of that firm's refusal to accept recommendations of the National Defense Mediation Board (NDMB). The Navy was encountering many difficulties that the War Department fortunately had escaped at North American Aviation. Although the suggestion to centralize all seizure operations in one office was repeatedly advanced during subsequent months and at later stages of the war, the idea was unfortunately never adopted.(3)

The Federal Shipbuilding case stimulated further consideration of the general subject of plant seizures since it presented the first World War II instance of management defiance similar to that of the 1918 Smith and Wesson Company case. Because of the War Department's experience at North American Aviation, the Navy naturally turned to it for advice. Much of the early thinking on the nonlabor aspects of the Federal Shipbuilding case were joint products of the two services. This was fortunate because within two months the War Department was deeply involved in a comparable situation at Air Associates. The case also furnished the occasion for certain additional theoretical considerations of the nature and objectives of any plant seizure.(4)

Air Associates, Inc.

The case of Air Associates, Inc., was comparable to the North American Aviation seizure only in its dramatic beginning. It was infinitely more complex than its predecessor because of the impossibility of retaining the company's top operating personnel and because the business was in serious financial difficulties. The case represented the first instance in the World War II period, where the War Department seized an industrial facility because of a strike that resulted directly from a company's refusal to accept the recommendations of a government agency, in this case the NDMB. While Air Associates was in many respects entirely unique in the history of plant seizures, it raised new issues and required the disposition of a large number of important problems that recurred elsewhere.

Description of the Company

Air Associates was a small company employing less than one thousand persons at its principal plant in Bendix, New Jersey, and at seven branch establishments located in Lodi and Belleville, New Jersey; Chicago and Rockford, Illinois; Dallas, Texas; Marshall, Missouri; and Los Angeles, California. The latter were assembly points, warehouses, and distribution centers. Before the wartime emergency it had been an unimportant jobbing house dealing in small but standard-manufacture aircraft parts. As the aircraft program got under way, however, its business mushroomed and it contracted for additional manufacturing operations. Orders flowed in at a rapidly increasing rate, and the company accepted them beyond its probable ability to deliver. By the fall of 1941, 30 percent of its total backlog was represented by some forty prime contracts with the Army Air Forces (AAF), with an aggregate value of approximately $1,445,000. It also had substantial Navy contracts, with the balance of its business consisting of orders from several major aircraft companies.(5)

The company was owned by the ten men who constituted its board of directors. Six of these had other more important business or professional interests and knew little about the operation of the enterprise. To them it was a sideshow to which they gave little attention. The other four were Leroy Hill, its president, a strong-minded individual who personally ran the business and established its policies; H. I. Crowe, the executive vice president, and G. S. Kleverstrom, the secretary-treasurer, both Hill supporters; and Roy Acre, who handled operations on the West Coast and apparently was not on the best of terms with Hill. The company had been experiencing financial difficulties, largely because its working capital, sufficient for its volume of business in 1939, was insufficient for purposes of its greatly expanded 1941 operations. An effort to refinance through floating an issue of preferred stock had failed, and the company had been forced to borrow increasingly large amounts.

Background of the Dispute

In July 1941 the CIO-affiliated United Automobile Workers of America (UAW) had been certified as the exclusive bargaining agent at Air Associates after a close election, in which a large minority of the employees voted in favor of no union. The company immediately laid off certain UAW members, ostensibly because of a lack of materials. The CIO construed this action as antiunion and called a strike. The dispute was certified to the NDMB, and the men returned to work. For the next two months the board endeavored unsuccessfully to resolve the dispute while also undertaking the more basic problem of assisting the parties in negotiating their first collective bargaining agreement. The company, on the rare occasions when its representatives appeared at scheduled board meetings, objected to the reinstatement of the affected men and to the negotiation of an agreement, repeatedly challenging the National Labor Relations Board's certification of the UAW.

These delays and other further acts on the part of the company brought about a new strike early in October, at a time when Professor Harry Schulman of Yale University, at the request of the NDMB, was undertaking an independent investigation of the case. When company officials walked out of a conference searching for a way to end this new strike, the NDMB recommended, on 9 October 1941, that the union call off the strike, that the company immediately return all strikers to their former jobs without discrimination, and that the parties attend a further hearing before the NDMB in order to work out a general collective bargaining contract. These were standard NDMB recommendations in every case where a strike was in progress, which had received almost universal acceptance in prior disputes. The union promptly accepted, but the company, while agreeing to reemploy the strikers, stated that it would only do so over a period of thirty days and then without any guarantee that the persons concerned would be restored to their former jobs. The board construed this conditional acceptance as a rejection and announced that it was turning the entire case over to the Executive Branch for action.(6)

War Department Efforts To Forestall a Crisis

Paralleling these unfavorable developments were material deteriorations in both production and financial situations at the plant. The company became 130 to

150 days delinquent in its deliveries to the Army. AAF representatives repeatedly met with the company's president and threatened to terminate Army contracts unless the situation was promptly improved, and the possibility of shifting these orders elsewhere was carefully explored. Early in October conditions became so serious that War Department representatives attended a board of director's meeting and demanded a change in management based on the grounds that deliveries were delinquent, financial conditions were critical, and management's continuing labor relations difficulties threatened Army procurement. Representatives of the under secretary of war also made repeated appeals to the president and directors for compliance with the NDMB's recommendations, stating that failure to do so would result in the termination of Army contracts.(7)

Development of the Final Labor Crisis

Almost simultaneously with the NDMB's announced referral of the case to higher authority, the Army Air Forces came to the unexpected conclusion that it could not transfer its orders elsewhere within any short period and that many aircraft concerns would have difficulty obtaining parts if the Bendix plant shut down. This eliminated the possibility of permitting the strike to run its course. The government was face to face with the necessity of taking more drastic steps. Hopeful that a direct appeal to the owners might avert a takeover,(8) the entire board of directors was asked to meet with William S. Knudsen[1] and Under Secretary Patterson on 24 October. This meeting took place when the situation at the plant gave every indication of reaching a bloody crisis, with mass picketing in progress and large groups of militant nonunion employees staging demonstrations and endeavoring to break into the plant.(9) After many hours of haggling the company agreed that "all employees on strike will be returned to the payroll at their former pay on Monday, October 27, and will be placed in their former positions as fast as possible."(10) This announcement postponed the crisis, and the plant operated without pickets the following day. When the strikers presented themselves for reinstatement the company offered to place them on the payroll with pay on the basis of a standard work week until a specific job was found. This precluded any possibility of these men receiving overtime earnings, which normally constituted a very large portion of take-home pay at this plant. Furthermore, there was no assurance when, if ever, employees would be placed in their former jobs. The union immediately threatened to restore the picket lines, and over the next two days the situation quickly deteriorated. At a hurriedly convened conference on 29 October it was decided that a representative of the War Department should be sent to the plant to physically supervise the rein-

---

[1]William S. Knudsen (1879–1948) emigrated to the United States from Denmark in 1899. He joined General Motors Corporation in 1919, serving as vice president and later president of Chevrolet and then as executive vice president and later president of the company. In 1940 Knudsen became a member of the National Defense Commission and in 1941 director general of the Office of Production Management. Recruited by the War Department, he served from January 1942 to June 1945 as director of production with the rank of lieutenant general.

statement in specific jobs of the persons who had been out on strike, even though that meant displacing replacement workers.(11)

On the morning of 30 October Col. Roy M. Jones, chief of the AAF's Eastern Procurement District, and his assistant, Maj. Peter Beasley, proceeded to Bendix. They found an almost hopeless situation. A large number of nonstriking employees, wearing the badge of the "Air Associates Benevolent Association," were on site protesting the return of the strikers. It was evident that there would be trouble, and as soon as striking employees began to return to their former jobs under Army supervision the other employees struck. After one returning striker had been injured in a scuffle, the CIO representative withdrew all his men. Conditions were so bad that Beasley and Jones felt it inadvisable to address the workers in the plant in an attempt to restore some semblance of order.

Lt. Gen. William S. Knudsen
(Photographed in 1942)

These events were repeated at the beginning of the night shift, and the picket line had been reestablished. New and more serious trouble appeared to be in the offing as the picket line grew. Reports came in that sympathy strikes were occurring at neighboring plants and that sympathizers were mobilizing in great force to march on Bendix. By 8:15 P.M. the county sheriff, who had placed twenty policemen around the properties, advised Jones that the crowd would soon be out of his control. At 9:15, after picketers had set fire to the grass adjacent to the plant, burning down several small buildings, the sheriff called the governor for assistance, stating he could no longer assume responsibility for the safety of the nonunion members in the plant who were now conducting a sit-down strike. Word came that the crowd was planning to forcibly invade the plant and throw out its occupants. County police mounted machine guns on the roof of the building and issued sawed-off shotguns and pistols to recently employed workers. According to Colonel Jones, the police were wholly out of sympathy with the CIO and "there is little doubt that had the strikers continued to carry out their threats there would have been a massacre, the proportions of which would have been terrible to contemplate."

Colonel Jones, having concluded that people were about to be killed and government property destroyed, directed that the plant be shut down and asked the sheriff to smuggle the nonunion employees out of the plant through a back entrance and transport them in unlighted cars across a meadow to safety. This was accomplished at the same time that a skirmish line of CIO members could be seen advancing on the plant. Fortunately, this movement was stopped by their leaders, and the group, having learned either of the departure of the nonunion employees from the plant or of developments in Washington, became less menacing and undertook to organize what they termed a victory parade. Jones and Beasley continued a lonely vigil in the plant awaiting further instructions.(12)

The Decision To Take Over

Special consultant McGrady foresaw these events and advised Under Secretary Patterson on 28 October that seizure of the facilities was the only satisfactory answer from the government's standpoint and from that of the public, the employees, and Air Associates' management.(13) He reasoned that "seizure and operation of the plant . . . would enable the War Department to utilize to capacity the facilities of this plant for the production of items needed by the War Department and by War Department prime contractors and would at the same time enable us to uphold the Mediation Board and reestablish collective bargaining and satisfactory labor relations. . . ." By the afternoon of 30 October no one questioned this view, particularly after the UAW's Richard Frankensteen had advised President Roosevelt that riots would occur unless the government immediately intervened. Jones and Beasley continued to plead for such action. All day, officials in the War Department, the Department of Justice, and the NDMB worked on the preparation of papers. At 9:30 P.M. Under Secretary Patterson recommended seizure to the president(14) and at 10:15 an executive order was signed. Roosevelt simultaneously issued a statement, castigating the company for its failure to accept the NDMB's recommendations and calling for an immediate return to work. At 2:00 A.M. on 31 October Colonel Jones announced that he had taken possession of the plant as the War Department representative, with Major Beasley serving as his deputy. By this time a staff of technical assistants—including McGrady, Maj. Karl R. Bendetsen, a judge advocate; Lt. Donald Ipson, a labor officer; and Maj. Robert S. Pickens, a public relations advisor—were en route by plane and several thousand troops were moving to the plant. Before dawn notices of government possession had been posted and some two thousand soldiers were deployed.

Problems Confronting the Army

Unlike at North American Aviation, the task of obtaining a prompt return to work did not appear to be overly difficult. While fights the preceding afternoon between reinstated strikers and nonstrikers indicated the existence of strong feelings between the two groups, there was reason to believe that the presence of federal troops would prevent any repetition of violence. On the other hand, the problem of working out a permanent solution of the conditions that precipitated the seizure loomed very large. Hill, his immediate associates, and the company's attorney, Mr. Challaire, seemed determined to prevent compliance with the

NDMB's recommendations or settlement of other points with the union. Even before government intervention the only solution seemed to lie in obtaining new management and having this new group negotiate a collective bargaining agreement, with the certified union under the direction of the NDMB. Since the directors at the preceding week's Washington conference had supported Hill and his labor policies, it was determined that such a solution might take a long time to work out, and in the meantime the plant had to be run, probably without management cooperation. This raised a series of business problems that had been absent at North American Aviation and that were complicated by the company's financial situation. Colonel Jones' instructions—almost identical to those of Colonel Branshaw—did not provide ready-made answers.

Col. Karl R. Bendetsen
(Photographed in 1944)

Restoring Production

Since most of the employees had not slept during the preceding turbulent night, Jones decided to postpone manufacturing operations until the middle of the day and to use the intervening hours to prepare for a full restoration of production. At 8:00 A.M. he addressed a large number of employees assembled at the plant. He informed them that he was speaking in the president's name, that he had taken possession of the plant and would operate it for the United States, that all former employees should return to their jobs, and that each person would be placed in his former position on an individual basis and without discrimination as soon as certain details could be worked out.(15) This appeal was supplemented by a radio broadcast, in which Jones and McGrady told of the purpose of the seizure and the status of the plant and by telephone calls to employees informing them of the reopening. During the morning office workers were admitted and "hired" to carry on in their normal positions. A rapid survey was made of plant conditions and preliminary plans were developed for the control of operations, for the recording of all business transactions, and for an inventory. At noon Jones began to admit employees in groups of five. Each employee was interviewed, required to sign an employment application, and assigned as far as possible to his former position. By the end of the day shift more than 60 percent of the production force was at work and some shipments of materials had been made to meet critical shortages. By the following afternoon production and the work force had returned to normal.(16)

The one real obstacle to keeping the work force intact was the strong feelings of persons in the nonunion group, but any real danger of an incident or of a walk-out seemed remote. A petition signed by 502 employees, alleging that the pre-seizure disorders were entirely the work of a small minority of strikers and outside agitators, requested that the United States immediately withdraw from possession so that the former "loyal American management" of the company might continue to operate the plant. Investigation disclosed that this petition had been written by a publicity man for Hill.(17) Colonel Jones and other War Department officials believed that Hill was trying to enflame worker conflicts, and Jones decided to exclude him, Crowe, and Challaire from the plant and to keep 300 soldiers on guard duty as late as December 3.

Immediate Operating Problems

Colonel Jones called a directors' meeting early on the first morning of the seizure. This meeting was friendly and company representatives agreed to cooper-ate fully with the government. Jones and Beasley were willing to test this pledge, but as realists they nevertheless went about the job of making plans for direct gov-ernment operation. They faced several types of difficulties, including practical questions concerned with the taking of an inventory, the establishment of an accounting system, the development of procurement procedures, and the financing of the enterprise with government funds; problems relating to the proportion of the company's total business the War Department would endeavor to carry on; prob-lems created by the company's prior production and planning decisions; and prob-lems growing out of the company's financial condition. All these dilemmas were interwoven with and had to be solved in the light of the ultimate task of developing a permanent solution permitting the early return of the plant to private ownership.

By 9:00 on the first morning of occupation an inventory was under way—a difficult job because the plant contained hundreds of thousands of small items of the kind to be found in any jobbing house. Because a physical count could require weeks of extensive labor, which could interrupt or delay operations,(18) an inno-vative procedure was adopted. The closing balance sheet of the company as of 30 September 1941, the end of its fiscal year, and the record of all shipments received and made during the subsequent thirty days were obtained and com-bined, providing a satisfactory estimate of the value of the properties taken.(19) This work was turned over to a New York accounting firm engaged on the morn-ing of the seizure under a contract that also provided for a complete audit of the company's books and the opening of a new set of books to reflect War Department operation.(20) The Army Air Forces immediately furnished finance officers to Colonel Jones, and AAF funds were credited to his account. It was rec-ognized that he would have to make expenditures that might not be approved by the General Accounting Office (GAO) and that in such event special legislation to reimburse him would be necessary.(21) Fortunately, many of these problems were largely avoided by converting the operation into one that was essentially for the account of the company,(22) and the final cost to the government was only $8,008.(23) As the company initially indicated no desire to continue its normal procurement, Major Beasley was designated as contracting officer with instructions to purchase materials through the channels ordinarily used by Air Associates but for the account of the government.(24)

The War Department continued both the commercial and military work of the company because the character of the business was such as to make segregation of the two types of transactions very difficult. Most of the commercial business was indirectly for defense purposes, and it seemed undesirable to destroy a going enterprise and its goodwill, particularly if there was any hope that the plant could be restored to private control.(25)

A more fundamental question related to whether the War Department would extend its control to the company's seven branches nationwide for which the Bendix plant was the central office and control point for sales, purchases, and records. It was the consensus that from a business standpoint this integrated system should be operated as a unit. This view was strengthened by a belief that control over these additional properties strengthened the War Department's bargaining position with management. As matters stood, certain members of management believed that they could use this situation to embarrass the War Department, and there was some indication that they might be planning to set up a new central operating unit comparable to the Bendix plant that would service and tie in with the branch establishments. Failure to take over these branches might also lead to a company charge that the War Department had destroyed their business by failing to supply them with goods. The decision was made to supply these branches irrespective of War Department control.(26) This produced a number of accounting and bookkeeping problems.(27)

The company was quick to raise the question of control of the branches in a letter to Secretary Stimson that unwittingly argued the best possible case for extension of government possession.(28) It pointed out that the Bendix plant controlled all branch operations, filled more than a hundred branch requisitions for materials daily, carried on the entire company's accounting and bookkeeping work, made funds available for local branch payrolls, and performed all engineering, designing, and experimental work necessary to meet the requirements of branch office customers. In addition, one half of its manufacturing was in response to orders received from these branches. The letter demanded an arrangement under which the company could continue to use the facilities of the Bendix plant. The War Department came to a prompt decision,(29) but Judge Advocate General Maj. Gen. Myron C. Cramer[2] was doubtful whether the executive order was sufficiently broad to permit

---

[2]Maj. Gen. Myron C. Cramer (1881–1966) was born in Connecticut and was educated at Wesleyan University and Harvard Law School. He entered the Washington National Guard for duty on the Mexican border in 1916 and served with the 41st Division, American Expeditionary Forces (1917–18). After the war he was assigned to the Judge Advocate General's Department (1921), taught at West Point (1921–22), and was staff judge advocate of the Philippine Department (1935–37). He was the judge advocate general from 1 December 1941 to 30 November 1945, when he left to take part in the Far East War Crimes Tribunal.

Maj. Gen. Myron C. Cramer

the taking of these properties. After conferring with President Roosevelt, however, Secretary Stimson moved forward with the plan to seize the remaining facilities.(30) Taking the other properties presented a practical organizational problem that was solved by issuing new instructions to Colonel Jones and by issuing separate instructions to AAF officers located near the branch properties, ordering them to seize and operate each under Jones' direction and control.(31) The additional properties were in the possession of these officers by the afternoon of 7 November, and arrangements were immediately made through a New York accounting firm and the accounting offices of the appropriate procurement districts to take an inventory and to handle other financial details.(32) These properties had no labor problems and operation of them caused no difficulty.(33)

A third question concerned whether new construction work under a Defense Plant Corporation lease with Air Associates should be continued. Since the new facilities adjacent to the Bendix plant were for defense purposes, and because of the adoption of the policy of not disrupting the company's normal business, the War Department decided that this work should go forward.(34)

Major Beasley stated that he found the plant in a worse condition than any other plant he had ever seen, with 43 percent of the machinery "blacked out" because of lack of direction and 63 percent of the work requiring redoing.(35) The firm's delinquencies on orders were already well known. Accordingly, Jones was authorized to make any changes in the plant and to purchase any machinery he felt would be desirable in the interests of full and efficient production.(36) The job to be done was largely of an engineering character, and Beasley, who was an old hand at this sort of thing, methodically reorganized the plant. By the end of War Department possession eight weeks later production was approximately 30 percent higher and sales had increased. During the second month of government operation the net income of the business exceeded that of any previous month in the company's history.(37)

The company's lack of adequate capital was quickly apparent. Its prewar annual sales of about $1.8 million quadrupled in 1941. Capital adequate for its 1939 business was not adequate to meet the fourfold increase. When the attempt to float stock failed, the company resorted to bank loans obtained from the Irving Trust Company and Bank of Manhattan.(38) The company was short of cash and the

War Department, by operating its business, was cutting off its principal source of income. Since the bank loans were made against accounts receivable, the banks immediately wished to know government intentions with respect to remittances in payment of such accounts. They were advised that the government had no interest in any current accounts receivable nor in any remittances received in payment of shipments made prior to government possession, but that remittances reflecting payment for shipments made during or as a result of government operations would, to the extent that they reflected government effort, be covered by the Treasury of the United States. The banks were also concerned over the possibility that trade creditors with delinquent accounts might precipitate insolvency proceedings and, with this in mind, they declared their intention of calling in outstanding loans and offsetting deposits of the company against them. War Department representatives took the position that this decision was up to the banks but suggested that no other single action would precipitate insolvency proceedings more quickly, ending any possibility of government aid through advance payments on outstanding company contracts. The banks were impressed by these arguments. The financial situation provided the key to the discovery of a technique for operation without the use of government funds, while simultaneously serving as a powerful weapon in forcing a solution of the case.(39)

Method of Operation

Since Hill and his associates were excluded from the premises, there seemed no alternative except to operate the plants with government funds and managing personnel.(40) For all the reasons foreseen, direct government operation immediately gave every evidence of proving unsatisfactory. There would be difficulties in carrying out day-to-day procurement in accordance with Army regulations, including deductions and payments of social security and related taxes and benefits; in reconciling private employment practices with Civil Service rules or, conversely, in applying Civil Service rules to employees; in employing salesmen and sales engineers to maintain the company's commercial business and goodwill; and in making the kind of expenditures required to run a private enterprise consistent with GAO procedures. The formation of a government corporation similar to the National Operating Corporation of World War I was therefore considered. Attorneys Joseph Bishop and Arthur F. Tripp, Jr., prepared a study of the steps necessary for creating such a corporation, its advantages, and its method of operation.(41) With the exception of Colonel Greenbaum, everyone was of the opinion that if no other arrangement could be worked out quickly, either for the return of the properties to Air Associates or for some operating arrangement that would end the need for using federal funds, the general procedure urged in the Bishop and Tripp report should be adopted.(42)

The necessity for such action was eliminated on 22 November. After three weeks of negotiations a unique arrangement between the company, its creditors, and the War and Navy Departments was effected, making it possible to operate the properties without further use of federal funds and to reimburse the government for all expenditures. The agreement served as a means of providing working capital for the business until equity funds could be obtained. Under the agreement special accounts were established, to which the banks that had extended credit to Air Associates transferred all monies from the company's regular accounts. The banks agreed to extend their loans at 4 percent instead of the former 2.5 percent interest. The War and Navy Departments agreed (43) to make advance payments for deposit in these special accounts in the amount of 30 percent of their outstanding contracts with the company (approximately $500,000), and the company agreed that all its future receipts, with the exception of small accounts required locally for the operation of branch establishments, would be similarly deposited. The amounts in the special accounts might be used for any business purpose, including the reimbursement of the government for all expenses incurred by it in operating the properties, but not including the cost of troops and other strictly seizure expenses. Until all advance payments deposited in such accounts had been liquidated, any withdrawals were subject to the approval of the War Department representative,(44) and extensive security provisions were included to protect creditors. Most important, the contract contained a promise by the company to obtain a new president or general manager as soon as possible at the War Department's option within twenty-one days.(45) It was expected that government advances would be liquidated as contracts were performed and that sufficient working capital would be provided until the company could be refinanced. This agreement was doubly significant from a War Department standpoint because it meant that future expenses would be paid out of company rather than government funds and that prior federal expenditures in running the business would be reimbursed. The complicating factor of government financing was now out of the picture, and any need for creating a government operating corporation was gone.

Finding a Permanent Solution

Colonel Jones and his associates were convinced that new management was needed to permanently solve the troubles at Air Associates, and they sought to persuade company directors of the need for this move. Irrespective of the very persuasive fact of government possession, this might have proved very difficult if the company had been solvent or if the War Department had indicated a willingness to relinquish control with the former management in place.

In spite of initial assurances of cooperation, it was plain that the faction represented by Hill maintained a running fight against the War Department both privately and in the press, and the Air Associates board in its 5 November meeting supported Hill and his lieutenants, even though it concluded that too much policy discretion had been vested in them. In the succeeding days four of the directors visited the plant and talked to Colonel Jones. For the first time they learned of the circumstances leading up to the government's action, and they expressed shock and surprise. They were further advised of the War Department's determination to remain until acceptable managerial personnel were substituted for Hill and, later, of the dependency of the proposed financial agreement upon a promise to this effect.(46) By the middle of the month the majority of the board yielded, and on 18 November they forced both Hill and Crowe to resign.(47) Hill's reaction was very negative, and he undertook a press campaign(48) against what he termed the arbitrary action of the War Department in forcing his resignation. He attempted to enlist the support of several congressmen,(49) of local businessmen, and of the National Association of Manufacturers.(50) He made a personal visit to the War Department(51) and issued such strong statements concerning the Army that the War Department felt impelled to issue a lengthy statement to the press defending its position.(52)

The directors went about the business of finding a new general manager to replace Hill, and within a few days had selected F. G. Coburn(53) with the understanding that he would work unobtrusively under the direction of the War Department representative until the situation could be stabilized. It was now possible to tackle the company's labor troubles and to undertake the refinancing of the business through a new security issue. As a practical matter, solution of the labor dispute was related to this refinancing because of doubt as to the company's ability to meet the union's wage demands.

Coburn undertook a series of meetings with the union, at which War Department labor consultant Robert F. Gaffney was present.(54) There was considerable question as to whether Gaffney should actively participate in the discussions and what part, if any, he should play in the solution of the dispute. A decision was reached that he should remain wholly inactive and neutral,(55) a decision that was difficult to follow because of Coburn's attempts to obtain the department's position on particular points.(56) Coburn was generally handicapped in these negotiations by an incomplete knowledge of the company and the frequent necessity for financial consultation with his bankers. The slowness of the negotiations was such that the War Department decided on 18 December that it would withdraw from the plant by the end of the year regardless of Coburn's progress.(57) This decision was possible because most of Air Associates' business had been transferred elsewhere when the nation went to war. It was thought these factors might incline both parties toward concluding a labor agreement.(58) The decision was made in spite of the fact that in the absence of such an agreement a strike would probably follow the War Department's withdrawal.(59) This stand had its effect: Shortly before Christmas an agreement was reached.

Termination of Possession

The War Department had advised the company very early of its hope that the entire operation could eventually be concluded by the exchange of mutual releases. In addition, the War Department would assign to the company all contracts that it had made during its possession and offset against sums due the company from the government the cost of government-purchased materials in stock. Any accounts payable would be assumed by the company, and the company would be given the benefit of accounts receivable after the total cost of government operation had been deducted.(60) The Army was prepared, if an arrangement could not be effected when it relinquished possession, to reserve the right to make a complete inventory as of the date of relinquishment and to obtain a certified balance sheet audit in order to protect itself against any claims the company might subsequently assert.(61)

The company initially appeared reluctant to accede to the proposal for mutual releases, believing it might have some claim against the government by reason of the seizure as such, but it indicated its willingness to enter into the second type of arrangement. In addition, it was prepared to fill orders, to file social security and unemployment insurance returns, and to preserve intact all books, records, and other data relating to the period of Army occupation. At the last moment it agreed to the plan first suggested, and on 29 December 1941 letters of release were exchanged. That same day, after obtaining President Roosevelt's concurrence, the Army withdrew.(62) The terms of this withdrawal were carefully set forth in special instructions from Under Secretary Patterson to Colonel Jones(63) that called, among other things, for a letter from the company agreeing to preserve records; to take care of social security, state unemployment compensation, group insurance, and hospitalization payments for employees for the period of government operation; and to advise insurers of the changed status of the company's properties.(64)

The War Department was commended by many of the company's contractors and by the board of directors.(65) Coburn remarked that the company would have gone into receivership if the Army had not occupied and operated the properties.

Operating Labor Problems

While the War Department was obviously obliged to dispose of day-to-day labor difficulties that arose, it did not try to correct basic conditions on the theory that their rectification was a company matter. Sweatshop conditions had existed in the plant, and there were less than forty-five men who received more than 45 cents per hour.(66) In fact, the history of the company had been one of difficult labor relations. During the Army operation the employees were considered government employees and, in contrast with the North American Aviation case, were required to sign an application for employment when they returned to work.(67) These applications were designed to clarify the terms and conditions of employment but, more important, were intended to obtain the employees' consent to deductions for social security and workman's compensation, deductions which would have been required by law if the company had been operating the properties but which were not required in the case of a government business. Although considered government employees, workers were not treated as such, or at least not as ordinary government employees. The terms and conditions of employment were the same as before the seizure, and it was decided that such federal laws as the eight-hour day and Saturday half-holiday laws should not be construed as applicable.(68)

In spite of War Department objections, the executive order included the same provision as in the North American Aviation order requiring the employment of a civilian advisor on labor relations. Considerable difficulty was experienced in obtaining such an individual because of the uncertain tenure of the job, and it was only after an exhaustive search that Robert Gaffney was finally secured.(69) While Gaffney did an excellent job, the difficulty finding him further strengthened the War Department's desire to exclude such a provision in any future executive order.

Post-termination Developments

Because the agreement with the banks provided for approval by the War Department representative of all withdrawals from the special accounts, the War Department continued to have special obligations even after termination of possession. These obligations continued until the company was refinanced and the necessity for the agreement removed. War Department officials were not satisfied with the way Coburn ran the company, and Crowe was brought back as president. He did a good job, and by July all government funds had been withdrawn and the business was on a reasonably sound financial basis in private hands.

Significance of the Case

The case of Air Associates, Inc., was significant because it raised a large number of basic problems that were likely to arise in any case where management refused to cooperate. It also provided an excellent opportunity for exploring and reaching tentative conclusions concerning many fiscal, procurement, inventory, accounting, and Civil Service problems incident to direct War Department operation. The Air Associates case clearly demonstrated the great difficulties of a seizure and showed that even in management noncompliance cases there was a possibility of financing the operation without the use of government funds.

Endnotes

(1) Memo, Ohly for Amberg, 21 Jul 41; Memo, Bishop for Amberg, 31 Jul 41, sub: Proposed Directive Establishing a Section in the OUSW To Handle the Seizure and Operations of Plants (App. I–1); Memo, Bishop for Ohly, 26 Jul 41, same subject.

(2) Western Cartridge Company, East Alton, Ill., and Aluminum Company of America. Vancouver, Wash.

(3) Memo, Ohly for Amberg, 22 Sep 41, sub: Plant Requisition Section; Memo for file by Ohly, 25 Sep 41, sub: Plant Requisition Section (App. I–2).

(4) See App. I–3, an informal analysis prepared in the Labor Section.

(5) Exhibit H of Memo, Ohly for Under Sec War, 24 Oct 41, sub: Air Associates; and Memo, Bishop for Ohly, 23 Oct 41, sub: Miscellaneous Data on Air Associates.

(6) As to the background of this dispute, see Memo, Ohly for Under Sec War, 21 Oct 41, sub: Air Associates, Inc.; Memo, Ohly for Under Sec War, 24 Oct 41, and attachments thereto, particularly Exhibit C, being a summary of the case prepared by the NDMB on 14 Oct 41; Findings and Recommendations of NDMB, 9 Oct 41, in the Matter of Air Associates, Inc., and UAW of America, CIO, NDMB Case No. 51.

(7) Exhibit H of Memo, Ohly for Under Sec War, 24 Oct 41; Memo, Ohly for Under Sec War, 21 Oct 41; Memo for file by Ohly, 19 Oct 41, sub: Air Associates; unsigned and untitled Memo, 18 Oct 41, summarizing telecons Hill and Ohly; Memo for file by Ohly, 11 Oct 41, sub: Strike at Air Associates.

(8) Memo for file by Ohly, 23 Oct 41, sub: Air Associates.

(9) These events are described by Professor Nunn, Chairman of the New Jersey State Mediation Board, in Telecons with Ohly, 24 Oct 41.

(10) War Department Press Release, 24 Oct 41.

(11) Memo, McGrady for Under Sec War, 27 Oct 41, sub: Air Associates, Inc.; Memo, Lewis Gill of NDMB for Ohly, 29 Oct 41; Telg, Under Sec War to Hill, 29 Oct 41.

(12) 1st End, Col Jones for Under Sec War, 2 Dec 41, to Memo, Under Sec War for Eastern District Supervisor, Air Corps Procurement, 29 Oct 41; Telecons, Col Jones and Maj Beasley with various War Department officials in Washington, 30 Oct 41, at 1100, 1630, 1700, 1750, 1900, and 2135.

(13) Memo, McGrady for Under Sec War, 28 Oct 41, sub: Air Associates (App. J–1).

(14) Memo, Under Sec War for President, 30 Oct 41, sub: Air Associates, Bendix, New Jersey.

(15) Telecon, McGrady and Battley, 31 Oct 41, at 1130.

(16) Memo, Lt Ipson for Battley, 3 Nov 41, sub: Seizure of Air Associates, Inc., Bendix, N.J., which carefully described labor events from 0220 on 31 Oct to 1300 on 1 Nov; Memo, Col Jones for Sec War, 6 Nov 41, sub: Initial Report, Operation of Bendix, New Jersey, Plants of Air Associates, Inc., par. 7; Telecons, Col Jones and Smith, 31 Oct 41, at 0945, Col Battley, McGrady, and Maj Bendetsen, 31 Oct 41, at 1130, Smith and Maj Bendetsen, 1 Nov 41, at 0915, and Ohly and Maj Bendetsen, 1 Nov 41, at 1145.

(17) "A Petition for the President, the Speaker of the U.S. House of Representatives and the President of the United States Senate," 26 Nov 41, referred to the War Department on 1 December 1941 by the Secretary to the President; Telecon, McGrady, Ohly, Col Jones, and Gaffney, 3 Dec 41.

(18) Instructions for Col Jones from Acting Sec War, 30 Oct 41.

(19) Initial Rpt of Col Jones to Sec War, par. G.

(20) Memo, Maj Beasley for Phagan, Tillison, and Tremble, approved and accepted by them, 7 Nov 41, sub: Auditing Services.

(21) Memo, Amberg for Under Sec War, 3 Nov 41, sub: Air Associates, Incorporated, par. 4 (App. J–2).

(22) Method of Operation, par. 9.

(23) Memo, Col Jones for Under Sec War, 11 Feb 42, sub: Report Submitted in Connection With Government Occupancy of Air Associates, Inc., Bendix, New Jersey, par. 6.

(24) Initial Rpt of Col Jones to Sec War, par. 1.

(25) Memo for file by Ohly, 8 Nov 41, sub: Air Associates—Conference of Nov. 2nd, 1941, par. 2; Memo, Amberg for Under Sec War, 3 Nov 41, par. 3 (App. J–2).

(26) Memo for file by Maj Bendetsen, 4 Nov 41, sub: Operation of Bendix Air Associates Plant.

(27) Memo, Amberg for Under Sec War, 3 Nov 41, par. 4 (App. J–2).

(28) Ltr, Hill to Acting Sec War, 3 Nov 41 (App. J–3).

(29) Memo for file by Ohly, 8 Nov 41 (App. J–4); Memo, Amberg for Under Sec War, 3 Nov 41, pars. 1 and 2 (App. J–2); War Department Press Release, 5 Nov 41.

(30) Ltr, Acting Sec War to President, 3 Nov 41 (App. J–5) on which the president noted his approval.

(31) Ltr, Under Sec War to Col Jones, 4 Nov 41 (App. J–6); Memo, Under Sec War for Lt Col Branshaw, 5 Nov 41, sub: Possession of Branch Plants of Air Associates, Incorporated (App. J–7).

(32) See Memo, Col Jones for Sec War, 7 Nov 41, sub: Supplemental Report Concerning War Department Operations, Air Associates Plants.

(33) Memo, Col Jones for Sec War, 11 Nov 41, sub: Relinquishment of Government Possession of Air Associates, Marshall, Missouri, Property; Ltr, Col Jones to Gilbert Colgate, Jr., 11 Nov 41.

(34) Continuation of this work necessitated legal arrangements that were worked out with the Defense Plant Corporation (DPC). The expedient was used of having Colonel Jones exercise the contractual rights of the company under the DPC lease, giving approval in lieu of the company to vouchers submitted by the building contractor. The directors of the corporation met and authorized this procedure. The lease was even modified during War Department possession. See Memo, Brig Gen O. P. Echo for Col Jones, 4 Nov 41, sub: Lease Air Associates, Inc., With Defense Plant Corp.; Memos for file by Ohly, 8, 22, 26, and 28 Nov 41 and 12 Dec 41, variously titled.

(35) Memo for file by Ohly, 22 Dec 41, sub: Air Associates—Developments (App. J–8).

(36) Memo for file by Ohly, 8 Nov 41 (App. J–4).

(37) Memo, Col Jones for Under Sec War, 11 Feb 42; Memo, Ohly for Under Sec War, 9 Jan 42, sub: Air Associates.

(38) Memo for file by Ohly, 22 Dec 41 (App. J–8); Memo, Col Jones for Sec War, 9 Nov 41, sub: Report of Developments Touching Termination of Government Possession (App. J–9).

(39) Memo, Col Jones for Sec War, 9 Nov 41 (App. J–9); Memo, Amberg for Under Sec War, 4 Nov 41, sub: Air Associates, Inc.; Memo, Under Sec War for Lovett, 5 Nov 41, sub: Air Associates, Inc.

(40) Memo for file by Ohly, 8 Nov 41 (App. J–4).

(41) Memo, Tripp and Bishop for Amberg, 4 Nov 41, sub: Outline of Contractual Relations Between the Government and Corporation Operating the Plant of Air Associates, Inc. (App. J–10).

(42) Memo, Amberg for Under Sec War, 6 Nov 41, sub: Air Associates, Incorporated (App. J–11); Memo, Amberg for Under Sec War, 7 Nov 41, sub: Air Associates, Inc.

(43) Pursuant to the authority contained in Sec. i, par. (c) of Public Law 703, 67th Cong., approved 3 Jul 40, as amended.

(44) Such withdrawals were also subject to approval of the Navy Department, but the latter designated the War Department representative to act for it.

(45) The contract, without exhibits, surety annex, and signatures, is contained in Appendix J–12.

(46) Memo, Col Jones for Sec War, 9 Nov 41 (App. J–9); Memo for file by Ohly, 8 Nov 41, sub: Air Associates—Conference With Palmedo.

(47) Memo for file by Ohly, 18 Nov 41, sub: Air Associates, Inc.

(48) Statement of Hill to Press, 19 Nov 41; Ltr, Hill to Under Sec War, 24 Nov 41; Memo for file by Ohly, 22 Nov 41, sub: Air Associates—Statements by Mr. Hill.

(49) Telg, Rep J. Parnell Thomas of New Jersey for Under Sec War, 17 Nov 41; Ltr, Rep Leland Ford for Under Sec War, 15 Dec 41; Memo for file by Ohly, 22 Nov 41.

(50) Telecon, McGrady, Ohly, Gaffney, and Col Jones, 3 Dec 41.

(51) Summary of Interview With Mr. Hill, Former General Manager of Air Associates, Inc., Mr. McGrady, and Col Battley, 18 Nov 41, 10:30 A.M., signed by Battley and McGrady.

(52) War Department Press Release, 26 Nov 41 (App. J–12A).

(53) Ltr, Coburn to Under Sec War, 21 Nov 41; Memo, Amberg for Under Sec War, 22 Nov 41; Memo for file by Ohly, 22 Nov 41, sub: Air Associates—Choice of New Management.

(54) Memo for file by Ohly, 3 Dec 41, sub: Air Associates— Developments in the Labor Situation.

(55) Telecon, Ohly, McGrady, Gaffney, and Col Jones, 3 Dec 41.

(56) Memo for file by Ohly, 22 Dec 41 (App. J–8).

(57) Memo, Col Jones for Under Sec War, 20 Dec 41, sub: Army Evacuation of the Plants of Air Associates, Inc.; Memo for file by Ohly, 22 Dec 41 (App. J–8); Memo, Under Sec War for Amberg, 19 Dec 41; Memo, Amberg for Under Sec War, 19 Dec 41; Memo, Ohly for Under Sec War, 24 Dec 41, sub: Army Withdrawal From Air Associates; Memo, Under Sec War for Ohly, 24 Dec 41; Memo for file by Ohly, 17 Dec 41, sub: Air Associates—General Developments.

(58) The disregarding of this fact is in direct contrast with the relevancy given to similar facts in later cases, where, in spite of the unimportance of production, the Army remained in possession until the danger of another strike passed. This change in attitude was a direct outgrowth of the no-strike pledge and the formation of the NWLB.

(59) Memo, Col Jones for Sec War, 9 Nov 41 (App. J–9).

(60) Memo, Col Jones for Under Sec War, 20 Dec 41.

(61) Ltr, Under Sec War to Air Associates, 29 Dec 41 (App. J–13); Ltr, Air Associates to Sec War, 29 Dec 41 (App. J–14); Memo, Col Jones for Under Sec War, 30 Dec 41, sub: Termination of Government Occupancy of Air Associates, Inc.; Ltr, Under Sec War to President, 26 Dec 41, and approved by the president (App. J–15). It should be noted that the president signed no executive order directing termination as in the North American case, the Department of Justice being of the opinion that the president's written approval of the under secretary's proposal to withdraw as set forth in this letter was sufficient. See Ltr, Newman A. Townsend, Acting Asst Solicitor General, to Maj. Charles P. Burnett, Jr., 6 Jan 42; Memo, Ohly for Under Sec War, 9 Jan 42, sub: Air Associates.

(62) Ltr, Under Sec War to Col Jones, 29 Dec 41 (App. J–16).

(63) Ltr, Air Associates to Sec War, 29 Dec 41 (App. J–17).

(64) Ltr, Col Jones to Under Sec War, 5 Dec 41; Memo, Col Jones for Under Sec War, 11 Feb 42; Memo, Ohly for Under Sec War, 9 Jan 42.

(65) Memo for file by Ohly, 8 Nov 41 (App. J–4).

(66) App. J–18.

(67) Memo for file by Ohly, 12 Nov 41, sub: Air Associates—Eight-Hour Law and Saturday Half-Holiday Law.

(68) Memos for file by Ohly, 12 and 17 Nov 41.

(69) Memo, Col Jones for Under Sec War, 11 Feb 42; Memo, Col Jones for OUSW, 19 Feb 42, sub: Air Associates, Inc. (Countersigning of Checks on Special Lien Fund); Memo, Ohly for Under Sec War, 25 Mar 42, sub: Recent Developments at Air Associates; Memo, Ohly for Amberg, 2 Jul 42, sub: Air Associates, Inc.

CHAPTER 4

The Captive Coal Case, November 1941, and General Developments, October 1941 to August 1942

The Captive Coal Case

Although the strike of the United Mine Workers of America (UMW) against the steel company owners of the captive coal mines in the fall of 1941 never actually required a War Department seizure, planning for such an eventuality did take place.

The first phase of this strike began in October 1941, when the steel companies, after months of negotiations, refused to grant the closed-shop demand of John L. Lewis,[1] president of the UMW. The stoppage had the immediate effect of seriously reducing bituminous coal supplies at steel mills, and this in turn threatened steel output, perhaps the most critical of all war programs at that time. There was a short respite late in October, when, at President Roosevelt's request and with a promise of expeditious consideration of the case by the National Defense Mediation Board (NDMB), Lewis suspended the strike and the NDMB took the matter under consideration. In prior cases the NDMB recommended maintenance of membership in cases where unions asked for union security. Such recommendations were uniformly accepted, but in this instance there was a real danger of rejection. Therefore, when it became clear that the NDMB would again follow this policy in spite of bitter opposition from CIO members, a major crisis appeared imminent. Conferences of War Department and other government officials were called by the public members of the NDMB to discuss what to do in the event that the miners struck upon the rendering of such a decision.(1) As a result, the War Department undertook the preparation of a plan to seize and operate the captive mines.

Under the plan responsibility was divided between a troop commander—Lt. Gen. Robert Richardson, Jr.[2]—and a director of operations—Col. David

---

[1] John L. Lewis (1880–1969), was an Iowa-born labor leader and early UMW member, AFofL organizer (1911–17), UMW vice president (1917–21), and UMW president from 1920 onward. Lewis was influential in William Green's election to the presidency of the AFofL after Samuel Gompers' death in 1924, but broke with Green a decade later over the issue of industrial organization. In 1935 Lewis founded the CIO and served as its president until 1940.

[2] Lt. Gen. Robert Richardson, Jr. (1882–1954), was born in Charleston, South Carolina, was graduated from West Point (1904), served with the 14th Cavalry in the Philippines (1904–06), and was an instructor at West Point
Continued

McCoach, Jr.[3]—with final responsibility vested in neither one. General
Richardson prepared an elaborate program that called for large numbers of combat troops, armed with tanks and heavy artillery, to be deployed to the mining areas
to guard the persons, properties, and families of nonstrikers and to serve as a threat
to strikers. Colonel McCoach's plan was similarly elaborate, calling for the establishment of a central War Department office in Pittsburgh with a director of operations and technical experts in mining, public and industrial relations, and fiscal
matters. He also urged creation of regional offices with a similar director and
group of technicians in each affected mining area,(2) as well as the designation of
a War Department representative to act as manager of the coal mines of each company. Specific nominees for nearly every one of the several hundred jobs listed
were included. McCoach's plan contemplated only token seizure until the War
Department could determine to what extent the companies would make their managers and finances available to the government during the latter's period of control. The first step in the plan was a meeting with steel executives, where they
would be asked to operate the properties for the government with their own funds.
If they refused, direct operation with federal funds would result. Most of these federal funds, however, would in reality be supplied by the steel companies through
payments to the government for any coal furnished from seized mines. The operating plan was ably conceived and well drawn insofar as its legal, fiscal, production, safety, public relations, and administrative aspects were concerned. It failed
entirely, however, to deal with the crucial question of how the War Department
would induce the miners to return to work if the mere fact of the government
seizure did not do so.(3)

The dependence of the plan on expectations of an automatic and voluntary
return to work purely as a result of a simple seizure and the division of responsibility contemplated led the Labor Section, OUSW, to take exception to its
implementation. McCoach was convinced of the wisdom of the Labor Section's
view, which gained further support when Lewis ordered a second walkout following the adverse decision of the NDMB and the failure of further negotiations. Lewis stated bluntly, "If the soldiers come, the mine workers will remain
peacefully in their homes, conscious of the fact that bayonets in coal mines will
not produce coal." The Labor Section emphasized that the problem was a psychological one, a problem of convincing the miners that they should return to

---

(1906–11). After one year with the 23d Infantry and service with the American Expeditionary Forces (1918–21),
he returned to the Philippines (1921–23) and later served as military attache in Rome (1926–28), as commander
of the 5th and 1st Cavalry Divisions (1939–41), as a staff member of the War Department Public Relations Office
(1941), and as commander of the VII Army Corps (1941). His final post before retirement in 1946 was as commanding officer of the Hawaiian Department (1943).

[3]Maj. Gen. David McCoach, Jr. (1887–1951), was a 1910 West Point graduate, born in Philadelphia,
Pennsylvania. An engineer, he served in the Panama Canal Zone; at Fort Leavenworth, Kansas; Texas City, Texas;
and with the American Expeditionary Forces. Following the war he was assigned to the Operations Division of
the War Department General Staff (1919–21) and commanded engineer units throughout the United States. He
began duties with the Office of the Chief of Engineers in 1941, becoming commander of the Ninth Service
Command, ASF, in October 1943. In September 1944 he became the chief of the Engineering Section, Allied
Force Headquarters, North African Theater. On his return to the United States he commanded the Sixth Service
Command.

Lt. Gen. Robert Richardson, Jr.   *Col. David McCoach, Jr.*

work voluntarily. Seizure was a technique that should be exclusively directed toward that objective and patterned in every detail with that goal in mind.(4) Before there was any need for resolving these basic differences in approach, or the need to put either to an actual test, President Roosevelt proposed arbitration, which was agreed to by both parties. The UMW called off its strike and the crisis passed.

Both in 1943 and again in 1945 the War Department was confronted with the possible task of seizing coal mines on an industrywide scale when it was doubtful whether the mere act of seizure would end strikes. In each instance it undertook the preparation of an extensive plan as formidable in character as that developed for the captive coal dispute. The framers of the 1943 plan sought to remedy the primary defect of the 1941 program—its failure to deal with the question of how to get the men back to work. The plan called for the induction into the armed forces, either on a voluntary basis or under the Selective Training and Service Act, of all workers in idled coal mines and further provided for the commissioning in the Army of supervisory personnel.(5) The mines were to become military installations, with officers in charge and enlisted men mining coal. While many recognized that such an experiment might be necessary as a last resort, it was severely criticized by the Labor Branch, Industrial Personnel Division, Headquarters, Army Service Forces, as being unrealistic, unworkable, and probably illegal. While perfect in its every military detail, it overlooked the all-important factor of human nature.(6) Very fortunately, it was Secretary of the Interior

Harold L. Ickes,[4] rather than Secretary of War Stimson, who was ordered to take over the mines. After many very crucial days, during which time only nominal possession of the mine properties was assumed, Ickes restored production. However, the return to work did not result from the fact of seizure as such, but because Lewis had obtained what he wanted through direct negotiations with Ickes—negotiations that not only bypassed the National War Labor Board (NWLB)[5] but also ignored established government labor policies.

The coal crisis of 1945 produced a third War Department plan.(7) This time plans were developed in close cooperation with the Labor Branch. The doubtful features of the 1943 plan were eliminated or modified and an entirely different approach was adopted, based upon the then extensive War Department experience in individual plant seizures. This new approach was spelled out in various memoranda for Maj. Gen. Glen E. Edgerton,[6] the proposed War Department representative, and in proposed instructions for labor officers.(8) Considerable thought was given to the possibility of nationalizing the mines for the remainder of the war in the same fashion as had been done in Great Britain.(9) The Department of the Interior, rather than the War Department, was again placed in charge and, after some uncertain days, Lewis, satisfied that he was obtaining desired concessions, ordered the men back to work.

General Developments, October 1941 to August 1942

The mine strike revived demands for restrictive labor legislation. Congress was aroused and President Roosevelt was reported as feeling that some form of antistrike law was necessary. A wide variety of proposed remedies was developed as embodied in bills introduced in Congress or as widely discussed plans in various official circles. Some would have outlawed strikes completely for the duration or would have imposed a cooling-off period, pending mediation in any labor controversy. Others sought to amend the Sabotage Act to include strikes within it scope, and still others proposed compulsory arbitration of disputes. There were also renewed pleas for the enactment of a specific law authorizing plant seizures. Some law seemed inevitable. But before Congress acted, the end of the mine strike, the outbreak of war, and other events completely changed the picture,

---

[4]Harold L. Ickes (1874–1952) was a Pennsylvania-born lawyer and politician, who was prominent in Republican Party politics in the 1920s but worked for Roosevelt's presidential campaign in 1932. He served as secretary of the Interior (1933–46), as administrator of public works (1933–39), and as petroleum administrator for war and solid fuels administrator (1941–45).

[5]Following a conference of labor and industry representatives held at Roosevelt's behest on 17 December 1941, the National War Labor Board was established within the Office of Emergency Management by Executive Order 9017, 12 January 1942. It superseded the National Defense Mediation Board and was assisted by twelve regional boards. For NWLB records, see Record Group 202, NARA.

[6]Maj. Gen. Glen E. Edgerton (1887–1976) was born in Kansas and educated at Kansas State College and at West Point. He served in a variety of engineer and command positions in the Panama Canal Zone, with the American Expeditionary Forces, and throughout the United States (1908–44) before being assigned to the Army Service Forces in May 1944 as deputy director of materiel. Edgerton became the director of materiel in August 1945. He retired in April 1949 after forty-four years of military service.

Secretary of the Interior Harold L. Ickes

Maj. Gen. Glen E. Edgerton

diverting attention away from attempts to secure labor legislation for almost eighteen months.(10)

During the nine months that followed the captive coal crisis there were no further War Department seizures, but other important developments took place materially affecting the character of all subsequent takeovers.

First, the American entrance into the war changed public attitudes toward strikes and most labor groups. Almost immediately, the number and the average size and duration of strikes decreased sharply,(11) and the strikes that did occur were clearly contrary to the great weight of public opinion. While the fact of war became less and less of a restraining influence as time went on, particularly by 1945, one could almost always depend upon the underlying patriotism of the great majority of workers and capitalize significantly on this fact in any plant seizure. Both public and labor opinion usually supported a return to work under government auspices.

Second, in early December 1941 President Roosevelt convened a conference of management and labor leaders for the purpose of developing the machinery and policies to resolve industrial disputes without resort to force. Out of this conference came the no-strike pledge, by which management and labor agreed to avoid lockouts or strikes for the duration. The parties further agreed to submit all disputes not resolved by direct negotiations or through conciliation to a tripartite board, equally representative of management, labor, and the public, whose decisions should be accepted by the parties as final.(12) There was nothing legally binding about this pledge, nor did the decisions of the newly created NWLB (13) have any legal force and effect. However, the recommendations of this conference set a certain moral tone for management-labor relations for the duration, and the commitments of the conferees represented covenants that could not be lightly disregarded. Whereas previously strikes had often been condoned, and in some instances actively supported, by some organized labor leaders, and whereas the NDMB's recommendations were occasionally flouted by important segments of industry and labor, the representative leaders of both groups had now solemnly declared themselves as squarely behind the new policy.

General support of this policy by national leaders of labor and industry in later years proved a tremendous asset in cases where an irresponsible local labor leader or some uncooperative management official deviated from the pledge to such an extent that government seizure was necessary. Moreover, the establishment of an agency whose decisions were accepted as final and binding by all persons if the voluntary no-strike, no-lockout pledge was to work, but which were nevertheless not enforceable through court process, eventually resulted in the actual, though never admitted, use of plant seizures not merely as an instrument for maintaining critical war production but also for the purpose of upholding this pledge and the proposition upon which it was dependent—that the NWLB decisions must be accepted in every case. Lacking judicial remedy in cases where the attitudes of labor or management threatened the cornerstones of the government's labor policy, the NWLB and the president occasionally invoked plant seizure to secure what in effect constituted specific performance of an NWLB decision in a case where a threat to war production, while perhaps present, was extremely remote or indirect.

The advent of war could not indefinitely postpone a violent eruption of industrial disputes seriously threatening the war effort. Controversies muted by the patriotic fervor that followed Pearl Harbor gradually came to the surface, and by June 1942 there was again a scattering of strikes affecting important procurement. The War and Navy Departments became concerned lest this rash of disorders result in a whole series of plant seizures to settle disputes that the government should be able to handle by other means. This concern developed at about the same time as a feeling, frequently expressed in editorial columns and also shared by many government officials, that it was improper to use the same remedy in every case—that is, plant seizures—irrespective of whether labor or management was at fault. It was asked why management should have its business confiscated when labor was in the wrong, or why labor should suffer when management was at fault. While much of this public feeling was based upon a wholly erroneous conception of the purpose and character of plant seizures, the feeling that seizures punished the innocent was widely held and it seemed desirable to change this perception.(14) Both these developments were largely the product of experiences with the seizures of the S. A. Woods Machine Company, South Boston, Massachusetts, and the General Cable Corporation, Bayonne, New Jersey, in August 1942, cases that revealed other matters deserving of attention, namely, serious, though unintended, lack of coordination between the NWLB and the procurement agencies. In the General Cable case, for example, President Roosevelt, at the NWLB's insistence, signed an executive order directing Navy seizure not only without submitting the order to the Navy Department but also without the latter's knowledge. Moreover, it was later generally agreed that the order to seize was ill-timed and probably unwarranted and that proper staff work among the agencies involved would have prevented it. Likewise, the S. A. Woods order never received War Department clearance, and in both cases the orders had been abominably drafted.

In light of all the foregoing circumstances, and faced with the imminent possibility of a takeover of the Vernon, California, plant of Alcoa, the War and Navy Departments asked for a conference with the NWLB's public members to review the use of plant seizures as a technique and to agree upon standard procedures.(15) The resultant conference, attended by Secretary of the Navy Knox, Assistant Secretary of War McCloy, Col. Edward S. Greenbaum, and Wayne Morse,[7] the acting NWLB chairman and later a senator from the State of Oregon, discussed a general procedure that might be jointly recommended to the president by their three agencies for use in all cases. There was little difficulty in reaching such an agreement, and on 22 August 1942 a memorandum was transmitted to Judge Samuel I. Rosenman,[8] who forwarded it to President Roosevelt.(16) This memorandum made the following recommendations:

(1) In cases where an employer defies a decision of the War Labor Board, the President will direct the Army or the Navy to take possession of the plant and cause it to be operated in a manner which effectuates the purpose of the decision of the WLB.

(2) In cases where employees strike, or otherwise interfere with production, in defiance of a decision of the WLB, the President will notify the strikers that unless they return to work at once, they will lose their occupational deferments under the Selective Service law and will also be ineligible for employment in war industries. Whether the President will also direct the Army or the Navy to take possession of the plant and cause it to be operated will be dependent upon the circumstances in each case.

There was substantial conflict within the War Department on the second point, but it expressed a view, reiterated on many occasions by Under Secretary Patterson, that the best way to deal with strikes in war plants was to induct the striking workers into the Army and not to undertake plant seizure. President Roosevelt did not agree. He was unwilling to issue a work-or-fight order in the absence of a seizure but he was ready, in conjunction with a seizure caused by labor defiance, not only to clearly place the blame where it belonged but also to invoke the Selective Training and Service Act and to threaten the blacklisting of any person who failed to return to work.(17) Following this advice during the Alcoa strike, the original conferees devoted themselves to the preparation of an

[7]Dr. Wayne Morse, who was born in 1900, was an educator, lawyer, and labor arbitrator. He was educated at the Universities of Wisconsin and Minnesota and at Columbia University. He held academic positions (1924–36) until accepting a post as a special assistant to the U.S. attorney general (1936–38). He served as an arbitrator for the Department of Labor (1938–40) before being appointed to the National Defense Mediation Board in July 1941. He became an NWLB public member in January 1942.

[8]Samuel I. Rosenman (1896–1973) was a Texas-born jurist and justice of the New York State Supreme Court (1932–43). He served as a special counsel to Roosevelt between 1933 and 1945.

executive order and an accompanying statement that would conform to President Roosevelt's wishes.(18) The end of the strike made the particular order and state-ment academic, but Rosenman asked that they be processed in the normal fashion through the Bureau of the Budget and the Department of Justice for approval as a model for use in subsequent cases.(19) However, it was more than a year before the Army or Navy was involved in another seizure, and during the interim these papers were nearly forgotten. They were later resurrected by Colonel Greenbaum for internal use in the War Department, and an effort was made to use them for the purposes for which they were originally intended.

Endnotes

(1) Memo, Ohly for Under Sec War, 6 Nov 41, untitled.

(2) Memo, Col McCoach for Under Sec War, 2 Dec 41, sub: General Plans Under the Proposed Executive Order Pertaining to the Coal Mines Owned and Operated by Steel Companies or Subsidiaries.

(3) Encls 12 and 13 to ibid. (attached respectively as Apps. K–1 and K–2).

(4) See unaddressed and unsigned Memo, 12 Nov 41, sub: The Coal Strike (App. K–3), and Memo, McGrady for Under Sec War, 14 Nov 41, sub: The Coal Strike (App. K–4).

(5) Plan for Operation of Army Controlled Coal Mines, 1943. A general summary of the plan is contained in pages 1–6 thereof (App. K–5).

(6) Memo, Ohly for Col Monntford [*sic*], Off of Dep CofS for Service Commands, ASF, 6 Mar 45, sub: Plan for Operation of Army Controlled Coal Mines, 1943 (App. K–6); Memo, Brig Gen Green for Dep CofS for Service Commands, 16 Mar 45, sub: War Department Plan for the Operation of Army Controlled Mines, 1943 (App. K–8).

(7) War Department Plan for Operation of Coal Mines, distributed 4 Apr 45.

(8) Memo, Lt Col Boland for Maj Gen Edgerton, n.d., sub: Method of Handling Labor Problem in the Event of a Seizure of the Bituminous Coal Mines (App. K–9).

(9) Unaddressed and unsigned Memo, n.d., sub: The Case for Actual Government Possession and Operation of All Coal Mines for the Duration of the War (App. K–7).

(10) See page 1 articles in the *New York Times*, 28 Oct 41, and the *Washington Post*, 16 Nov 41.

(11) App. E–2.

(12) The substance of the report of the conference is contained in a letter addressed by the president to the conference at its conclusion (App. L–3).

(13) EO 9017, 12 Jan 42.

(14) For a discussion of this misconception, see Ltr, William P. Witherow, President, National Association of Manufacturers, to George W. Taylor, Vice Chairman, NWLB, 14 Aug 42 (*New York Times*, 15 Aug 42, p. 1); editorial in *Washington Evening Star*, 14 Aug 42, entitled "The Navy Takes Over"; and column by David Lawrence entitled "Strike Again Puts Penalty on Firms," which appeared widely on 14 Aug 42 (*Washington Evening Star*).

(15) Memo for file by Ohly, 23 Aug 42, sub: Prevention of Strikes—Seizure of Plants (App. L–1).

(16) Memo, Sec War, Sec Navy, and Acting WLB Chairman for President, 22 Aug 42 (App. L–4); Memo for file by Ohly, 23 Aug 42 (App. L–1); Memo, Col Greenbaum for Under Sec War, 21 Aug 42 (App. L–5).

(17) Memo for file by Ohly, 23 Aug 42 (App. L–1).

(18) Draft EO, sub: Authorizing the Secretary of War To Take Possession of and Operate the Plant of the Aluminum Company of America [Alcoa] at Vernon, California (App. L–2), and proposed statement for the president in connection therewith (App. L–6).

(19) Memo for file by Ohly, 23 Aug 42 (App. L–1). The matter was the subject of further correspondence between Judge Rosenman and the War Department, in which Patterson kept hammering for a stronger statement on work-or-fight. In this connection see his memo for Rosenman, 25 Aug 42.

CHAPTER 5

The S. A. Woods Machine
Company Case, August 1942

The seizure of the S. A. Woods Machine Company plants in August 1942 was the only seizure directly involving the War Department in the two years following Pearl Harbor. It was the first instance following adoption of the no-strike pledge in which a company adamantly refused to conform with the country's recognized policy. It was also the forerunner of a series of similar takeovers that grew out of the refusal of a company to comply with a directive order of the National War Labor Board (NWLB). The case is of particular importance in the history of plant seizures because for the first time the government faced a situation where a business flatly refused any form of cooperation. The case raised all the difficulties anticipated under such circumstances and provided a real test for several different methods of government operation. Fortunately, the passage of the War Labor Disputes Act made academic in future cases many of the difficult problems the War Department encountered directly operating S. A. Woods.

Description of the Company

The S. A. Woods Machine Company was a small corporation with sixteen stockholders. It was largely controlled by H. C. Dodge, its president and owner of 40 percent of the stock; Kingsland Dunwoodie, a vice president, whose wife owned one-fifth of the stock; and Ralph Lowe, Jr., its secretary and the owner of 10 percent of the outstanding shares. Among this group Dodge was the dominant figure.(1) The company had seven buildings located in South Boston, Massachusetts, consisting principally of those constituting the so-called A and B plants, engaged in the production of woodworking machinery and induction motors, and a shell plant, established in 1940, designed to produce shells and shot for the British and American governments. In 1941 the A and B plants, representing the ordinary peacetime premises of the company, had no direct government contracts, although many of it products were of importance to the war effort, particularly to the lumber industry. In addition, the company had leased certain property in Natick from the State of Massachusetts to be equipped with government machinery and operated by the company for the production of shells. In all, the company had more than a half-dozen contracts for the manufacture of ordnance for the United States and Britain.(2)

The company employed around one thousand workers, six hundred fifty in the shell plant alone. Both plants were organized by the CIO-affiliated United Electrical Radio and Machine Workers of America,[1] but each plant constituted a distinct bargaining unit covered by separate contracts. The Natick plant was not yet in operation and had no certified collective bargaining agent.(3)

Background of the Dispute

Following its certification by the National Labor Relations Board (NLRB) as the exclusive bargaining agent for the employees and inspectors at the shell plant on 15 May 1941, Local 272 of the United Electrical Workers entered into a collective bargaining agreement with the company providing, among other things, for a voluntary checkoff, a 10-percent basic wage increase, and an automatic renewal of the contract from year-to-year unless written notice of termination was given by one of the parties thirty days before the contract's expiration date. In April 1942 the union gave the appropriate notice and advised the company of various provisions it desired to have incorporated in the new contract. These included maintenance of membership clauses, provision for arbitration of all matters arising under the terms of the contract, and modifications in the standard rates of production in the case of changes of materials or manufacturing methods or the introduction of new products or machines.

After unsuccessful efforts by both parties and a federal conciliator to adjust several contested issues, the case was certified to the NWLB on 16 May and heard by a mediator during early June 1942. A large number of matters were settled during the mediation proceedings, including agreements on certain wage increases and the effective retroactive date and processes for any adjustments that might subsequently be agreed upon with respect to changes in standards. Upon conclusion of the proceedings the parties agreed to submit the unsettled issues to a fact-finding panel. The panel recommended maintenance of membership, arbitration of all matters arising under the contract, and resolution of the controversy involving changes in standards through a type of arbitration proceeding specifically described on 3 July 1942.(4) When the company failed to accept the panel's recommendations, the board itself, on 1 August 1942, issued a order unanimously approving the action of the panel.(5) Two weeks later the company advised the NWLB that it would not comply with this order, setting forth the argument, which it was to repeat and publicize for many months, that maintenance of membership and the requirement of arbitration were essentially un-American. Employer members of the NWLB subsequently failed to persuade S. A. Woods to accept the board's decision.(6)

The War Department showed great interest in the negotiations and NWLB proceedings because it had placed some $15 million worth of contracts at South

---

[1]The United Electrical Radio and Machine Workers was organized in 1936 as an AFofL affiliate. It subsequently joined the CIO in 1937. Its 1941 membership numbered 133,300, which increased to 210,000 by mid-1942.

Boston and additional contracts of approximately $5 million at the Natick plant. This interest was heightened because of substantial evidence of a slowdown on the part of the employees that interfered with production and led to frequent assertions by the company that this prevented timely fulfillment of its contracts. Ordnance branch concerns were repeatedly evidenced in memoranda submitted to Headquarters, Services of Supply (SOS).(7)[2] Upon the NWLB failure to achieve a settlement, and with the prospect of a possible seizure looming, the War Department undertook to obtain company acceptance of the government's decision.(8) Under Secretary Patterson conferred with Governor Leverett Saltonstall of Massachusetts, who, through his commissioner of conciliation, a Mr. Moriarity, endeavored to persuade Dodge.(9) When he was unsuccessful, Patterson appealed directly to Dodge in a strong telegram,(10) but the latter again refused to accede and repeated his challenge to the government to test the legality of the NWLB order in the courts. At the same time, he indicated no objection to cooperation with the government should it decide to condemn and operate the shell plant.(11) On 18 August the NWLB referred the matter to President Roosevelt.(12) Meanwhile, the union had withheld strike action upon NWLB assurance that the government would exhaust its powers to place its order into effect.(13)

On 19 August Roosevelt signed an executive order directing Secretary Stimson to take possession of the company's properties.(14) Stimson promptly issued a statement describing the history of the case and the character of the War Department's mission under the president's order. In condemning the company he indicated that the purpose of the seizure was not just to restore war production but also to employ the War Department as an instrument of the NWLB. "No company and no labor organization," he said, "can be permitted to defy the mandate of this impartial tribunal [the NWLB] with impunity."(15) At 8:00 P.M. on the same day War Department representative Maj. Ralph F. Gow of the Boston Ordnance District, acting under instructions similar to those issued in previous cases, occupied the shell plant after advising Dodge of his intentions. The actual seizure was uneventful, although a platoon of military police was on hand if needed to maintain order or to afford protection to persons and property.(16)

Basic Problems

Since the plant was operational when Major Gow took possession and since the executive order provided that Secretary of War Stimson was to implement the "purposes of the directive order of the NWLB of August 1, 1942," there was no problem of restoring or maintaining production in the sense of persuading men to return to or remain at work. To the contrary, the War Department's primary prob-

---

[2]The Services of Supply was the designation for the Army Service Forces prior to the War Department reorganization of 12 March 1943 (GO 14). See John D. Millett, *The Organization and Role of the Army Service Forces* (Washington, D.C.: Office of the Chief of Military History, 1954). For SOS records, see Record Group 160, NARA.

Col. Ralph F. Gow
(Photographed in 1944)

lems during the first weeks of operation were to convince the company by persuasion or threat to accept the NWLB's decision or, failing that, to persuade the company to negotiate some agreement acceptable to the union that, although at variance with the NWLB's order, would not be objectionable to them. Second, the War Department had to obtain the company's cooperation in operating the properties consistent with the legal parameters of the executive order. Third, the War Department had to determine whether and by what means War Department possession should be extended from the seized shell plant to the other commercial facilities of the company in South Boston and Natick, and how to provide an interim basis of operation while the foregoing problems were examined.

The First Weeks of Operation

When Major Gow advised Dodge of the projected seizure, the latter agreed to cooperate fully with the government if seizure was limited to the shell plant. He also stated, however, that he would use every means at his disposal to oppose the seizure if the A and B plants were affected. Gow, unfamiliar at that time with the interrelationship of the two properties, was noncommittal and, on the basis of instructions received by telephone from Washington, limited his 20 August seizure to the shell plant and corporate records pending further investigation. A few hours later Dodge and his attorneys reiterated their position and agreed, at Gow's suggestion, to submit to the under secretary of war a statement of their contentions.(17) This letter was presented and read over the telephone to Colonel Greenbaum in Washington the following morning.(18) At 11:00 A.M. Greenbaum was advised that the under secretary's instructions contemplated the seizure of all properties of the company in South Boston.(19) This unplanned decision greatly disturbed management, which was advised that it could choose between direct War Department operation or operation by the company for its own account as an agent for the War Department in compliance with the NWLB's order. Dodge was belligerent and demanded immediate payment for the properties taken, but, together with other company representatives and at the urging of his attorney, agreed to take the matter under advisement.(20)

In view of Dodge's reactions Gow assumed that he would not be able to obtain the company's cooperation. Therefore, he immediately took the precaution of hiring certified public accountants to prepare a balance sheet of the company at the hour and date of seizure, to take an inventory of all merchandise and work in progress, and to set up a system of accounting to record all transactions embraced in the government's operation of the properties.(21) Similarly, notices were forwarded to all suppliers and purchasers advising them of the government's seizure and stating that, while the War Department did not assume the contract obligations of the company to accept supplies or to deliver merchandise, it did intend to place orders and continue the manufacture and sale of the same products. Shippers were advised that goods would be accepted upon arrival, even though War Department shipping orders had not actually been transmitted. In addition, each employee was required to sign an employment application form similar to that used at Air Associates and to take an oath not to overthrow the government,(22) the assumption being that since this was probably a direct government operation with federal funds the persons concerned were being given employment on an unclassified Civil Service basis.(23) Insurers were notified of the fact of government possession. Preparations were made to meet the regular payroll out of government funds if necessary, and Gow obtained fiscal and disbursing personnel for this purpose.(24)

During the next few days various operating matters were discussed with company representatives. These included the company's right to gain access to its records; management's decision to terminate its employee group insurance program; arrangements for mail sorting; definition of government intentions with respect to the Natick plant and supply contracts; the status of the company's nationwide sales organization, branch offices, and War Department contracts; and resolution of the company's potentially embarrassing financial situation that would result if the government failed to pay for seized inventories. The character and tone of these conferences gave government representatives the impression that the company intended to refuse cooperation and to engage in a long and bitter fight over the seizure, thus laying the basis for a later damage suit against the government. The company attitude prompted Major Gow to take further steps toward complete War Department operation, such as negotiating with insurance companies for the maintenance of workmen's compensation, health, and accident insurance; the revision of all invoices, bills, and other company papers to carry Gow's name as the War Department representative; and the initiation of a search for someone who could manage and direct plant production. Consideration was also given to extending War Department operations to cover the Natick plant. Following this conference, it was decided that Dodge and Dunwoodie should be excluded from the properties.(25)

Labor problems emerged immediately. There had been serious concerns among some government representatives concerning the extent to which the government could legally continue to enforce all the existing terms and conditions of employment existing when the properties were taken or to implement the provisions of the NWLB order with which the executive order had demanded compliance.(26) There was doubt, for example, as to whether the War Department could legally continue the voluntary checkoff, and even more doubt as to whether it could apply maintenance of membership to employees on a federal payroll. A still more difficult question was whether government funds could be employed to pay the retroactive portion of wage increases as agreed to by Dodge during the course of his negotiations with the union preceding the NWLB directive. Inability to do one or more of these things might affect the attitude of the company or the union toward continued government possession and the negotiating positions of the two parties. If, for example, the union could obtain neither the benefits of the NWLB order nor the very substantial retroactive wage payments from the War Department but could obtain these payments from Dodge, there would be a very strong argument for settling with the company on a compromise basis. The same factors would influence Dodge, as well as the timing and the nature of War Department decisions concerning the best method of operating the properties. Every War Department official agreed that some technique should be sought whereby these benefits could be made available to the employees without delay, but the department continued to vacillate.(27)

The problem with respect to Natick, like the unresolved labor issues, played an important role in subsequent developments. The Natick property was clearly not within the scope of the executive order, yet its operations were closely related to those at South Boston. First, the engineering work for Natick was being done at South Boston. Furthermore, a small amount of equipment for the furnishing of the Natick property was being supplied from South Boston. Third, the purchasing department at South Boston covered both plants. Fourth, the records and books covering both plants were kept at South Boston, and, fifth and finally, production scheduling for both plants was closely related and was carried out at South Boston. At the same time, it seemed likely that if the Natick plant was seized under a new order or by condemnation the company would seek to convince the public that this step was simple persecution. The production integration argument used at Air Associates for seizing branch plants was not deemed sufficiently strong to fully counteract such a charge at S. A. Woods.(28) The matter was not settled until September.

A strategy conference was called in Washington at which Under Secretary Patterson and Lt. Gen. Brehon B. Somervell,[3] commanding general, SOS, agreed to make one last effort to persuade Dodge to reconsider. It was hoped that some face-saving formula might be worked out, and a few broad hints concerning the possibility that the government might move into Natick, which looked like a profitable venture for Dodge, might provide the necessary leverage. Another factor that seemed to place the government in an excellent bargaining position concerned the firm's poor cash position. If current liabilities were to be met, the company had to take action to recover its plant or promptly enter into some agreement with the government to provide funds.(29) Dodge and his lawyers readily responded to

---

[3]Lt. Gen. Brehon B. Somervell (1892–1955) was born in Little Rock, Arkansas, and was graduated from West Point in 1914. He served as the district engineer in the District of Columbia (1926–30), as the chief of the Construction Division of the Quartermaster Corps (1940–41), as the assistant chief of staff, G-4 (1941–42), and as the commander of the Services of Supply (later Army Service Forces) from 9 March 1942 to 18 April 1945. He retired in 1946.

Patterson's invitation but remained firm, despite the best efforts of Patterson and Somervell.(30) It was clear that the company was not going to comply with the NWLB order or cooperate with the government.

Almost simultaneously with the failure of this conference, however, there was a development that gave encouragement to a belief that the entire matter could be solved without continued government possession. This was the sudden resumption of negotiations between the union and the company.(31) Dodge was willing to grant virtually every union demand that the NWLB had granted, including the payment of retroactive wage increases, but insisted that the arbitration provision be slightly modified. In addition, Dodge categorically refused to accept maintenance of membership. As previously indicated, he had an important talking point

Lt. Gen. Brehon B. Somervell

because he knew—and capitalized on the fact—that the War Department was having difficulty deciding how maintenance of membership and retroactive wages could be provided under government operation. The union in turn was worried by government procrastination, particularly on the issue of retroactive wages that loomed as the most important feature of the dispute to the average worker. These questions were discussed at length by the local unions, the international union, and War Department officials.(32) Concurrent conversations were going on between the War Department and the NWLB to insure that the latter had no objection to the parties freely negotiating an agreement at variance with the NWLB order.(33) For a few days the likelihood of a settlement appeared so good that the War Department prepared a press release.(34) However, fears on the part of the international union that any concession on maintenance of membership could create a dangerous precedent in other cases led to a final union rejection of the company's proposal on 28 September. This rejection was made even though the union had no assurance that the War Department would deal with the problem of retroactive wages.(35) The complete breakdown in negotiations left the War Department with no alternative but to proceed with plans to permanently operate the entire facility.(36)

Technique of Operation

From the very first day it was apparent that operating the S. A. Woods plants directly with government funds would produce innumerable difficulties, particularly involving labor and carrying on the company's commercial business.(37) As early as 31 August, therefore, Major Gow submitted alternative recommendations to Under Secretary Patterson. He wrote that direct government operation for an indefinite period was undesirable because of the expense, the number of War Department personnel required, the difficulty of operating an industrial plant in accordance with Army regulations and, most important, the dangers of attempting to operate the properties in conformity with the NWLB's order.(38) In fact, long-term direct government operation was caused by the recurrent hope that the union and the company would reach agreement, permitting the return of the properties to private ownership and obviating any need for continued government involvement. During this period alternative plans to direct government operation went forward, specifically a study of Gow's 31 August report recommending that the government condemn a leasehold interest in the South Boston and Natick properties and arrange continued operation with another private corporation on a cost-plus-a-fixed-fee basis by subleasing the condemned properties and contracting with the new firm for the manufacture of the supplies previously furnished by Woods. The new operator would carry on the commercial business with working capital provided by a War Department guaranteed loan and enter into a contract with the union conforming to the NWLB order. Gow further recommended that supply contracts with S. A. Woods be canceled, while at the same time the government should exercise its rights under such contracts to require the transfer to it of materials, supplies, and rights acquired by Woods.

The problem was repeatedly discussed during September and consideration was given to establishing a government corporation to operate the properties in lieu of adopting Gow's suggestion, but this idea was abandoned. As hope of any settlement dwindled, feelers were put out to several private companies, including the Murray Company of Dallas, Texas.(39) On 24 September Patterson forwarded to Somervell Gow's earlier recommendations and, in an accompanying memorandum, directed that Chief of Ordnance Maj. Gen. Levin H. Campbell, Jr.,[4] "take prompt steps to select an established company having satisfactory manufacturing experience and labor record with which it may contract, for the operation of the plant upon terms to be agreed upon."(40)

A general plan was approved that called for condemnation proceedings to be instituted to acquire a leasehold interest in and the right to use real and personal property of the company. Hopefully, through such proceedings an agreement could be reached with S. A. Woods not only for the acquisition of the necessary assets but also for the disposition of such claims as the company might have against the government for the use and occupancy of its premises and equipment. Furthermore, the

---

[4]Lt. Gen. Levin H. Campbell (1886–1976) was born in the District of Columbia and attended the U.S. Naval Academy (Class of 1909). He transferred to the U.S. Army's Coast Artillery Corps in 1911 and spent the next twenty years at the Rock Island and Frankford Arsenals. Early in World War II he was in charge of the construction and operation of new ordnance plants, becoming the Chief of Ordnance in June 1942. Following his retirement as a lieutenant general in 1946, Campbell served as the executive vice president of International Harvester, as the director of the Automotive Safety Foundation, and as a director of American Steel Foundaries Company, the Universal Oil Products Company, and the Curtiss-Wright Aircraft Corporation.

plan called for the seizure of Woods' inventory and the use of its patents and other intangible rights required for operations. It was believed that such an agreement might also make possible a solution to the problem of retroactive wages payments. An important reason for this decision to condemn was the desire to place the government's possessory interest beyond any possibility of legal attack for a fixed period so the balance of the plan calling for the lease and operation of the facilities by another private company could be carried out. Obviously, such a company would wish positive assurances that its tenure in the properties would be undisturbed for a definite time. The plan also called for the cancellation of existing supply contracts and subsequent placement of similar orders with the new operating company. The chief of ordnance, rather than the War Department

Maj. Gen. Levin H. Campbell, Jr.

representative, would administer the plan after its implementation.

After considerable investigation by the Office of the Chief of Ordnance, the Murray Company, a small corporation engaged in the manufacture of cotton processing machinery, was selected to run the Woods properties provided its labor policies were above reproach,(41) a fact that was verified by the Labor Relations Branch, Civilian Personnel Division,[5] Headquarters, SOS (see Chart 1), and confirmed by the international union.(42) Accordingly, the War Department forwarded a proposed contract to the Murray Company(43) in mid-October stating that the War Department was condemning the South Boston and Natick properties of S. A. Woods and would make shot and shell contracts with the Murray Company similar to the existing ones with Woods. The government would turn over its interest in the condemned properties and goods to the Murray Company, while real estate, machinery, and other durable goods would be rented at a certain percentage of the appraised value. Inventory on hand would be transferred at cost except that consisting of woodworking machinery and repair parts, which would be paid for by Murray only if used. The company would enter into a collective bargaining agreement with the United Electrical Workers that contained the provisions of the NWLB order and conditions Woods previously agreed to, except to the extent that

---

[5] Shortly after the creation of the Services of Supply in March 1942, the day-to-day functions of the Labor Section in the Office of the Under Secretary of War were absorbed by the new headquarters' Civilian Personnel Division. The division had three branches: Manpower, Labor Relations, and Civilian Personnel.

CHART 1—ORGANIZATION OF THE LABOR RELATIONS BRANCH, CIVILIAN
PERSONNEL DIVISION, HEADQUARTERS, SERVICES OF SUPPLY, AUGUST 1942

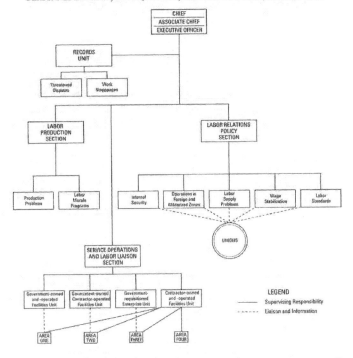

Source: Adapted from Organization Chart, Labor Relations Branch, file (OM) Organization
Charts and Statement of Functions, 1942, Box 740, Entry 174, Record Group 160, NARA.

some or all of these might be modified through mutual agreement. The company
would continue the manufacture and sale of woodworking machinery and electrical motors in the commercial plant as though it were the owner, provided, however, that if the continuance of such work should result in loss, the company could
insist that its contract be modified so Murray was obligated to carry on such work
only on a cost-plus-a-fixed-fee basis. The government agreed to hold the company
free from liability in the event that any suits were brought against it by Woods,
including any suits for the infringement of patent rights. The company further

agreed to take care of workmen's compensation, social security, and other like matters from the date of initial War Department occupation until the commencement of Murray's operations of the plants. The War Department in turn obligated itself to turn over to Murray all amounts deducted from salaries or set aside as a reserve for such purposes. This agreement was then incorporated in a formal contract.

The arrangement entered into differed materially from those employed during World War I. At that time the American Can Company and the American Rolling Mill Company were appointed to operate certain properties as agents for the government on a cost-plus-a-fixed-fee basis, with the fee being a purely nominal amount. In the S. A. Woods case the government leased the properties involved on a strictly commercial basis to a third party, with a definite commitment to place supply contracts in a certain amount with this party. The third party was an independent contractor and not an agent. Its only obligations were to use the properties to fill contracts and, provided it did not suffer a loss, to do the same with the commercial business of the company, as well as to enter into a specified contract with the labor union. Subsequent difficulties with this arrangement raised doubts as to the wisdom of using this concept in other comparable situations. At the time of adoption opinions differed widely within the War Department as to which was the better arrangement.(44)

Pursuant to a memorandum from Under Secretary Patterson to General Campbell, the government canceled its contracts with S. A. Woods in early October 1942.(45) These contracts carried the usual provision permitting cancellation for the convenience of the government upon payment to the contractor of all costs incurred by him in preparation to meet such commitments. Termination of these contracts permitted the government to capture, at cost, shell inventories on hand in the contractor's plant at the time of seizure. Shortly thereafter the War Department, through the Corps of Engineers, filed a condemnation petition for the lands, buildings, machinery, equipment, papers, books, patterns, and other possessions of the company, and still later the department filed a declaration of taking. Simultaneously, negotiations were under way with S. A. Woods, covering all disputed matters between Woods and the War Department and looking toward a final liquidation of any claim against the government by the company. Through these negotiations Dodge pressed for a payment on account of the canceled supply contracts and for other legitimate claims, largely, it appears, because of trouble with creditors. The company was unable to meet their debt payments since its assets were frozen by the government's seizure.(46)

The government rejected a partial payment, fearing that Dodge, once he had solved his immediate problem of indebtedness, would procrastinate and resist every disputed item. The government wanted a complete agreement that would cover both disputed and undisputed matters at the earliest date. The matter was further complicated by questions of price renegotiation of the supply contracts.(47) Finally, on 30 December, a contract was signed providing for government acquisition of S. A. Woods inventory then on hand, its land, buildings, machinery, equipment, patent rights, and other intangible properties until 1 June 1945. The value of the property acquired was set forth in the agreement, as was the rent to be paid by the government for properties merely used during the lease-hold period.(48)

Responsibility for the case was then transferred from Major Gow to the chief of ordnance,(49) operating through the Boston Ordnance District, and subsequent operations were based upon the agreement and condemnation proceedings rather than on the executive order. This obviated the need for a War Department repre-sentative and staff and, as it turned out, many of them were relieved as soon as the Murray Company took over.

Subsequent Problems

The Murray Company held the South Boston plants until after V–J Day,(50) but this did not preclude the development of numerous problems requiring the attention of many people or recurrent suggestions for the termination of the Murray arrange-ment and return of the properties to S. A. Woods. These problems were of two var-ieties. First, the Ordnance Department's shell needs varied greatly. The situation was such that the department, given a free choice, would have placed no business with Murray at all. Secondly, the woodworking operations turned out to be of far greater importance to the war effort than shell-making, although less profitable.

The Ordnance Department, annoyed by problems with the Woods facility and in a position to fill its entire shell and shot requirements from other sources at lower costs, repeatedly proposed termination or nonrenewal of the supply con-tracts. The War Production Board (WPB),[6] however, was insistent that the wood-working machinery business be continued because of a serious national shortage in this area. Moreover, a large part of the lumber industry used Woods' machines and frequently needed spare parts obtainable only in South Boston. The wishes of both could not be fulfilled because Murray was under no obligation to operate the woodworking property if it were not supplied with shell contracts. Furthermore, the whole purpose of the takeover was the settlement of a labor dispute at the shell plant that did not extend to the A and B plants. If the shell plant were closed, and if Murray refused to operate the commercial plant, the only practicable alternative was a return of the properties to S. A. Woods. This would leave the executive order unfulfilled and probably cause a strike halting all production.

Such dilemmas were constantly being presented as Ordnance and WPB inter-ests in Woods varied, and strong disagreement existed within the War Department as to the proper course of action. The Labor Relations Branch insisted that the

---

[6]The War Production Board was established within the Office of Emergency Management by Executive Order 9024, 16 January 1942. It exercised the authority vested in the president by Section 120 of the National Defense Act of 1916 to oversee the war procurement and production programs of federal departments. WPB powers were extended by Executive Order 9040, 24 January 1942, with the transfer of duties of the now defunct Office of Production Management, and also by Executive Order 9125, 7 April 1942. The WPB chairman in 1942 was Donald M. Nelson, and its vice chairman for labor production was Wendell Lund. The WPB had more than a hun-dred regional and district offices nationwide. See Civilian Production Administration, *Industrial Mobilization for War*, and Calvin L. Christman, "Donald Nelson and the Army: Personality as a Factor in Civil-Military Relations During World War II," *Military Affairs* 37 (October 1973): 81–83. For WPB records, see Record Group 179, NARA.

War Production Board. Chairman Donald M. Nelson is seated second from the right.

Ordnance Department use the facility even though it might prefer another for reasons of convenience or cost, arguing that too much was at stake from the standpoint of national labor policy to permit closing the plant. The necessity for keeping the commercial plant in operation made abandonment of shell contracts impractical. Ordnance was instructed to continue contracting with Murray as long as its requirements called for the shell and shot manufactured there.(51)

The woodworking operation led to other problems. On several occasions the Murray Company intimated that it was losing money on this portion of the business and sought to invoke the contract provision allowing it to conduct the commercial business on a cost-plus-a-fixed-fee basis. Fortunately, more detailed analysis disclosed that there was no such loss. A more serious problem resulted from the position into which Murray found itself drifting with respect to inventories of woodworking machinery, consisting largely of spare parts. Murray was protected in regards to the woodworking inventory it had originally received from the War Department by the contract provision requiring them to pay only for the inventory used. This provision did not apply to inventory subsequently produced by Murray in the course of its operation of the commercial plant, and as time went on the original inventory was largely replaced by newly manufactured spare parts. Murray, aware that its South Boston tenure was temporary and having no future desire to conduct this type of business at its own plants, felt that this highly specialized inventory represented a potentially serious liability. The only possible purchaser was S. A. Woods, and the company would undoubtedly attempt to obtain the inventory at salvage prices. Murray sought relief by requesting that the Ordnance Department accept a bill of sale for this material in lieu of payment in cash for tools and parts that the department had furnished it. When this suggestion was rejected, Murray proposed to dispose immediately of such inventory as salvage so that it could offset for tax purposes the losses incurred in such a transaction against excess business profits at its other plants. The war importance of this inventory precluded government approval of this proposal. The problem was finally worked out through a so-called pool-order agreement with the Defense Plant Corporation, by which Murray agreed to make an immediate cash settlement for all inventory it had used and to segregate the balance of the inventory for the government. It further agreed to continue operating the commercial business at a certain rate per month, to dispose of the products of that business and the segregated inventory, and to pay the Defense Plant Corporation for any item withdrawn from the segregated portion for disposal.

These numerous difficulties frequently led to rumors within the plant concerning layoffs, a halt of shell operations, and a return of S. A. Woods control, resulting in many inquiries to the War Department by the United Electrical Workers. In each instance it was possible to assure the union that the rumor was false or to give it a frank appraisal of the situation. As a consequence, relations with the union were always excellent.

In early spring 1945 serious consideration was again given to separating the woodworking and shell businesses, returning the former to Woods and maintaining the latter under Murray as long as Ordnance needs required it. A thorough investigation by the Production Division,[7] Headquarters, Army Service Forces, concluded, however, that separate operations were impossible unless the two managements cooperated, which they did not. Even if the two companies worked together, the transition would require $150,000 worth of alterations, resulting in the loss of two weeks' production, increased operating costs, and serious labor trouble. The proposal was abandoned.(52)

With V–E Day the Ordnance Department no longer needed to conduct business with Murray. Since the sole purpose of the seizure was the settlement of a labor dispute in the shell plant and since that plant was no longer needed, the War Department, the NWLB, and the Office of Economic Stabilization[8] concluded that

---

[7]In July 1942 the Services of Supply created the Resources and Production Divisions to monitor production in war industries and to coordinate with them on military requirements. Four months later the two elements were combined into one, which was redesignated as the Production Division. In November 1943 the division became a separate section under the Army Service Forces' director of material. Brig. Gen. Charles Hines was the division chief from July to September 1942, when he was replaced by Brig. Gen. Hugh C. Minton. Minton held the position until September 1945.

[8]The Office of Economic Stabilization (OES) was established within the Office of Emergency Management by Executive Order 9250, 3 October 1942. Its first director was James F. Byrnes. The OES was to control inflation and economic dislocations that threatened the war effort and the domestic economic structure. It was authorized to formulate policies controlling civilian purchasing power, prices, rents, wages, salaries, profits, rationing, and subsidies. It also sought to prevent increases in the cost of living and unnecessary movements of workers. It was abolished by Executive Order 9620, 20 September 1945, and its duties were transferred to the Office of War Mobilization and Reconversion. See Herman M. Somers, *Presidential Agency, OWMR: The Office of War Mobilization and Reconversion* (Cambridge, Mass.: Harvard University Press, 1950). For OES records, see Record Group 250, NARA.

continued government possession was unnecessary. The fact that restoration to private ownership might result in labor difficulties in the A and B plants was not sufficient to justify continued government control.(53) This decision came at a propitious moment since the government's leasehold interest in the Woods' properties expired on 30 June and further condemnation proceedings or another agreement with Dodge would have been necessary. On 20 June notice was given to the Murray Company, terminating the supply contracts effective 30 June. The company was given two months to remove equipment and restore the plant to its former condition. It proved possible to make amicable arrangements with S. A. Woods for a continuance of government possession during this period without any necessity for further condemnation proceedings. Before the two months had expired, V–J Day occurred and an order of President Harry S. Truman relieved the War Department of any responsibilities it still had under the original executive order.(54)

Company Criticism and Congressional Investigation

From the beginning Dodge carried his bitter opposition to the government's seizure to the public. Throughout most of the period of War Department possession he undertook a one-man crusade directed not so much at the seizure as such but against the government's allegedly arbitrary and pro-labor policy of forcibly jamming such fundamentally undemocratic policies as maintenance of membership and arbitration down employers' throats. His arguments were set out in a widely circulated, printed pamphlet "The Fifth Freedom—Freedom To Work," under the name of the S. A. Woods Machine Company. He was particularly bitter about the extension of government possession to the woodworking plant and Natick. He was sufficiently persistent and forceful in his protests to stir up a small amount of congressional interest, which in the fall of 1943 was reflected in an investigation of the matter by Virginia Congressman Howard W. Smith's Special Committee To Investigate the Practices of Certain Agencies, including the NWLB. This was the only instance where a War Department seizure was directly scrutinized by Congress. The hearings and investigation eventually petered out, and no War Department policy changes were made.

Labor Problems Incident To Direct Government Operation

Labor problems played an important part in patterning the techniques for operating the S. A. Woods plants and are illustrative of the difficulties of direct government operation under an executive order in the absence of a law, such as the War Labor Disputes Act, defining the status of employees in a seized plant. The principal labor problems fell into two classes. The first group concerned the application to S. A. Woods' employees of the terms and conditions of employment in effect at the time of seizure that were previously agreed to by the company and the union during negotiations and those ordered by the NWLB, since many were at variance with Civil Service laws and regulations. The second was the problem of the payment of retroactive wages for the period preceding War Department occupation.

The first set of problems was created by the assumption that the employees fell under the unclassified Civil Service, which raised two further questions: Did the War Department, under laws relating to government employment and appropriating funds to the department, have the legal authority to apply such terms and conditions of employment? Assuming such authority, was it wise, as a matter of policy and precedent, to introduce these private industrial practices? The controversy centered principally around continuation of the voluntary checkoff that was in effect, the arbitration of matters arising under the contract as ordered by the board, and the application of maintenance of membership. Under federal law, was it permissible to make a deduction from wages not authorized by statute even though voluntarily agreed to? Could the government agree to submit any dispute between itself and an outsider, particularly an employee, to final binding arbitration by a third party? Was tenure in a government position dependent on continued union membership? If so, didn't this completely upset the idea of a competitive, independent Civil Service System? Everyone in the department agreed that these benefits should be available to the employees and that failure to provide them vitiated the purpose of the seizure and unfairly strengthened the company position. At the same time, there was sharp division between those who feared setting such a dangerous precedent and those who held that the distinctions between the two groups were so obvious, and the circumstances so unique, that the government could safely proceed to treat S. A. Woods' workers as private employees. Major Gow expressed the former view:

> More important than this [other arguments for operation by a private company], however, is the fact that the War Labor Board directive contemplates that the management will enter into written agreements for compulsory arbitration and maintenance of union membership. Further, the previous management had already obligated itself to the voluntary checkoff, certain rates for overtime, and other matters which the union would expect to be accepted by succeeding management. These provisions are without precedent in direct military operations as, for example, government arsenals. The problem of meeting the purpose of the War Labor Board Directive will be awkward and embarrassing to the War Department, if direct government operation continues for any prolonged period.(55)

The final answer to these differences lay in the arrangement with the Murray Company, although before such arrangement was worked out, the War Department reinstated the voluntary checkoff as a result of the continued representations by the financially embarrassed local union.(56) The issues of maintenance of membership and arbitration were never crucial enough during the period of direct operations to force a final War Department decision on the matter.(57) Other terms of employment were handled without too much difficulty, including implementing certain NWLB-mandated or previously agreed upon wage increases and the observance of certain overtime rates. This was easily rationalized because as ungraded Civil Service workers payment to the employees in accordance with generally prevailing practices was permitted.(58) Such problems as social security, workmen's compensation, and group insurance, however, continued to present the same fundamental difficulties experienced in earlier cases and were only worked out in the final arrangement with Murray.(59)

The problem of retroactive pay was far more difficult and crucial. The NWLB order had not covered this point, but the parties had reached preliminary agreement during negotiations, although it was doubtful that any company promise created a legal obligation. Could the War Department use appropriated funds to pay for services not rendered to it, services that were performed for and accrued to the benefit of another organization at an earlier time? This was a constantly recurring question, culminating finally in the explosive Montgomery Ward situation. The answer appeared to be no, and the only solution appeared in the possibility that their payment by the government might be justified in the interest of the war effort and to preserve good labor relations. Therefore, pressure was used on Dodge in settling with the government to make him agree to allow the amount to be charged against him. In the end, the latter course of action was followed in substance.(60)

Day-to-day labor problems were disposed of directly by the government representative, including all grievances. Major Gow was fortunate in having the very able assistance of Joseph Miller of the Personnel Department of the National Broadcasting Company, who was designated as the civilian advisor on industrial relations as required by the executive order.

Significance of the Case

The S. A. Woods case is of particular significance because it furnished the best real test of the feasibility of direct government operation in the face of noncooperative management in the absence of the War Labor Disputes Act. It also represented the only case in which the War Department experimented with the use of a private corporation to run any of its seized properties.

Endnotes

(1) Memo for file by Ohly, 17 Aug 42, sub: Plant Seizure—S. A. Woods Co.

(2) Statement by S. A. Woods Machine Company before the NWLB, Mediation Section.

(3) Rpt of the Panel, attached to NWLB Panel Recommendations, 3 Jul 42, in the matter of S. A. Woods Machine Company and Local 272 United Electrical Radio and Machine Workers of America (CIO), Case No. 160.

(4) NWLB Recommendations, 3 Jul 42; Statement by S. A. Woods Machine Company before the NWLB, Mediation Section.

(5) NWLB Directive Order in the matter of S. A. Woods Machine Company and United Electrical Radio and Machine Workers of America (CIO), Local 272, 1 Aug 42. The opinion, and the special concurring opinion with respect to the union security issue by the industry members, both of which accompanied the Directive Order and were issued 1 August 1942, give further background.

(6) Memo, Lewis M. Gill, Asst Exec Sec, NWLB, for Wayne Morse, 15 Aug 42, summarizing the company's letter and the efforts of employer members. See also Telg, 14 Aug 42, employer members of the board to Dodge (NWLB Release B–152), and reply of S. A. Woods Machine Co., same date.

(7) Memos, M. H. Pettit, Off of CofOrd, for Labor Relations Branch, CPD, SOS, 6 and 16 May 42, subs: Alleged Slowdown at S. A. Woods Machine Company, Boston, Mass. Further extensive materials on this general subject are to be found in the general strike records of the Labor Relations Branch, CPD, SOS.

(8) Memo, Dir, CPD, SOS, for the CG, SOS, 15 Aug 42, sub: S. A. Woods Co.

(9) Memo, Col Greenbaum for Under Sec War, 17 Aug 42, sub: S. A. Woods Machine Co.

(10) Telg, Under Sec War to H. C. Dodge and to Leverett Saltonstall, 17 Aug 42.

(11) Telg, S. A. Woods to Under Sec War, 17 Aug 42 (App. M–1).

(12) Ltr, Wayne Morse to President, 18 Aug 42 (NWLB Release B–157).

(13) Memo, Gill for Morse, 15 Aug 42.

(14) EO 9225, 19 Aug 42, 7 F.R. 6627.

(15) Statement of Robert P. Patterson, Acting Sec War, 19 Aug 42.

(16) Rpt, Maj Gow to Sec War, 20 Aug 42, sub: The Seizure of the Plants and Facilities of the S. A. Woods Machine Company by the United States Army (App. M–2).

(17) Ltr, S. A. Woods Co. to Under Sec War, 20 Aug 42.

(18) Rpt, Maj Gow to Sec War, 20 Aug 42 (App. M–2); Log of Col Greenbaum, titled "S. A. Woods Machine Co." Verbal instructions were supplemented by a telegram from the acting secretary of war to Major Gow on 20 August 1942.

(19) Rpt, Maj Gow to Sec War, 20 Aug 42 (App. M–2).

(20) Ltr, Maj Gow to Patterson, Toole, and Dennis, Public Accountants, 21 Aug 42.

(21) Second Rpt, Maj Gow to Sec War, 23 Aug 42, sub: The Seizure of the Plants and Facilities of S. A. Woods Machine Company at South Boston, Mass. (App. M–3), and Encls 1 and 2 to said report, being form letters for the signature of Major Gow to suppliers and customers, respectively, 22 and 21 Aug 42 (App. M–4 and M–5).

(22) App. J–18.

(23) Rpt, Maj Gow to Sec War, 20 Aug 42 (App. M–2).

(24) Ibid., and Second Rpt, Maj Gow to Sec War, 23 Aug 42 (App. M–3).

(25) Second Rpt, Maj Gow to Sec War, 23 Aug 42 (App. M–3).

(26) See subsection *Labor Problems Incident To Direct Government Operation* below.

(27) Memos for file by Ohly, 31 Aug 42 (App. M–6) and 4 and 7 Sep 42, subs: S. A. Woods Co.—Developments; Memo, Bishop for Ohly, 4 Sep 42, sub: Suggestion [*sic*] Solution to the Problem of Retroactive Overtime Pay in the S. A. Woods Plant (App. M–12).

(28) Telecon, Maj Gow and Ohly, 26 Aug 42; Memo by Col Greenbaum, 25 Aug 42, sub: S. A. Woods Co., being a resume of a telephone conversation between himself and Major Gow; Greenbaum Log. See also, for an example of bitter opposition to the extension of possession expressed in some War Department circles, Memo for file, Lt Col Edgar Lewis, OUSW, 12 Sep 42, sub: S. A. Woods Machine Co., South Boston, Mass.

(29) Telecon, Maj Gow and Ohly, 29 Aug 42; Second Rpt, Maj Gow to Sec War, 23 Aug 42 (App. M–3), and Greenbaum Log. With respect to the calling of a conference with Dodge, see Memos for file by Ohly, 23 and 27 Aug 42, respectively, subs: S. A. Woods Co.—Miscellaneous Notes and S. A. Woods Co.—Developments. With respect to discussions held and decisions reached at the Washington strategy meeting, see Memo for file by Ohly, 31 Aug 42 (App. M–6). With respect to the general line to be taken with Dodge, see unaddressed and unsigned Memo, n.d., sub: Various Arguments That the Under Secretary May Make (App. M–7).

(30) Memo for file by Ohly, 31 Aug 42 (App. M–6).

(31) Memo for file by Ohly, 4 Sep 42, sub: S. A. Woods Co.—Developments.

(32) Memos for file by Ohly, 7 and 28 Sep 42, subs: S. A. Woods—Developments; Memo for file by John L. Saltonstall, Jr. (of the Labor Relations Branch), 23 Sep 42, sub: Conversation With United Electrical Workers Representatives re S. A. Woods Company

(33) Memo, Col Greenbaum for Under Sec War, 14 Sep 42, sub: S. A. Woods Machine Co.

(34) Memo, Ohly for Bishop, 16 Sep 42, sub: S. A. Woods Company—Return of Plant to Management Press Release, and Memo, Bishop for Ohly, 18 Sep 42, sub: Press Release on Return of S. A. Woods Plant.

(35) The negotiations, with all their ups and downs, are very fully reported in Greenbaum's Log.

(36) Memo for file by Ohly, 19 Sep 42, sub: S. A. Woods Co.— Developments (App. M–8).

(37) Greenbaum Log.

(38) Memo, Maj Gow for Under Sec War, 31 Aug 42, sub: S. A. Woods Machine Company (App. M–9).

(39) Greenbaum Log.

(40) Memo, Under Sec War for CG, SOS, 24 Sep 42, sub: S. A. Woods Machine Company

(41) Memo, Maj Gen T. J. Hayes, Off of CofOrd, for CG, SOS, 28 Sep 42, sub: Operator for the S. A. Woods Co. Plant, and 1st End, Maj Gen W. D. Styer, CofS, SOS, to CofOrd.

(42) Memo for file by Ohly, 4 Oct 42, sub: S. A. Woods Co.— Investigation of Murray Co.; Memo, CPD, SOS, for CofS, SOS, 8 Oct 42, sub: Labor Relations Record of the Murray Company

(43) Ltr, Under Sec War to Murray Co., 10 Oct 42.

(44) Note should be made of the fact that immediately after the War Department took possession, the international union suggested that the plants be operated by a joint War Department–Union Production Committee. See Ltr, Neil Brant to Ohly, 24 Aug 42. The issue was carefully avoided and a noncommittal reply forwarded to the union after extensive delay. See Ltr, Dir, CPD, SOS, to Brant, 28 Aug 42.

(45) Memo, Under Sec War for CofOrd, 28 Sep 42.

(46) Ltr, Dodge to War Dept, Attn: Brig Gen B. O. Lewis, 28 Nov 42.

(47) Telecon, Majs Gow and Hammond, 16 Dec 42.

(48) Contract No. W–SW–1130, 30 Dec 42.

(49) Memo, Col Greenbaum for CofOrd, 23 Jan 43.

(50) Memo for file by Ohly, 5 Feb 43, sub: S. A. Woods Co.— Developments.

(51) Memos, Ohly for J. P. Mitchell, 13 and 18 Nov 42, subs: S. A. Woods; Memos for file by Ohly, 7 Dec 43, 23 Mar 44, 20 Mar 45, subs: S. A. Woods Co.—Developments; Memo for file by Ohly, 14 Oct 43, sub: Plant Seizure—S. A. Woods Co.; Memo, Lt Col Hammond for Brig Gen Greenbaum, 22 Mar 44, sub: S. A. Woods Plant; Memos for file by Brig Gen Greenbaum, 23 Mar and 7 Apr 44, subs: S. A. Woods Plant and S. A. Woods Machine Co.; Memo for file by Ohly, 22 Jan 45, sub: S. A. Woods Co.—Developments; Memo for file by Col Gow, 23 Jan 45, sub: S. A. Woods Co; Memo for file by Ohly, 29 Mar 45, sub: S. A. Woods Co.—Developments; Memo, Maj Gen Campbell for Under Sec War, 6 Apr 45, sub: Contract With Murray Co., Boston, Mass. (S. A. Woods Co.).

(52) Memo, Brig Gen Greenbaum for Howard Bruce, Dir of Materiel, 28 Feb 45; Memo, Col R. H. Tatlow, Exec to Bruce, for Under Sec War, 13 Mar 45, sub: S. A. Woods Co., Boston, Mass.; Memo, Brig Gen Greenbaum for Col Woods, Production Div, ASF, 17 Mar 45.

(53) Memo for file by Ohly, 18 Jun 45, sub: S. A. Woods Co.— Developments (App. M–10); Ltr, Acting Sec War to Dir, OES, 27 Aug 45 (App. M–11).

(54) EO 9603, 25 Aug 45 (App. Y–1). See also Ltr, Acting Sec War to Dir, OES, 27 Aug 45 (App. M–11); Memo, Acting Sec War for CG, ASF, and CofOrd, both 31 Aug 45, subs: Termination of War

Department Possession and Control of Certain Plants and Facilities of S. A. Woods Company, Located at South Boston, Mass.

(55) Memo, Maj Gow for Under Sec War, 31 Aug 42 (App. M–9).

(56) With respect to the checkoff, see Memos for file by Ohly, 23 and 25 Aug 42, subs: S. A. Woods Co.—Checkoff, and 31 Aug 42 (App. M–6).

(57) Memo for file by Ohly, 31 Aug 42 (App. M–6).

(58) Ibid.

(59) Memo, Under Sec War for Gow, 13 Oct 42. For further discussion of Social Security problems, see Social Security Board Memo, 6 Dec 41 (App. M–13).

(60) On the retroactive wage question, see Memo for file by Ohly, 31 Aug 42 (App. M–6); Memo, Bishop for Ohly, 4 Sep 42 (App. M–12); Memo for file by Ohly, 7 Sep 42, sub: S. A. Woods Co.—Developments; Memo for file by Saltonstall, 23 Sep 42. Authority to pay these retroactive wage adjustments was contained in two memos, Under Sec War for Maj Gow, 13 Oct and 28 Nov 42, and Memo, Under Sec War for the Chief, Boston Ordnance Dist, 4 May 43, sub: S. A. Woods Machine Co., et al.

CHAPTER 6

The Fairport, Painesville, and Eastern Railroad Case, November 1942

The seizure of the Fairport, Painesville, and Eastern Railroad in November 1942 is the only case in which a seizure took place without a presidential executive order and the only case where military personnel operated a seized facility. The case has no parallel in the history of plant seizures and came about only because of a unique combination of circumstances: the availability of qualified military personnel, the urgency of timely government intervention, the nonavailability of the president, and the threat of immediate damage to government equipment.(1)

Description of the Railroad

The Fairport, Painesville, and Eastern Railroad was a ten-mile belt line that operated between Fairport Harbor and Perry, Ohio, connecting the New York Central and Baltimore and Ohio tracks. In 1942 it was engaged in bringing limestone, dolomite, and other raw materials to the Diamond Magnesium and Diamond Alkali Companies in Painesville and in carrying out the finished magnesium and chlorine. The railroad served a dozen other war plants of lesser importance, including a facility of the Industrial Rayon Company, and was the sole transportation link for many firms.(2)

Background of the Dispute

The background of the labor dispute is not clear. In 1936, when the operating personnel of the railroad were organized by one of the railway brotherhoods, a strike of engineers and firemen occurred. The company fired some of the strikers and replaced them with other individuals. Inconceivable as it may seem, the discharged workers were still striking and receiving strike benefits five years later in 1942, although their replacements had long since joined the brotherhood and achieved respectability. Meanwhile, the United Mine Workers of America, District 50, had slowly organized the workers in the maintenance department and were eager to enroll the operating personnel as well.

The situation was still somewhat confused both as to facts and motives in 1942, but at 6:30 A.M. on 6 November a strike occurred to force the train crewmen from the railway brotherhood into the United Mine Workers, although it was justified as a means of requiring the company to lay off the "scabs" and reinstate the discharged workers. Rail transportation halted, and within hours the potentially dire implications of this stoppage were made known to War Department headquarters by a number of the technical services, by the companies served by this railroad, and by the War Production Board. The Diamond Alkali and Diamond Magnesium Companies depended on a virtually continuous flow of raw materials that could not be stockpiled and on an unbroken outflow of processed materials for which there were no local storage facilities. A break in the transportation network shutting off either incoming supplies or outgoing shipments would force an almost instantaneous shutdown. By the afternoon of 6 November company employees were being laid off and operations curtailed.

Not only did this strike immediately stop the urgent production of chlorine and magnesium, it also threatened to cause millions of dollars of damage to irreplaceable equipment within hours in particular chlorine cells. The loss of such equipment by two major producers could delay key war programs for months, and since much of the equipment was government-owned or -financed, a serious federal financial loss could result. It was deemed imperative to get the railroad back in operation at once.

The strike occurred so suddenly that the government was powerless to avert it, and the period between its occurrence and the time when irreparable damage to machinery would occur was so short that the possibilities of employing ordinary techniques were limited. The National War Labor Board (NWLB) promptly sent perfunctory telegrams to the local union officials, urging them to return to work and to utilize the facilities of the Railway Labor Act.[1] This action promised few results, so in spite of the unquestioned jurisdiction of the NWLB and the known antipathy of the United Mine Workers toward the board, NWLB Chairman William H. Davis[2] was asked to intervene. All through the late afternoon and evening War Department labor officers worked frantically to persuade local labor leaders to take their men back to work, as did officials of the Labor Relations Branch, Civilian Personnel Division, Headquarters, Services of Supply, who forwarded a strong message from Under Secretary Patterson. As the prospects for any return to work became dim, and with the knowledge that the danger of irreparable damage to equipment would be acute the following morning, the

---

[1]The Railway Labor Act (44 Stat. 578) became law on 20 May 1926. It stated that railroad workers had a right to select collective bargaining representatives without interference, influence, or coercion by employers. It also established a board of five members who encouraged mediated settlements or binding arbitration, applicable in this case, and emergency boards to settle disputes not covered by the act. The law prohibited the checkoff, the closed shop, and maintenance of membership and was upheld by the U.S. Supreme Court in *Texas and New Orleans RR vs. Brotherhood of Railroad and Steamship Clerks* (US 548, 570 [1930]).

[2]William H. Davis was a New York patent lawyer, with experience in labor relations. He was a member of the National Defense Mediation Board (NDMB), serving as its chairman following the resignation of Clarence Dykstra and continuing in this role when the NDMB in January 1942 became the NWLB. In May 1945 Davis was appointed the director of the Office of Economic Stabilization.

National War Labor Board. Chairman William H. Davis is seated in the center.

Labor Relations Branch proposed that the Army seize and operate the railroad with a railway labor battalion.

Three steps were necessary before such a plan could be made operative. In the first place, it was essential to locate qualified military personnel within a short time and distance of Painesville. While this seemed like a hopeless task at the outset, the 730th Engineer Railway Operating Battalion was stationed in the Fifth Service Command.[3] In the second place, the NWLB had to be convinced of the need for this action when it had had no opportunity to even superficially examine the case. The board was in session that evening, and while unwilling to recommend a seizure, Davis stated that if President Roosevelt asked for his advice he would unhesitatingly support the War Department position. He was insistent, however, that the operation be conducted by soldiers rather than civilians who were willing to return to work because the latter course might place the

---

[3] On 22 July 1942 the corps areas were redesignated service commands of the Services of Supply (later Army Service Forces). The Fifth Service Command consisted of the states of Indiana, Kentucky, West Virginia, and Ohio, with headquarters in Columbus. In November 1942 Maj. Gen. Fred C. Wallace commanded the approximately 42,600 military and civilian personnel of the Fifth Service Command.

government in the position of taking sides with either the union or the so-called scabs in a controversy the government had not yet studied. This view had already been advanced by the War Department, and in any event an operation with troops seemed the only practical method of making certain that the trains would actually run. In the third place, some form of clearance from the White House appeared essential in view of the extraordinary nature of the intervention. Roosevelt was unavailable and there was no time to draft, process, and obtain approval of an executive order. The Labor Relations Branch sought some other legal basis than a specific order of the president for the proposed action, although it was likely because of the urgency of the situation that the takeover would have occurred even if no rationalization was found.

The theoretical justification for seizure used was Executive Order 8972,(3) which authorized and directed the secretary of war, whenever he deemed such action to be necessary or desirable, to establish and maintain military guards and patrols and to take other appropriate measures to protect from injury or destruction national defense utilities. The equipment in these plants was of the type contemplated by the order, much of it was government-owned and -financed, and it was now clearly threatened. If similar actions were threatened by a saboteur or some act of God, the secretary certainly would have had authorization to act. Why, then, could he not use the authority of the order to take steps to avert imminent injury from an equally serious though different form of threat? This argument was recognized as somewhat tenuous, but after Assistant Secretary McCloy received the informal approval of White House officials the decision was made to proceed.(4)

The Takeover

The 730th Engineer Railway Operating Battalion and the 735th Military Police Battalion were moved during the night of 6 November, and by 9:30 the following morning they began operating the facilities of the railroad. Simultaneously, telegrams were dispatched by the under secretary of war to company and local union officials, advising them of the reasons for the seizure and appealing to them to arrange for an immediate resumption of transportation under private control while their dispute was processed through the ordinary channels.(5) From the outset the troop commander operated the railroad exclusively with military personnel, except that he temporarily retained certain nonstriking workers as pilots for the trains and to instruct military personnel in the routes to be followed. There were protests against this exception from several sides, but the briefest explanation for the measure and its temporary character was sufficient to silence them. In accordance with previous plans, these workers were relieved the same evening and the operation continued on a purely military basis. Service was near normal by the afternoon of the same day with materials being delivered to the alkali and magnesium plants and their employees being recalled to work. A fear that the men at these plants, who were mostly members of the United Mine Workers, might, in sympathy with the striking railroad workers and as a protest against the government's order, refuse to return to work or to load or handle materials transported by the Army did not materialize.(6)

Settling the Labor Controversy

Concomitant with the seizure, the War Department successfully urged the NWLB to take jurisdiction of the case, and a board representative immediately went to the scene.(7) Over a period of several days, in spite of initial union opposition, he succeeded in obtaining an agreement, whereby the status quo was restored and Dr. Steelman, director of the Conciliation Service, and NWLB Chairman Davis agreed to appoint an arbitrator to settle the dispute with the settlement appealable by either party to the NWLB.(8) This agreement was reached at 11:00 P.M. on 9 November, and at 6:30 A.M. on 10 November the War Department withdrew and private operation resumed. The only aftermath was a belated and somewhat anxious inquiry from the NWLB as to why the department had intervened in the first place.(9)

Endnotes

(1) Memo for file by Ohly, 10 Nov 44, sub: Formulation of Labor Policies To Govern the Operation of Clinton Engineering Works; Memo, Ohly for [Lt] Col Hebert, 24 May 45, sub: Plant Seizure—Manhattan District (App. N–1); Memo, Brig Gen Green for Ohly, n.d., sub: Plan for Seizure and Operation by the War Department of Facilities Operated in Connection With Manhattan District Projects (App. N–2); and Memo, Ohly for Lt Col Hebert, 10 Jul 45, sub: Plan for Seizure and Operation by the War Department of the Facilities Operated in Connection With Manhattan District Projects (App. N–3).

(2) Teletype, Becker, AAF, Cleveland, to HQ, AAF, 6 Nov 42; Telecon, Col Dillon and Maj Gen Styer, 7 Nov 42, at 1055; Telecon, Maj Gen Styer and Eastman, Dir, ODT, 7 Nov 42, at 0940; Labor Relations Branch, CPD, SOS, strike files.

(3) App. N–4.

(4) See EO draft in official files. Also see statement by the War Department to the local union at Painesville, Ohio, 6 Nov 42; Memo for file by Ohly, 7 Nov 42, sub: Fairport, Painesville, and Eastern Railroad Strike—Miscellaneous Notes; G–2 teletype re Fairport, Painesville, and Eastern Railroad, Ohio, 7 Nov 42.

(5) Telg, Under Sec War to C. Baughman, President, Fairport, Painesville, and Eastern Railroad, William Ulle, and Wolfert H. Duck, 7 Nov 42; War Department Press Release, 7 Nov 42, sub: Army Ordered To Move Vital Materials When Labor Dispute Halts Railroads (App. N–5).

(6) Memo for file by Ohly, 8 Nov 42, sub: Fairport, Painesville, and Eastern Railroad Strike—Developments, Nov. 7, 1942 at 4:00 P.M. to Nov. 8 at 2:00 P.M.

(7) Ltr, Under Sec War to W. H. Davis, 12 Nov 42.

(8) Memos for file by Ohly, 7, 8, and 10 Nov 42, subs: Fairport, Painesville, and Eastern Railroad.

(9) Memo for file by Ohly, 24 Nov 42, sub: Fairport, Painesville, and Eastern Railroad. The effectiveness and promptness of the Army's action was highly praised in Ltr, Francis G. Allen, Aluminum and Magnesium Br, WPB, to Lt Col Edgar Lewis, OUSW, 11 Nov 42.

Chapter 7

General Developments, November 1942 to November 1943

From November 1942 to November 1943 there were no War Department plant seizures. Other notable events took place, however, profoundly affecting the handling of subsequent takeovers. These developments, which constituted the prelude to the modern phase of plant seizure, included the enactment of the War Labor Disputes Act, the issuance of Executive Order 9370, the revamping of the War Department's organization for seizing plants, and the creation of a plant seizure manual.

Enactment of the War Labor Disputes Act

The June 1943 passage of the War Labor Disputes Act(1) had a significant effect on the development of plant seizure techniques. Without this law the history of seizures would probably have been very different. Curiously, the character and extent of these effects were not appreciated by the government at the time, and some of the law's most advantageous features were opposed by the War Department for two years due to much confused thinking.

War Department attention was first directed toward the question of such legislation in the spring of 1941 during the Allis-Chalmers case. Both the War and Navy Departments believed that Section 9 of the Selective Training and Service Act, as amended, authorizing the seizure of plants under certain circumstances, was not applicable to labor disputes.(2) At the same time, military leaders believed that the aggregate and inherent emergency powers of the president as commander-in-chief were sufficient to permit the seizure of strike-bound properties of importance to the war effort.(3) In addition they had doubts whether such authority existed in cases in which an interruption of production was only threatened, management defiance compelled seizure, or condemnation or confiscation proceedings were necessary. These doubts, as well as a recognition that distinct advantages might come from reinforcing and clarifying presidential authority through additional legislation, resulted in the War and Navy Departments preparing several draft bills. Some of these drafts, along with proposals to confer additional power on the president to seize plants, called for the strict application of the Civil Service and Classification Acts and regulations to employees in any plant seized.(4) These drafts never took the form of officially sponsored legislation but, following several informal conversations between congressmen and procurement officials during the Allis-Chalmers strike, bills were introduced proposing amendments to Section 9 of the Selective Training and Service Act to authorize seizure when an interruption of vital production was caused or threatened by a labor disturbance or any other cause.(5) These bills were bare grants of broad power to the president and did not attempt to spell out, as the War Labor Disputes Act did, any guidelines for government operation of a seized plant, nor did they spell out penalties against those who interfered with such operations. The War Department showed an active interest in these measures and urged their adoption, believing that they "would place in the hands of the President the power to assure the uninterrupted production of defense supplies."(6)

Senator Tom Connally[1] of Texas, then and later the principal congressional proponent of this legislation, succeeded on 12 June 1941, during the North American Aviation controversy, in obtaining Senate adoption of his proposals in the form of an amendment to Senate Bill 1524. The House Committee on Military Affairs, while purporting to support the principle of Connally's proposal, developed a bill that substantially altered it.(7) The committee's version proposed that "a refusal in any labor dispute to utilize existing Government conciliation and mediation facilities in an effort to settle such dispute on the part of any individual firm . . . with which an order has been placed for defense materials" was to be construed as a refusal to comply with a compulsory order under Section 9 of the Selective Training and Service Act. It further suggested that in the event of a production stoppage from "subversive influences or otherwise," the president could order a resumption of production and enforce his order by directing the Army or Navy to "afford protection to all persons engaged in the operation [of the plant] . . . who voluntarily desire to work in such plant." Finally, it stated that nothing contained in the preceding provisions should be construed "to authorize the president or any Government agency to seize or operate any plant or industry, or to give any persons affected thereby, in any respect whatsoever, the status of government employees." The amended bill went a step further than its predecessors and provided for criminal penalties against anyone who by force or violence attempted to prevent persons from working in any defense plant. Such a bill would certainly have covered situations like North American Aviation and Air Associates, but it would not have applied to the S. A. Woods case or to any of the dozen later cases involving management defiance of a National War Labor Board (NWLB) order. According to the House report on the bill, the administration and the War and Navy Departments thought it wise to obtain legislation making clear and unmistakable the right of the president to intervene in cases like the North American Aviation situation, and legislation was proposed "in response to an earnest request by the War Department" stating that strikes were

---

[1]Tom Connally (1877–1963) was educated in law at Baylor University and the University of Texas. He was involved in Texas state politics before entering the House of Representatives as a Democrat in 1917. Following military service in World War I, he returned to Congress and gained election to the Senate in 1928. An ardent internationalist, Connally supported Roosevelt's foreign policies but staunchly opposed most New Deal social welfare and labor legislation. The War Labor Disputes Act of 1943, popularly known as the Smith-Connally Act, was a product of Connally's collaboration with Congressman Howard W. Smith (D-Va.).

seriously interfering with war production. In spite of this statement it appears that the War Department did not do anything more than emphasize the serious character of the labor situation and indicate the desirability of adopting measures like Connally's. The War Department was not in full sympathy with restrictive measures but seems to have favored, at least unofficially, the idea of amending Section 9 of the Selective Training and Service Act to cover failures and refusals by a manufacturer to produce.(8)

The House deleted provisions relative to plant seizures and the matter was referred to a conference committee. At this stage the War Department strongly urged the administration to press for a compromise measure to carry out Connally's purpose.(9) In doing so, the War Department was influenced by the fact that Connally's amendment permit-

Senator Tom Connally

ted seizures in nonlabor situations of the kind experienced in World War I—cases of insolvency or of inefficient or subversive management. The War Department also argued that even though the president's power to take custody of a plant in order to permit willing workers to return to work, as at North American Aviation, might be clear, it was doubtful whether this power authorized seizures and direct operations of properties when management refused to enter into fair labor agreements. There was a distinct advantage in spelling out for the benefit of government agencies and all others concerned a clear statement of the nature and extent of such power. The administration did not act on the War Department recommendations and the bill died.(10)

The captive coal strike revived proposals for the handling of strikes, and the fall of 1941 was marked by intense congressional debate. Senator Connally introduced a new bill containing features from the previous bill and new additions providing that the terms and conditions of employment in any seized plant were to remain frozen during government possession except upon petition of the majority of employees. The bill called for the creation of a three-man defense wage board that could authorize wage increases with presidential approval.(11) Under Secretary Patterson strongly supported the general principles of the proposed measure before the Senate Judiciary Committee. While stating that the president already had the authority to take such action, he added that enactment of the bill would give "legislative sanction to such procedure and govern details of its operation such as we do not have now." He defended the bill against critics who charged that it was drastic and vested arbitrary and potentially abusive powers in the administration. He also endorsed the provisions freezing terms of employment on seizure,(12) although the War Department later questioned the wisdom of this endorsement because it could limit the operating agency during a long takeover.(13)

The Senate Judiciary Committee reported favorably on Senator Connally's measure,(14) but before it was brought to a vote the House sent the Senate an entirely different measure, which, while including many of Senator Connally's provisions, provided for extensive controls over labor activities and called for the establishment of elaborate machinery for the resolution of industrial disputes.(15) The House measure was referred to the Senate Committee on Labor but never advanced. Before action could be taken on either bill, however, Congress was swamped with far more critical problems following Pearl Harbor. In rapid order the captive coal strike was settled, management and labor agreed to a no-strike pledge, and President Roosevelt announced his intention of creating a national war labor board.

During the spring of 1942 Connally again renewed efforts to enact his bill. He was faced, however, with the facts of a substantial decrease in the number of strikes, a lack of administration support, and a widespread desire to give the NWLB an opportunity to work out industrial problems on a voluntary basis. He was unable to bring the measure to a vote as interest in Congress and the War Department waned.(16) Strikes and seizures were not as numerous as anticipated, the no-strike pledge and the NWLB were proving effective, and Congress had passed the War Powers Acts of 1941 and 1942,[2] which vested in the government broad powers of condemnation and requisition that could be used in emergency labor situations. Thus in May 1943, in commenting upon H.R. 2027, an act similar to Connally's proposed law, the War Department stated that it had no objections but saw little need for such legislation.(17) There were even those in the department who wished to submit an unfavorable report on the mistaken belief that the provision of the bill freezing employment conditions, except as modified by the NWLB upon application, would unduly restrict the freedom of an operating agency.(18)

It was another coal crisis, this time in the late spring of 1943, that again compelled Congress to consider antistrike legislation. Senator Connally introduced a new bill, which differed greatly from his last version. First, it substituted the NWLB for the defense wage board. Second, it gave the NWLB the power to change wages and all other terms and conditions of employment in any seized plant and similar rights to employees and their representatives to apply for such changes. Third, it gave the government an agency to operate such plants. Fourth

---

[2]The War Powers Act of 1941 authorized the president by executive order to direct the secretary of war to take possession and operate any industrial facility for the production of war materials or materials that affected the war effort. The War Powers Act of 1942 (56 Stat. 176) extended this authority to the acquisition by purchase, donation, or condemnation of any property, private or personal, or temporary use thereof, deemed necessary for military purposes in accordance with the Act of 1 August 1888 (25 Stat. 357) and Section 1b of the Act of 2 July 1940 (54 Stat. 712).

and finally, the bill made it a crime for any person to instigate or aid, by giving direction, guidance, or funds to, any strike, lockout, or other interference with production in a seized plant.(19) The last-mentioned addition resulted from the government's demonstrated inability, even after seizure, to secure an immediate return to work in the coal mines.

The Senate quickly passed Connally's measure, but the House Committee on Military Affairs revised it into a very strong antistrike measure.(20) The changes omitted the basic provision authorizing seizure, apparently on the assumption that such authority already existed, but retained those sections relating to employment conditions and penalties for interfering with government operation of a seized plant. The House version of the bill was not subjected to hearings, and its sudden appearance prompted a concerted administration effort for its defeat. Labor Secretary Perkins called a conference of the labor and procurement agencies, and all agreed to send a joint letter to the Majority Leader of the House, the Speaker of the House, and the Military Affairs Committee chairman,[3] setting forth their united opposition supplemented by individual agency letters relative to specific parts of the bill.

The government's letter was in general terms, and because of conflicting views among its authors it did not address the plant seizure provisions as such.(21) The War Department submitted no separate comments, but the report of the four NWLB public members is of interest because it strongly attacked the provision of the bill permitting either the government operating agency or the majority of company employees or their representatives to apply to the NWLB for changes in terms and conditions of employment.(22) The NWLB wrote:

The inevitable result of permitting a governmental operating agency to formulate terms of employment for submission to the WLB would be to put the Government into the business of collective bargaining, which ought to be left to the parties alone, and which might well result in the engineering of stoppages to compel government seizure in the hope of obtaining, from negotiations with government operating officials, terms which might not be obtainable through the normal processes of collective bargaining. In addition, the clause, if enacted, might lead to conflicts between the operating officials and the WLB as to what the terms of settlement should be. These terms should be left to the parties to work out with Board approval or, failing agreement, should be determined by the Board through the application of its basic policies to the facts as found, without the interposition of some other governmental agency. The provision which permits a union, representing a majority of the workers in the seized plant, to apply to the Board for changes in the terms of employment is a privilege not extended to employers and is calculated further to invite the very interruption of production which the bill seeks to prevent. It is the Board's firm policy not to entertain union complaints while men are on strike and, if a plant is taken over, not to consider proposals for changes in the terms of employment, except such as may be presented jointly as a result of collective bargaining or such as the Board may determine to direct, after a hearing, for the purpose of terminating the controversy. We believe that any

---

[3]The Majority Leader of the House in May 1943 was John W. McCormack (1891–1980), a Democrat from Massachusetts. The Speaker of the House was Sam Rayburn (1882–1961), a Democrat from Texas, and the Military Affairs Committee chairman was Andrew J. May (1875–1959), a Democrat from Kentucky.

impairment of this policy, such as Section 12 would bring about, would have the most unfortunate effect on the maintenance of industrial peace.

The resort to this extraordinary procedure whereby the executive agencies appealed over the head of the responsible committee to the House of Representatives so angered the committee that several agency heads were summarily called to a hearing. Assistant Secretary McCloy and James P. Mitchell,[4] director of the Industrial Personnel Division (IPD), Headquarters, Army Service Forces, both appeared and explained the background of the government's letter. They also reiterated the War Department's opposition to the features of the amended bill not relating to plant seizures and expressed concerns similar to those of the NWLB relating to changes in the terms and conditions of employment in a seized plant.(23)

Administration opposition made little impression upon a House of Representatives aroused by a further coal strike. All but minor administration amendments were defeated and additional provisions of an even more drastic character were added and passed by a substantial majority. The conferees met at once and, after acrimonious debate, reported a compromise measure retaining the plant seizure provisions of the Senate bill and a large number of other provisions specifically opposed by the executive agencies.

The conference bill was promptly passed by both chambers while President Roosevelt requested the views of the several departments on the question of a veto. The matter was the subject of extensive War Department discussions. It was agreed that the seizure provisions were generally desirable and that most of the other provisions, such as those giving legal recognition and subpoena powers to the NWLB, were unwise but not issues meriting War Department comment. The majority believed that the War Department should point out the bill's advantages and disadvantages without a final conclusion, contrary to the wishes of Under Secretary Patterson, who favored the bill but only as it applied to the current coal crisis. Secretary Stimson, however, finally insisted that the War Department urge Roosevelt's approval, believing that Section 6 (dealing with criminal prosecution of violators) would help in dealing with the likes of John L. Lewis. Stimson further thought the bill would boost the morale of soldiers overseas who were allegedly anxious about growing labor unrest at home. In a joint letter with Navy Secretary Knox, Stimson recommended against a veto.(24) Other agencies took the opposite position, and Roosevelt followed their advice, although his veto message indicated his substantial approval of the plant seizure sections.(25) The veto was promptly overridden by an overwhelming majority in both houses, and on 25 June 1943 Congress passed the War Labor Disputes Act.(26)

The consequences of this law to subsequent plant seizures were great, although not entirely understood at the time. First, the War Labor Disputes Act put plant seizures beyond the probability of successful legal attack. While serious

---

[4] James P. Mitchell had been a civilian labor advisor to General Somervell for some years by the time of the events described here.

legal questions arose with the Montgomery Ward seizure, in which the relation of the business to the war effort seemed remote, it was a unique and unprecedented situation. Second, the law gave employees in a seized plant a definite status in that the terms, conditions, and other attributes of employment were prescribed. It was no longer germane whether they were governmental or nongovernmental employees, and the doubts that existed in the S. A. Woods case as to whether a plant could legally be operated under such provisions as maintenance of membership and voluntary checkoff were now gone. Third, the law prescribed only one procedure for changing the existing terms and conditions of employment, which proved extremely well adapted to seizure operations. The procedure provided a convenient means by which an operating agency could initiate noncon-

James P. Mitchell

troversial changes necessary to the effective operation of a facility and at the same time did not force seizing agencies into collective bargaining because it compelled employees or their representatives to refer their demands directly to the NWLB. Fourth, the criminal penalties established proved useful in later cases, where events might otherwise have careened out of control. Finally, the law provided that in any seized plant all existing state or federal laws relating to health, safety, security, and employment standards remained applicable. This meant that social security and workmen's compensation problems, which had complicated the seizures at S. A. Woods and Air Associates, could be handled simply because operations were to conform with the law irrespective of whether workers were government employees. Thus, not only were the terms and conditions of employment prescribed, but there was also a legal framework for operation.

Revamping the War Department's Plant Seizure Organization

Increasing industrial unrest and the widely prevailing view that the passage of the War Labor Disputes Act invited takeovers led to an extensive examination by both the IPD's Labor Branch and Brig. Gen. Edward S. Greenbaum of the desirability of reallocating War Department plant seizure responsibilities in the summer of 1943. Until then seizures were more or less supervised by the Office of the Under Secretary of War (OUSW) with respect to both policy and operational details, although the Labor Relations (later Labor) Branch of the Civilian (later

Industrial) Personnel Division[5] did most of the work in an informal and somewhat haphazard manner. Greenbaum, in line with his policy of restricting the under secretary's office to policy questions, felt that the time was ripe to relieve the OUSW of operational supervision.

The first plan considered(27) was very similar to that urged by Patterson in 1941, and although it was discussed for several months, it was abandoned because of Greenbaum's belief that the unsettled nature of the plant seizure concept made it more desirable to handle takeovers informally and in a manner assuring maximum flexibility and minimum amount of paperwork.(28) In its place Greenbaum submitted a far less revolutionary plan embodied in a directive from Patterson to the commanding generals of the Army Air Forces and Army Service Forces on 9 August 1943.(29)

Under the procedure outlined in the new directive, Patterson's office had the general responsibility for insuring that technically qualified people were available and for preparing and revising an operating manual and other useful materials. Patterson was to call on special consultant McGrady, the director of the Industrial Personnel Division; the chief of the Industrial Services Division,[6] the representatives of the assistant chief of staff for materiel, maintenance, and distribution, AAF, and the director of materiel, ASF; the fiscal director of administration; and the judge advocate general to perform these duties.(30) When a seizure became imminent, the under secretary would make seizure plans, including alerting of personnel; selection and briefing of a War Department representative; holding conferences with the NWLB, Justice Department, and other agencies relative to the preparation of an executive order; and perfecting any arrangements with the ASF's chief of staff for troops. As soon as the executive order was signed, the entire operation of the facility, with the exception of high policy matters, devolved from the under secretary to the AAF and ASF commanding generals and staffs, depending on the installations.

The memorandum of 9 August 1943 was of considerable significance, although not a basic reform. It might have become such had it been properly implemented by the two commanding generals through the centralization in one office of all operating responsibility. At the outset both commanding generals, their chiefs of staff, and their immediate advisors were utterly unfamiliar with

---

[5]In January 1943 the Civilian Personnel Division, Headquarters, SOS, was redesignated as the Industrial Personnel Division. At this time, two of its three branches—Labor Relations and Manpower—were combined into one element, the Labor Branch, with four sections: Policy, Information, Research, and Labor Operations. The latter section was geographically organized, with two officers for each of three regions. These officers were the sole channel of communication with the field on labor problems, and they worked in close cooperation with the Labor Branch simultaneously established at each service command.

[6]The Industrial Services Division (ISD) was formed in the War Department's Bureau of Public Relations on 14 August 1942, with the mission of formulating programs that would enhance morale and productivity among labor and management. One of its major activities was the awarding of the Army-Navy "E" to industrial plants achieving outstanding war production records. It cooperated on specific projects with the ASF's Industrial Personnel Division, the Office of War Information, the labor division of the War Production Board, and the War Manpower Commission. Maj. Ralph F. Gow, the War Department representative for the S. A. Woods seizure in August, also served as the ISD director. He remained in that position until September 1944, when he transferred to the Industrial Personnel Division.

Lt. Gen. Wilhelm D. Styer   *Maj. Gen. LeRoy Lutes*
(Photographed in 1942)

plant seizure and its implications, and even though relative documents later flowed to and from them, the job was carried on, as in the past, by the under secretary's office and the Labor Branch. Fortunately, the two wartime chiefs of staff of the Army Service Forces, successively, Lt. Gen. Wilhelm D. Styer[7] and Lt. Gen. LeRoy Lutes,[8] had the capacity for understanding these operations and eventually were able to make very substantial contributions and to take some of the burden off Patterson. The real trouble lay in the fact that matters that were of sufficient

[7]Lt. Gen. Wilhelm D. Styer (1893–1975) was born in Salt Lake City and was educated at West Point, Class of 1916. He served on the Mexican border (1916) and with the American Expeditionary Forces. Between the wars he was an engineering instructor, a district engineer, and a consulting engineer for the American Battle Monuments Commission and the Works Progress Administration. He served in the Panama Canal Zone (1936–39) and, in January 1941, was deputy chief of the Construction Division of the Office of the Quartermaster General. In March 1942 he was appointed chief of staff, SOS, and in May 1943 chief of staff and deputy commander, ASF. In May 1945 he became the commanding general, ASF, Western Pacific, and later served as a military governor during the Japanese occupation. He retired in 1947.

[8]Lt. Gen. LeRoy Lutes (1890–1980) was born in Cairo, Illinois, and was educated at the Wentworth Military Academy (1908). He joined the Illinois National Guard in 1906 and received a Regular Army commission in 1917 while serving on the Mexican border. Between 1921 and 1939 he served with the Coastal Artillery Branch in the United States and its possessions. In January 1940, following four years with the National Guard Bureau, he was made the assistant chief of staff, G–4, with the Third Army in Atlanta, where he was involved with the 1940 and 1941 Louisiana maneuvers. He joined the War Department General Staff in February 1942 as the director of operations, SOS, becoming the acting chief of staff, ASF, in September 1943, and the director of plans and operations, Headquarters, ASF, that October. In April 1945 Lutes was made chief of staff and deputy to the commanding general, ASF, and on 1 January 1946 he assumed the duties of commanding general, ASF. He retired in January 1952.

importance to merit their personal consideration also deserved consideration by
the OUSW, and they did not make provision for the regular disposition of less
important questions by anyone other than themselves.

The under secretary's office proceeded to perform all of the functions allotted
to it under the memorandum. These functions were almost exclusively discharged
by General Greenbaum, who continued to carry on many of the nonpolicy activities he had performed before the memorandum became effective. However, from
a routine standpoint the reorganization did reduce the work of the OUSW, and it
might have been still further reduced if so many of the problems referred to headquarters had not involved important policy questions.(31)

Perhaps the most important consequence of this memorandum was making the
War Department components that were responsible for handling the technical
aspects of seizures and for furnishing seizure teams more responsive. Although the
advisors specified in the memorandum met only once as a committee, each was
active in making certain that the duties of his own office were properly discharged.
Furthermore, these individuals or their representatives were normally present at
the briefing sessions preceding the departure of any seizure team. In this way they
succeeded in keeping abreast of general developments on the subject and facts
about particular cases necessary to the solution of the technical problems constantly being referred for the consideration of headquarters.

The principal defect of the reorganization was not the plan itself but the ASF's
and AAF's failure to fix responsibilities. In neither command was there any bureau
officially designated to supervise all seizure operations. This failure resulted in
some confusion concerning the chain of command and for a time caused the
annoyance of the chiefs of staff and commanding generals on minor matters that
would otherwise have been of no concern. Lack of centralized authority was at
times a handicap in obtaining personnel, in assuring proper administrative coordination, and in keeping a War Department representative in line. The organization
of each seizure team, its supervision in the field, and the handling of headquarter's
problems continued on a somewhat informal basis, and it was only after the technical people came to know one another intimately, to work as a team, and to look
by tacit understanding to the Labor Branch for coordination that well-defined
administrative procedures developed. In time, through this casual process and the
chiefs of staffs' acceptance of the fact, the Labor Branch assumed direct supervision of most of the work.

Eventually a standard clause was inserted in the War Department representative's instructions ordering communication with the commanding general responsible through the director of the Industrial Personnel Division. This arrangement
assured proper supervision and coordination once an operation was under way but
never surmounted the difficulties experienced in planning and preparation. Almost
without fail, responsibility for planning in the really tough situations was given to
some office or to some person who was completely unfamiliar with the subject and
who usually thought of seizure in terms of a military mission, completely over-
looking its basic objective. This was illustrated in the preparation of the three coal
plans and in the Philadelphia Transportation, Montgomery Ward, and American

railroad cases. Each case was ultimately successful, but only after an incredible waste of time, many anxious moments, and the nearly complete jettisoning of the plans. Communication instructions of the character mentioned were not included when the AAF was designated to conduct an operation. However, in practice the same procedure of reporting through the Industrial Personnel Division was followed informally. By V–J Day the Labor Branch was serving in two capacities—as director of field operations on all seizures for the AAF and ASF commanding generals and as staff policy advisors to the under secretary.

The memorandum did not, however, sufficiently convince the AAF and ASF production groups of the importance of seizures to insure that the most qualified War Department representatives were selected. It was many months before they were properly familiarized with seizure activities and commenced furnishing the kind of War Department representatives who were needed. While there were several good War Department representatives in the interim, their choice was often the result of accident rather than intelligent planning, and several were very inferior.

The memorandum of August 1943 represented the last serious attempt to effect a major formal reorganization of the responsibilities for handling War Department plant seizures. The Labor Branch often reiterated its proposal that all seizure matters be centralized in a separate section located at a high level in the Army Service Forces,(32) but the successive Industrial Personnel Division directors[9] were unwilling to press this idea.

Publication of a Labor Manual

As early as summer 1942 the Labor Relations Branch had considered the preparation of a plant seizure manual, and Joseph Bishop had completed a proposed outline. Bishop's induction temporarily halted this work, which was revived in the spring of 1943, when General Greenbaum requested that the judge advocate general undertake the assignment. Its preparation was placed under the direction of Lt. Col. Paul M. Hebert and Maj. Victor Sachse, both judge advocates. Passage of the War Labor Disputes Act gave the project further impetus, and after many conferences and drafts the first edition was issued on 31 October 1943. This document contained in an organized form a wealth of information and experience gained from the North American Aviation, Air Associates, and S. A. Woods cases and integrated these experiences with the changes caused by the War Labor Disputes Act and the memorandum of 9 August. Standard forms and pertinent extracts from important laws, executive orders, and memoranda were appended. The document constituted a useful operating guide, summarized the purposes and philosophy of a takeover, set forth the important policies, and outlined the routine of a seizure. It could be used to train personnel in the technical aspects as well as to indoctrinate War Department representatives in the nature of their job and to serve as a guide in meeting specific problems. Publication of this manual was the

---

[9]Mitchell's successors were W. A. Hughes (April 1944), Col. Ralph F. Gow (September 1944), and Col. Foster L. Furphy (September 1945).

Maj. Joseph W. Bishop, Jr.

first step in placing the administration of plant seizures on an orderly, methodical basis. The manual was revised in March 1944 to incorporate the experiences of subsequent cases and, as so revised, in effect constituted the department's standard operating plan for the duration. Its one major defect was the failure of the Labor Branch to prepare a section on the many labor aspects of seizures, due to the difficulty of standardizing material on what was the most variable factor from case to case.

Issuance of Executive Order 9370

On 16 August 1943 President Roosevelt issued Executive Order 9370, authorizing the director of economic stabilization to take certain actions for the enforcement of NWLB orders.(33) It was twofold in purpose. In the first place the order was designed to provide alternatives to plant seizures in cases of employer noncompliance with NWLB directives. It authorized the director of economic stabilization to order any department or agency to withhold or withdraw from any noncomplying employer priorities, benefits, privileges, or contracts entered into by executive action of the government until compliance was effected. The order was intended to bring economic pressure to bear on employers who failed to cooperate with the government on the reasoning that persons who refused to conform to the country's wartime policy should not be accorded a share of the nation's scarce materials or benefit from government contracts. The theory was excellent, but as a practical weapon it had four weaknesses vitiating its effectiveness. First, it was impossible for the government to apply these sanctions against any important war contractor without hurting its own war procurement. Federal use of the order was of necessity restricted to unimportant, relatively small, and nonessential producers. Second, such sanctions adversely affected not only the employer against whom they were directed but equally his employees—the very people for whose benefit the action was being taken. Third, the legality of some of the sanctions was doubtful, and the War Production Board refused to honor orders of the director of economic stabilization for withholding priorities. This issue was never fully resolved. Finally, the practical problems of administering the order and of determining whether the government could actually afford to shut off a particular plant or activity tended to severely limit its usefulness. While the existence of this portion of the order may have had a salutary effect on certain employers, it appears

War Manpower Commission. Chairman Paul V. McNutt is seated in the center.

that among the several score of cases in which its use was considered the sanctions were actually applied only three times and only once successfully.(34) Their application was considered and rejected in several cases that later developed into full-blown plant seizures.(35)

The second portion of Executive Order 9370 contained two parts directed at employees and unions who refused to accept NWLB directives. Under the first part the director might instruct a government agency operating a seized plant to apply to the NWLB under Section 5 of the War Labor Disputes Act for an order withholding or withdrawing from a noncomplying labor union any benefits, privileges, or rights accruing to it under the terms and conditions of employment in effect when possession was taken until such time as the union demonstrated its willingness to comply. The Navy Department used this technique with considerable success in two cases, but the War Department never had occasion to use it.(36) The second part permitted the director to order the War Manpower Commission[10] to cancel or modify recalcitrant workers' employment privileges

---

[10]The War Manpower Commission (WMC) was established within the Office of Emergency Management by Executive Order 9139, 18 April 1942, to assure effective mobilization and utilization of national manpower. Among the agencies it controlled and directed were the Labor Division of the War Production Board, the National Youth Administration, and the Selective Service System. It was abolished by Executive Order 9617, 19 September 1945. The WMC chairman was Paul V. McNutt (1942–45). For WMC records, see Record Group 211, NARA.

or draft deferments or both. Techniques of blacklisting and cancellation of deferments of strikers were never used in the absence of a seizure, although they were repeatedly urged and occasionally threatened by the War Department. When used in conjunction with seizures, Executive Order 9370 was not required to permit their use, although it was several times mentioned in such connection. Nevertheless, formalizing sanctions in a executive document had a salutary effect and had the definite virtue of centralizing authority in the director of economic stabilization, who was in a position to order sanctions if the heads of the Selective Service System and War Manpower Commission refused to invoke them. The sanctions themselves were used most effectively in a number of critical cases.

As a result of Executive Order 9370 being virtually impossible to apply in employer noncompliance cases, and because it really was unnecessary as a basis for applying sanctions against defiant employees and unions, the order never played a particularly significant part in government efforts to secure compliance with NWLB directives. Early hopes that it might lessen the burden of plant seizures never materialized.

Development of the Service Commands

By the end of 1943 the service commands were well-established organizations responsible for a large share of the Army's nonprocurement activities. In time the question of their relationship to and responsibilities for plant seizures arose. It was natural, for example, for a service commander to consider that a plant seizure within the territorial limits of his command, particularly if it involved the use of troops, was a matter for him to handle, and on several occasions this feeling led to considerable friction between a War Department representative and a service commander. At the same time, the existence of a large military organization in the area of any seizure provided an excellent means of furnishing a seizure team with supplemental assistance. The service commands served as an invaluable and excellent source of nontechnical military personnel for use as occupation or riot-control troops or service troops providing supplies and equipment, communications, secretarial assistance, intelligence, and local contacts (*Chart 2*).

The Modern Phase of Plant Seizure

Enactment of the War Labor Disputes Act and related events set the stage for the modern phase of plant seizure. This phase, extending to V–J Day, was marked by increased takeovers and the establishment of well-defined patterns for handling each situation. The variety of experiences gained in the first three seizure cases; the standards and procedures fixed by the War Labor Disputes Act; the publication of the plant seizure manual; the preparation of standard operating procedures for judge advocates, War Department representatives, and service commands; and the gradual training of specialists made the establishment of management patterns relatively easy. These factors enabled the War Department to handle, although not without dif-

CHART 2—TYPICAL ORGANIZATION OF A SERVICE COMMAND HEADQUARTERS,
DECEMBER 1943

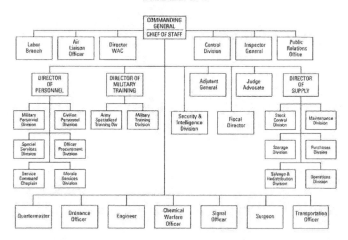

Source: Adapted from Millett, *Army Service Forces*, p. 334.

ficulty, the large volume of cases assigned to it by the president. Procedures eventually were so streamlined that operations became routine in character, and it was often possible after the initial occupation of the premises for the judge advocate, public relations, disbursing, and fiscal officers to return to their permanent stations.

The War Department's standardized approach makes it simple to categorize the subsequent twenty-five seizures into one of three types, with four notable exceptions. The first and largest class comprises cases where the seizure was caused by labor noncompliance with the government labor policy and where the takeover was token in character. The second category covers situations where seizures resulted from management noncompliance with an NWLB order but where management agreed to operate the plant as an agent of the War Department in conformity with its labor orders. This class of seizure was also token in character, except to the extent that direction on labor matters was involved. The third class embraces the small number of cases where seizure resulted from management noncompliance with an NWLB order and where management refused to cooperate in running the business. Token seizure was impossible and varying degrees of active business control by the War Department was necessary.

Within each of the three types of seizure cases, most of the variations were found in the nature of the labor problems involved and the techniques required for their solution. While the general seizure approach was standardized, and while legal, fiscal, public relations, and technical phases were often routine, nearly every seizure presented novel labor questions.

As seizures became frequent in the closing weeks of 1943, the War Department sought to have the seizure responsibility placed elsewhere in government and to this end arranged a conference with Wayne Morse of the NWLB, Benjamin "Ben" Cohen[11] of the White House, and a representative of the Justice Department. It argued that the government should find some means of securing labor peace other than plant seizures; that seizures should be turned over to some existing agency like the War Production Board, except in cases where the military interest was direct and urgent; and that the Reconstruction Finance Corporation[12] should create a group to handle all such questions. Representatives of the other agencies expressed the belief that the War Department, both from the standpoint of prestige and personnel, was normally the best-equipped agency to undertake a seizure, causing War Department efforts to come to naught.

[11]Benjamin "Ben" Cohen (1894–1983) was born in Indiana and was educated at the University of Chicago and Harvard Law School. He practiced law in Chicago and New York (1922–33) before coming to Washington, D.C., at the behest of Felix Frankfurter to work on New Deal securities legislation. He joined the Department of the Interior as associate general counsel to the Public Works Administration (1933–34) and later served on the National Public Power Committee (1934–41). He left the Interior Department in 1941 to become a counsel to John G. Winant, the U.S. Ambassador to Great Britain. He spent the years 1943–45 as a general counsel to the director of the Office of War Mobilization and as a special advisor to Roosevelt.

[12]The Reconstruction Finance Corporation (RFC) was formed under Section 201e of the Emergency Relief and Construction Act, 22 January 1932 (47 Stat. 5; USC 601 et seq.). It was grouped with other agencies in 1939 to form the Federal Loan Agency before being transferred to the Department of Commerce by Executive Order 9071, 24 February 1942. In connection with defense programs, the RFC provided financing for plant conversion and construction, working capital for mining operations and other activities, as well as war production facilities and supplies of strategic and critical war materials. For RFC records, see Record Group 234, NARA.

Endnotes

(1) Act of 25 Jun 43 (Public Law 89, 78th Cong., 1st Sess.). This law is also commonly referred to as the Smith-Connally Act.

(2) This is reflected in correspondence between the under secretary and the attorney general, who held a somewhat contrary view: Memo for Under Sec War, 5 May 41, sub: Proposed Regulations Under Sections 9 and 10 of the Selective Service Act; Memo, Under Sec War for Atty Gen, 13 May 41, same sub (App. O–1); Memo, Atty Gen for Under Sec War, 20 May 41, same sub (App. O–2). Section 9 of the Selective Training and Service Act is set forth in Appendix O–6.

(3) Ltr, Under Sec War to Sen Reynolds, 24 Jun 41. See also studies by Bishop discussed in Chapter 1. The Department of Justice held a similar view.

(4) See Navy Department's draft of proposed amendment to Section 9 of the Selective Training and Service Act of 1940 (App. O–3), commented upon in Memo, Amberg for Thom and Ohly, 20 Mar 41 (App. O–4), and draft of undetermined source of a more extensive proposed bill on this subject (App. O–5).

(5) H.R. 4257, 77th Cong., 1st Sess., introduced by Rep Vinson of Georgia on 1 Apr 41; S. 1600, 77th Cong., 1st Sess., introduced by Sen Connally on 5 Jun; and amendment proposed on 9 Jun 41 by Sen Connally to S. 1524. This amendment was similar to S. 1600.

(6) Proposed letter to the House Military Affairs Committee for signature by Sec War, commenting on H.R. 4257, transmitted to the Dir, Bureau of the Budget, 29 May 41.

(7) H.R. 785, 77th Cong., 1st Sess., to accompany S. 1524, 17 Jun 41.

(8) Ltr, Under Sec War to Baruch, 6 Jun 41.

(9) Memo, Amberg for Coy, 16 Jul 41, sub: Connally Amendment (App. O–7).

(10) S. Doc. 92, 77th Cong., 1st Sess., 1941.

(11) S. 2054, 77th Cong., 1st Sess., 1941.

(12) Testimony of the Under Secretary of War before the Senate Judiciary Committee, 21 Nov 41. See *Washington Post*, 22 Nov 41, p. 3.

(13) Statement of War Department Views on H.R. 6058 and H.R. 6070 (App. O–8).

(14) S. Rpt. 846, 77th Cong., 1st Sess., 1 Dec 41.

(15) *New York Times*, 29 Nov 41, p. 1.

(16) *Washington Post*, 3 Mar 42, p. 1; *New York Times*, 20 Mar 42; and *Washington Post*, 31 Aug 42, p. 1.

(17) Ltr, Sec War to Honorable Mary T. Norton, Chairman, House Labor Committee, 5 May 43.

(18) Draft Ltr, Sec War to Norton, commenting on proposed bill H.R. 2027 (App. O–9). Similar views are contained in the proposed draft report, dated 25 March 1943, to the House Committee on Military Affairs on H.R. 2022.

(19) S. 796, 78th Cong., 1st Sess., 1943.

(20) H.R. 440, 78th Cong., 1st Sess., on S. 796, 1943.

(21) Ltrs to Honorable Sam Rayburn, Speaker of the House, Majority Leader McCormack, and Chairman May of the House Military Affairs Committee, each signed jointly by the War, Navy, and Labor Departments, the Maritime Commission, the National Labor Relations Board, and the NWLB public members, and the War Production Board, 17 May 43 (App. O–10).

(22) Ltrs to the Speaker of the House, the Majority Leader, and Chairman May from William H. Davis on behalf of the four NWLB public members, 15 May 43.

(23) Statement proposed for delivery by McCloy to the House Committee on Military Affairs relative to S. 796 as amended by the committee and summary prepared for him on the War Department position on this amended bill (Apps. O–11 and O–12). See also *New York Times*, 2 Jun 43, p. 1.

(24) Ltr, Sec War and Sec Navy to Dir, Bureau of the Budget, 17 Jun 43 (App. O–13). For a summary of the discussion within the War Department preceding the dispatch of this letter, see Memo for file by Ohly, 22 Jun 43, sub: S. 796 Developments.

(25) Msg, President to Congress, 25 Jun 43.

(26) Sections 3 through 6 of this law (PL No. 89, 78th Cong., 1st Sess., 1943) are set forth in full in Appendix O–14.

(27) Memo, Brig Gen Greenbaum for Under Sec War, n.d., sub: Procedure in Handling the Seizure and Operation of Private Industrial Facilities, prepared in the Labor Branch on 9 Jun 43 (App. O–15).

(28) Memo, Col O'Gara, Labor Branch, for Mitchell, 4 Aug 43, sub: Organization To Handle Plant Seizure Problems.

(29) Memo, Under Sec War for CGs, AAF and ASF, 9 Aug 43, sub: Procedure for War Department Operation of Industrial Facilities Under Executive Orders (App. O–16).

(30) The following individuals were named respectively by the director of materiel, the director of administration, the fiscal director, the judge advocate general, and the assistant chief of Air Staff to serve as their representatives: Lt. Col. John A. Sargent, Lt. Col. J. C. Boyer, Col. Andrew Stewart, Colonel Hebert, and Colonel Volandt.

(31) See Memo for file by Ohly, 15 Dec 43, sub: Plant Seizure—Lessons of the Massachusetts Leather Manufacturing Case (App. P–5).

(32) The writer has been unable to locate any of the several proposals advanced by the Labor Branch, but late in the war an interesting study of this and other problems was submitted in Memo, Capt Chapman, Labor Branch, for Ohly, 16 Jul 45, sub: Emergency Operations of Industrial Facilities by the War Department, particularly par. 4 (App. O–17). See also App. P–5.

(33) EO 9370, 16 Aug 43 (App. O–18).

(34) More than a fifth of the cases of noncomplying employers were referred by the board to the director of economic stabilization, who in turn sent them to the several procurement agencies, including the War Department, for information as to whether the application of sanctions would adversely affect the war program. Appendix O-19 contains an almost complete list of the companies involved together with a statement of War Department views with respect to the application of sanctions against each. Sanctions were applied unsuccessfully in the case of Wentworth Bus Lines, Inc., of Lover, N.H., and in the combined case of McClaren Sportswear Company of Phillipsburg, Pa., and the Standard Trousers Company, an affiliate, of Buchannon [Buckhannon], W.Va. See two Ltrs, William H. Davis, Dir, OES, to Sec War, 23 May 45, sub: McClaren Sportswear Company, Phillipsburg, Pa., and Amalgamated Clothing Workers of America, CIO, WLB Case III–4417–D, and sub: Standard Trouser Company, Buchannon [Buckhannon], W.Va., and Amalgamated Clothing Workers of America, CIO, WLB Case III–4418–D, together with accompanying directive orders dated 23 May 45. See also two Memos, Brig Gen Greenbaum for CG, ASF, 24 May 45, in which, in conformity with Davis' instructions, it was ordered that contracts with these two companies be canceled and no further orders placed with them. In the case of E. A. Laboratories of Brooklyn, N.Y., the sanctions were effective, and the following documents with respect to this case may be of interest: Ltr, Brig Gen Greenbaum to Fred M. Vinson, Dir, OES, 8 Dec 44 (setting forth War Department interest); Memo, Lt (j.g.) Smith for Ohly, 20 Jan 45, sub: E. A. Laboratories, Inc., Brooklyn 5, N.Y. (describing OES discussion); Ltr, Vinson to Under Sec War, 31 Jan 45, sub: E. A. Laboratories, Inc., Myrtle Ave. and Spencer St., Brooklyn 5, N.Y. (directing cancellation of War Department contracts in the event the NWLB did not advise of the company's compliance before 10 Feb); identical memoranda, Col Gow for the Dir of Materiel, ASF, and the Asst CofAirS for M.M.&D., 7 Feb 45, sub: E. A. Laboratories (advising of Vinson's letter and requesting that they be prepared to make specific action in accordance with such letter upon receipt of further instructions); similar identical memoranda from Brig Gen Greenbaum, 14 Feb 45 (directing cancellation of contracts); Memo, Ohly for Brig Gen Greenbaum, 20 Feb 45, sub: E. A. Laboratories (in which the sudden discovery of vital War Department procurement is reported); Memo, Ohly for Col Fred Foy, n.d., sub: E. A. Laboratories Army Activity in Connection With Cancellation of This Company's Contracts (summarizing more important developments in the case); Memo, Amberg for Brig Gen Greenbaum, 16 Mar 45, sub: E. A. Laboratories, Inc. (being a summary of a protest meeting by company officials); identical memoranda, Brig Gen Greenbaum for Dir of Materiel, ASF, and the AsstCofAirS for M.M.&D., 13 Apr 45, sub: E. A. Laboratories, Inc. (revoking prior order due to company's compliance with the NWLB order). The inherent difficulties of making these sanctions work were the subject of an OES conference, which is reported in detail in Memo, Ohly for Brig Gen Greenbaum, 21 Apr 45, sub: Compliance With NWLB Directive Orders (App. W–9).

(35) Among these were Gaffney Manufacturing Company, Cocker Machine and Foundry Company, and Mary-Leila Cotton Mills.

(36) The two Navy cases involved the San Francisco machine shops and the Goodyear Tire and Rubber Company. The War Department considered its use in the American Enka seizure, but decided against it. See Ltr, Brig Gen Greenbaum to George W. Taylor, Chairman, NWLB, 24 Mar 45 (App. O–20).

CHAPTER 8

The Salem-Peabody Leather Manufacturing Case, November 1943

The takeover of the Salem-Peabody leather manufacturing plants in November 1943 was the first case to follow the enactment of the War Labor Disputes Act, the publication of the plant seizure manual, and the issuing of Under Secretary Patterson's procedural directive in his memorandum of 9 August. The case established the general pattern for all subsequent seizures where token operations were possible. The nonlabor phases of seizure—those relating to fiscal, legal, public relations, operating, and procedural problems—were reduced to almost a precise science so that in later cases of this type their handling was routine. Out of the experience gained in this operation came many practical operating reforms, including important developments in the establishment of the team method of seizure management. Finally, the case initiated the practice of creating and distributing the daily reports of the War Department representative to the provost marshal general and all interested War Department headquarters components.

Description of the Companies

Thirteen companies, all located in the neighboring communities of Salem, Peabody, and Danvers, Massachusetts, were involved in the takeover.(1) They were part of the Massachusetts Leather Manufacturers Association, a group of some thirty manufacturing establishments engaged in the initial processing of leather. Even though all of them were involved in the same labor dispute, the decision to seize the plants of only thirteen was completely arbitrary—the result of the existence of strikes at these properties when the executive order was drafted. At any other time the list would have been quite different, and it was thought impossible to solve the problems of any single plant or group of plants without dealing with the whole group.

The plants were tanneries rather than producers of finished consumer leather products, and this fact made evaluating their importance to the war program difficult. Initially, it was believed their production was crucial to quartermaster inventories (that is, mukluks, helmet headbands and chin straps, military gloves, heel pads for coats and gloves, and arctic felt shoes), even though the War Department had no direct contracts.(2) This view changed as alternate sources of supply were discovered, but at a point too late to affect seizure. In the final analysis War Department interest in these facilities proved inconsequential because alternate sources were adequate and available and because the majority of production was for nonessential civilian purposes. At least one of the plants produced nothing for the armed forces, and only three produced more than 10 percent for war uses. The lack of war interest was so obvious that once the facts became known the customary public posting of the executive order was omitted for fear that its recitations about vital war production would make the government appear ludicrous.(3)

Background of the Dispute

In 1933, as the result of a general strike, an autonomous union named the National Leather Workers Association was formed and entered into collective bargaining contracts with the companies making up the Massachusetts Leather Manufacturers Association. The union was not affiliated with any national labor organizations, but in 1937 it was admitted to the CIO as a independent affiliate. In April 1939 it merged with the International Fur Workers Union to form the International Fur and Leather Workers Union of the United States and Canada (IFLWU),[1] headed by Ben Gold[2] of New York. In subsequent years this union negotiated all contracts for the companies with the Manufacturers Association, including two-year contracts signed in December 1942.(4) The contracts contained peculiar union shop clauses, including provisions on giving hiring preference to union members so long as the union could make available qualified persons satisfactory to the employer within twenty-four hours.(5) If no qualified new employee was furnished by the union, the employer might hire from any source, but that employee must become a member of the union within three weeks after the date of his hiring. Furthermore, in the event that any applicant before or after joining the union became "unfinancial," the union might simultaneously notify the employer and the Massachusetts State Board of Arbitration and Conciliation. If the unfinancial status was not corrected within seven days, the latter would order the individual's discharge. Employees who were not members of the union at the time the contract was signed were exempted from the requirement of joining the union.

The amalgamation of the unions was not a happy one, nor were the relations between the two distinct groups of employees found in each tannery. One group, which favored affiliation with the International Fur Workers Union, was composed of the so-called downstairs workers, persons who performed the wet, unskilled, dirty work and who were generally of recent foreign extraction—Armenians,

[1] The National Leather Workers Association had approximately 5,000 members in 1938, the year before the merger, while the International Fur Workers Union had 20,000 members that same year. By 1943 the IFLWU had over 39,000 members. It was expelled from the CIO in 1948 for alleged Communist leanings.
[2] Ben Gold (1898–1985) emigrated to the United States from Bessarabia in 1910. He joined the Furriers Union of the United States and Canada, the forerunner of the International Fur Workers Union (IFWU). A socialist, he led the union's left wing in the 1920s. A Communist by 1937, he ran unsuccessfully for several New York political offices and became president of the IFWU, taking that organization into the CIO in 1937.

Turks, and Poles. The other group, which opposed affiliation, was made up of the so-called upstairs workers, primarily Irish Catholics, whose skilled jobs were performed in dry, relatively pleasant surroundings. Racial, religious, and nationalist feelings between the two factions was strong, a reflection of the prevalent feelings in many Boston communities at this time.

The upstairs group controlled the local for six months after the merger, and it was its subsequent loss of leadership that caused a separatist movement on the part of its members, many of whom never had joined the CIO. This schism was sharpened by the distrust, dislike, and resentment of the upstairs group for the New York crowd that dominated the parent international union and interfered in local union affairs. The growing differences finally evidenced themselves in an open split in August 1943, when a number of employees left the CIO and reconstituted the old independent National Leather Workers Association. In the process they succeeded in getting hold of the local union's funds in the amount of $30,000, a step that led to an immediate lawsuit by the IFLWU in the Superior Court of Massachusetts. The National Leather Workers Association defended its move by alleging that it legally held these assets because the merger with the International Fur Workers Union was illegally consummated and was therefore void. As expected, the court in late October ruled for the IFLWU, while the Leather Workers Association began steps for an appeal.

The August revolt signaled open warfare between the groups, and during the next two months there were frequent stoppages in a number of the plants as one group or the other jockeyed for position. Most of the stoppages emanated from efforts of the Leather Workers Association to collect dues on the premises of the various companies in spite of the fact that the IFLWU had exclusive bargaining rights under contracts providing for a union shop. The continuation of these efforts gradually led to a threat of a general strike, which the National War Labor Board (NWLB) was able to stave off by negotiating an interim settlement favorable to the fur workers.

But the truce was short-lived because of the CIO's efforts to consolidate its position, and in early November the Leather Workers Association called a general strike when two of its members, employees of the Richard Young Company, were sent home. The cause of this action was somewhat obscure at the time, and it was unclear whether the men had been discharged, suspended, or merely laid off. It did appear, however, that CIO workers at this plant had refused to work with these individuals on the grounds that they were antagonizing their fellow employees and engaging in provocative acts. It was also true, however, that the individuals affected were in arrears in their dues and were said to have participated in several slowdowns. The action brought the entire question of jurisdiction between the two groups to a head.

The Regional War Labor Board[3] summoned the parties to a hearing to show cause and directed that the strike be terminated at once and the issues submitted to a board panel. The Leather Workers stated that they would call off the strike when several conditions were met, including the reinstatement of the two fired employees,

---

[3] The chairman of the Regional War Labor Board, Massachusetts Region No. 1, was Saul Wallen.

James F. Byrnes

the guarantee of no further discharges for any reason until after the appeals court ruling, and confirmation of the right of the union to collect dues from its members on company premises. The conditions were obviously unacceptable, and the board promptly sent a back-to-work order promising a tripartite panel inquiry into the merits of the case of the two employees as soon as full production was restored. This telegram produced no results, and the matter was referred to the NWLB. An NWLB order to return to work, to disband picket lines, and to refrain from interfering with access to the plants was quickly answered by a telegram from the rebel group stating that all the strikers were willing to resume work immediately if the order applied to the two discharged employees. The NWLB ignored this demand and on 17 November unanimously referred the case to President Roosevelt. The board believed the case constituted one of the most flagrant challenges to the government's no-strike policy yet seen and merited drastic action.(6)

On receipt of the NWLB letter, President Roosevelt, in a highly unusual move, made a personal appeal to the strikers that they return to work.(7) It made no impression but did make seizure almost inevitable. War Department representatives set to work on a draft executive order for a takeover and cleared it with the Department of Justice, but they learned on 22 November(8) that another completely inadequate document had already been signed by Roosevelt.(9) Armed with this information, and by now fully aware of its lack of interest in these plants, the War Department initiated efforts to prevent the seizure or to obtain a more adequate order from the president. The NWLB, while apologetic about the form of its order and its lack of coordination, insisted that seizure was essential whether or not direct war production was involved because the particular case was of great importance to the government in rebuilding the pledges and structures destroyed by the unfortunate handling of the 1943 coal case.

James F. Byrnes,[4] director of the Office of Economic Stabilization, was sympathetic to the War Department viewpoint, agreed that the order was inadequate

[4]James F. Byrnes (1879–1972) was a jurist, politician, and statesman from Charleston, South Carolina. He served in the House of Representatives (1911–25) and Senate (1931–41); on the U.S. Supreme Court (1941–42); as the director of economic stabilization (1942–43); as a member and director of the Office of War Mobilization and its successor agency, the Office of War Mobilization and Reconversion (1943–45); as secretary of state (1945–47); and as governor of South Carolina (1951–55).

and perhaps unworkable, and sought to avoid seizure if possible. While the first difficulty was beyond rectification because Roosevelt was out of the country, Byrnes agreed to hold the order for several days pending independent and anonymous efforts by special consultant McGrady to persuade the dissidents to return to work. Unfortunately, McGrady faced a hopeless task, although he did find that both factions would return to work if the Army took possession. Agreement was reached to seize the plants on the afternoon of 24 November or the morning of Thanksgiving Day and to direct efforts toward obtaining a return to work on 26 November. An information leak, however, forced an acceleration of the government's time schedule.(10)

The Takeover

While the negotiations and investigations proceeded, headquarters perfected takeover arrangements. After a poor initial choice of a War Department representative, Col. Curtis G. Pratt was designated the seizing officer. His selection was one of the most fortunate single occurrences in the entire history of plant seizures, as Pratt, far more than any other War Department representative, initiated substantial and far-reaching reforms. Assigned to assist him were top War Department technicians, and this group constituted the first of a series of hard-hitting, closely cooperating teams used so effectively in seizure missions. Pratt took advantage of the fact that for the first time an executive order did not require a civilian labor advisor, and in all subsequent seizures a War Department labor relations officer acted as a part of the seizure team.

The time lag between the first hint of seizure and the final takeover was long enough to permit some advance preparation. Most of the War Department technicians left for Boston with McGrady and had several days to discreetly tap local sources of information. In Washington there was time for some fruitful discussions with the NWLB on general strategy and time to obtain what in effect amounted to instructions on managing issues that were bound to arise. The board had two principal ideas. First, the two fired employees should not be reinstated unless the regional board so directed after it had processed their cases in accordance with the established procedures and, second, that the independent union must be convinced that it had only two lawful means of recourse—to accept and comply with the existing contract while legally electing officers from the faction it represented and to petition the National Labor Relations Board for an election. These suggestions constituted an important part of the basic War Department operational framework.

The Washington conferences prior to Colonel Pratt's departure also addressed the possibility of conflicts between him and the commanding general of the First Service Command,[5] and the utmost care was taken in drafting instructions relative to federal troop use. These efforts largely failed, and the service commander

---

[5]The commander of the First Service Command was Maj. Gen. Sherman Miles. The First Service Command, headquartered in Boston, consisted of the states of Maine, New Hampshire, Vermont, Massachusetts, Connecticut, and Rhode Island.

bristled at his slight role in the seizure and objected strenuously to the decision not to use troops. Except for Colonel Pratt's skill as a diplomat, the relations between the two might have developed in such a way as to have prevented effective cooperation.

Upon arriving in Boston at 7:00 A.M. on 24 November, Colonel Pratt went about the business of organizing his staff, gathering intelligence, preparing documents, and developing a precise and efficient operational plan, actions facilitated by prior high-quality staff work. The newspapers had reported that a seizure was imminent, and that same morning the White House announced government intentions. It is a tribute to the efficiency of Pratt and his staff that at 2:00 P.M. the same day the plants of all thirteen companies were in War Department hands. Both Under Secretary Patterson and Colonel Pratt issued appeals for a return to work on 26 November, and when the plants opened that morning 82 percent of the work force was on the job—an unusually high rate for the day after a holiday.(11)

Problems Presented

Important fiscal, procurement, management, production, and legal problems never arose because of excellent planning and the use of the plant seizure manual. Along with the aid of cooperative managers, problems were quickly solved by the use of prepared forms, a nominal inspection of books, and the posting and sending of various notices. The real difficulties were of a labor character, and they appeared formidable in spite of the earlier pledges of each group to return to work without prompting. Both groups gambled that government possession would strengthen their respective positions and therefore sought to capitalize on the Army's presence. The first problem was to prevent any sort of crisis that might come from these efforts until the regional board could dispose of the issues before it, a difficult task as both parties sought to press the War Department for an interim solution to their differences, especially the right of the Leather Workers Association to collect dues on company premises. This problem was complicated by rabble-rousing speeches on both sides and by the likelihood that the slightest incident could so inflame one or the other group that a new strike would occur.

It was obvious that a more fundamental and difficult labor problem existed than the possibility of a strike taking place before the board could act, however. The issues before the NWLB were merely symptomatic of a deep schism in worker ranks, and there was no assurance that either party would accept NWLB solutions to these questions or to others that might arise during the short period of Army operation. Except for trying to convince the independent group that it must seek recognition through orderly and established channels and obtain NWLB settlement of some of the more immediately explosive issues, little more could be done. From the outset, the War Department stressed these objectives by trying to persuade both sides to show restraint and by trying to prevent any incidents that could complicate existing issues—such as dues collection by the independent group, CIO requests for further discharges, and the disposition of issues before the NWLB.(12)

The Operation

The formal aspects of the seizure were quickly disposed of. Standard contracts were executed with the various companies and their implementation obviated any need for an inventory or more than a cursory examination of corporate records. The report of the fiscal advisor was limited to a simple finding that company records were adequate to reflect operations during the time of War Department possession without any necessity for a separate set of books.(13) Plant managers were promptly designated, in each instance the regular general manager of the plant involved, and all matters such as the notification of insurers were handled through these individuals rather than directly by the War Department. Liaison was established with the Federal Bureau of Investigation (FBI), with the mayors and chiefs of police of Peabody and Salem, and with other state and local officials.(14)

Conferences were promptly held with labor representatives, who reiterated worker intentions to return to the job. These conferences, however, clearly revealed that critical labor issues were about to boil over. The CIO threatened to submit the names of unfinancial members to the State Board of Arbitration in accordance with the contracts, and the independent union announced its intention of obtaining permission to collect dues on company premises. Both groups pressed Colonel Pratt with a series of difficult questions, but Pratt avoided any answers until work resumed. At the same time, the companies and the independent union expressed concern about the other leather plants where similar issues existed and where strikes had occurred or were threatened that could seriously affect the operation of the plants in War Department possession.

The anticipated labor difficulties quickly materialized and the labor officer was kept busy straightening out a series of incidents threatening production including one instance on 6 December resulting in a short strike. These incidents involved a variety of questions—the status of certain employees, threatened discharges of unfinancial workers, the right of the independent union to collect dues on company premises, its right to have shop stewards, the application of Executive Order 9240 relating to overtime, call-in pay, and other similar issues. The prevailing tensions and differences between the parties were such that there was never any assurance that solving one issue would prevent the emergence of a dozen others. Some of the most portentous difficulties arose in plants not under government possession, but the clear interrelationship of events in the two groups of plants was such that Colonel Pratt felt fully justified in intervening regardless. In fact, the apparent futility of attempting any final solution not encompassing all of the leather manufacturing plants in the area led to serious considerations of extending the operation through an amendment to the executive order. This consideration was given impetus by the inability of the unions to understand the reason for the artificial distinction causing the seizure of only thirteen plants. Extending the takeover was discussed with the national and regional labor boards, and the ultimate decision not to act was largely the result of Pratt and his labor officer's successful efforts in putting out brush fires in the privately operated plants and in convincing the unions that it was to their advantage to keep working. This was a noteworthy accomplishment in view of the inflammatory speeches made from time to time by members of both groups.(15)

Once the plants were actually operating the next step was to press for quick NWLB action, and an informal meeting with the chairman of the regional board was arranged. The chairman stated that the certification of the case was sufficiently broad to cover the issue of the two men, a matter not previously clear, and revealed further facts about the events surrounding their layoff. The IFLWU had apparently informed management that the men were unfinancial, and the company had advised them that they must pay their dues. When the men left the manager's office, it was erroneously believed that the entire question had been straightened out. To the contrary, the men took an unauthorized holiday, and upon their return some of the fur workers struck and management, apparently in self-defense, suspended the men. The case was then referred to the State Board of Arbitration, which scheduled a formal hearing and then postponed it when the strike occurred. It was not clear what issues were before the state board or whether that board had jurisdiction. The regional board proposed to get at the missing facts, and the chairman agreed to set a hearing for 30 November.(16)

Representatives of all three parties participated in the hearing and told highly conflicting stories. All agreed that the principal issues involved the two discharged men, but no agreement existed about NWLB jurisdiction to hear the matter or as to the actual course of events. It still remained unclear whether the men had been discharged, suspended, laid off, or merely permitted to take a holiday. At the conclusion of the meeting the parties were given until 10 December to file briefs covering their positions for a further hearing on 16 December.(17)

This postponement represented a serious setback to the War Department's plans because the NWLB could take as much as a month to reach its decision. The War Department was forced to reorient its thinking and consider other ways of stabilizing the situation before that time so the properties could be relinquished without having to deal with the difficult issues raised by the parties involved. This situation prompted Colonel Pratt to offer a series of alternatives to headquarters.(18) These recommendations, the War Department's analysis,(19) and the department's final decisions are of considerable importance in the history of plant seizure. In the process of finding a solution here, the War Department partially defined its functions with respect to the labor problems involved in seizures.

Pratt's memorandum had several premises. First, Pratt recommended that the War Department itself determine appropriate action on labor matters during the period before an NWLB decision. Second, he concluded that all parties had confidence in the War Department and were likely to acquiesce to its recommendations, and third, he suggested that the anticipated affiliation of the independent group with the AFofL be welcomed by the War Department as a stabilizing influence. The War Department proposed, subject to prior clearance by the company and both unions, that until the NWLB rendered a decision the IFLWU would not invoke the unfinancial clause or seek to enforce the contract provision requiring new workers to join the union and that the Leather Workers Association would not collect dues on the premises. Pending a final decision by the state court, the

Leather Workers Association would question neither the validity of the existing collective bargaining contracts nor the right of the IFLWU to act as the collective bargaining agent. Both parties would avoid strikes and abide by the decisions of the State Board of Arbitration, the NWLB, and the courts. The plan's merits were elaborately and forcefully presented and, while admittedly imperfect, it was argued that the plan could keep the peace and allow a quick Army withdrawal before its prestige and usefulness diminished.

Headquarters took strong exception to the proposals, arguing that Army operations were bound by the existing terms and conditions upon seizure and could not deviate from them except as provided by Section 5 of the War Labor Disputes Act. Specific objections were raised concerning the fact that concessions required from the CIO constituted a victory for the Leather Workers Association, and the mere fact of any agreement gave the latter a qualified type of recognition. Under such circumstances it was unlikely that the CIO could afford to enter into a formal agreement as suggested. In addition, the War Department's sponsorship and negotiation of such an agreement, even though of an interim nature and made with the NWLB's acquiescence, might embarrass the board in its disposition of the case, weaken board policy against concessions in face of a threat of force, and undermine the principle of supporting collective bargaining agreements. Sponsorship of such an agreement also placed the War Department in the middle of a complicated and bitter labor dispute that could have the unfortunate long-range effect of causing other unions to press for seizures with hopes that the War Department might provide a better or quicker decision than the NWLB.

The nature and pressing character of Colonel Pratt's difficulties were fully understood, and headquarters agreed that he was entitled to some kind of help in the form of an alternative program. Pratt accepted a new program that included the following points. The War Department would obtain for the parties specific NWLB instructions concerning the interim disposition of some of the most immediate and troublesome issues. Efforts would be made through the NWLB to have the CIO international union deter the local from invoking contract rights concerning the discharge of unfinancial members and to have the AFofL international union restrain their local. If necessary, the NWLB would assume jurisdiction over plants not under War Department control, pending seizure under an amended executive order. The government would use troops, criminal prosecution, and other sanctions to prevent or terminate any strike or disorder. The War Department further insisted that the NWLB accelerate disposition of the basic dispute.

That same day a War Department representative appeared before the NWLB and obtained instructions,(20) forbidding the Leather Workers Association from collecting dues or soliciting members on the premises at any time and ordering that the status quo be maintained pending final disposition of the basic dispute. This meant that new employees who had not joined the union within three weeks, even though replacement workers were available, could not be discharged until final NWLB action.

The parties accepted these decisions in spite of claims by the Leather Workers Association that they were unfair and inflammatory.(21) The decision, nonetheless, cleared the air. Certain rules of operation were established, and a set procedure developed to deal with the settlement of new issues. While the onus for applying the rules fell to the War Department, the latter had avoided any involvement in their formulation. The War Department could now claim neutrality and thereby retain the respect and confidence of both groups, which proved of great importance in permitting it to quickly and successful terminate the seizure.

Although the NWLB decisions placed matters on a more even keel, the possibility of further incidents had not disappeared. Perhaps only Colonel Pratt's speed and firmness in dealing with a short strike intended as a test by the Leather Workers Association on 6 December prevented the situation from again becoming dangerous. The strike was short-lived due to quick War Department intervention, and Pratt called in union leaders for the purpose of making very plain that any further such actions would result in government sanctions, including prosecutions under Section 6 of the War Labor Disputes Act. In these efforts Pratt gained reluctant support from the FBI and the attorney general's office.(22)

The turning point occurred when the anticipated affiliation of the independent with the AFofL was finalized. This had a visibly salutary effect and promptly set the stage for Army withdrawal. The appearance on the scene of this experienced organization acted as a restraining influence on hotheads in the local as these wiser union leaders counseled against provocative acts that could only cause trouble and impressed members with the importance of the no-strike pledge and the necessity of adherence to orderly procedures. More important, they stressed with respected authority that the group's only course under the law, and in view of its doubtful strength, was to wait until it was in a position to seek and win an NWLB-sponsored election.

With this favorable development, and the disposition of more pressing issues by NWLB instructions, Colonel Pratt concluded that the Army should gamble on continuing labor peace even if it withdrew before the NWLB decision. On 8 December Pratt formally recommended withdrawal,(23) stating that the root of the trouble could only be solved with an election months or years off, that the intervention of the AFofL would temporarily restrain the contending parties, and that all groups were impressed with the need of ending the disputes through normal legal channels. His recommendations admitted the possibility of the return of the Army, but this possibility was balanced against the desirability of getting the War Department out of a situation where it ran the risk of becoming involved in day-to-day union quarrels. The NWLB, with whom these recommendations were thoroughly discussed, indicated they had no objection to an Army withdrawal under these circumstances.(24) Meetings held at the national level with the representatives of the AFofL international and local unions were reassuring, and on 10 December Army possession was relinquished.

Epilogue

The judgment of Colonel Pratt proved correct. No strike followed the Army's withdrawal. It was mid-January before the regional labor board finally rendered its decision, calling for the reinstatement with pay of the two men if they became "financial" within a specified period.(25) This decision was accepted with protests by both sides,(26) but the parties quickly settled down to the business of orderly recruiting as a preliminary to the anticipated election when the CIO contract expired. The State Board of Arbitration ruled that it had no jurisdiction in the case of unfinancial members,(27) and the state courts held for the CIO in its suit to recover the union funds and validated its collective bargaining status. There was no further trouble until the beginning of 1945, when the contract between the IFLWU and the companies expired and the AFofL petitioned the National Labor Relations Board for an election. This contest precipitated the kind of incidents usually accompanying any bitter fight for union control, but the war ended without another major strike.(28)

Significance of the Case

The Salem-Peabody case became the model for the modern phase of plant seizure and produced a series of recommendations for improved techniques from the field(29) and headquarters.(30) Although the token method of operating a seized plant was employed in a crude way at North American Aviation, the Salem-Peabody case represented the first real instance of a refined and conscious application—a technique by which private management, under a more or less standard contract, continued its normal operations and furnished capital, retaining profits or bearing losses. Management was the War Department's agent and subject to its legal control, but such control was only infrequently exercised with respect to labor matters. While the legal arrangements between companies and the War Department changed slightly in later cases to meet unusual circumstances, and although the character and extent of War Department control of labor was further defined, the Salem-Peabody operation was the general type of operation the War Department sought in subsequent cases. In situations where labor's failure to comply with government policy caused a seizure, the War Department was uniformly successful in this objective. Even in seizures resulting from management noncompliance with NWLB orders the War Department usually succeeded in effecting a token operation similar to that at Salem-Peabody.

Although War Department representatives in prior cases were usually assisted only by judge advocate, fiscal, public relations, and industrial relations officers, Colonel Pratt subsequently perfected the idea of a small, well-organized, expandable, and highly coordinated group of experts operating as a team of equals rather than as a military organization. Additional members of these teams included an executive officer, a service command liaison officer (usually doubling as transportation officer), a deputy War Department representative, and sometimes an operations officer. It was not so much the composition of the staff, however, but the way it operated that was important. Pratt made decisions only after discussing problems—irrespective of whether they were of a public relations, labor relations, or legal character—with all key members of his staff. This continuous informal interchange of ideas allowed exploration of every question from every possible

angle, achieved unity of effort and approach, developed team spirit, and prevented staff members from working at cross-purposes. The effectiveness of this concept depended in some measure upon the personality of the War Department representative. Nevertheless, even in those cases where a representative could not
adapt himself to this mode, the technical staff itself operated on this general principle. The fact that the staff operated this way was in part the result of another of
Pratt's recommendations: the formation of headquarters cadres for future missions. While specific cadres as such were never created, small groups of individuals competent in each phase of the work, who were familiar with one another and
trained in the team approach, did develop, and from these groups teams for particular cases were quickly selected and organized.

The Salem-Peabody case raised sharp differences of opinion between headquarters and the field about labor matters, leading to tentative formulations of
basic policies regarding the extent and manner in which the War Department
should directly intervene in these problems. The question was not new, but it came
up more acutely than in previous cases and in a different context. At North
American Aviation day-to-day labor problems, apart from the question of firings,
were overshadowed by the major dispute between management and labor over a
contract. This dispute was the National Defense Mediation Board's responsibility
and not the War Department's. At Air Associates and S. A. Woods the Army was
management and could not avoid responsibility for labor problems.

These differences of opinion were natural and typical of those appearing in
later seizures,(31) in which field personnel were close to problems and were constantly being pressed for their solution. They were keenly aware of the explosive
features of the situation and witnessed daily incidents that were difficult to
describe to people hundreds of miles away. These representatives knew the local
disputants and could evaluate their capabilities and intentions and held direct
responsibility for maintaining production, often under conditions likely to provoke work stoppages. At the same time, their very closeness to the scene sometimes skewed their perspective and caused them to unconsciously exaggerate the
urgency of the local picture. They tended to press for interim and compromise
solutions directed solely at the local dispute and forgot or minimized the effects
on national labor policy, on the attitude of employers and employees, on the prestige of government agencies, and on other War Department seizures.
Headquarters personnel thought primarily in terms of these broader issues and
were often unaware of the tense local situation. Headquarters could not hope to
capture the local atmosphere and tended to discount field descriptions of impending trouble. These differences were usually bridged by close personal relations
between field and headquarters groups and by extensive telephone exchanges of
ideas and information.

Out of these differences in the Salem-Peabody case two general propositions
developed. First, the War Department should never negotiate toward a decision on
the merits of any disputed issue when that issue was or would be placed before
another government agency. Second, when the terms and conditions of employment or when the labor policies in effect at the time of possession were in doubt,

the points in question should be referred to the NWLB or some other federal labor agency. Some of these propositions were modified, and in several extreme cases disregarded, but by and large they became basic guidance in subsequent seizures.

Salem-Peabody was the last instance of any serious lack of coordination between the War Department and the NWLB concerning the initial seizure. The War Department vigorously protested the NWLB handling of this matter,(32) and these protests were responsible for a reorganization of internal NWLB procedures that provided a reasonable assurance against further recurrences.(33) While there were often serious differences of opinion between the two agencies about the propriety of seizure and the designation of an operating agency, these differences were always discussed freely and fully. It was rare for either to embark upon an independent course of action without consulting the other.

This case marked the development by the NWLB and the War Department of the practice, followed so successfully in the next two years, of constantly interchanging information and ideas concerning the operation itself. It also witnessed the War Department's adoption of the policy of treating the NWLB as its advisor on controversial labor issues involved with seizures.

The Salem-Peabody case demonstrated the difficulty that arose time and time again of obtaining the NWLB's quick disposition of underlying disputes. While bridged at Salem-Peabody, there were other situations where NWLB delays prolonged Army operations.

The FBI followed a policy of nonintervention in this and most other cases,(34) based on a specific and long-standing order by Attorney General Jackson. The FBI adhered to this order in spite of violations of such federal laws as the War Labor Disputes Act, removing authority from local FBI representatives to act. Whenever such authority was sought the Justice Department and the FBI tried to sidestep involvement. When in extreme cases they were required to give assistance, they reacted with far less enthusiasm than the War Department might have desired. After the Salem-Peabody case the War Department obtained a definite commitment from the attorney general to authorize his field representatives to make investigations and arrests in any seizures where violations of the War Labor Disputes Act occurred and otherwise to render assistance. Nevertheless, the commitment did not remove the FBI's reluctance about intervening in labor affairs when required.

As in many other cases, both the Navy and the Army had an interest in Salem-Peabody, and poor coordination here and in several later takeovers created a feeling on the part of Navy field representatives that they were being denied access to information concerning operational progress. While the War Department regarded the Navy's complaints as unfounded, steps were taken to insure, in writing, better coordination in the future.(35)

In the aftermath of the Salem-Peabody case, and following the suggestions made by Colonel Pratt and his staff for the training of additional plant seizure technicians, apprentices were sent with each plant seizure team. Frequently, an apprentice eventually took over the work of his principal and the latter could then be released, subject to recall in an emergency. Through this system it was possible to create a sizeable group of individuals thoroughly familiar with theoretical and practical seizure phases of their own technical spheres and their relationship to the mission as a whole.

The Salem-Peabody case illustrated the desirability of planning an operation as far in advance as possible and of attempting to assemble beforehand a complete picture of the labor problems involved. In spite of the rather thorough investigation preceding this seizure, Colonel Pratt was initially seriously handicapped by a lack of reliable information and strongly recommended that a better job be done in the future. He emphasized thorough familiarity with any applicable labor contract, a knowledge of the views of the NWLB concerning problems likely to arise, and an understanding of the underlying issues in dispute. This meant that pre-seizure conferences should take place involving representatives of the War Department, including a labor officer and a judge advocate; representatives of the NWLB; the local service command labor officer; and local, state, and federal officials. After a time it became the practice for the labor officer of the service command to prepare a full resume of the entire case for use by the seizure team and to arrange for any conferences with local people to orient the team.

The Salem-Peabody case demonstrated the importance of clarifying the relationships and responsibilities of the service commander and War Department representative, leading to the adoption of four basic policies and procedures. First, subject to the exceptions noted, full control over and responsibility for any takeover was vested in a War Department representative, and the line of command ran directly from Washington headquarters to him. However, the War Department representative would report to the service commander for purposes of administration, supply, transportation, and discipline, and he might call upon the latter for troop assistance. Conversely, and with the exceptions noted, the service commander was to have no control over the seizure. This policy was adopted because operations of this character called for experienced and specially trained people, which no service command could possibly be expected to furnish, and because it was unwise to place a local person in charge for fear of being accused of partisanship. Second, the War Department representative would maintain the closest possible contact with the service commander, and the latter, in order to facilitate such liaison, would supply an officer for the staff of the War Department representative. The reasons for this practice were obvious in view of the possible need of the War Department representative for troops or other services the service commander could furnish. Furthermore, it was deemed proper that the person having military jurisdiction in the area should be kept fully apprised of important developments within his command. With minor exceptions, usually where a new service commander was involved or where the War Department representative was either impolitic or much junior in rank, satisfactory relations were maintained. Third, the service commander was responsible for furnishing secretarial and other administrative personnel, occupation officers, technicians, office equipment and space, printing facilities, transportation, and other similar services to the War Department representative. In some cases funds were furnished through the service command for certain incidental operational expenses. Fourth,

Industrial Personnel Division, ASF. Ohly is standing (far left).

service commanders would be informed in a general manner of the nature of plant seizures and the reasons why they were to be handled by specialized teams rather than by the service commands. A considerable amount of educational work along these lines was done by successive teams and by the deputy chief of staff for service commands. This was largely responsible for the development of the kind of cooperation ultimately achieved.

The question of the command function with respect to the use of troops came to the forefront before, during, and after the Salem-Peabody case. It was natural for a service commander to feel that decisions concerning deployments, when and if carried out, were his. However, the policy followed at North American of placing sole discretion about troop use with the War Department representative was adopted in this case and written into all later instructions to War Department representatives. Troop use was incidental to the main mission of a seizure and therefore the War Department representative was given the final say.(36)

Salem-Peabody was the first case after the adoption of the memorandum of 9 August and illustrated the continuing need for greater headquarters coordination. Although most communications from the field to headquarters went, as before, to either General Greenbaum or the Labor Branch of the Industrial Personnel Division, this was the choice of Pratt and his staff and not a formal order. He later recommended that the Labor Branch should act as the central coordinating office in all cases or that a small branch be established in the Army Service Forces to perform such functions. While the first alternative was often followed in practice, it only gradually became standard procedure.

Colonel Pratt's organizational talents led him to formulate detailed administrative procedures for plant seizure teams. These were incorporated in a checklist,

covering such matters as the installation of central switchboards and a direct private wire to Washington, the development of a standard filing system, the keeping
of a log, the furnishing of plainclothesmen, the standards to be met by administrative personnel furnished by a service command, and the specific duties of each
member of the staff.

The Salem-Peabody case demonstrated once more that the character of the
War Department representative could greatly influence the nature of a plant
seizure and the likelihood of its success. An unfortunate mistake had almost been
made at the beginning through cavalier treatment of the matter of selection and a
misunderstanding on the part of persons making the choice as to the type of person required. At the conclusion of this case it was strongly urged that measures be
taken to assure the selection of men of Colonel Pratt's stature for subsequent
takeovers. This presented a difficult problem as those desired were probably
already doing other valuable War Department work, making it difficult to shake
them loose on a few hours' or few days' notice for a job of indefinite duration. As
a result, until late in the war, when the director of materiel was finally convinced
of the importance of careful choices, War Department representatives were selected on a rather haphazard basis, usually by requesting the technical service most
concerned to furnish a man but without giving the service selection criteria. Many
of the selections turned out very well, but in other cases it was only the high degree
of competence of the supporting staff that assured successful missions.

This case established the pattern followed in all other seizure cases resulting
from labor noncompliance with government labor policy(37) and in several others with slight variations.(38) The extent of control in even a token operation
varied from case to case, depending on the intensity of the dispute and the duration of War Department possession. In some instances a vigil by a large staff was
necessary, while in others a mere symbolic indication of government possession
was enough.

Endnotes

(1) Verza Tanning Company, Trimount Leather Company, Nathan H. Poor Company, Richard Young Company, Hunt-Rankin Leather Company, B. E. Cox Leather Company, and Morrill Leather Company, all in Peabody; Salem Leather Company, John Flynn and Sons, Inc., Helburn Thompson Company, Puritan Tannery, and Leach-Heckel, all in Salem: and Creese and Cook of Danvers.

(2) Memo, Maj Boland, Labor Branch, for Mitchell, 17 Nov 43, sub: Peabody Mills; Memo summarizing telecon, Maj Boland and Capt Gagliardo, QM Labor Branch, 17 Nov 43.

(3) Memo, Mitchell for Under Sec War, 25 Nov 43, sub: Production Information Peabody Tanneries; Memo for file by Ohly, 24 Nov 43, sub: Plant Seizure of Massachusetts Tanneries—Developments, par. 8a; Memo, Col Pratt for CG, ASF, 4 Dec 43, sub: Restoration of Normal Production War Department Possession and Operation of Thirteen Leather Manufacturing Plants in Salem-Peabody Area.

(4) Mimeographed standard form 1942 contract for signature by individual companies and International Fur and Leather Workers Union of the United States and Canada (Leather Division) (CIO).

(5) Ibid., art. 7.

(6) Telecon, Maj Boland and Navy Comdr Nader; Ltr, William H. Davis to Roosevelt, 17 Nov 43; Memo, Saul Wallen, Chairman, Regional WLB, for Clyde Mills, principal NWLB Mediation Off, 12 Nov 43, sub: Report of Facts in Strike Involving Massachusetts Leather Manufacturers Association; Telg, Isador Rickman, Sec-Treas, IFLWU, CIO, to Davis, 16 Nov 43; Telgs, National Leather Workers Association to Wayne L. Morse, 16 and 17 Nov 43; Telg, Morse to Joseph P. Harrington, 16 Nov 43; Telgs, Morse to James Dunn, Isador Rickman, Harrington, and others, 15 Nov 43; Memo, Col Pratt for CG, ASF, 4 Dec 43.

(7) Telg, Roosevelt to Dunn and Harrington, 17 Nov 43.

(8) Ltr, Under Sec War to Harold C. Smith, 22 Nov 43.

(9) EO 9395B, 20 Nov 43, 8 F.R. 16957.

(10) Memos for file by Brig Gen Greenbaum, 22 and 23 Nov 43, subs: Peabody-Salem Strike Situation; Memo for file by Ohly, 24 Nov 43.

(11) Memo for file by Ohly, 24 Nov 43; Memo for file by Brig Gen Greenbaum, 26 Nov 43; PMG Rpt No. 1, 25 Nov 43; Memo, Col Pratt for CG, ASF, 30 Nov 43, sub: War Department Possession and Operation of Leather Manufacturing Plants in Area of Salem and Peabody, Massachusetts, Under Executive Order of the President, being his initial report; Memo, Col Pratt for CG, ASF, 4 Dec 43.

(12) Telecon, Brig Gen Greenbaum and Col Pratt, 25 Nov 43, in which labor problems are analyzed.

(13) Memo, H. A. Wythes, Fiscal Advisor, for Col Pratt, 25 Nov 43, sub: Fiscal Aspects of Tannery Plant Occupation (Rpt No. 1), being Tab F of Rpt, Col Pratt to CG, ASF, 30 Nov 43.

(14) These aspects of the seizure are thoroughly discussed and documented in Rpt, Col Pratt to CG, ASF, 30 Nov 43, and its attachments. See also PMG Rpts Nos. 1 and 2, 25 and 26 Nov 43.

(15) As to the issue of call-in pay, see Memo for file by Brig Gen Greenbaum, 26 Nov 43, sub: Salem-Peabody Strike Situation; on the issue of EO 9240, see Memo for file by Ohly, 27 Nov 43, sub: Plant Seizure of Massachusetts Tanneries—Labor Developments; Memo for file by Maj Sachse, 26 Nov 43, sub: Application of Executive Order 9240 to Saturday Work (Nature of Work Relating to Overtime), being Tab A of Memo, Col Pratt for CG, ASF, 30 Nov 43; as to various incidents, see Memos for file by Brig Gen Greenbaum, 26 and 30 Nov 43, subs: Salem-Peabody Strike Situation; Memos for file by Ohly, 27 Nov and 4 and 7 Dec 43, sub: Plant Seizure of Massachusetts Tanneries—Labor Developments; Memo for file by Maj Sachse, 6 Dec 43, sub: Seizure Massachusetts Tanneries (in which a strike in the Verza Tanneries is discussed). As to consideration given to extending possession, see Telecon, Col Pratt and Brig Gen Greenbaum, 25 Nov 43; Memo for file by Ohly, 25 Nov 43, sub: Plant Seizure of Massachusetts Tanneries—Developments; Memo for file by Brig Gen Greenbaum, 26 Nov 43, sub: Salem-Peabody Strike Situation. For early conferences with labor groups, see PMG Rpt No. 1, 25 Nov 43.

(16) Memos for file by Ohly, 27 Nov 43 and 4 Dec 43, sub: Plant Seizure of Massachusetts Tanneries—Labor Developments, particularly par. 2 of the former and par. 1 of the latter.

(17) Memo for file by Majs Sachse and Hill, 30 Nov 43, sub: Special Hearing by WLB Panel on the Case of Poss and Horrigan 1050, 30 Nov 43; and Memo for file by Ohly, 4 Dec 43, par. 8.

(18) Memo for file by Ohly, 2 Dec 43, sub: Plant Seizure of Massachusetts Tanneries—Telephone Conversation Between Ohly and Colonel Pratt, 1700, 1 December 1943 (App. P–1).

(19) Memo for file by Ohly, 2 Dec 43, sub: Analysis of Colonel Pratt's Proposed Recommendations Concerning the Handling of Labor Problems in the Tanneries Strike (App. P–2).

(20) Ltr, Morse to Ohly, 3 Dec 43, which contains instructions and to which is attached a transcript of pertinent portions of the NWLB record.

(21) Memo for file by Ohly, 4 Dec 43, sub: Plant Seizure of Massachusetts Tanneries—Labor Developments, pars. 17 and 18.

(22) Memo for file by Maj Sachse, 6 Dec 43, sub: Seizure Massachusetts Tanneries; Memos for file by Ohly, 7 and 14 Dec 43, subs: Plant Seizure of Massachusetts Tanneries—Labor Developments; Memo, Lt Col Schieffelin for Brig Gen Greenbaum, 10 Dec [43], sub: Mr. Tom Clark, Department of Justice. See also PMG Rpts.

(23) Memo, Col Pratt for the CG, ASF, 8 Dec 43, sub: Termination of Government Possession—War Department Operation of Thirteen Leather Manufacturing Plants in Area of Salem-Peabody, Massachusetts, Under Executive Order of the President (App. P–3).

(24) Memo for file by Ohly, 14 Dec 43, sub: Plant Seizure of Massachusetts Tanneries—Labor Developments.

(25) Panel Report and Recommendations, 24 Dec 43, in the Matter of Massachusetts Leather Manufacturers Association and International Fur and Leather Workers Union of the U.S. and Canada, CIO, and United Leather Workers International Union, Local 21, AFofL (Formerly National Leather Workers Union, Independent), Case No. 111–3957–D of Regional WLB for Region I. The report was upheld by the Regional WLB on 6 January 1944.

(26) Memo, Maj W. D. English, OQMG, Industrial Relations Off, for Maj Boland, IPD, 27 Dec 43, sub: Peabody-Salem Tanners Strike.

(27) Memo for file by Ohly, 14 Dec 43; Memo for file by Majs Hill and Sachse, 10 Dec 43, to which are attached as Tabs A and B, a copy of a Ltr of 9 Dec 43 from the State Board to Martin J. McGrady (CIO business agent) and a summary of applicable statutes.

(28) Two Summaries of Information, 8 Jan and 13 Feb 45, sub: Leather Workers Controversy in Peabody-Salem-Danvers and Woburn, Massachusetts, submitted by Lt. Col. Gerald M. Coxe, Chief, Labor Branch, First Service Command, to the Labor Branch, IPD.

(29) Memo, Col Pratt for Maj Gen Styer, n.d., sub: Suggestions for Consideration in Connection With Army Operation of Plants or Other Industrial Facilities Under Executive Order of the President (App. P–4).

(30) Memo for file by Ohly, 15 Dec 43, sub: Plant Seizure—Lessons of the Massachusetts Leather Manufacturing Case (App. P–5).

(31) This was particularly true in the Fall River textile mills, Western Electric, Springfield Plywood, and Hummer cases.

(32) Ltr, Under Sec War to Morse, 29 Nov 43.

(33) Ltr, Morse to Under Sec War, 15 Dec 43.

(34) Difficulties with the FBI were marked in the Fall River textile mills, American Enka, Farrell-Cheek, Cleveland Graphite, Hughes Tool, Montgomery Ward, Western Electric, and Springfield Plywood cases. On the other hand, very full cooperation was received in the Philadelphia Transportation and Toledo MESA strikes.

(35) See Plant Seizure Procedure (App. BB–1) and Memo for file by Ohly, 12 Feb 45, sub: Plant Seizure—Liaison With Navy (App. BB–2).

(36) See Memo, Col Gow for the CG (All Service Commands), n.d., sub: Labor Officers for Plant Seizures (App. BB–6). See also War Department Circular 57, 20 Feb 43.

(37) These cases were: Western Electric Company, Cleveland Graphite Bronze Company, Cleveland Electric Illuminating Company, Fall River textile mills, the Toledo MESA case, International Nickel Company, Bingham and Garfield Railway Company, U.S. Rubber Company,

Diamond Alkali, Springfield Plywood Company, and American Enka Corporation. Because these cases fall within one pattern except as to their labor phases, only their labor phases are discussed in any great detail in this history. However, brief summaries of most of them, prepared in the Office of the Judge Advocate General, with other descriptive documents, are included in Appendix Z.

(38) With slight variations the pattern was followed in takeovers involving American railroads, the Philadelphia Transportation Company, and the Department of Water and Power of the City of Los Angeles.

CHAPTER 9

The Seizure of American Railroads, December 1943

The seizure of the entire American railroad system, comprising some 750 different lines, was the only industrywide War Department takeover during World War II and involved numerous difficulties never previously encountered.

Events Leading up to the Seizure

In the summer of 1943 negotiations covering wage increases, overtime pay, vacations, and travel expenses between the fifteen non-operating and five operating railway labor organizations and the nation's carriers broke down. Strike votes were taken. The machinery of the Railway Labor Act was invoked, but to no avail. Subsequently, recommendations were put forth by President Roosevelt's two special emergency boards—the Stacy Board[1] for the operating group and the Shaw Board[2] for the non-operating group. In September the Stacy Board recommended an increase of four cents an hour, whereas in December the Shaw Board suggested a sliding scale hourly increase of four to ten cents. The unions uniformly refused to accept these recommendations, which were limited exclusively to the basic wage issues and did not cover fringe benefits. Strike orders were sent out calling for a complete cessation of nationwide railroad transportation at 6:00 A.M. on 30 December.

On 23 December the president asked the contending parties to rescind their strike orders and agree to accept him as the final arbiter of the disputes. He warned that the government could not permit the strike and would seize the railroads if necessary to prevent a stoppage. The next day two of the operating unions, the Brotherhood of Locomotive Engineers[3] and the Brotherhood of Railroad Trainmen,[4]

[1]The Stacy Board, appointed by Roosevelt on 31 May 1943 pursuant to the Railway Labor Act and Executive Orders 9172 and 9299, consisted of three members. Its chairman was Judge Walter P. Stacy, who had experience in railroad labor-management negotiations dating from 1927. The board issued its report, with recommendations, on 25 September 1943.

[2]The three-member Shaw Board, first appointed by Roosevelt in 1942 under Judge Elwyn R. Shaw and then again on 31 May 1943, reconvened pursuant to Executive Order 9413 in December. At this time, the board issued its recommendations.

[3]The Brotherhood of Locomotive Engineers, founded in 1863 as the Brotherhood of the Footboard, adopted its current name in 1864. This independent union had a membership of 74,000 in late 1943.

[4]The Brotherhood of Railroad Trainmen (BRT), founded in 1883 as the Brotherhood of Railroad Brakemen, adopted its current name in 1890. An independent union, the BRT was not affiliated with either the AFofL or CIO. Its membership in 1943 was approximately 199,000.

accepted the president's proposal and recalled their strike orders. The other three operating unions, the Brotherhood of Locomotive Firemen and Enginemen,[5] the Order of Railway Conductors[6] and the Switchmen's Union,[7] rejected the president's request, while the non-operating group hedged, largely due to a disagreement with the carriers about the scope of the arbitration.(1) President Roosevelt ordered the War Department to prepare for seizure within ninety-six hours, his instructions ultimately going to Chief of Transportation Maj. Gen. Charles P. Gross.[8] The presidential orders largely bypassed the under secretary's office and those persons in the Army Service Forces most familiar with plant seizures—another instance of the tendency to ignore the department's experience and to resort instead to standard command lines. It also indicated the negative consequences of failing to create a single, centralized plant seizure authority in the War Department. Because the technicians were eventually consulted, the chief of transportation and the deputy chief of staff for service commands,[9] with the energetic and talented assistance of Lt. Col. Luke W. Finlay, developed a plan for the president before the deadline.

The Plan of Operation

The plan called for the acquisition or possession of all properties involved by a mere public declaration of taking by Secretary of War Stimson, although the declaration was followed as soon as possible by personal notices of possession being served on all carriers.(2) Token seizures were the goal, along with the execution of standard contracts with each carrier. The nature of the subsequent operations depended upon whether employees remained at work, and the plan proposed a series of measures designed to induce the men to choose this alternative. These were largely of a public relations nature, including a proposed statement by President Roosevelt and a radio address by Stimson, and were intended to capitalize on the patriotism of the workers.

---

[5]The Brotherhood of Locomotive Firemen and Enginemen was led during World War II by David B. Robertson (1922–53) and had a 1939 membership of 82,500, a figure that grew to 121,000 by 1945. This independent union was founded as the Brotherhood of Locomotive Firemen in 1873 and adopted its current name in 1906.

[6]The independent Order of Railway Conductors (ORC) was founded as The Conductor's Union in 1868. It took its present name in 1878. Under Harry W. Fraser, the ORC grew from 33,000 in 1939 to 37,800 members by 1945.

[7]The Switchmen's Union of North America was founded as the Switchmen's Association in Chicago in 1877. It took its present name in 1894. The union joined the AFofL in 1906, and was the only operating railway union to do so until the mid-1950s. Its membership in 1939 was 7,800, growing to 9,700 by 1945.

[8]Maj. Gen. Charles P. Gross (1888–1975) was a New York City native educated at Cornell University and West Point (Class of 1914). He served with the American Expeditionary Forces and between 1920 and 1939 was an engineer and instructor in the United States and Nicaragua. He was the district engineer at Rock Island, Illinois, when called in March 1941 to become the chief of transportation, G–4 (Supply) Section, War Department General Staff. He became the SOS G–4's chief of transportation in February 1942 and the chief of the newly organized Transportation Corps, with the rank of major general, the following August. He retired from the Army in November 1945 and became chairman of the New York City Board of Transport. Recalled to duty in 1948, he worked for the Office of the Military Government of Germany and became the military governor of Baden-Wuerttemberg in 1949. He retired for a second time in 1952.

[9]The deputy chief of staff for service commands at the time was Brig. Gen. Clarence H. Danielson, who was replaced on 6 January 1944 by Col. Joseph F. Battley. Battley was promoted to brigadier general on 22 February.

Maj. Gen. Charles P. Gross   *Lt. Col. Luke W. Finlay*

If the strike were canceled because of the takeover, the token character of the seizure would continue until the dispute was settled or assurances were given that the strike would not recur if the government withdrew. If the strike occurred, three elaborate steps were planned. The first step called for breaking the strike by the invocation of the War Labor Disputes Act and its penalties, including the cancellation of occupational deferments, provision of protection for nonstriking workers, and further appeals to patriotism by all local and national media. The second step called for providing Army-furnished transportation wherever needed by employment of railway service units, by screening of all American military personnel for railroad experience in order to replace strikers, and by mobilization and use of all government and privately owned nonrail transportation equipment and personnel in place of the railroads. Finally, the last step called for instituting an extensive transport priority system.(3) The importance which the War Department attached to this mission is illustrated by the fact that, in spite of desperate needs abroad, every person and every type of transportation nationwide not specifically scheduled for overseas shipment before 15 February was made available.(4)

The War Department representative was General Gross in Washington. He was assisted by a staff, including his own transport technicians and those from Army elements familiar with plant seizures—the deputy chief of staff for service commands, the directors of the Military and Industrial Personnel Divisions, the fiscal director, and the judge advocate general, among others. In addition to military personnel, he had special advisors including Martin W. Clement,[10] president of the Pennsylvania Railroad; Alvanley Johnson[11] and Alexander F. Whitney,[12] respectively presidents of the Locomotive Engineers and the Railroad Trainmen; John J. Pelley[13] and Charles H. Buford[14] of the Association of American Railroads; and James M. Hood[15] of the American Short Line Railroad Association. Many of these individuals participated in drafting the War Department plan. Field operations were the responsibility of seven regional offices embracing the lines of designated carriers assigned according to operating interests rather than on the basis of a mere geographical division. The regional director in each instance headed one of the principal railroads allocated to the area and was promptly commissioned without physical examination or any other formality as a U.S. Army colonel for the mission. Each regional director was assisted by an Army staff composed of an assistant, an executive officer, a judge advocate, a service command liaison officer, and public relations, labor relations, and fiscal advisors. Most of the technical personnel were supplied by Army components having normal responsibility in these fields and, insofar as possible, prior plant seizure experience. The service commands were responsible for selecting and alerting the officers needed to provide an Army representative to each railroad system.

The service commands received extensive instructions, supplemented by a Washington conference of representatives from each command concerning the mobilization of personnel and equipment in the event of a strike, the furnishing of administrative services to the various regional directors, and the use of troops in emergencies to protect life or property. Each service command in turn established programs and special staffs for these functions.(5)

The Industrial Personnel Division's Labor Branch, however, considered the plan defective in its general conception(6) and argued that it was naive to discuss

---

[10]Martin W. Clement (1881–1966) was a Pennsylvania-born civil engineer who began working for the Pennsylvania Railroad in 1901. He worked his way up in the company, becoming its president in 1935. He heartily approved of the War Department railroad seizure.

[11]Alvanley Johnson (1875–1951) was a Canadian-born railway union official. He began work with the Great Northern Railroad in 1892 and was active in the Brotherhood of Locomotive Engineers after 1909, serving as its president between 1924 and 1950. He was a labor consultant to Roosevelt before becoming the railroad representative to the Combined War Labor Board.

[12]Alexander F. Whitney (1873–1949) was an Iowa-born labor leader who started work with the Illinois Central Railroad in 1888. He joined the Brotherhood of Railroad Trainmen in 1896, becoming its vice president in 1907 and its president in 1928. He was also the chairman of the Railway Labor Executives Association (1932–34) and co-sponsored the Railroad Retirement Act in 1935.

[13]John J. Pelley (1878–1946) was president of the Association of American Railroads from 1934 until his death in 1946. Prior to 1934 he was president of the New York, New Haven, and Hartford Railroad. For his role in organizing the nation's rail system in support of the war effort, he received the Medal of Merit (1946) and citations from the War, Navy, and Treasury Departments.

[14]Charles H. Buford (1886–1960) was born and educated in Arkansas. He worked for the St. Paul and Pacific Railroad between 1907 and 1939 and was vice president for operations and maintenance of the Association of American Railroads (AAR). Following wartime service with the AAR in Washington, he returned to executive positions with his former railroad employer.

[15]James M. Hood (1891–1974) was born in Ohio and began working for the Baltimore and Ohio Railroad at age twenty-one. He was later employed by the Wheeling and Lake Erie Line and was chief operations officer for the Akron, Canton, and Youngstown Line. Hood accepted a post with the American Short Line Railroad Association, a railroad trade group, in 1932 and served as its president from 1935 to 1960.

the plan's second phase—that is, what to do if men struck—because the Army lacked sufficient equipment and personnel to do the job with only 6,200 officers and men in stateside military service units.(7) If the railroads were to run, professional railroaders had to do the job, and the seizure must be conceived with the idea of keeping men working, with the seizure being merely one phase of a government plan. The Labor Branch warned against assuming that employees would continue working under a mere token seizure as planned, unaccompanied by other measures such as the use of troops, and suggested a study of what factors not in conflict with national labor and wage policies would keep them on the job. The seizure plan should then capitalize on those factors.

Although theoretically sound, these criticisms were practically without substance as the likelihood of a post-seizure strike was nonexistent. The assumption that the mere fact of a takeover would prevent a stoppage was fully justified and the plan was adapted to this assumption. Part II of the plan met many of the criticisms, and while the Army could not have run all or even a substantial portion of the national rail system with military personnel, it is by no means certain that the measures planned in the event of a strike would not have quickly solved the situation. In any event, criticisms that might have been justified if there had been any real threat of a strike during government possession were unwarranted under the circumstances.

Seizure and Operation

As the strike deadline of 27 December approached, President Roosevelt concluded that seizure was necessary, although the non-operating unions rescinded their strike orders and agreed to arbitration. "I cannot," he said in announcing his signature of the executive order,(8) "wait until the last moment to take action to see that the supplies to our fighting men are not interrupted." Shortly before he had announced his award as arbitrator in the case of the two operating brotherhoods. This award affirmed the four-cent-per-hour increase of the Stacy Board already being paid and in consideration of claims not previously presented, such as those for expenses while away from home and for time and a half for work in excess of forty hours per week, granted an additional five cents.(9)

The War Department plan proceeded after Secretary Stimson signed the seizure order and delivered a nationwide broadcast explaining its purpose and urging public cooperation.(10) Within two days every carrier but one was served by one of the six hundred Army officers selected as federal representatives with the individual railroads. Transportation continued to move normally with virtually no evidence of a government presence, except occasional notices advising of War Department possession.

The nominal character of the operation is illustrated by an incident that incensed the chief of transportation but amused the participants. General Greenbaum, waiting in Baltimore for a Washington-bound train that was several hours late, sought to board a north–south train not normally taking passengers for stops north of Virginia. He was stopped by a conductor and brakeman. Upon explaining that the Army was running the railroads and that he was in charge of the operation for the War Department, they simply laughed and remarked: "Don't be silly; we are running these trains and you don't get aboard." The operation was completely token, and even the original plan for executing a standard operating contract with each carrier was abandoned as unnecessary under the circumstances.

Sections 4 and 5 of the War Labor Disputes Act being inapplicable,(11) the executive order included provisions with respect to labor matters. Executive Order 9412 stated that under Section 6 of the act:

> The Secretary is authorized to prescribe the compensation to be received by applicable statutes, executive orders and regulations relating to economic stabilization. To the extent deemed practical by him, he may maintain the working conditions which are specified in existing contracts between the carriers and their employees. He may recognize the right of the workers to continue their membership in labor organizations, to bargain collectively through representatives of their own choosing with the representatives of the owners of the carriers, subject to provisions of applicable statutes and executive order, as to matters pertaining to wages to be paid or conditions to prevail after termination of possession, control and operation under this order; and to engage in concerted activities for the purpose of such collective bargaining or for other mutual aid or protection, provided that in his opinion such concerted activities do not interfere with the operation of the carriers.

And further under Section 7 of the act:

> Except as this order otherwise provides and except as the Secretary otherwise directs, the operation of the carriers hereunder shall be in conformity with the Interstate Commerce Act, as amended, the Railway Labor Act, the Safety Appliance Acts, the Employers' Liability Acts, and other applicable Federal and State laws, executive orders, local ordinances and rules and regulations issued pursuant to such laws, executive orders and ordinances.

In spite of the discretion vested by the order in the secretary of war over Labor Branch opposition, there was never much call to exercise it. No action was required to make the 27 December arbitration award effective since by formal agreement on 29 December these increases took effect on a date prior to the seizure and were thus part of the terms and conditions of employment the War Department inherited.

The three holdout unions did not immediately withdraw their outstanding strike orders but on the evening of 29 December, eight hours before they were to become operative, and after an conference with General Somervell and informal meetings with McGrady, they postponed these strikes for the duration of government possession.(12) This action removed all threats of interruption, and the unions continued negotiating with the carriers on the issues they had previously refused to submit to the president. On 14 January 1944 they reached an agreement identical with Roosevelt's award in the arbitration proceeding involving the two other operating unions. The strike votes were declared null and void(13), and on 15 January a War Department order directed the carriers to make this agreement effective.(14)

The non-operating group, after no mutually satisfactory definition of the scope of arbitration could be found, had its claims heard by a special board appointed by the president. This board worked out a settlement agreeable to all parties and to the director of economic stabilization. The adjustments were placed in effect by War Department order on 18 January, and the same day the Army withdrew.(15)

The railroad dispute was a national matter for national disposition and did not cause any acute local problems or incidents affecting the Army. Bitter charges were hurled at President Roosevelt by some of the unions, which he denied, that wages were frozen for the duration of the war. The unions also wrangled among themselves, with the three holdout operating unions accusing the two agreeing to arbitrate with betrayal.(16) This battle of words, with the exception of the statement of Chief of Staff General George C. Marshall that the strikes were causing unnecessary troop casualties, did not involve the War Department.(17) Within days of the seizure many of the officers assigned to the railroads were released, and in less than two weeks over two-thirds of them were back at their normal assignments. In a cautionary move, however, technical staffs attached to the regional directors were kept intact until the end of the operation although only the judge advocates had substantial duties—preparing releases for all the carriers, a desirable step seeking to forestall claims against the government. By 31 January nearly 90 percent of the releases were obtained, with delays of the remaining releases being attributed to the need for court approval in the case of roads in bankruptcy reorganization and receivership or to the inability to convene boards of directors.

Endnotes

(1) *New York Times*, 23 Dec 43.

(2) Rpt, CG, ASF, to Sec War, 27 Dec 43, sub: Plan for the Possession, Control and Operation of the Railroads by the Army.

(3) Tabs X and DD to ibid.

(4) Memos, ACofS, G–3, for CGs, ASF, AGF, and AAF, 23 Dec 43, subs: Preparation for Army Operation of Public Transportation Systems.

(5) Tab DD to Rpt of CG, ASF, 27 Dec 43.

(6) Unsigned and unaddressed Memo, n.d., sub: Basic Issues Involved in Any Seizure of the Railroads (App. Q–1).

(7) See Tab I (List of Military Railway Service Units) to Rpt of CG, ASF, 27 Dec 43.

(8) EO 9412, 27 Dec 43, 8 F.R. 17395

(9) White House Statement on Seizure of the Railroads, reprinted in *New York Times*, 28 Dec 43, p. 1, and Rail Arbitration Ruling in same place.

(10) Transcript of Stimson's broadcast, *New York Times*, 28 Dec 43, p. 8.

(11) Sections 4 and 5 of the War Labor Disputes Act apply only to plants and facilities taken over pursuant to Section 3 of that act. The railroads were taken over under the authority of the Act of August 1916, 39 Stat. 645. Section 6 of the War Labor Disputes Act has no such limitation and was considered applicable to this operation. This conclusion was upheld in prosecution arising under Section 6 during the Philadelphia Transportation strike.

(12) *New York Times*, 30 Dec 43, p. 1.

(13) *New York Times*, 15 Jan 44, p. 1.

(14) War Department Press Release, "Three Rail Unions Cancel Strike Call," 15 Jan 44, which contains copies of pertinent documents.

(15) Monthly Progress Rpt, Control Div, Transportation Corps, 31 Jan 44.

(16) *New York Times*, 31 Dec 43, p. 1, and 1 Jan 44, p. 1.

(17) *New York Times*, 31 Dec 43, p. 1; "Marshall statement," an anonymous statement by a "high Army official," in 31 Dec 43, *Washington Post*, 1 Jan 44, p. 1.

CHAPTER 10

The Department of Water and Power of the City of Los Angeles, February 1944

The seizure of the facilities of the Department of Water and Power of the City of Los Angeles in early 1944 would have fallen into the Salem-Peabody pattern if the employer had not been a municipal government. This unusual circumstance(1) raised several questions concerning federal authority to intervene in local government affairs, National War Labor Board (NWLB) jurisdiction, the applicability of the War Labor Disputes Act, and the status of municipally employed workers.

Description of the Employer

In 1943 the Department of Water and Power was one of a large number of departments under the supervision of a mayor and a fifteen-man elected council. This resulted from a consolidation under a reform administration of the separate bureaus of water and power after almost two decades of intense political controversy centering around the issue of private versus government utilities ownership. These differences were still evident among certain key employees who were holdovers from the pre-reform days when the department was part of the political machine. The department was administered by an appointed five-member commission.[1] It controlled a $500 million utility system, had proved profitable, and supplied water and electricity to more than 650,000 residences and nearly all business and industrial establishments within the city limits. Most of its power came from the Boulder Dam over hundreds of miles of power lines maintained by the department, but there were also standby steam plants in Los Angeles itself.

With a few exceptions, the six thousand department employees were hired in accordance with seniority from a master Civil Service list, prepared by the independent Civil Service Commission after competitive examinations. However, the department's board of commissioners had almost exclusive jurisdiction over the character of the department's relations with these employees from the standpoint of wages, hours, and working conditions once they were hired. The city charter,

---

[1] For more on Los Angeles during this period, see Martin J. Schiesl, "City Planning and the Federal Government in World War II: The Los Angeles Experience," *California History* 59 (1980): 126–43.

for example, vested in the commissioners—without any right of review by the mayor or the city council—the sole power to determine wages, and this power was subject only to the requirement that wages not be lower than those prevailing for similar private work in the area. The department was thus nearly autonomous and held the mayor and his council in disregard, as well as the other departments of the city, even though the incumbent reform mayor, Fletcher Bowron, had appointed outstanding citizens as commissioners to correct this pattern. Officially at least, the department did not bargain collectively with its employees or any employee representatives. There was, however, a considerable amount of informal negotiation on minor issues, such as hours of work, working conditions, and assignments between division chiefs and representatives of the eight labor organizations representing employees. The most powerful of these employee groups was Local B–18 of the International Brotherhood of Electrical Workers (IBEW),[2] which had strong political connections and active support within the department and city council. This union was behind the 1943 strike.(2)

Background of the Dispute

Prior to the strike, as a result of meetings between representatives of the department and some of the employee groups, the commissioners approved a $15 per month wage increase. This raised employees wages up to or above the wage levels of private utility companies to a point some 20 percent over the average rate of pay prevailing on 1 January 1941, the base date of the Little Steel Formula.[3] Subsequently, employees of other city departments had received a $20 per month increase in the form of a bonus to meet the rising cost of living. This action had led to an immediate IBEW demand for a further $5 monthly raise for the department's workers. The general manager of the department favored a $10 increase, but the commissioners were more cautious, fearing the effect of any large increase on other city employees and perhaps on private utilities as well, which might be forced to match the increase. In addition, they requested that Mayor Bowron hold any action in abeyance pending a survey of all municipal wages. Accordingly, on 10 February 1944 they voted to limit the additional increase to $5 until completion of a detailed wage commission investigation.

This vote signaled trouble. On 14 February one thousand workers with the IBEW as their spokesman failed to report for work. This partial strike resulted in

---

[2]The AFofL-affiliated International Brotherhood of Electrical Workers was organized in 1891 as the National Brotherhood of Electrical Workers of America, adopting its present name in 1905. Its membership in 1944 numbered 350,500.

[3]The Little Steel Formula, developed by the NWLB, was intended to control wage increases and to bring wages in line with wartime inflation and cost-of-living increases. Under the formula, general wage increases made because of cost-of-living changes would be limited to a total 15-percent increase in wage rates since 1 January 1941, the base date. It became effective on 16 July 1942, and those workers who had not had wages adjusted since the base date were entitled to have them adjusted. The formula was not applicable automatically to offset cost-of-living increases after May 1942, and it was found that over 67 percent of manufacturing industries already had made the necessary increases. The formula dealt with only general wage movements in response to the cost of living and was a small part of the federal government's overall wage stabilization program.

some interference with electrical services to certain residential districts and small shops, but it had no immediate effect on war production. The strategy of the union was to generate sufficient pressure among the affected civilian groups to force a showdown with city officials, but at the same time to provide no basis for any charges that it was interfering with the war effort. Mayor Bowron promptly refused negotiations until the men returned to work and privately expressed his desire to fire every man who was off the job. The stalemate continued with neither side making concessions. On 19 February thirteen hundred additional workers joined the strike. This included employees at the standby plants and patrolmen on the Boulder Dam power line. This new development created a serious hazard. If anything should break the flow of power from Boulder Dam, Los Angeles, with its heavy concentration of war industry, would be totally blacked out. Although war production was still unaffected, the War Department in Washington became concerned over the implications of the situation. It alerted the 751st Military Police Battalion at Camp Williston, Nevada, and, in addition, directed an occupational check among personnel of the Ninth Service Command[4] for persons who could replace strikers.

The crisis might have passed without government intervention had it not been for an act of God. The following day one of the worst storms in the history of Los Angeles struck the city and continued for three days. Wide areas were flooded, and many power lines were broken. Almost at once 75,000 homes and several plants were plunged into darkness, with at least a hundred war plants idled within hours. Some of these plants were key aviation subcontractors, and their production was essential to the operations of big airframe manufactures in the vicinity. Although promises were quickly made by some of the union leaders to provide enough men to repair the lines to any plant certified by the Army and Navy as critical, the promises were never carried out and the leaders conveniently became unavailable.

The War Department promptly urged the NWLB to take the case, but the board was unsure of its jurisdiction in a municipal government dispute and voted not to intervene unless requested to do so by the city. War Department and NWLB efforts to persuade city officials to ask for such intervention or to accept board mediation services were unsuccessful. Attempts by Joseph D. Keenan[5] of the War Production Board and by IBEW President Edward J. Brown[6] to end the strike evoked solemn commitments but produced no results. A strong War Department statement was equally ineffective.

On 22 February, following a conference with War Mobilization Director Byrnes and NWLB Chairman Davis due to the rapidly deteriorating conditions, the War

---

[4]The Ninth Service Command consisted of the states of Washington, Oregon, Montana, Idaho, Utah, Nevada, Arizona, and California. The commander in February 1944 was Maj. Gen. David McCoach, Jr., who was succeeded by Maj. Gen. William E. Shedd on 1 September.

[5]Joseph D. Keenan was vice chairman and associate director for labor production of the War Production Board between 1943 and 1945.

[6]Edward J. Brown (1893–1950) was a Chicago-born labor official educated in law at the University of Chicago. He joined the IBEW in 1911, worked as an organizer, and served on the IBEW executive council (1937–40). He was a regent of the University of Wisconsin (1935–38), IBEW president after 1940, and a member of the National Defense Mediation Board.

Joseph D. Keenan

Department alerted Col. Rufus W. Putnam of the Los Angeles district engineer's office about possible assignment as the War Department representative. He was briefed by telephone on plant seizure, and late in the afternoon Colonel Hebert and Brig. Gen. Theodore Weaver of the ASF's Production Division departed by plane from Washington to give Colonel Putnam technical assistance. There was no time to assemble a regular team but arrangements were made to recruit an interim staff from among officers in the Ninth Service Command and the AAF's Western Procurement District.[7] That evening Justice and War Department representatives improvised an executive order designed to meet the peculiar conditions presented by municipal involvement. This task was rendered easier by the mayor's promise to Under Secretary Patterson to send a telegram requesting such action. Armed with the consent of the local government, basic problems of intergovernmental relations were largely solved.

The situation did not improve during the night, and early the following morning President Roosevelt signed the necessary executive order.(3) At 1:00 P.M. Pacific War Time Colonel Putnam took possession, a seizure that was purely token in character, with military occupation officers assigned only to some of the department's key properties.(4)

Principal Problems and Their Solutions

Getting the men back on the job and restoring full power distribution presented no real difficulties. The union agreed to terminate the strike when the federal government intervened, and an elaborate plan to restore service on a war priority basis was complete. The union delivered on its pledge, and the emergency plan was promptly made operational. In addition, the coincident abatement of the storm and the recession of the flood aided the work of repair. By the morning of 24 February employment was back to the usual level, and all war

---

[7]The Western Procurement District, headquartered in Santa Monica, California, was one of the three original geographically organized districts. The others were the Eastern Procurement District, headquartered in New York City, and the Central Procurement District, headquartered in Chicago. Three more districts were added by 1945—the Midwestern Procurement District, headquartered in Wichita, Kansas; the Mid-Central Procurement District, headquartered in Chicago; and the Southeastern Procurement District, headquartered in Atlanta.

plants were in full operation. Within forty-eight hours service in the city was normal.(5)

With operations restored, only two major problems remained—one technical and legal, the other involving the labor dispute. The first concerned the establishment of some sort of formal relationship between the Department of Water and Power and the War Department. All agreed that the board of commissioners and the department manager, subject to the broad general power of Colonel Putnam, should continue management duties as before. Was it possible, however, for a municipal agency to execute the standard operating contract employed in other seizures, and, if so, who must approve it? Could and would the city agree in advance to furnish the War Department with a general release at the termination of possession?

The War Department was anxious to prevent an open council hearing, fearing that discussion of these issues might provoke an airing of the labor dispute itself with harmful repercussions. It, therefore, worked informally with city officials and did not press for a written contract. On receiving an opinion by the city attorney that a legal contract was possible and that the board of commissioners had the power to consummate it without reference to the city council, an agreement similar to that in other token cases was made that solved all legal, fiscal, procurement, and operating problems.(6)

The labor dispute itself was approached with the recognition that the workers were municipal employees, whose terms of employment were determined by various city laws and administrative policies. In this case, unlike others where an independent tribunal, such as the NWLB, was present, only the City of Los Angeles had the power or jurisdiction to make a settlement. The city could refer the case to an outside agency but was unwilling to surrender its sovereignty. Consequently, employees had to seek justice from the very persons against whom they were complaining.(7)

Recognizing the complicated character of the problem and its political ramifications, Colonel Putnam and his staff avoided involvement for several days and instead proceeded to gather information on the general situation. They also set forth three War Department objectives: the restoration of city property as soon as conditions made a new strike unlikely, the avoidance of the appearance that either side gained any advantages from the seizure, and the avoidance of involvement in collective bargaining or arbitration of the dispute. The first objective resulted from the real and justified fear that the War Department could become embroiled in prestige-damaging local politics. The second objective focused on the fact that this seizure was the first wartime case on the West Coast and was being carefully scrutinized by management and labor. A false step might necessitate a series of California seizures if employers or employees believed that such a takeover was an easy road to benefits unobtainable through ordinary channels. It was also feared that municipal employees in similar situations in other parts of the country might conclude that seizure was a means of going over the heads of municipal employers. The third objective was common to all cases in that the employees, lacking any other means of relief, wanted the War Department to fill the role of arbiter.(8)

After a very thorough investigation, which included a long meeting with the board of commissioners, Colonel Putnam's staff submitted a long and detailed analysis of the situation, concluding that department employees were well paid and that demands for a wage increase, though real, were likely a screen for something else such as exclusive union recognition, genuine collective bargaining, or some political end. They further concluded that there was no agency other than the board of commissioners that could decide the issues involved and that a majority of the board was bitter about the strike and wanted disciplinary action to prevent a recurrence. Putnam's staff further determined that the commissioners had no intention of granting a wage increase during Army possession and looked to the War Department for a solution. They would take no action, however, without prior consultation with Putnam. The commissioners favored an impartial study of the wage situation by an outside authority whose reputation and integrity was beyond question and had no objection to discussing disputes with a committee "representative of all employees," although not with any particular union. The War Department report also stated that the Water Department's handling of personnel problems had been poor and that the local IBEW representatives were possibly closely tied to a department group that sought for political reasons to reestablish the Bureau of Power and Light as a separate entity. Indeed, the dispute itself was possibly related to a larger IBEW struggle for recognition of the union as the exclusive bargaining agent for all city employees, which extended to other agencies including the police and fire departments. It was obvious to War Department officials that there was insufficient employee understanding concerning their vital war role and that public opinion, unbeknownst to the strikers, was very strongly against them.

Based on this, Colonel Putnam submitted three alternative plans. Under the first plan the War Department, without publicity, would informally attempt to persuade the commissioners to retain an outside authority to make a wage survey, to remove confusion as to the duration of the $5 increase previously granted, to authorize the organization of an employee committee to represent employees in any dispute, and to notify all employees of its action. If the commissioners agreed with the plan, an employee no-strike pledge would then be sought and, once obtained, the Army would withdraw. This line of action had the advantage of making another strike unlikely, but it had the disadvantage of giving the strikers the appearance of a victory because they had gained a distinct concession. Nonetheless, such a plan appeared acceptable to the commissioners.

Under the second plan the War Department would ask the NWLB to take jurisdiction of the wage issue and obtain employee agreement to abide by its decision. Army withdrawal would follow. This plan had little to recommend it because even if the NWLB took jurisdiction, which was unlikely, it would set a dangerous precedent for exploitation by other municipal employees. Furthermore, any NWLB decision would assuredly violate the Little Steel Formula limitations and trigger a rejection of employee demands that could create another crisis.

The third alternative was a four-step plan favored by Colonel Putnam. Its first step consisted of War Department efforts, through the IBEW president, to obtain a no-strike pledge from the local union after Army withdrawal. Following this action the War Department would commence a short, intense campaign to impress workers with the essential character of their work, followed by a sudden, prompt, and unannounced Army withdrawal on the grounds that the emergency was over. Finally, the War Department would give informal advice to the commissioners concerning subsequent steps it anticipated taking to resolve the dispute. This plan represented a gamble but was likely to succeed because of local public opinion and because it permitted Army withdrawal while prestige remained high, obviated War Department involvement in the dispute, and prevented setting a precedent leading to further municipal seizures. The only disadvantage was the risk of possible failure and further War Department intervention.(9)

After careful study the third plan was adopted(10) with refinements, the first of which included a proposal for War Department representatives to meet separately with the mayor and commissioners, with the Water Department, and with the latter's employees for the establishment of a representative employee committee. Further suggestions included making an independent wage survey, preferably after consultation with the employee committee; hiring an industrial relations expert; and improving the classification analysis system. No reprisals were to take place against the strikers, and the department was to undertake an extensive publicity program announcing these steps.

The plan was carried out with speed and precision. The board indicated a willingness to give favorable consideration to the suggestions, and key union leaders guaranteed labor calm. At noon on 29 February 1944, without advanced notice, the War Department announced that its mission was fulfilled and withdrew.

Epilogue

No further strikes followed, but for a considerable period the War Department's solution appeared of doubtful value. The IBEW charged the War Department with a breach of faith and threatened a new strike unless a settlement was reached.(11) The board of commissioners reacted violently to this new challenge, and it appeared that Colonel Putnam's suggestions would be set aside. Luckily, cooler heads prevailed, and the Department of Water and Power scheduled a meeting on 3 March to announce an employee representation plan, employee committee elections, and a wage survey. Even then, because some of these matters were ineptly handled and impossible commitments were made by the department manager to the IBEW, another strike appeared likely. This threat was removed on 13 March, when the commissioners voted an additional $5 increase, over vocal opposition.

Army labor officers were active throughout this post-seizure period, and their assistance prevented another strike.(12) These same officers later counseled the commissioners and assisted them in implementing the reforms.(13)

Endnotes

(1) Memo for file by Ohly, 1 Jan 44, sub: Railroad Seizure—Labor Developments, par. 3; Memos for file by Ohly, 10 and 14 Jul 45, subs: Minnesota Grain Weighers Strike; Memo for file by Lt Shermer, Labor Branch, IPD, 11 Jul 45, sub: Minnesota State Grain Weighers Local 603 (AFL); Memo for file by Ohly, 12 Jul 45, sub: Minnesota Grain Weighers Strike—Developments; Memo, Maj Moiselle, Labor Off, Dist 1, Seventh Service Command, for CG [sic], Labor Branch, IPD, ASF, 6 Aug 45, sub: Minnesota Railroad and Warehouse Commission, St. Paul, Minn.

(2) A brief summary of the organization and history of the Department of Water and Power and of the Los Angeles municipal government and a description of the employment and labor relations background of this case are contained in Memo for file by Ohly, 25 Feb 44, of telecon (edited) with Maj Burroughs, same date, 5:30 P.M. (App. R–1).

(3) EO 9426, 23 Feb 44, 9 F.R. 2113.

(4) A detailed description of the dispute and of the other events leading up to the takeover is to be found in the following documents: Memo, Ohly for Maj Hill, 17 Feb 44, sub: Strike of Los Angeles Municipal Employees; Memos for file by Ohly, both 22 Feb 44, subs: Los Angeles Power and Light [sic] Strike—Developments; Memo, Labor Disputes Unit, Labor Branch, 22 Feb 44, sub: Los Angeles Bureau of Power and Light [sic], Los Angeles, Calif.; Memo for file by Maj Hill, 22 Feb 44, sub: Resume of Telephone Conversation Between Maj. Adams and Maj. Hill, 12:30; Memo for file by Maj Hill, 22 Feb 44, sub: IBEW Strike, Los Angeles Bureau of Power and Light [sic]; Telg, Mayor Fletcher Bowron to Under Sec War, 23 Feb 44; Memo for file by Maj Hill, 24 Feb 44, sub: Los Angeles Power and Light [sic]; Memo for file by Ohly, 25 Feb 44 (App. R–1). The labor disputes files of the Labor Branch contain considerable additional information. See also PMG Rpt No. 1, 23 Feb 44.

(5) PMG Rpts Nos. 2 and 3, 24 and 25 Feb 44; Memo for file by Maj Hill, 24 Feb 44, sub: Los Angeles Power and Light [sic]; Memo, J. B. for Ohly reporting telecons with Maj Adams of Col Putnam's staff during the course of 23 Feb 44. See also Col Putnam, 3 Mar 44, "Report Covering War Department Possession and Operation of the Properties in California and Nevada of the Department of Water and Power of the City of Los Angeles" (hereafter cited as Putnam Rpt).

(6) Memo for file by Ohly, 25 Feb 44 (App. R–1); PMG Rpts Nos. 2, 3, and 4, 24, 25 and 26 Feb 44; Putnam Rpt.

(7) Tab D to Putnam Rpt; Telg, E. P. Taylor to Under Sec War, 1 Mar 44; Memo, Brig Gen Greenbaum for Maj Gen Styer, 1 Mar 44, sub: Los Angeles Strike; Telecon, Maj Gen Styer and Col Putnam, 2 Mar 44, at 1820; Memo for file by Ohly, 3 Mar 44, sub: Los Angeles Water and Power—Developments.

(8) Memo for file by Ohly, 25 Feb 44 (App. R–1).

(9) Memo, Seizure Staff to Ohly, 26 Feb 44, sub: Special Labor Rpt No. 2 (App. R–2).

(10) Memo, Col O'Connell, Dep Dir, IPD, for CG, ASF, 27 Feb 44, sub: Termination of War Department Possession and Operation of the Properties of the Department of Water and Power of the City of Los Angeles, which transmitted a memo telephoned by Maj Burroughs on behalf of Col Putnam (App. R–3).

(11) See note 7.

(12) Memos for file by Ohly, 3, 6, 10, and 11 Mar 44, subs: Los Angeles Water and Power—Developments; Memo, Maj Burroughs for Ohly, 16 Mar 44, sub: Los Angeles Department of Power and Water Strike.

(13) Memo for file by Ohly, 15 Aug 44, sub: Los Angeles Power and Light Post Mortem [sic].

CHAPTER 11

The Ken-Rad Tube and Lamp Corporation Case, April 1944

The 1944 seizure of the Ken-Rad Tube and Lamp Corporation of Owensboro, Kentucky, was the first instance of a War Department takeover following enactment of the War Labor Disputes Act caused by a company's noncompliance with a National War Labor Board (NWLB) order. The War Department originally hoped to gain management cooperation, permitting a token seizure like that at Salem-Peabody, but this hope went unrealized and direct government management was necessary. The case represented one of a very small number of situations occurring late in the war where direct government operation was required and where the inherent difficulties in the takeover process, even after passage of the War Labor Disputes Act, were still evident. This case, for example, resulted in a lawsuit attacking the legality of a government seizure.

Description of the Company

The Ken-Rad Tube and Lamp Corporation employed approximately 3,300 people, 90 percent of them women. Its 150,000 outstanding shares were distributed among some seven hundred stockholders. No one individual had a controlling interest, but the company was dominated by the Burlew family, and more particularly by President Roy Burlew, who owned the largest single block of stock. In addition to the Owensboro facility the company had four smaller and closely integrated plants situated in Bowling Green, Kentucky, and Tell City, Rockport, and Huntingburg, Indiana.(1)

In 1944 these plants were of considerable importance to the Signal Corps, producing a large proportion of the nation's total output of certain types of radio and radar sending and receiving tubes. The company was one of two suppliers of metal receiving tubes, and its 1944 production schedules called for 12 million of the 36 million units scheduled for production by the entire industry. Its general quota for transmitting tubes was smaller, but in the case of two types it was to provide more than half of the Army's requirements, and it was further allocated 15 percent of the annual objective for miniature tubes. The use of alternate sources of supply was out of the question because of a lack of facilities, trained personnel, and capacity.(2)

Although Local 783 of the AFofL-affiliated United Automobile Workers of America[1] (UAW) was the certified bargaining agent at the Owensboro plant, it had never successfully negotiated a contract. The takeover grew from its attempts to do so. In the spring of 1944 three of the other plants were almost wholly unorganized, but at Tell City the CIO-affiliated United Electrical Radio and Machine Workers of America[2] had filed a petition with the National Labor Relations Board (NLRB) for an election.(3)

Background of the Dispute

The controversy between the company and the UAW went back to 1942, when the union began seeking an agreement. Initially, this controversy covered the whole scope of collective bargaining but by the spring of 1944 the only unresolved issues were wage rates, the length of probation for new employees, and union security. In November 1942 the case was certified to the NWLB, which recommended wage increases averaging ten cents per hour as well as other benefits the following April. The company was paying an average wage of forty-five cents an hour, about fifteen cents below the industry average. The NWLB recommendations were modified by the full board in a directive order of 22 July 1943 to conform with a newly issued executive order relating to wage stabilization that limited wage increases to those found at the local level.(4) Specifically, the directive provided for a learner's rate of forty cents per hour, with automatic increase to fifty cents an hour after forty-five days of employment; the establishment of a minimum rate of fifty cents an hour; an across-the-board pay increase of three cents per hour for all employees except those in three classifications; equal pay for equal work; a one-week paid vacation; and standard maintenance of membership. Wage increases were to be retroactive to 4 September 1942. Both the company and the union petitioned for a reconsideration of this decision, and both petitions were denied early in 1944. The company then flatly refused to comply, contending that the retroactive provisions would bankrupt the company, that the training period was too short, and that union security was improper. It further alleged that the NWLB lacked the authority to direct compliance. The employees, becoming increasingly impatient and dissatisfied, asked for a strike vote under Section 8 of the War Labor Disputes Act and on 21 March voted 1,938 to 581 in favor of a stoppage. The NWLB ordered Ken-Rad to show cause for noncompliance, and at a 31 March hearing the company repeated its position and again stated that it would not comply. The NWLB immediately issued another order identical with that of 22 July(5) and asked the company to inform the board not later than 3 April whether it intended to cooperate. When no word was received, the NWLB unanimously voted to refer the matter to President Roosevelt on 5 April 1944.(6)

---

[1] The United Automobile Workers (AFofL) was the smaller rump UAW organization created after the union split into AFofL and CIO factions in 1939.
[2] In 1944 union membership was 432,200.

William Green (left) and John L. Lewis

Preparation for Seizure

There followed ten days of vacillation and hesitation growing from the difficulties associated with drafting an executive order that would give effect to the retroactive pay provisions of the NWLB order. Additional difficulties were caused by President Roosevelt's absence from Washington and the recurrent hopes of an independent labor-management settlement without government involvement.

There were indications even before the matter was referred to the president that the company's opposition was based on the hope that by legal technicalities(7) it could maneuver the union into accepting an agreement more satisfactory to the company than that being considered by the NWLB. Ken-Rad attorneys allegedly communicated with Signal Corps officials and representatives of AFofL President William Green[3] and gave them the impression that they were trying to reach a set-

---

[3]William Green (1873–1952) was a labor leader who joined the United Mine Workers of America (UMW) in 1891 and was active in UMW affairs until becoming president of the AFofL in 1924 on the death of Samuel Gompers. He held this post until 1952. During the 1930s he served on the Advisory Council of the Committee on Economic Security and of the National Recovery Administration and on the governing board of the International Labor Organization, and also was a member of the original National Labor Board. As AFofL president he expelled the CIO in 1936. During the war he served in the Office of War Mobilization and Reconversion and on the Management-Labor Committee of the War Manpower Commission. For a biography, see Craig Phelan, *William Green: Biography of a Labor Leader* (Albany: State University of New York Press, 1989).

tlement with top union people that the local subsequently would be forced to accept. Although nothing came of these efforts, they were of importance later(8) and belief of their existence slowed takeover preparations.

The Ken-Rad executive order was drafted and submitted to the Bureau of the Budget, along with a similar draft involving the Navy Department and Jenkins Brothers, Inc., of Bridgeport, Connecticut. Both cases raised the question of what if anything an operating agency could do to enforce an NWLB order directing the payment of retroactive wages. The procurement agencies felt the executive order should cover this issue with specific instructions at the outset.(9) For almost a week representatives of the War and Navy Departments, the NWLB, the Bureau of the Budget, and the attorney general's office struggled with this question. The NWLB argued that the order should direct the operating agency to comply in full with their directive and that failure to do so destroyed the foundations of the no-strike policy. From its inception the NWLB emphasized the policy that money benefits directed in a board order should be retroactive to the date of certification or some other similarly appropriate time. Benefits employees gained by striking should not be foreclosed because they agreed to submit to board procedure, and if they were to forego strikes they must be protected from losses as long as two years. The War and Navy Departments were prepared to accept this proposition, but only if told beforehand where these funds would come from, as their own appropriations could not legally be used as payments for past services not rendered to the government. The Department of Justice supported this position, adding that funds and other intangible company assets could not be seized and converted to such a purpose.(10)

The conferees reached only an interim agreement that the operating agency was to be instructed in a letter from the president to pay the retroactive wages but only out of the net income derived from its own operations. In the event that this proved insufficient, the facts were to be reported to the president, who would presumably issue further instructions. The conferees hoped this plan would reassure employees, allay NWLB qualms, and give the government an opportunity to devote further study to the question and calculate the amounts due.(11) The first objective was realized but before the feasibility of the instructions themselves was tested both cases were settled, rendering the instructions academic. The second objective, that of finding a more permanent solution to the problem of retroactive wages, was never achieved, and the interim instructions accompanying the Ken-Rad and Jenkins Brothers orders were incorporated almost verbatim in the body of each succeeding executive order involving retroactive wages.

The delay in drafting an order had its good and its bad effects. From the standpoint of thorough preparation the time lost was in fact time gained. The seizure team went to Fort Knox, Kentucky; organized their affairs; briefed the designated War Department representative, Col. Carroll Badeau of the Lexington Signal Depot; and developed a plan of action. The availability of this relatively quiet planning and decision period was fortunate because of the well-justified expectation that Ken-Rad noncooperation would necessitate direct War Department operation and would complicate later decision making. During this time the team obtained funding from the allotment of Signal Corps moneys previously earmarked for contracts with Ken-Rad.(12) Similarly, the use of troops in the event of company resistance was discussed, and the decision was reached that if the War Department representative made his initial entry unaccompanied by any armed troops and encountered resistance he would withdraw and await further instructions. Any possible embarrassment occasioned by such a temporary withdrawal was thought better than setting a precedent where troops forcefully entered a plant before all other means were tried, including civilian authorities.(13)

Corporate relationships between Ken-Rad and other companies were discussed because of the unwarranted fear that the executive order might not cover all properties necessary to conduct the business.(14) Many difficult

Col. Carroll Badeau

questions confronted the War Department. In deciding the best time for action, it sought to continue operations, prevent strikes, and avoid meeting a payroll shortly after takeover. Because of the serious mechanical problem involved, it was decided to dispense with applications forms and any oath of office for employees even if government funds were used.(15) The seizure team prepared for Ken-Rad legal action by having originals of all documents dispatched by special courier from Washington to Colonel Badeau.(16) As in other cases the problem of retroactive pay caused difficulties. The War Department decided it would improve its bargaining position if the company were advised that the Army would pay retroactive wages and charge the amount to the Ken-Rad account.(17) The seizure team carefully studied the question of retaining managers if the company refused to cooperate and developed a plan outlining which supervisory personnel were essential, whether replacements were available, how loyal the managers were to the top boss, and whether a threat of firing might help settle the issue.(18) The question was quickly answered when the top company officials walked out on their own accord.(19)

A less desirable effect of the delay in drafting the executive order was increasing employee restlessness. The War Department wanted to take over while the employees were still working, and urgent appeals were made to the NWLB to keep the employees in line while difficulties with the executive order were being ironed out. The NWLB and War Mobilization Director Byrnes worked effectively with representatives of the parent international union to postpone any strike. In spite of these efforts, however, the employees met on 11 April 1944 and voted to strike on 14 April if government intervention had not occurred. Seizure became possible several hours before the scheduled time to strike.(20)

The Takeover

When word was received that the executive order had been signed,(21) Colonel Badeau and his staff, at 1600 on 14 April, entered the Ken-Rad properties without resistance to serve Roy Burlew notice of government possession. Burlew and other top officials were present in anticipation of Badeau's arrival and the initial meeting was friendly. There was every indication that at least some measure of cooperation would be forthcoming and a conference to work out the necessary relationships was scheduled for the following morning. Immediately thereafter, union officials assured the War Department of their full support and indicated their complete satisfaction with its policies. The situation seemed well in hand until late that night, when Burlew canceled his scheduled appointment the next day because of pressing business in Louisville. This word was followed in the morning mail by a letter completely destroying all previous hopes of cooperation and strongly intimating that the company intended to file a lawsuit. It stated categorically that Colonel Badeau lacked authority to take over the plants and that he operated them at his peril.(22)

Problems Presented

Within twenty-four hours of the initial occupation several facts appeared certain. First, it seemed clear that the company would not cooperate with the Army; second, the company would probably file suit; third, it appeared that management wanted a settlement with the union on its own terms and was negotiating toward this end; and fourth, the union would cooperate wholeheartedly with the Army. Under these circumstances the War Department's problems fell into four categories: first, problems associated with operation and management of the business without key personnel; second, a response to the threatened lawsuit; third, the application and enforcement of the NWLB order; and fourth, the disposition of the underlying dispute by getting Ken-Rad to accept the NWLB order or by encouraging the parties to reach some other agreement.

Direct Operation of the Business

When Burlew and his associates quit the Owensboro premises, the Army took over actual as well as titular control of the business. It had possession of all the necessary physical properties, although not the principals who normally directed the business. This problem was further complicated by difficulties in obtaining information that any business manager requires. Burlew had done a good job of teaching his supervisory personnel his own philosophy, and they were not responsive to Army requests for data. Moreover, because of their lack of technical information, War Department representatives were not certain that information that was supplied was reliable. The problem at first appeared so staggering that consideration was given to the possibility of engaging some outside company to operate the properties for the War Department as at S. A. Woods. Any decision on this question was postponed for thirty days on the hope that the company and the union would reach an agreement within a shorter period and because of the discovery that sufficient supervisors, as distinguished from corporate officials, were on hand to keep production going until the War Department obtained its own production men.(23) The decision to operate the plants directly involved the War Department in a series of complicated business and legal questions.

Almost immediately after occupation Colonel Badeau discovered that the Owensboro property was inseparable from the operations of the four feeder plants. Within three days he requested authority to seize these plants as well.(24) All raw materials were purchased through, and all finished products were shipped from, the main facility at Owensboro. Moreover, there was a constant, daily flow of partially finished goods from Owensboro to these outside installations, and the latter, after certain essential processing and assembly work, reshipped the goods to Owensboro for still further work and for final inspection and delivery. Colonel Badeau concluded that the five plants constituted one enterprise that was incapable of division and his conclusion was conveniently, although inadvertently, supported by company letters to the War Department. These letters demanded immediate arrangements to furnish the other plants with all necessary materials and held the War Department responsible for damages to the corporation resulting from any failure to do so.(25) The War Department quickly concluded that they had no alternative but to permit the normal flow of goods among these facilities. This same decision plunged the department into almost insolvable problems of inventory and accounting. It was impossible to keep a record of shipments in and out of the main plant, and the War Department was in the position of shipping out government seized property without knowing its character and quantity and without any assurance of receiving payment.(26) Consequently, after checking with the Justice Department concerning the legality of such a move, the necessary authorization was given(27) and at 7:00 A.M. on 19 April the four outlying plants were seized.(28) These seizures added no new problems to the War Department's long and growing list of difficulties and in fact removed many of the most serious questions.

The issue immediately arose as to whether the War Department should continue the company's nationwide sales organization. It was agreed that it should, for the time being at least, partly to minimize damages if the lawsuit were lost, partly because the function of this sales organization in relation to Ken-Rad's war production was unknown and partly to avoid disrupting a going business. This did not prevent the use of a greater amount of the capacity of the business for war production. Such action served the double purpose of expanding war capacity and pressuring the company to settle before it lost its civilian market.(29) It was decided that since government funds were being used, travel and other expenses of salesmen would be limited to the amounts paid to persons traveling at government expense, a precedent not subsequently followed.(30) This decision was deemed questionable because there was no valid reason for treating sales personnel differently from other employees.

Although the plant manager stayed at his post, Colonel Badeau nevertheless wanted a staff officer on site who understood the production process and could actually supervise the business. This conclusion was motivated by uncertainty as to the extent to which Badeau could trust the plant manager and other supervisory personnel and by the expected retirement of this Ken-Rad manager within a matter of weeks. Colonel O'Shea of the Signal Corps, an expert in production engineering and plant management, was assigned to the job after a careful headquarters study.(31)

In view of the company's noncooperation and lawsuit, the War Department created separate accounting books and conducted an inventory of the Ken-Rad properties with the aid of a well-known accounting firm. In addition, the Corps of Engineers was asked to make a survey of all the real property involved. Fortunately, the company books reflected fairly all items on hand and their value as of the date of government seizure.(32)

One arrangement of considerable importance, meeting the first payroll, was worked out between the War Department and Ken-Rad. The War Department took possession at the beginning of the second shift on a pay day, and the company met not only that payroll but also the payroll for all shifts the following week. While this undertaking was subject to the War Department's commitment to reimburse the company for amounts paid during the Army's operations, it was nevertheless of great benefit. The War Department could not have established the elaborate machinery necessary to meet these payrolls on time out of federal funds. Actually, because of the usual time lag in preparing a payroll, the amounts paid by the company were payments of its own obligations arising from operations prior to the seizure. Ken-Rad made no effort to incorporate the wage increases ordered by the NWLB in these payments. Within two weeks the War Department took over payroll functions, a task requiring many people who encountered numerous complications in computing the wage increases and incorporating them into individual pay checks.(33)

A going corporation like Ken-Rad pays a wide variety of state and federal transportation, sales, and excise taxes, as well as more general levies like income and franchise taxes. After a thorough study by Judge Advocate General Cramer the decision was made not to pay federal taxes and to use the government frank in lieu of postage in transmitting mail.(34)

Since Ken-Rad's operations were being conducted entirely for the account of the federal government, it was necessary to allocate War Department funds for this purpose. This extremely complicated process required a large staff of individuals and necessitated revisions in accounting procedures, purchase forms, and other practices. To protect the War Department and the individual officers involved, arrangements were made with the General Accounting Office for the assignment of a special field auditor so that disbursements could be made in accordance with commercial rather than government practices. The government had to conform to many ordinary business practices in running the plant, but it was feared that in the absence of some such procedure the comptroller general might later disallow certain of the required expenditures.(35)

As at Air Associates, there was a lease agreement between the Defense Plant Corporation and Ken-Rad, and it was necessary to arrange for the substitution of the War Department for the corporation. A similar situation existed with a contract between the Navy Department and the company covering a facility expansion at one of the feeder plants.(36)

The War Department was faced with the necessity of doing business with itself because the Signal Corps made further demands on Ken-Rad production facilities. Ordinarily, the War Department would have placed a contract covering this work, but in view of the seizure it was decided that for the purpose of new orders the Signal Corps would treat the Ken-Rad facilities like a federal arsenal.(37)

As virtual owner of the facility, the War Department had to make many operating decisions, including those relating to priorities, production scheduling, materials, manpower, relaxation of labor laws, and facility expansions. Although many problems were either solved or were being solved by the time private control resumed, these problems clearly demonstrated that direct operation was difficult at best, requiring at one point the services of a hundred officers and enlisted men. It was likely that if a solution to the underlying dispute were not obtained quickly, the operation would require contracting with a private corporation to run the plants.

The Lawsuit

On the afternoon of the first full day of War Department possession the company filed a multipurpose lawsuit in the United States District Court for the Western District of Kentucky against the War Department representative.(38) The suit claimed that Colonel Badeau was acting unlawfully to enforce an illegal NWLB order providing for retroactive and inflationary wage increases, in contravention of Section 7 of the War Labor Disputes Act because employees had participated in the hearings preceding the NWLB decision; that adequate legal hearings were not held; and that the NWLB decision was not fair and equitable as required by Section 7 of the War Labor Disputes Act. The plaintiff asked that the court hold the NWLB order unlawful, restrain the defendant from possessing or operating the plaintiff's properties, and provide general relief. The phrasing of the petition obviously indicated that it had been drafted in anticipation of a government seizure and was also an integral part of a Ken-Rad plan to strengthen its bargaining position with the union.

Soon after this the plaintiff filed a motion for a preliminary injunction, and a hearing was set for 26 April. Still later the complaint was amended to add an allegation that Colonel Badeau, in violation of Sections 4 and 5 of the War Labor Disputes Act, was placing in effect, to the irreparable injury of the plaintiff, terms and conditions of employment not in effect at the time of the seizure—namely the provisions of the NWLB order. In making this allegation Ken-Rad relied heavily on a position previously stated by Badeau that the War Department intended to pay a million dollars in retroactive wages and charge the company with the amount. This amendment was very disturbing since the War Department was not certain whether an NWLB order not in effect prior to government possession constituted part of the conditions of employment at the time of the takeover, and NWLB orders usually provided that the secretary of war continue the conditions of employment present upon seizure.(39)

The Justice Department was asked to defend this action(40) and closely cooperated with the War Department in the field and at headquarters for a number of weeks preparing affidavits and briefs, with the Army judge advocates, particularly Major Sachse, taking as much responsibility for the character of the defense as the Justice Department itself.(41) An elaborate affidavit drafted for the signature of General Somervell constituted the principal defense submission.

The government never entertained any real doubt as to its ultimate victory but was uncertain about what kind of a decision a district court judge could render. It was necessary to anticipate the possibility of an adverse ruling in the first instance—a ruling against Colonel Badeau covering all possession and operation of the properties or one limited to enforcement of the NWLB's order in whole or in part. These possibilities raised three important questions. First, what action should be taken to vacate such an order? The Justice Department developed detailed plans and was prepared to execute them immediately. Second, what should Colonel Badeau do when served with a copy of such an order? Should he ignore it, should he withdraw, or as a further alternative, should the War Department change the basis of possession by condemning a leasehold interest in the company's properties and requisitioning all necessary personnel? No final decision was ever reached, but the Corps of Engineers was instructed to make arrangements for a condemnation. The third question related to the most appropriate course if the court should merely direct Colonel Badeau to refrain from instituting the wage increases ordered by the NWLB on the grounds that to do so without following the procedures provided in Section 5 of the War Labor Disputes Act would violate Section 4 of that law.(42)

These problems were never actually encountered. On 10 May, two weeks after the all-day hearing on 27 April, the court handed down a sweeping decision upholding government possession and dismissing the complaint.(43) The decision was never appealed.

*Application of the NWLB Order and the Conduct of Day-to-Day
Labor Relations*

Immediately after the seizure War Department labor officers prepared a statement of the terms and conditions of employment, including the provisions directed by the NWLB order. This proved difficult for two reasons. First, the NWLB order was too vague to allow direct application without further interpretation, and the War Department had to ask for further instructions and explanations on five occasions. The points in question related to the NWLB's interpretation of words, the method of incorporating wage increases and minimum rates into piece-rate structures, the time frame for payment of retroactive wages, and other technical questions directly affecting payroll preparation.(44) These difficulties seriously complicated the already heavy burdens of fiscal and disbursing officers.

The absence of any prior labor contract was the second reason why the drafting of terms and conditions of employment proved troublesome. Although the company and union had intermittently negotiated for several years and had agreed on many proposed contract provisions, the War Department was unable to obtain reliable information on past practices or the results of these negotiations. In addition, during the course of mediation and other proceedings before the NWLB, and under the auspices of a United States conciliator, they had concurred on many other points. The union representatives were uncertain of the precise character of many of these agreements, however, and had entrusted the initialed copies of the accepted provisions to the company. Naturally, Ken-Rad was not eager to furnish the War Department with any information. Wanting to avoid direct confrontation, the War Department asked the NWLB to undertake this job. The NWLB acquiesced, but before the individual designated could complete his work the War Department terminated its possession.(45)

The War Department quickly encountered further difficulties due to a lack of a grievance procedure that could be clearly considered a part of the existing terms of employment at the time of seizure. Although these difficulties were merely a part of the larger problem, they demanded immediate attention as a government-run operation could not condone an inadequate grievance procedure. As a result, Colonel Badeau, with NWLB approval, developed a most satisfactory interim grievance procedure until final terms and conditions of employment were established.(46)

The problem of discharges came up at Ken-Rad when a foreman fired eight individuals for excessive absenteeism. The action seemed strange since in the preceding year only three persons had been discharged for any cause. An order was immediately issued preventing further discharges except after a review by a labor officer, while prompt action was instituted to reexamine the particular cases to assure remedial action should the discharges prove arbitrary and unwarranted, as they later did. The firm position of the War Department had a perceptible effect on the attitude of foremen and other supervisory employees but clearly showed the need for more fundamental instruction in personnel management techniques.(47)

Ken-Rad management and union representatives were informed at the outset that retroactive wages would come from net operating income derived during the period of possession and that the War Department intended to charge these payments to the company account even though they were initially from government funds. Initial estimates indicated that perhaps eleven or twelve thousand workers were entitled to roughly $1 million of retroactive wages. The many questions incident to this payment were given early consideration by Badeau and his labor staff, but it was known that it would take many weeks to calculate the amount due each employee, particularly since the calculations depended upon a series of NWLB interpretations. Moreover, it required a further lengthy period to determine whether the War Department had earned sufficient net operating income to make the payments. The problem was still being considered when the War Department terminated possession.(48)

There were other labor problems encountered in the course of normal daily operations. Absenteeism, for example, was high prior to War Department intervention, but the aggressive measures taken to combat it were remarkably successful. Another problem was the petition of the United Electrical Workers for an election at the Tell City plant, which raised the question of the status, position, and obligations of the War Department with respect to an NLRB proceeding at any plant under its control. A scheduled hearing on this petition and on a subsequent intervening UAW petition was delayed to provide an opportunity for consideration of this novel point by the NLRB, which decided, based upon an interpretation of the provisions of Section 9 of the Selective Training and Service Act, that the National Labor Relations Act was applicable to Ken-Rad operations and that the hearing should proceed. This decision raised a number of issues. The War Department was anxious to avoid taking any position in the hearing but did not wish to prejudice Ken-Rad by preventing the submission of testimony that a private employer normally had the right to present. To meet this dilemma, Army officers attended the hearing as observers. The general managers under the Army and of Ken-Rad testified concerning undisputed facts, and were not permitted to give any opinions. Ken-Rad officials were advised that they were privileged to participate independently should they wish to express the company's attitude.(49)

Another operating labor problem of a very practical type—found also in many subsequent cases—resulted from the existence of gross wage inequities, which caused a high turnover rate and adversely affected morale. Typically, such inequities occurred among workers outside the bargaining unit, especially among lower supervisory personnel who were placed at a disadvantage by an NWLB order applying only to production employees. To remedy this situation at Ken-Rad, the War Department instituted proceedings under Section 5 of the War Labor Disputes Act for a change in the terms and conditions of employment of the persons concerned. Such proceedings in this and other cases did not involve the War Department in controversial matters since normally the application for change was made with the tacit consent and usually the approval of management and the affected employees were not represented by any union. At Ken-Rad the proceedings were never completed due to the termination of the War Department's possession, but the company later implemented the proposed change with NWLB approval.(50)

The Ken-Rad case resulted in some important NWLB rulings on what constituted changes in the terms and conditions of employment under Section 5 of the War Labor Disputes Act. The necessity for such rulings illustrated again the many technical problems requiring action by any operating agency. The NWLB ruled that Ken-Rad's pre-seizure merit wage increases did not constitute changes in terms and conditions of employment within the meaning of the War Labor Disputes Act.(51) Still another question, partly of a legal and partly of an industrial relations character, was raised by the company's War Bond Purchase Plan, under which regular amounts were deducted from employee wages for war bond purchases. The War Department continued this plan but found that at the time of takeover individual credit balances in the war bond purchasing account already aggregated more than $50,000 and that the company, which physically controlled the funds, showed no inclination to take any action. The employees affected were naturally disturbed, having received neither the bonds nor the refunds. Colonel Badeau's instructions were modified to authorize the use of general funds for purchasing bonds or, upon request, of refunding any amount owed an employee. In order to protect the War Department, Badeau obtained receipts from each employee so claims could later be asserted by the War Department against Ken-Rad.(52)

By and large, day-to-day labor relations were conducted in a satisfactory manner, and the training given supervisory employees improved personnel management and industrial relations practices throughout the plants. The only difficulties stemmed from differences of opinion between production manager Colonel O'Shea, who thought in terms of the most economical and efficient way to run the plant, and War Department labor officers, who felt that the predominantly labor nature of the mission justified extraordinary measures not normally found in a well-run, wholly private plant. To some extent these labor-management differences reflected those common to any private industrial enterprise.

Disposition of the Underlying Labor Dispute

The War Department's top objective was gaining either company compliance with the NWLB order as issued or a negotiated settlement between the company and the union acceptable to the board. The company's attitude made the first alternative unlikely. The second alternative seemed more hopeful since Ken-Rad had indicated a strong desire, and actually made overt moves, to reach a settlement on more favorable terms than those in the NWLB order. Unfortunately, this alternative had inherent dangers. It was considered unjust, ironic, and poor precedent to have a noncompliant party benefit at the expense of employees as a result of a War Department seizure. It was obvious that the War Department could not exert pressure on the union to reach an agreement at variance with the NWLB order. Such an agreement had to be the result of free bargaining on the union's part. At the same time, however, the War Department could pressure Ken-Rad to accept the NWLB order or a reasonable alternative settlement.

The company was expected to employ any technique to get the union to accept a less favorable settlement. The lawsuit was one of those techniques, designed to convince the employees that it was hopeless for them to expect government enforcement of the NWLB order. Ken-Rad publicity was carefully framed to develop these convictions and was facilitated by the close friendship between the owner of the only local newspaper and Roy Burlew. Stories were circulated that the War Department faced eviction or was about to terminate possession and that employees might just as well meet management on management's terms. In addition, a strained construction of President Roosevelt's letter was used as a basis for the claim that the War Department had no intention of paying retroactive wages.

The company further attempted to capitalize on its political contacts in Washington to discredit the War Department and to introduce further doubts into the minds of employees. Kentucky Senator Albert B. Chandler, for example, in a statement appearing in the *Congressional Record*, charged that War Department intervention was retarding production. After the seizure was terminated, Secretary Stimson wrote Chandler, providing figures proving an actual increase of productivity under Army jurisdiction.(53)

From the outset the War Department actively pressed for quick company action. On the first day Under Secretary Patterson appealed to Burlew to reconsider his position and accept the NWLB order,(54) but the only reply received came ten days later and expressed regret about the government's seizure of Ken-Rad.(55) Efforts were also undertaken through Dean Graham, a leading Kentucky citizen and War Department consultant, and through Kentucky's governor[4] to convince friends and business associates of Burlew to persuade him that it was good sense and a patriotic duty to reach a settlement. When this type of persuasion and reasoning quickly appeared futile, the War Department turned to other means. In doing so, it had to remember that production, not punishment, was its goal and that nothing should be done that the company could properly construe as persecution or as the exercise of a sanction to compel compliance with an NWLB order that was not legally binding. Measures taken had to have other legitimate objectives, and their effects in terms of pressure had to be merely incidental.

A study of Ken-Rad's financial condition disclosed that a group of banks held a substantial note against the company. The calling of this loan might embarrass Ken-Rad considerably, and the company showed some concern about this. Ways of capitalizing on this fact were explored, and while no measures were ultimately taken by the War Department, there is reason to believe that the mere existence of this condition constituted a substantial pressure on Ken-Rad.(56) In addition, immediate steps were taken to reopen Ken-Rad's negotiated agreement for the preceding year after it was discovered that the company had deducted as expenses the amount of the retroactive wages ordered by the NWLB, even though it had refused to pay them. Other persuasive steps discussed(57) included the seizure of feeder plants, the elimination of advertising, the reduction of salesmen's expense accounts, and the reorganization of personnel policies. Incentives of a more positive nature were likewise considered. The Office of Price Administration,[5] for example, was asked to expedite its determination of whether Ken-Rad might be

---

[4]The Republican governor of Kentucky in April 1944 was Simeon Willis (1879–1965), who held that office from 1943 to 1947.

[5]The Office of Price Administration and Civilian Supply, later the independent Office of Price Administration (OPA), was created within the Office of Emergency Management by Executive Order 8734, 11 April 1941, to stabilize prices and prevent speculative, unwarranted, and abnormal increases in prices and rents; to eliminate or prevent profiteering, hoarding, manipulation, and speculation resulting from wartime market conditions or scarcities; to assure that defense appropriations were spent properly; and to protect persons on fixed or limited incomes from undue economic fluctuations. The OPA was assisted in its efforts by 9 regional offices, 90 district offices, 259 rent control boards, and 5,500 war price and rationing boards throughout the nation. The OPA directors were Leon Henderson (1941–42), Prentiss M. Brown (1943), and Chester Bowles (1944–45). For OPA records, see Record Group 188, NARA.

entitled to price relief if it adopted the wage rates directed by the NWLB. Furthermore, the company was made aware that in the event of an early settlement—but only in such event—the War Department was prepared on reimbursement for its expenditures to turn over the entire operating profits to Ken-Rad in exchange for a release—that is, to treat the entire affair as a token operation. Finally, when negotiations began to drag interminably, Ken-Rad was flatly told that the War Department proposed to obtain another manager, perhaps a competitor, to operate the properties for the duration.(58)

It is impossible to estimate the amount of influence War Department actions had on the negotiations between Ken-Rad and the union. During the first few weeks, even though the company claimed it was negotiating with the union and making progress, there was little evidence of this fact, and it appeared that Ken-Rad was intentionally stalling to capitalize on the lawsuit and to exploit Washington political contacts. However, once the parties actually began serious negotiations, all disputed issues were satisfactorily worked out in a little over two weeks.(59) The settlement reached varied considerably from the NWLB order.(60) First, the learners period preceding the date when a new employee would receive the minimum going rate of fifty cents per hour was increased from forty-five to eighty-four days. Second, the retroactive wage payments were limited to those employees on the payroll as of the date the agreement was reached and to persons who had left to join the armed forces. Third, the checkoff of union dues and maintenance of membership was granted, and, finally, it was agreed that the settlement covered all Ken-Rad facilities. The company had materially scaled down its monetary liability, and the union obtained extensive union security and exclusive bargaining rights at four additional plants where it would not have won elections. From a union standpoint it was an attractive deal. The only major concession was the waiver of retroactive pay for persons who were no longer employed in the plant and who were consequently of no particular union interest.

Should this settlement, which did such violence to the NWLB order, be permitted to stand? There was doubt as to what jurisdiction the NWLB might have over such a settlement and what it would do if the contract were submitted for approval. The extension of the new wage rates to the feeder plants and the modification of the learners period, and perhaps even the reduction of retroactive wage liability, were matters for the NWLB's cognizance under its wage stabilization duties. In any event, the union and the company decided that NWLB approval was desirable, and a joint application requesting approval of the modifications of the NWLB order and of their contract was filed. The War Department was careful to avoid any involvement in this proceeding. With labor members dissenting, the NWLB, on 23 May, approved the portion of the agreement amending the order relating to the Owensboro plant.(61) The NWLB, which had always adhered to the principle that a collectively bargained settlement was preferable to an imposed one, could hardly have taken any other position. If the parties voluntarily desired a form of settlement different from that worked out by the NWLB that was their business, provided of course that no laws were violated. Acting purely in its capacity as the federal wage stabilization authority, the NWLB approved the extension of the wage provisions to the other four Ken-Rad plants.(62) In the case of Tell City, however, the NWLB specified that its approval did not in any way constitute an official board opinion on any issue of representation. This reservation followed from a fear that the United Electrical Workers might criticize any NWLB action that could be construed as recognizing the UAW at Tell City, and the board refused to pass on the contracts.

Termination of Possession

Belief that Ken-Rad and the union would eventually negotiate a settlement prompted discussions concerning different types of termination agreements. It was the consensus that the simplest method of adjustment was to consider Ken-Rad a token government operation in which, after reimbursing the War Department for all expenses incurred, the company became entitled to any profits realized during the period of occupation, thus meeting company claims for fair and just compensation for the use and occupation of its properties. The entire affair could end with a mutual exchange of releases. The attorney general approved this tentative settlement(63), and it was discussed with Ken-Rad, not only to expedite the Army's withdrawal but also to prod Ken-Rad into making an agreement with the union.(64) Shortly after the NWLB approved the labor agreement, the War Department plan was implemented and the Army withdrew.

Other Cases in the Ken-Rad Pattern

It is hard to draw specific conclusions about the influence of the Ken-Rad case on the history of plant seizures or its significance in other employer noncompliance cases involving uncooperative management. None of the three cases of management noncooperation were precisely the same because of varying degrees of management resistance, and each operation required specific tailoring to fit the size and nature of the business and the character of the labor issues involved. At Ken-Rad there were five separate plants, each in a different community, employing around six thousand workers total. Twentieth Century Brass Company,(65) Minneapolis, Minnesota, owned one small foundry, with fifty workers managed by three equal co-owners. The Gaffney Manufacturing Company,(66) Gaffney, South Carolina, also had only one plant, which employed seven hundred workers, but it was controlled by absentee owners belonging to the Deering-Milliken textile brokerage concern in New York.

In spite of these significant differences there are enough similarities to consider the Ken-Rad case illustrative of all three. In each case the War Department sought management cooperation toward operating properties on a token basis and promises to carry out applicable NWLB orders. When this failed in every case, the War Department undertook actual management, the extent and character depending on the degree of owner cooperation. At Ken-Rad top officials walked out but lower supervisors remained, including the plant manager. At Gaffney the plant manager quit. At Twentieth Century Brass the co-owners stayed as War

Department employees. In all three instances the War Department was inevitably forced to handle many labor relations, production scheduling, and other general business management problems.

In each of these cases uniform efforts were made to persuade or force management to comply with applicable NWLB orders or to negotiate some other mutually acceptable agreement. At Ken-Rad and Twentieth Century Brass these efforts were successful in one and six months, respectively. The end of the war cut short the Gaffney operation after three months of possession, but it was unlikely that any settlement could have been reached irrespective of the length of the Army's tenure. In all three cases the government, either before or after the termination of possession, reached settlements with the respective owners that included the mutual exchanges of releases. Each agreement converted operations from a government account to a company account, with the government turning over its profits after each firm relinquished all claims for the use and seizure of their property.

Each of the cases demonstrated the difficulties inherent in direct government operation of a seized facility. While the War Labor Disputes Act removed some labor problems, it could not eliminate many of the fiscal, legal, and operational problems associated with running any business. With experience, however, these difficulties became less troublesome in subsequent cases. Similarly, in each individual case the longer the period of government tenure the simpler was the handling of such questions. All three cases clearly demonstrated that the government could conduct operations successfully irrespective of obstacles, and it is significant that in each instance production was higher on termination than when possession was taken.

In each situation labor peace was obtained for the duration of government occupancy. Applicable NWLB orders were made effective, except provisions for the payment of retroactive wages, although at Twentieth Century Brass the War Department was prepared at termination to pay these wages from realized net operating income. The techniques used to convince management of the desirability of labor agreements varied only slightly from case to case. In each the threat was made to turn the business over to an outside company for the duration, and in each the War Department hoped that on achieving a labor settlement the profits accured during the period of possession could be transferred to the company in exchange for a complete release. Other forms of persuasion were not available except at Twentieth Century Brass, where it was learned that the three co-owners were largely dependent for their livelihoods upon the dividends and salaries from the business. The source of any substantial dividends was cut off by the War Department's operation of the business, and consequently the threat of dismissal or drastic salary reduction was used most effectively. In all these cases it was necessary to exercise the greatest care to make certain that employees were not pressured to accept a less favorable settlement than that contained in the NWLB order, but at the same time it was prudent to encourage labor-management negotiations and to apprise workers of the long-range desirability of obtaining a decent working arrangement with the company that went beyond the period of Army possession. They were made to understand that they must find some way of getting along with their employer other than counting on indefinite federal control to maintain good working standards.

Endnotes

(1) Pertinent facts on Ken-Rad and labor dispute (App. S–1).

(2) Memos, Lt Col Wheeler for Under Sec War, 19 and 24 Apr 44, subs: Ken-Rad Tube and Lamp Corporation, with attachments.

(3) App. S–1.

(4) EO 9328, 8 Apr 43.

(5) NWLB Directive Order, 31 Mar 44, in the matter of Ken-Rad Tube and Lamp Corporation and International Union, UAW, Local 783, AFL, Case No. 2942–CS–D (815).

(6) Ltrs, Davis to Roosevelt, 5 and 6 Apr 44; App. S–1.

(7) The nature of these legal technicalities was brought out in the lawsuit. They related to the legality of the NWLB order.

(8) Memo by Lt Col Johnson, 5 Apr 44, sub: Ken-Rad Tube and Lamp Corporation, Owensboro, Kentucky, which traces some of the company's maneuvering in the preceding days.

(9) Memo, Brig Gen Greenbaum for Titus, Bureau of the Budget, 6 Apr 44, sub: Ken-Rad Company [*sic*]

(10) Ltr, Atty Gen to Dir, Bureau of the Budget, 6 Apr 44 (App. S–2). For an extremely able analysis of some of the many problems involved, see Informal Staff Memo, [Lt] Col Hebert for Ohly, 10 Apr 44, sub: Labor Considerations in Take-Over (App. S–3). It should be noted that the War Shipping Administration, in taking over the Atlantic Basin Iron Works in Brooklyn, New York, did in fact seize all of the firm's intangible assets and that such action was of material assistance in causing the company's rapid compliance with the NWLB order it had previously refused to accept. Furthermore, prior executive orders that had been approved by the attorney general before their submission to the president contained language that on its face authorized seizure of virtually any property of a seized company. On the problem of retroactive wages, see the discussions of the subject in the chapters on S. A. Woods and Montgomery Ward.

(11) See successive drafts of the proposed executive order contained in the official files; Ltr, Acting Atty Gen Fahy to Roosevelt, 8 Apr 44; Memos, Dir, Bureau of the Budget, for Roosevelt, both 11 Apr 44, one transmitting the Jenkins order and the other the Ken-Rad order; Memo for file by Ohly, 12 Apr 44, sub: War Department Operation of Ken-Rad—Developments, particularly par. 1; Ltr, Roosevelt to Sec War, 13 Apr 44 (App. S–4). For further consideration of the history and meaning of the retroactive wage provision that was developed in this case, see Memo, Lt Gen Styer for War Department Representative at Montgomery Ward, 9 Jan 45, sub: Interpretation of Executive Order No. 9508.

(12) Memo for file by Ohly, 12 Apr 44, pars. 1(d), 2(e), and 3(b), (c), (m).

(13) Memo for file by Ohly, 12 Apr 44, pars. 2(d) and 3(a), (e). This same philosophy was adopted in all subsequent cases. At Twentieth Century Brass, where the seizure was made late in the evening, the properties were locked up. The War Department representative, upon seeking instructions, was advised that he should not break in but that instead he should try to find some company official who would admit him. Similarly, at Montgomery Ward the War Department took a very strong position in favor of the use of police authorities (local or federal) in the event that the Army had difficulty in entering or encountered other forms of interference.

(14) Memo for file by Ohly, 12 Apr 44, par. 2(g).

(15) Memo for file by Ohly, 14 Apr 44, sub: War Department Operation of Ken-Rad—Developments, 13 April, par. 4(c).

(16) Memos for file by Ohly, 12 and 14 Apr 44.

(17) Memo for file by Ohly, 14 Apr 44, par. 4(a).

(18) Ibid., par. 4(b).

(19) The problem of retroactive wages required some special attention in the instructions (Memo, Lt Gen Somervell for Col Badeau, 14 Apr 44, sub: War Department Possession and Operation of the Plants and Facilities of Ken-Rad Tube and Lamp Corporation, par. 8). A new paragraph was also added on public relations (ibid., par. 19), and provision was made for the exemption of officers and enlisted personnel assigned to the mission from the general War Department thirty-day limitation on

per diem for officers away from their permanent station (Memo, Under Sec War for CG, ASF, 14 Apr 44, same sub, par. 5). This latter provision, while seemingly technical, was actually of the greatest importance to this and subsequent missions. Officers and enlisted personnel were often required to be away on these cases for a good many weeks, and it would have been a serious hardship to them and undoubtedly have seriously impaired their morale if they had not been permitted to collect per diem. There were many interesting ramifications of this problem in terms of drafting the most satisfactory clause possible. The form finally adopted is to be found in instructions in the later cases. Further changes in the form of instructions to War Department representatives in subsequent seizures came about as a result of experiences in this case and will be noted at the appropriate point.

(20) Memo for file by Ohly, 12 Apr 44, pars. 1, 2(a) and (f), 3(d) and (h); and Memo by Ohly, 14 Apr 44.

(21) EO 9436, 13 Apr 44, 9 F.R. 4063.

(22) Ltr, Roy Burlew, President, Ken-Rad, to Col Badeau, 14 Apr 44 (App. S–5). For events on the day of entrance, see PMG Rpt No. 1, 15 Apr 44; and Memo for file by Ohly, 16 Apr 44, sub: War Department Operation of Ken-Rad—Developments, 15 April.

(23) Memo for file by Ohly, 18 Apr 44, sub: War Department Operation of Ken-Rad—Developments, 17 April, par. 1(h).

(24) Memo, Col Badeau for CG, ASF, 17 Apr 44, sub: Extending Army Possession, Control, and Operation of Plants and Facilities of Ken-Rad Tube and Lamp Corporation to the Feeder and Processing Plants of the Company Located at Tell City, Indiana, Huntingburg, Indiana, Bowling Green, Kentucky, and Rockport, Indiana (App. S–6).

(25) Ltr, E. Sandidge, Atty for Ken-Rad, to Col Badeau, 15 Apr 44; and Ltr, Burlew to Col Badeau, 18 Apr 44.

(26) Telecon, Lt Col Hebert and Ohly, 17 Apr 44; Memo for file by Ohly, 18 Apr 44, par. 3; Memo for file by Ohly, 22 Apr 44, sub: War Department Operation of Ken-Rad—Developments, 18 April, pars. 1, 2, and 5.

(27) Finding and Order of Acting Sec War re Ken-Rad, 18 Apr 44 (App. S–7); Memo, Under Sec War for CG, ASF, 18 Apr 44, sub: Extension of War Department Possession, Control, and Operation of the Plants and Facilities of Ken-Rad Tube and Lamp Corporation to the Feeder and Processing Plants of the Company . . . ; and Memo, Lt Gen Somervell for Col Badeau, same date and sub.

(28) PMG Rpt No. 6, 19 Apr 44.

(29) Memo for file by Ohly, 16 Apr 44, par. 4(a).

(30) PMG Rpt No. 5, 19 Apr 44, par. 8.

(31) Memo for file by Ohly, 18 Apr 44, pars. 1(a) and 4(c).

(32) PMG Rpt No. 2, 15 Apr 44, par. 6; PMG Rpt No. 3, 17 Apr 44, par. 6; PMG Rpt No. 6, 19 Apr 44, par. 8; Memo for file by Ohly, 29 Apr 44.

(33) PMG Rpt No. 2, 15 Apr 44, par. 7; and many labor memoranda relating to the application of the NWLB decision.

(34) PMG Rpt No. 3, 17 Apr 44, par. 3; Memo, Maj George Tackabury, Dep to War Department Representative, for CG, 15 Jan 45, sub: Report Containing Financial Statements of Results of War Department Operation of the Plants and Facilities of the Twentieth Century Brass Works, Inc., From 9 September to 31 December 1944, and Memo of Procedures Employed in Preparation of Physical Inventory. This memo was approved by the Industrial Personnel Division director (Memo from him for the CG, 22 Jan 45), the fiscal director (Memo from him for the CofS, ASF, 29 Jan 45), and the ASF commanding general (Memo, Lt Gen Styer for Col Lynn C. Barnes, 1 Feb 46). See also Memo, Lt Col Hebert for Dep JAG, 10 Feb 45, sub: Montgomery Ward and Company, Inc.

(35) PMG Rpt No. 21, 5 May 44, par. 3; PMG Rpt No. 3, 15 Apr 44, par. 7.

(36) Memo, Col Badeau for CG, ASF, 2 May 44, sub: Ken-Rad Tube and Lamp Corporation, Plancor #1668 Defense Plant Corporation Effect of War Department Operation; PMG Rpt No. 18, 2 May 44, par. 2.

(37) Memo for file by Ohly, 18 Apr 44, par. 5(b).

(38) Complaint for injunction and declaratory relief in the matter of Ken-Rad Tube and Lamp Corporation Plaintiff vs. Carroll Badeau Defendant, filed 15 Apr 44 (App. S–8). See also PMG Rpts Nos. 2 and 3, 15 and 17 Apr 44.

(39) Ltr, Under Sec War to Dir, Bureau of the Budget, n.d., commenting on the executive order in the Hummer case (App. S–9). See Appendix S–10 for amendment to complaint.

(40) Ltr, Acting Sec War to the Atty Gen, 14 Apr 44.

(41) Unsigned Memo, prepared by Maj Sachse, 2 May 44, sub: Legal Matters (Comments on Ken-Rad Brief for Mr. Faneilli, Department of Justice).

(42) PMG Rpt No. 10, 24 Apr 44, par. 1; and PMG Rpt No. 11, 25 Apr 44, pars. 1, 3, and 4.

(43) Ken-Rad Tube and Lamp Corp. vs. Badeau, 55 F. Su 193 (D.C., W. D. Ky., 44).

(44) Special Labor Rpt No. 1 from Lt Col Johnson and Maj Boland, 19 Apr 44; Ltr, Brig Gen Greenbaum to Davis, 19 Apr 44; and reply from William Berg, Jr., of the Board to Brig Gen Greenbaum, 20 Apr 44; Special Labor Rpt No. 2 from Maj Boland, 21 Apr 44; Special Labor Rpt No. 3 from Maj Boland, 22 Apr 44, and reply from Berg to Brig Gen Greenbaum, 24 Apr 44; Memos, Maj Boland for Ohly, both 26 Apr 44, subs: The Method of Computation of Payroll Now Being Followed by Payroll Section and The Piece Rate System Incorporation of Wage Increase; Ltr, Brig Gen Greenbaum to Davis, 27 Apr 44, and reply from Berg to Brig Gen Greenbaum, 28 Apr 44; Ltr, Under Sec War to Davis, 8 May 44, and reply from Berg to Under Sec War, 12 May 44.

(45) Special Labor Rpt No. 2; Ltr, Brig Gen Greenbaum to Davis, 24 Apr 44; PMG Rpt No. 16, 29 Apr 44, par. 5.

(46) Interim Grievance Procedure (App. S–11); Ltr, Brig Gen Greenbaum to Davis, 24 Apr 44, and reply from Berg to Brig Gen Greenbaum, 24 Apr 44.

(47) Memo for file by Ohly, 29 Apr 44, sub: War Department Operation of Ken-Rad—Developments, 20 April.

(48) Special Memo, Col Badeau for JAG, 22 Apr 44, sub: Additional Data Requested for Transmission to Attorney General for Preparation of Defense in Suit of Ken-Rad Tube and Lamp Corporation vs. Carroll Badeau, War Department Representative, Hearing Set for Thursday, 27 April 1944. See also App. S–3.

(49) PMG Rpt No. 25, 10 May 44, par. 4; and PMG Rpt No. 12, 25 Apr 44, par. 9.

(50) Ltr, Under Sec War to Davis, 17 May 44.

(51) Ltr, Jesse Freidin, General Counsel, NWLB, to Under Sec War, 13 May 44.

(52) Memo, Col Badeau for CG, ASF, 10 May 44, sub: Request for Authority Relative to War Bond Purchase Plan—War Department Operation of Plants of Ken-Rad Tube and Lamp Corporation (App. S–12); Memo, Lt Gen Somervell for Col Badeau, 11 May 44, sub: War Department Possession and Operation of the Plants and Facilities of the Ken-Rad Tube and Lamp Corporation—Authority Relative to War Bond Purchase Plan.

(53) *Congressional Record*, 28 Apr 44, p. 3855.

(54) Telg, Under Sec War to Burlew, 14 Apr 44.

(55) Telg, Burlew to Under Sec War, 24 Apr 44.

(56) Memo for file by Ohly, 15 Apr 44, par. 6; Memo for file by Maj Sachse, 16 Apr 44, sub: Revolving Credit Agreement; Memo for file by Ohly, 18 Apr 44, par. 4c.

(57) Memo for file by Ohly, 18 Apr 44, par. 6; Memo for file by Ohly, 22 Apr 44, par. 3; PMG Rpt No. 4, 17 Apr 44, par. 7.

(58) Telecon, Maj Gen Styer and Max Truitt, 15 May 44.

(59) Par. 1 of PMG Rpts. Nos. 19, 22, 23, 24, 27, 29, and 31, and par. 2 of Rpt No. 27 for the history of these negotiations and the subsequent steps to obtain NWLB approval.

(60) Joint Application of International Union, UAW, Local 783, AFofL, and Ken-Rad Tube and Lamp Corporation for Modification of Board's Directive and Approval of Contracts Between Said Applicants Before the NWLB in Case No. 2942–CS–D (815).

(61) Approval of NWLB, 23 May 44, in Case No. 2942–CS–D (815).

(62) Two Authorizations of NWLB, 23 May 44, in Case No. 2942–CS–D (815).

(63) Memo, Col Badeau for CG, ASF, 8 May 44, sub: Proposed Procedure for Termination of Government Possession of Plants and Facilities of Ken-Rad Tube and Lamp Corporation (App. S–13); Ltr, Acting Sec War to Atty Gen, 13 May 44 (App. S–14); Ltr, Atty Gen to Sec War, 15 May 44 (App. S–15); Memo, Lt Gen Somervell for Col Badeau, 18 May 44, sub: War Department Operation of the Plants and Facilities of Ken-Rad Tube and Lamp Corporation—Procedure for Termination of Government Possession (App. S–16).

(64) PMG Rpt No. 23, par. 2; PMG Rpt No. 30, par. 2; and PMG Rpt No. 31, par. 2.
(65) The Twentieth Century Brass Works case is summarized in Appendix Z–2a.
(66) The Gaffney Manufacturing Company case is very briefly summarized in Appendixes Y–6 and Y–7.

Chapter 12

The Hummer Manufacturing Division of Montgomery Ward and Company, Inc., May 1944

In operating the facilities of the Hummer Manufacturing Division of Montgomery Ward and Company, Inc., the War Department successfully and for the first time secured the cooperation of managers whose noncompliance with a National War Labor Board (NWLB) order had precipitated the seizure. In spite of the experiences at S. A. Woods, Air Associates, and Ken-Rad, the War Department had maintained hope that token arrangements would prove feasible in at least some management noncompliance cases. It was believed that a company's desires to receive profits and to prevent disruptions served as powerful incentives, but the one main obstacle always encountered was the requirement that the company, in doing government business, had to comply with NWLB orders they had previously refused to observe. While an insurmountable obstacle in cases where compliance entailed the substantial expenditure of money(1) or the sacrifice of strong personal convictions,(2) such an arrangement did permit a firm to carry out NWLB orders without losing face or completely abandoning its position. It was often argued that the company had refused voluntary compliance as long as it was free to exercise choice but that it could not object to operations undertaken in conformity with NWLB orders while the government was in lawful possession. At Hummer this line of reasoning proved justified.

Description of the Employer

The Hummer Manufacturing Division in Springfield, Illinois, formed a small and relatively unimportant segment of the nationwide retail and mail order business of Montgomery Ward. Hummer facilities were normally used for the manufacture of farm implements, but during the war it had taken on a number of Army subcontracts with Bendix and Frigidaire. In May 1944 its war business included the production of gun arms for upper turrets, carburetor nozzles, and propeller parts for the B–29, P–47, B–17, and B–24 aircraft, which accounted for 65 percent of its capacity. Considerable confusion about the importance of this work existed, and it was initially and mistakenly believed that these items were not available from other sources. In fact, before, during, and after seizure a mere transfer of certain machine tools, dies, and patterns to other facilities could have removed Hummer from the defense producer category with no effect on the war effort. This widely known fact proved troublesome throughout the seizure because Montgomery Ward could attempt to capitalize on the inconsequential nature of the plant's war production. The Army Air Forces constantly was seeking to rid itself of the responsibility of supervising a business in which it had no true interest.(3)

Background of the Labor Dispute

The plant employed approximately 525 workers represented by the International Association of Machinists (AFofL), which had referred a dispute with Hummer to the NWLB in August 1942. A panel report in April 1943 was followed by a series of contradictory Regional and National War Labor Board orders that pleased neither side. Montgomery Ward refused acceptance, and in January 1944 the NWLB directed it to show cause for noncompliance. The subsequent hearing developed into an argument on the merits and was followed in April by still another NWLB order, directing Montgomery Ward to implement maintenance of membership; wage adjustments; retention of the piece-rate system, with a review of rates through the grievance procedure; the resolution of the seniority issue by collective bargaining, with NWLB mediation in case of deadlock; and the establishment of a grievance procedure, having its terminal point in arbitration.(4) The company not only refused to comply but proceeded to vigorously press a lawsuit to restrain the NWLB and the director of economic stabilization from enforcing any order.

On 5 May 1944 the machinists struck, and five days later the NWLB voted unanimously to refer the matter to President Roosevelt.(5) At the outset War Department opposition to seizure was minor because of misinformation concerning the company's production. At the same time, however, the War Department quickly sought to transfer production elsewhere and was successfully completing this transfer when it realized the relative unimportance of the facility and the fact that seizure was inevitable because of its relationship to the overall situation at Montgomery Ward. It was forced to do an about-face and cancel instructions for the removal of machine tools and dies from Hummer to other plants.

Preparations for a Takeover

When the inevitability of the seizure became apparent, the War Department, fearing management noncooperation, undertook elaborate plans for the operation of the properties. This fear seemed well justified in view of Montgomery Ward's long fight with the NWLB, its bitter opposition to the seizure of its Chicago properties by the Department of Commerce a few months earlier, and the lawsuit already filed. A very large regular staff was assembled and augmented by a special group of AAF apprentices. The chief of the AAF's Central Procurement District, Lt. Col. Nelson S. Talbott, an extremely able and personable individual, was selected as the War Department representative to head the mission.

The Takeover

At 3:00 P.M. on 21 May Colonel Talbott took possession of the properties under an executive order signed the previous day(6) and was surprised to learn that in anticipation of such action Montgomery Ward had instructed its manager to cooperate. Indeed, the following day company officials indicated their intention to cooperate fully in a token type of operation, even though the War Department retained final control over all labor matters and insisted on compliance with the NWLB order.

Termination of the strike itself presented no difficulties. Seizure guaranteed the establishment of the terms and conditions of employment at the time of the strike, and the union promised an immediate return to work. Union efforts, plus the War Department's use of spot radio announcements, made it possible to restore production to 93 percent of normal the next day.(7)

Basic Problems and Their Solution

Operating problems were almost entirely removed when Hummer agreed to reduce to writing an understanding of the agreement reached in principle the second day.(8) This agreement, which took the form of an exchange of letters rather than of a standard operating contract, provided for company operation of the properties in accordance with its normal practices and the provisions of the disputed NWLB order. The agreement did not finally dispose of profit questions nor of the rights of the parties on termination of federal possession, but it provided an expectation that termination could be completed following the receipt of a release from Montgomery Ward in favor of the United States in consideration of a waiver by the latter of its rights to an accounting. The arrangement was terminable by either party upon reasonable notice.

While the company's decision to finance operations removed the primary reason for taking physical inventories, the precaution of reviewing book values on the date of seizure and obtaining certification from public accountants was considered a prudent step. Making physical inventories was considered unwarranted in view of the comprehensive book records of assets, the disruption to production this would have caused, and the agreement with the company.(9) The business end of the seizure went so smoothly that as time went on War Department control became negligible except in the labor field, and during the last nine of the twelve months of Army operation Colonel Talbott's visits to the properties were infrequent. Possession became nominal—the mere retention of a symbolic Army presence in the form of an occupation officer.

The War Department's three main problems were implementation of the NWLB order, disposition of day-to-day labor problems, and obtaining a settlement of the labor-management dispute, thus allowing it to terminate possession. The first was entirely technical in character. The NWLB had suggested leaving many questions open to negotiations that were now impossible, and the War Department encountered considerable difficulty in applying the general phrases of the NWLB order to specific situations.(10) Once interpretations were obtained, however, it was purely a matter of draftsmanship to embody them in published terms and conditions of employment.(11) The publication of this type of document became a standard practice in all cases involving the implementation of an NWLB order.

The second problem also presented no long-term difficulties. The general manager of Hummer was easy to work with and for the most part followed War Department instructions without much prompting. The few difficulties encountered were largely the result of this manager's unconscious loyalty to principles of industrial relations inconsistent with the administration of NWLB orders. Retraining supervisors and carefully policing their actions helped overcome these problems. Occasionally, the union or Hummer, or both, advised the War Department representative of a desire to change the terms and conditions of employment, and these requests were routinely processed through the machinery prescribed by the War Labor Disputes Act.(12)

The third problem was only solved because of the incredible patience and persistence of Colonel Talbott and his labor officer, Maj. (later Lt. Col.) Daniel L. Boland. The War Department had virtually no means of bringing real pressure on the company to accept the NWLB order. Threats to undertake direct government operation where the company would realize no profit was meaningless here because under the government's tax structure the profits of Hummer were too unimportant relative to the Montgomery Ward system as a whole to make any difference. Moreover, the company had previously demonstrated its willingness to expend money in its fight against maintenance of membership and other features of NWLB orders in comparable situations. If pressed too hard, they would probably force direct government operation with the loss of any benefits derived from a token operation.(13) The only alternatives were a duration-long occupation or an agreement disposing of the underlying labor-management dispute by some other means than that ordered by the NWLB. The latter course appeared to have some chance of success since both parties were in a frame of mind to negotiate, but it was hard to know what the War Department could do to encourage them. Its activities were more or less limited to appeals to negotiate for patriotic reasons; to continual emphasis of the fact that the union could never expect a permanent solution during an Army occupation; to instituting wage surveys for determining what wage increases were permissible under the wage stabilization program; to tactful suggestions of compromises; and to facilitating meetings between the parties. Time and again the parties met only to break up in complete disagreement, requiring the War Department to painstakingly repair any damages and arrange for further meetings on a different basis. Finally, after three months of such efforts, and due to the influence of a regional representative of the Machinists union, a contract covering all disputed issues was executed and approved.(14) In this agreement the union traded maintenance of membership, arbitration of grievances, and several other points for wage increases over and above those provided in the NWLB order. The wage increases were subject to NWLB approval under the wage stabilization program but were not dependent on such. The parties, coincident with the signing of the contract, prepared a Form 10 application requesting permission to institute the new wages and submitted it to the NWLB.(15)

Under normal circumstances execution of the contract meant the end of the case, but in this particular instance this was not true for a number of reasons. In the first place, the union's waiver of the various NWLB-directed benefits greatly perturbed the international union officials, who were not consulted and who disowned the contract. Second, the local union president, Joseph Winoski, and several of his conferees, who at this time were probably negotiating with the CIO, never liked the contract and resented regional union interference. They immediately charged that the agreement was illegally consummated and threatened to strike if it took effect and the properties were returned to Montgomery Ward. In the third place, as the company and possibly local union opponents suspected, a

Maj. Daniel L. Boland

substantial portion of the wage increases would not get NWLB approval under the wage stabilization program. If true, it meant that the union had waived substantial demands, irrevocably traded away NWLB-directed benefits for benefits that were wholly illusory, and gained virtually nothing.

Almost overnight the situation faced by the War Department completely changed. An agreement validly consummated had ostensibly disposed of the dispute, and management was no longer in noncompliance with the NWLB order since the latter was superseded by a contract. At the same time, if the War Department withdrew, it was clear that a strike would follow—putting labor in violation of an NWLB order. This crisis began developing a week after the contract's execution and led to serious considerations as to whether the War Department should go before the NWLB supporting the agreed wage increases in the hope that this approval would save the situation. After much discussion this plan was shelved, although the NWLB, in the event that it found the specific wage rates unacceptable, was asked to define what rates it could approve. The War Department hoped this would lay a foundation for a modified agreement which, though less favorable, might receive employee acceptance. While the NWLB did act on this suggestion, the contract modifications were rejected by the local union.(16)

Meanwhile, the international union entered the picture because of concerns about the contract and the possibility of a revolt that could push its local members into a rival union. The executive council of the Machinists union, while vocally disapproving of an agreement waiving NWLB-directed benefits, finally concluded that the contract was legally made and binding on the local irrespective of international wishes. They then assigned a representative to the task of straightening out the situation in such a way as to permit a rapid Army withdrawal because of growing evidence of local flirtations with rival organizations. Meanwhile, sentiment in the Army Air Forces for abandoning the whole operation steadily increased, but the possible relationship of Hummer to the larger Montgomery Ward situation and the knowledge that the War Department had not accomplished its mission led to repeated decisions to continue possession "just a little while longer." This attitude was materially influenced by international union requests for continued possession so the former could continue efforts to straighten out its own local.

The international union finally decided that the only possible solution was to remove or discredit the rebel leaders. To this end Winoski, the principal local leader, was tried with the idea of suspending him from the union for dual unionism and then invoking maintenance of membership to discharge him. Sufficient evidence to justify such action was lacking, however, and this approach was abandoned. A receiver was then appointed to take over the local union, but he met very strong resistance and found himself faced with a rapidly declining membership. Many employees were no longer paying their dues, and as a last resort, the union decided to invoke maintenance of membership against all delinquent members, now numbering seventy-five. As a result, most paid up and the four men who did not were suspended. This had a very salutary effect and seriously discredited Winoski, who had claimed that the War Department would never take this course of action. A subsequent War Department survey showed that withdrawal was possible, and on 2 July 1945 the Army left without incident.(17) One of the highlights of the seizure occurred when the company wrote an open letter to the secretary of war protesting continued War Department possession and enforcement of maintenance of membership. Considering the ramifications of this letter on the larger Montgomery Ward issue, it was never answered.(18)

The original understanding with Montgomery Ward left the final settlement open, but an agreement was quickly reached and approved by the Department of Justice. Montgomery Ward retained the profits of the business and furnished the War Department with a release and indemnity agreement.(19)

Other Cases in Which the Hummer Pattern Was Followed

In every other case of management noncompliance with an NWLB order an arrangement like that at Hummer was attempted. Only in situations where management continued to refuse cooperation were other procedures developed, and of the eight subsequent employer noncompliance cases the War Department succeeded in obtaining management assistance in five. Thus it was possible to use the Hummer technique to operate the plants of Hughes Tool Company, Farrell-Cheek Steel Corporation, Cudahy Brothers Company, Cocker Machine and Foundry Company, and Mary-Leila Cotton Mills, Inc.(20) The problems encountered in these cases were largely of a labor rather than of a general operating character. The labor problems ordinarily fell into the same three classes as at Hummer: application of a disputed NWLB order, general surveillance of the conduct of daily labor relations, and disposition of the underlying dispute.

The first two classes of problems usually consisted of technical questions. The pertinent NWLB order was usually difficult to apply to existing labor situations at the time of seizure or to contemplated labor-management negotiations, and frequent recourse to the NWLB was necessary for interpretations or modifications of its orders. The lengths of most of these operations were such that applications to the NWLB for changes in the terms and conditions of employment, particularly of wages, for individuals or groups of individuals were often necessary. Most changes were jointly agreed upon between the company as the War Department's manager and the union prior to their submission to the NWLB and were not matters of particular controversy. Difficulties experienced were usually technical in character and did not arise from War Department possession. These cases, which were generally characterized by labor-management conflict, also compelled the War Department to intervene in day-to-day labor relations to insure that grievance procedures operated properly and to prevent unfair or discriminatory disciplinary action. This always presented the opportunity for constructive work, and it was often possible for the Army to improve employee-employer relations, particularly through the education of supervisors. At Cudahy, for example, training courses for foremen were introduced at the War Department's suggestion, while at Cocker the manager was persuaded to provide additional sanitary and other facilities for workers.

Although this type of operation was successful in maintaining labor peace and, with one exception,(21) in securing enforcement of NWLB orders during War Department possession, it failed to solve the third category of labor problem, the disposition of the underlying labor dispute. This constituted the greatest weakness of the token technique as there was no way to bring these operations to a close. The employees usually enjoyed full benefits, stemming from an NWLB order, and seldom were in a mood to surrender them in exchange for a less favorable but more permanent arrangement. In this respect, Hummer was the exception. The employer, likewise, had little incentive to accept NWLB orders or any other settlement. He was virtually assured of uninterrupted operations during War Department possession, as well as higher productivity and all the profits of the business—often better profits than before. Under such circumstances there was little the Army could do to bring about negotiations or compromises or to change an employer's attitude toward an NWLB order, though efforts were made. A threat to cancel the operating agreement and cut off profits was likely to be disregarded and might result in the arduous task of undertaking direct operations—something the War Department did not want to risk.

Hummer was the only case where the War Department was able to reach a solution permitting the restoration of private ownership before the end of the war.(22) At Cudahy the company reached an agreement immediately after V–J Day, directly attributed to War Department efforts. At Cocker the parties reached substantial accord, although the union was unwilling to put the settlement in writing.

In five of the six cases the Hummer method of termination was employed. In the sixth situation, that involving Hughes, no exchange of releases was possible because of War Department insistence that one important disputed item be excluded. In all of these cases it was possible to considerably reduce staff size as soon token operations were established, and the only need thereafter was for a labor officer stationed in the area to make periodic visits to deal with any new problems.

Endnotes

(1) This was true at Ken-Rad, at Twentieth Century Brass, and at Gaffney. The fact that compliance involved heavy expenditures did not prevent such an agreement at Farrell-Cheek Steel Company, Cocker Machine and Foundry Company, Mary-Leila Cotton Mills, or Cudahy Brothers Company.

(2) This was an obstacle at Montgomery Ward but not at its Hummer Manufacturing Division. It was the most important obstacle at Gaffney and a lesser obstacle at Twentieth Century Brass.

(3) Telecon, Lt Col Talbott and Maj Boland, n.d.; Two Memos, Lt Col John K. Collins, Chief, Labor Branch, IPD, for Brig Gen Greenbaum, 11 and 13 May 44, subs: War Department Interest in Hummer Manufacturing Company [*sic*] and War Department Interest in Production at Hummer Manufacturing Company [*sic*], Springfield, Ill., respectively.

(4) NWLB Directive Order, 14 Apr 44, in the Matter of Hummer Manufacturing Company [*sic*] (Springfield, Ill.) and International Association of Machinists, Local 628 (AfofL), Case 2482–CS–D.

(5) Ltr, Davis to Roosevelt, 10 May 44. This letter also gives a brief history of the dispute.

(6) EO 9443, 20 May 44, 9 F.R. 5395.

(7) PMG Rpts Nos. 1 and 2, 22 May 44.

(8) Ltr, Lt Col Talbott to Montgomery Ward and Co., 23 May 44 (App. T–1); Ltr, Harold L. Pearson, VP and Treas, Montgomery Ward, to Lt Col Talbott, 25 May 44 (App. T–2); Ltr, Lt Col Talbott to Montgomery Ward and Co., 26 May 44 (App. T–3); Memo for file by Ohly, 22 May 44, sub: War Department Operation of Hummer Manufacturing Division—Developments, par. 1b.

(9) Interim, Supplemental and Final Rpts of Lt Col Talbott, in the form of Memos for CG, AAF, 1 Jun and 1 Aug 44, and 2 Jul 45; Memo, Lt Col Talbott for CG, AAF, 23 May 44, sub: Method of Taking Inventory, and reply from Brig Gen A. E. Jones, AAF, 26 May 44.

(10) Ltrs, Brig Gen Greenbaum to Davis, 27 and 30 May 44, and replies by William Berg, Jr., NWLB, 29 May and 6 Jun 44. See also Special Labor Rpts Nos. 1 and 2 from Maj Boland to Ohly, 24 May and 1 Jun 44.

(11) Terms and Conditions of Employment for Production and Maintenance Employees of Hummer Manufacturing Company [*sic*], Springfield, Ill., now in Possession of and Being Operated by the War Department, signed by Lt Col Talbott, 1 Jun 44.

(12) Memo, Maj Boland for [Lt] Col Talbott, 28 Jul 44, sub: Supplemental Report on Labor Matters (App. T–4).

(13) Memo for file by Ohly, 22 May 44, par. 1c.

(14) Contract of 16 Sep 44 between Montgomery Ward and Local 628 of the International Association of Machinists.

(15) The story of the negotiations is told in the following documents: Ltr, J. T. Farr and Joseph Winoski, International and Local Representatives, IAM, to J. J. Saxer, General Works Manager, 1 Jun 44; Memo for file by Ohly, 13 Jun 44, sub: Hummer Manufacturing Division of Montgomery Ward and Company—Developments; Telecon, Maj Boland and Capt O'Donnell, 14 Jun 44; Telecons, Brig Gen Greenbaum and Lt Col Talbott, 14 Jun 44, at 1540, and 17 Jun 44, at 1325 and 1340; Memo for file by Ohly, 19 Jun 44, sub: War Department Operation of Hummer Manufacturing Division of Montgomery Ward; Memo for file by Ohly, 4 Aug 44, sub: Hummer Manufacturing Company [*sic*]—Developments; Memo for file by Ohly, 10 Aug 44, sub: War Department Operation of Hummer Manufacturing Division of Montgomery Ward—Developments; Telecon, Brig Gen Greenbaum and Lt Col Talbott, 26 Aug 44; Memo for file by Brig Gen Greenbaum, 1 Sep 44, sub: Hummer Manufacturing Company [*sic*]; Memo for file by Ohly, 5 Sep 44, sub: Hummer Manufacturing Division of Montgomery Ward—Developments; Maj Boland's Supplemental Report on Labor Matters (App. T–4).

(16) Memo for file by Ohly, 27 Sep 44, sub: Hummer Manufacturing Company [*sic*]—Developments; Memo for file by Maj Krim, 14 Oct 44, sub: Hummer Manufacturing Company [*sic*]—Developments, 9–14 October; Memo, Maj Boland for Col Brennan, 18 Oct 44, sub: Hummer Manufacturing Division of Montgomery Ward and Company, Inc.; Memos, Maj Boland for Col Brennan, both 23 Oct 44, subs: Hummer Manufacturing Company [*sic*].

(17) The history of the last eight months of the occupation is contained in the following documents: Memo, Lt Col Boland for Ohly, 13 Dec 44, sub: Hummer Manufacturing Company [*sic*] (App. T–5); Memo, Maj William M. Ingles, Asst Dist Manpower Off, for CO, Mid-Central Dist, Air Technical Service Command, 9 Jan 45, sub: Hummer Manufacturing Company [*sic*] Springfield, Ill.—Report on Union Attitude Toward Army Withdrawal; Memo, Ohly for Brig Gen Greenbaum, 12 Jan 45, sub: Hummer Manufacturing Division of Montgomery Ward and Company—Present Status; Memo, Ohly for Brig Gen Greenbaum, 7 Feb 45, sub: Hummer Manufacturing Division of Montgomery Ward; Memo for file by Ohly, 5 Mar 45, sub: Hummer Manufacturing Division of Montgomery Ward—Analysis of Situation (App. T–6); Memo, Lt Col Boland for Lt Col Talbott, [15 Mar 45], sub: Analysis of Labor Situation at Hummer Manufacturing Company [*sic*]; Memo, Lt Walsh for Lt Col Boland, 11 May 45, sub: Labor Situation at Hummer Manufacturing Company [*sic*]; Memo, Ohly for Brig Gen Greenbaum, 17 May 45, sub: Hummer Manufacturing Division— Developments; Memo, Walsh for Ohly, 21 May 45, sub: Labor Situation at Hummer Manufacturing Company [*sic*], Springfield, Ill., After Notification to Delinquent Members Regarding Maintenance of Membership; Minutes of Meeting, 1 Jun 45, at which delinquent employees were summoned to explain their delinquency; Memo, Lt Col Boland for Ohly, 26 Jun 45, sub: Possibilities of Termination of Possession of Hummer Manufacturing Company [*sic*]; Memo for file by Ohly, 28 Jun 45, sub: Hummer Manufacturing Division of Montgomery Ward—Developments.

(18) Ltr, Sewall [*sic*] Avery to Sec War, 31 May 45 (App. T–7).

(19) Ltr, Sec War to Atty Gen, 28 Jun 45 (App. T–8); Ltr, Atty Gen to Sec War, 29 Jun 45 (App. T–9).

(20) See summaries on the Hughes Tool Company, Farrell-Cheek Steel Company, Cudahy Brothers, Cocker Machine and Foundry, and Mary-Leila seizures (Apps. Z–3a through Z–3e).

(21) The exception is the Hughes Tool Company case, where the War Department was fearful of the consequences to production of enforcing maintenance of membership.

(22) The thinking of the War Department on the problem of how to bring these token operations to an end is illustrated particularly well in various papers of the Cudahy (App. T–10), Farrell-Cheek (App. T–11), and Cocker (App. T–12) cases. Also see Memo for file by Ohly, 18 Dec 44, sub: Status of Take-Overs and Recommended Course of Action (App. T–13).

CHAPTER 13

The Philadelphia Transportation Company Case, August 1944

The seizure of the Philadelphia transit system in August 1944 was unique in that the War Department was forced to cope with a strike after it had taken possession.(1) The seizure technique was put to its most severe test and only proved effective after many tense hours and several serious challenges to wartime labor and racial policies. Failure in this mission would have been a serious blow to government prestige because the racial factors of the underlying dispute could have caused major domestic disorders in Philadelphia and other cities.

Description of the Company

The privately owned Philadelphia Transportation Company operated virtually the entire public transportation system of the city, with the exception of taxi fleets and suburban rail lines. Its operations were divided into a so-called high-speed transit system, a combination of subway and elevated railroads having a scheduled peak of 85 trains during rush hour; a surface car system with 1,932 trolley cars and 59 trackless trolleys; and a bus system with 564 vehicles. It employed 11,000 persons and moved between 1 and 1.5 million people daily.(2)

Background of the Dispute

In March 1944 the CIO-affiliated Transport Workers Union[1] won a State Labor Relations Board election against the independent Philadelphia Rapid Transit Employees Union after a bitter fight and was certified as the exclusive bargaining agent. The losing group, having represented employees for many years, immediately sought to regain control. While the newly elected union tried unsuccessfully to work out its first contract with the company, the independent union continued fighting for control.[2] In doing so it attempted to capitalize on racial

---

[1] Organized in 1934, the Transport Workers Union merged with the AFofL-affiliated International Association of Machinists in 1936. It withdrew from this merger and joined the CIO in 1937. Its 1944 membership was 31,700. See August Meier and Elliott Rudwick, "Communist Unions and the Black Community: The Case of the Transport Workers Union, 1934–1944," *Labor History* 23 (1982): 165–97.

[2] For background, see Allan M. Winkler, "The Philadelphia Transit Strike of 1944," *Journal of American History* 59 (1972): 73–89, and Gladys L. Palmer, *The War Labor Supply Problems of Philadelphia and Its Environs* (Philadelphia: University of Pennsylvania Press, 1943).

issues it had injected into its unsuccessful preelection campaign, specifically the proposed program for the training and use of blacks, previously employed only for shop work, on operating jobs.

This training and employment program was the result of an order issued by the Committee on Fair Employment Practice (FEPC)[3] on 27 December 1943 that directed the company to cease discrimination in the employment and promotion of blacks. The company, fearful of white reaction, only paid lip service to the order until 1 July 1944, when the War Manpower Commission promulgated a plan forbidding referrals to any employer whose practices were racially discriminatory. Noncompliance with an FEPC order was prima facie evidence of discrimination. The company, in urgent need of workers, capitulated, and on 8 July announced that it was accepting applications from blacks for employment as operators of cars and buses and for promotion to operator positions on the same terms as whites.

The company implemented this statement of intention by accepting applications and beginning the training program. This was the signal for further appeals to racial prejudice by the leaders of the independent union, who were finding fertile ground among the rank and file. Their speeches were all the more effective because they contained the unfounded charge that the program was being carried on in violation of seniority rules and that it would deprive returning veterans of jobs. Unfortunately, the leaders of the newly elected Transport Workers Union were still too inexperienced to successfully counter these charges.

The crisis came at 4:00 A.M. on 1 August 1944, when eight blacks who had completed their training course were scheduled to start trial runs. At that hour virtually all bus and streetcar operators reported ill, and the city awoke to find itself without public transportation. The impact of the stoppage on the city and its war activities was immediate. The Philadelphia Navy Yard recorded absenteeism of 72 percent and in many war plants less than 50 percent of the workers reported. Service employees in several downtown buildings joined the strike, and shortly after noon the high-speed transit system employees struck.

By evening every public transportation vehicle in the city was idle, stranding thousands of people. More serious still were indications that the labor dispute could turn into a race riot. The possible ramifications of the strike were promptly realized by federal and local officials, and the U.S. attorney in Philadelphia stated, "If this strike is not settled immediately Philadelphia will

---

[3]The original committee, first established within the Office of Production Management by Executive Order 8802, 25 June 1941, and then transferred to the War Manpower Commission on 30 July 1942, was abolished on 27 May 1943, when the independent Committee on Fair Employment Practice was created in the Office of Emergency Management by Executive Order 9346. The FEPC, through ten regional offices, promoted the full utilization of manpower and sought to eliminate discriminatory employment practices, especially those relating to race. Its chairman in 1944 was Malcolm Ross. See Herbert Garfinkel, *When Negros March: The March on Washington Movement in the Organizational Politics for FEPC* (Glencoe, Ill.: Free Press, 1959); Louis C. Kesselman, *The Social Politics of FEPC* (Chapel Hill: University of North Carolina Press, 1948); idem, "The Fair Employment Practice Movement in Perspective," *Journal of Negro History* 31 (1946): 30–46; Louis C. Ruchames, *Race, Jobs, and Politics: The Story of the FEPC* (New York: Columbia University Press, 1953); and William H. Harris, "Federal Intervention in Union Discrimination: FEPC and West Coast Shipyards During World War II," *Labor History* 22 (1981): 325–47. For FEPC records, see Record Group 228, NARA.

Committee on Fair Employment Practice

experience one of the worst race riots in the history of the country." As a contingency the mayor and the governor[4] called out ten thousand auxiliary policemen and alerted the Pennsylvania State Guard. The sale of all liquor was suspended. Leading citizens of both races and groups, such as the Action Committee of the National Association for the Advancement of Colored People (NAACP) and the Interracial Committee of the Federation of Churches, took moderating actions in areas of high racial tension, but their efforts were undermined by inflammatory articles in both the black and the white press. The Army and Navy promptly made arrangements to transport workers employed in military and naval establishments, transferring fleets of buses from other locations. As the petroleum administrator for war, Interior Secretary Ickes acted quickly to make more gasoline available, and car pools were hurriedly organized by employers, trade unions, and civic groups. The National War Labor Board (NWLB) took jurisdiction of the dispute and ordered a return to work. Representatives of the NWLB and of the Army, Navy, and other governmental agencies appeared at numerous workers meetings during the day and made fervent appeals. Their pleas were met with stony silence, and international and local officials of the CIO were booed off the platform.

---

[4]The mayor of Philadelphia in 1944 was Bernard Samuel (1880–1954), who served from 1941 to 1952. The governor of Pennsylvania was Edward Martin (1879–1967), a Republican, who served one term as governor (1943–47) before leaving state politics for the U.S. Senate (1947–59).

At a mass meeting on the evening of 1 August, 3,500 workers reaffirmed their intention of continuing the strike, and during that night sporadic racial disorders occurred. More than a dozen persons were hospitalized and several hundred others were arrested. There were increasing demands for the institution of martial law, and private groups began appeals to the federal government for combat troops.

The measures taken by the police, as well as the fortuitous outbreak of torrential rains, reduced the number of incidents on 2 August and lessened the likelihood of riots, but tension remained high and the strike continued. Efforts of a group of CIO workers to operate some of the transit lines during the early evening proved unsuccessful and were abandoned after acts of violence and intimidation. The heavy rains snarled auto traffic, which was eight times normal, and gasoline reserves were reported as running low. In spite of all these unfavorable developments, however, the situation in war plants improved as people found alternative means of getting to work. Attendance at Army and Navy installations rose to only 5 or 10 percent below normal and absenteeism in war plants was down to 18 percent.

Early on 2 August the NWLB gave up trying to obtain a settlement and by unanimous vote referred the matter to President Roosevelt.(3) The War Department, anticipating efforts to designate it as the seizing agency, wrote War Mobilization Director Byrnes, strongly recommending that some other agency be named while emphasizing that measures such as the allocation of additional gasoline and the use of military vehicles could effectively remove any threat to war production.(4) This request was disregarded. It was obvious that the situation could not continue, even if war plants were managing to limp along. No agency except the War Department was qualified to handle the emergency, and instructions were issued to prepare for an immediate seizure. A proposed executive order was radioed to Roosevelt, who was traveling in the Pacific.(5)[5]

Since it appeared likely that substantial numbers of combat troops would be required for protective and operational purposes, an exception to the usual policy was made in the choice of the War Department representative. Maj. Gen. Philip Hayes,[6] commander of the Third Service Command,[7] was selected, and in this way all troop control and operating functions were centralized in one qualified person. All of the principal War Department plant seizure technicians were immediately assigned to him, including two of the Army's best men on race relations.(6)

---

[5]President Roosevelt was in Hawaii from late July through early August 1944, meeting with Admiral Chester W. Nimitz and General Douglas MacArthur for the purposes of discussing the progress and future strategy of the war in the Pacific.

[6]Maj. Gen. Philip Hayes (1887–1949) was a Wisconsin-born West Point graduate (Class of 1909), who served in infantry and artillery units in the Philippines and United States (1909–18), in the War Plans Division of the War Department General Staff (1918), and as a military instructor (1919–35). He commanded the 19th Field Artillery (1935–37) and served as assistant chief of staff and chief of staff of the Hawaiian Department (1937–41), as chief of staff of the First Corps Area (later First Service Command) (1942–43), and as executive officer to the deputy chief of staff for service commands (1943). In December 1943 he was assigned as the commanding general of the Third Service Command.

[7]The Third Service Command, with headquarters in Baltimore, Maryland, consisted of Pennsylvania, Maryland, and Virginia.

By the morning of 3 August General Hayes and his staff were in Philadelphia, had perfected their program, and were conferring with top company officials. Their plan was essentially a token operation that involved appeals to CIO leaders to convince their members to return to work, while Hayes made similar, extensive press and radio appeals. The plan also included the summoning of the leaders of the independent union, who were likewise told that the War Department expected their cooperation in running the system and in getting the men back to work, although the union would receive no official recognition. If they should inquire about the War Department's proposed course of action with respect to the employment of the black employees, they were to be told that it was legally bound by the terms and conditions of employment at the time of seizure and that this included the FEPC orders. As soon as transit operations were normalized, the training program would continue but probably only after a delay of several days.(7) Finally, the plan called for local law enforcement authorities to furnish the necessary personnel to effect the takeover. The seizure was scheduled for noon on 3 August pending approval of President Roosevelt.

Brig. Gen. Philip Hayes
(Photographed in 1943)

First Phase: Nominal Occupation

The War Department experienced extreme difficulties in reaching the president, and a misunderstanding led to the premature posting of the notice of government possession at noon. Shortly thereafter, embarrassed officers hastily removed the bills from the carbarns, minimizing a mistake that could have had serious consequences considering the prevailing high degree of racial tensions. The incident was a clear example of the type of mix-ups that often occurred at the beginning of a takeover, which always required executive authorization. The difficulty from this arrangement stemmed in part from problems of communication, particularly when the president was on the high seas and security required radio silence, and the unsatisfactory orders resulting from cryptic transmissions coming from distant places in abbreviated form. On several occasions seizing officers were put into awkward situations such as those in Philadelphia. Toward the end of the war the Department of Justice prepared an executive order for inclusion with the president's traveling papers authorizing takeovers with a space left blank for insertion by the president of the name of the company involved, thus solving the problem. At 4:00 P.M., after hours of confusion, General Hayes was authorized to take possession.(8)

The planned steps were quickly executed. Before midnight the company approved an operating contract, notices were posted, and General Hayes broadcast radio appeals for a return to work.(9) Leaders of the rump union immediately called an emergency meeting and ordered their men back to work because of a misunderstanding as to the continuance of black training, but this action was reversed at a subsequent meeting after the facts were made plain in Hayes' broadcast. Nevertheless, many CIO members reported for work on 4 August, and while streetcar and bus operations were small, the high-speed subway and elevated system was going at 30 percent of normal by 10:00 A.M. Other groups congregated at the various carbarns and appeared willing to work provided they were protected, and CIO leaders called for such protection when reports of intimidation were received. Hayes promptly asked the chief of police to assign a patrolman to every car and indicated he would call on the governor for assistance if this request was not met. When municipal authorities agreed to this arrangement and provided the necessary personnel, Hayes publicly informed employees of the fact and intimated that the federal government would use all of the sanctions available to it against anyone interfering with operations.(10) The staff felt that this protection guarantee would effect a rapid return to work.

As these events unfolded, leaders of the insurgent union began demanding precise information about the War Department's contemplated course of action with respect to the racial issue. At a subsequent conference they were informed that the War Department supported immediate resumption of the black training program, that the issue was not open for discussion, and that they, the rump leaders, had no authority or status under any circumstances. The two-hour conference made a deep impression on the rump leaders, and the overoptimistic Army staff believed they would urge a return to work.

Meanwhile, the Army staff was having some initial difficulty overcoming the FBI's policy of nonintervention in labor disputes. FBI representatives and the U.S. district attorney met with General Hayes and a Mr. Schweinhaut, a special assistant to Attorney General Biddle and an expert on the War Labor Disputes Act. The public was advised of these developments.(11)

As the day went on it became evident that in spite of increased police protection the strike was getting worse. The Army representatives were making little headway during their repeated visits to the carbarns to urge the congregated workers to return to work and now demanded federal troops, alleging, perhaps not without some reason, that police protection was insufficient. Moreover, it was apparent that strong racial attitudes constituted a stronger deterrent against a return to work than any fear of injury. Late in the afternoon the operation of the high-speed system slowed and bus and streetcar transportation stopped. By midnight no vehicles were operating. That same evening the executive committee of the rump group, and a later gathering of three thousand of their supporters, defied the government by voting to remain on strike until a written guarantee denying employment to blacks as operators was obtained. Complete paralysis of the transit system throughout the following day seemed inevitable unless new measures were adopted.(12)

Second Phase: Invocation of Sanctions

General Hayes and his key personnel worked throughout the night on a plan to meet the situation. According to this plan, announced at 6:00 A.M. on 5 August, Hayes would call upon the governor for state troops to protect vehicle operators. The Army would then dispatch military personnel to operate vehicles and obtain extra buses to replace idle trolleys. Next, Hayes would call on the Justice Department to immediately arrest violators of the War Labor Disputes Act and on the Selective Service System to cancel striker deferments. Finally, Hayes would ask the War Manpower Commission to review striker certificates of availability to prevent their reemployment elsewhere and to have them dropped from company rolls unless they returned to work by Monday, 7 August.(13)

The plan was refined that morning and cleared with the War Department and other involved agencies, all of whom offered their cooperation. It was decided at noon to substitute federal troops for state guardsmen, and the first units of combat soldiers in battle dress (they were about to embark overseas) arrived early that afternoon.[8] Before nightfall six thousand federal troops were deployed at carbarns to guard property and to accompany buses and trains. The strikers were visibly impressed.

On the suggestion of General Somervell, the ASF commander, the leaders of the CIO and the rump groups were then summoned to General Hayes' office and threatened with arrest unless prompt and full cooperation was promised. The CIO leaders quickly appeared and pledged their wholehearted support but argued that a return-to-work deadline of 4:00 P.M. that same day should be postponed until the first Monday morning shift. Hayes accepted this recommendation on the knowledge that many employees were away from the city for the weekend and were impossible to contact. The rump leaders agreed to appear but never did.

The Army program was announced in a press statement by Hayes late that afternoon. The statement incorporated excerpts from simultaneous Washington releases of the Selective Service System, the War Manpower Commission, and the Justice Department specifying the actions each proposed to take.(14) Summaries were posted in all carbarns and read at all theaters and by Hayes in short radio addresses over the nine local stations.(15) Simultaneously, machinery was set in motion to obtain both troops to replace strikers and Army motor vehicles to furnish substitute transportation. By the end of the day two thousand additional troops and large numbers of vehicles were already en route. The 3 August agreement with the company was modified to compensate the government for the use of military personnel and equipment for transportation services.(16)

---

[8]Portions of five regiments of combat troops were sent to Philadelphia from the 102d Infantry Division, stationed at Fort Dix, New Jersey, and from the 78th Infantry Division, stationed at Camp Pickett, Virginia.

Though of doubtful legality, the Justice Department obtained arrest warrants for violations of the War Labor Disputes Act, and by midnight four rump group leaders were in custody. At the same time, the attorney general announced the convening of a federal grand jury to inquire into the causes of the strike, to determine if a criminal conspiracy was involved, and to decide whether further violations of the War Labor Disputes Act existed.

The combined effects of these actions were immediate. During the night and the following day the number of moving vehicles increased hourly. The strike was collapsing, and by 6 August the Army was able to run a sizeable portion of the system itself due to the large numbers of screened, tested, and qualified federal transportation troops that had arrived in the city. More than three hundred buses requisitioned from outside points, particularly from the Fifth and Seventh Service Commands,[9] were expected for supplemental emergency service before the deadline. As a further precaution, all projected vacations of regular company employees were canceled, and telegrams were sent to those employees already on leave urging them to return to work immediately.

All through Sunday a continual stream of publicity was issued through the press, radio, and movie theaters so that all workers were aware of the government's program, and repeated staff visits were made to the carbarns, where General Hayes' message was emphasized and reemphasized. Everywhere there was an inclination to return to work, although it was prompted more by fear than by any patriotic desire to cooperate. Army headquarters was flooded with reports from hundreds of workers who wished only to state that they were returning to work.(17)

The men flocked to their posts Monday morning. Absenteeism dipped to an all-time low as more than 98 percent of the employees reported in. By 10:00 A.M., after some mix-ups in the assignment of troops to ride on the cars, transportation was moving at levels greater than at any other time during the previous four months. The actual use of military vehicles and of federal troops as operators proved unnecessary.

Although the strike was over, the Army followed through with sanctions against the ringleaders and against the small minority of workers who failed to return to work, deeming it imperative to future operations to show firmness. General Hayes ordered the discharge of the four arrested strike leaders and promptly referred their cases to the Selective Service System and the War Manpower Commission. Two of these individuals were promptly reclassified by their local boards and ordered to report for physical examinations and induction.(18)

Approximately two hundred workers, only thirty-five of whom were operators, failed to report to work. General Hayes ordered their discharge but also asked company officials to recall the men to work and advise them that an Army board of three officers would review their cases. He knew that most of these men had

---

[9]The Fifth Service Command consisted of the states of Indiana, Ohio, Kentucky, and West Virginia, with Maj. Gen. James L. Collins commanding in 1944. The Seventh Service Command consisted of the states of Colorado, Wyoming, North Dakota, South Dakota, Nebraska, Kansas, Minnesota, Iowa, and Missouri. Maj. Gen. Frederick E. Uhl served as commander until January 1944, when he was replaced by Maj. Gen. Clarence H. Danielson.

valid excuses and wanted to give each a fair opportunity to justify their failure to return to work. The hearings themselves also constituted an excellent means of making it clear that the government intended to stand firm. One hundred and ninety-one workers actually appeared. Some were either on vacation or were late in returning, others were sick, many were ignorant of the order or, because they did not work on Monday, did not understand that the order applied to them. Although some borderline cases existed, Hayes sought to avoid creating undue hardships and upheld only four discharges. The names of these individuals, as well as twenty-four others who never appeared before the board, were dropped from company rolls and were referred to Selective Service for reclassification and to the War Manpower Commission for blacklisting.(19)

Third Phase: Laying the Groundwork for Government Withdrawal

With operations restored, the War Department set out to reinstitute the training program for blacks mandated by the FEPC and to lay the groundwork for continued post-termination operations.

General Hayes delayed the resumption of the training program until 9 August to give the system a chance to return to normal, to let emotions cool, and to provide an opportunity to investigate the training curriculum, the qualifications of instructors, and the condition of equipment. Seven of the eight trainees reported; the eighth was released because of conflicts unrelated to recent events. The first trial runs went off without incident. Hayes was careful to withhold all information concerning the tests to avoid demonstrations or celebrations, and the media cooperated in keeping publicity to a minimum. The training went well, and by 14 August several of the trainees were operating passenger cars.

An extremely effective and extensive intelligence system kept General Hayes thoroughly informed of the attitudes of employees and of the city as a whole, of the possibilities of another strike, and of the degree of racial tension. Reports showed, for example, that strikers returned to work not for patriotic reasons but from a genuine fear of being fired and inducted into the Army. It was apparent, however, that the workers had learned a lesson and that no strike sentiment remained. The entire affair had a sobering effect on the city, and racial tensions dropped to a point well below normal with civic groups uniting to prevent further violence.

The Army completed a tentative schedule for withdrawal on 9 August, calling for the relief of daytime guards from cars and buses on the tenth, of nighttime guards on the eleventh, of troops patrolling transportation routes on the twelfth or thirteenth, a complete withdrawal of all troops from the city on the fourteenth, and final termination on the fifteenth. This schedule in general was followed, although final withdrawal did not occur until the seventeenth. During the interim a number of preventative measures were necessary to protect against possible strikes or riots. Until the very last the Army continued in its course of treating arrested union leaders and those responsible for illegal incidents firmly, leaving a distinct impression of the consequences likely to follow from irresponsible strike actions.

It was clear to the War Department that the major cause of the outbreak was the unsettled labor relations picture and that the racial issue was only its most obvious manifestation. Company personnel policies had caused serious discontent among workers, the CIO local was still weak, negotiations for a collective bargaining agreement dragged on for months, and the independent union was strong, militant, and irresponsible. Immediate efforts were undertaken to strengthen the Transport Workers Union. The NWLB furnished a skilled mediator to assist with contract creation and to handle labor problems. A satisfactory contract was negotiated and executed within a few days, followed by an extensive union publicity program to regain worker support and a reconciliation with the independent union. Extensive War Department suggestions for reforms were submitted and accepted by the company, including the adoption of a $250,000 program for the improvement of the appearance of the system and of worker sanitary facilities. Simultaneously, War Department representatives met with small groups from the independent union to impress on them their patriotic duty to stay on the job, the penalties that would follow deviation from Army orders, the futility of seeking recognition except through the use of established procedures (set out by the National Labor Relations Act), and the desirability of working with the CIO. These measures improved CIO control, reduced employee discontent, and minimized the likelihood of interunion warfare.

Directly, and through cooperative civic organizations, a considerable amount of racial education work was done. Ill-founded beliefs that the black upgrading program violated seniority and deprived veterans of jobs were carefully dispelled. The convening of a grand jury investigation on 9 August also undoubtedly had a salutary effect. Large numbers of employees were called as witnesses, and there was real concern among many that their prior activities might result in indictments. Such individuals were unlikely to cause further trouble while the shadow of the investigation was still over them. State and local officials and representatives of civic groups also worked with the press and employed every possible means to emphasize restraint and to remove causes of racial friction.

While another strike over the training issue appeared unlikely there was no assurance that racial incidents would not occur. General Hayes did not view his mission as covering the prevention of racial outbreaks, except as they directly affected his work of operating the transit system, and he steadfastly insisted that municipal order was exclusively the domain of city and state authorities. This forced the latter to create their own program, and Hayes actively brought all local police groups together to create an extensive program of riot control for use in any foreseeable outbreak.

When the foregoing measures were carried out or were well under way, the War Department felt safe in leaving and terminated its possession at 11:00 A.M. on 17 August.(20)

Epilogue

The resumption of private operations was accomplished without incident. The training and use of blacks not only expanded to include twelve regular operators by November but included the enrollment of many others and the promotion of twenty-six more to higher mechanical classifications. The program worked so well that the FEPC closed its case, and its regional director wrote to an Army representative, "Those of us who have ridden with non-white operators have found the public either sympathetically interested or passively unconcerned, and no incidents of real importance have been brought to our attention."(21)

The grand jury slowly proceeded with its work and, after filing a general report, indicted some thirty employees for violation of the War Labor Disputes Act, including the four already arrested. The legality of this indictment was sustained against an attack questioning the applicability of Section 6 of the War Labor Disputes Act to government operation of a transit system. The defendants pleaded not guilty but on reconsideration changed their pleas to *nolo contendere*. With the exception of the two men in the armed forces and the three others against whom charges were dropped, these employees were fined $100 each.(22)

Several of the discharged men unsuccessfully sought reinstatement in their old jobs, and the four original ringleaders brought a bill in equity against the company to force their reinstatement with back pay. The court dismissed the case, holding that the men had been discharged by the president and were not employees of the system at the time the company regained possession.(23)

Endnotes

(1) See Apps. Z–1a and Z–1b.

(2) PMG Rpt No. 2, 4 Aug 44; Memo, Capt O'Donnell for Hughes, Dir, IPD, 1 Aug 44, sub: Strike Philadelphia Transportation Company (Privately-owned).

(3) Ltr, Davis to Roosevelt, 2 Aug 44.

(4) Memo, Under Sec War for War Mobilization Dir, 2 Aug 44.

(5) Memo, O'Donnell for Hughes, 1 Aug 44; Ltr, Davis to Roosevelt, 2 Aug 44; Memo, Under Sec War for War Mobilization Dir, 2 Aug 44; Intel Estimate of Philadelphia Transit Strike and Intel Rpt re Strike at Philadelphia Transportation Company, both 3 Aug 44, at 1200, both prepared by Chief, Intel Br, Security and Intel Div, Third Service Command; Progress Rpt on Philadelphia Strike, 2 Aug 44, prepared by Domestic and Counter-Intel Br, Intel Div, ASF; *New York Times*, 2 Aug 44; *Washington Post* and *Washington Evening Star*, 3 Aug 44; and Washington *Afro-American*, 5 Aug 44.

(6) Lemuel Foster of the Industrial Personnel Division and Louis Lautier of Secretary Stimson's office. These individuals were not part of the original team but were requested by General Hayes shortly after the takeover.

(7) Telecon, Ohly with Maj Boland, Col Long, and Maj Sachse, 3 Aug 44, at 1432.

(8) EO 9459, 3 Aug 44, 9 F.R. 9878.

(9) PMG Rpt No. 1, 3 Aug 44; and Preliminary Rpt, Maj Gen Hayes for CG, ASF, 11 Aug 44, sub: War Department in Possession and Operation of the Philadelphia Transportation Company Located in and Around Philadelphia, Pa. (hereafter Hayes Prelim Rpt), and particulary Tabs I–M; Memo for file by Ohly, 4 Aug 44, sub: Philadelphia Transportation Company—Developments, 3 August.

(10) See Tabs N and O of Hayes Prelim Rpt.

(11) See Tab P of ibid.; Justice Department release, containing attorney general's statement of 4 Aug 44 on Schweinhaut's appointment.

(12) PMG Rpts Nos. 1 and 2, 3 and 4 Aug 44; Three Memos for file by Ohly, 3 and 4 Aug 44, subs: Philadelphia Transportation Company—Developments, 3 August, Philadelphia Transportation Company—Developments, 4 August Until 1000, and Philadelphia Transportation Company—Developments, 1000–1500 on 4 August; Telecons, Brig Gen Greenbaum and Atty Gen Biddle, 4 Aug 44, at 0905, 0950, and 1050, sub: Philadelphia Strike; Hayes Prelim Rpt; *New York Times*, *Washington Post*, 4 Aug 44, p. 1; *PM* and *Washington Evening Star*, 4 Aug 44, p. 1; *Washington Post*, 5 Aug 44, p. 1.

(13) PMG Rpt No. 3, 5 Aug 44, par. 4.

(14) See Tab R to Hayes Prelim Rpt (App. U–1).

(15) See Tab S to ibid.

(16) See Tab E to ibid.

(17) For developments on 5 and 6 August, see PMG Rpts Nos. 2 and 3, 6 and 7 Aug 44; Memo for file by Ohly, 8 Aug 44, sub: Philadelphia Transportation Company—Miscellaneous Developments, 6 August Through 1000 on 8 August; *New York Times, Washington Post*, and *Philadelphia Inquirer*, 6 Aug 44, p. 1; *Inquirer*, 7 Aug 44, p. 1.

(18) PMG Rpt No. 5, 7 Aug 44; Memo for file by Ohly, 8 Aug 44; *Philadelphia Inquirer, New York Times*, and *PM*, 8 Aug 44.

(19) Hayes Statement to Press, 14 Aug 44, being Tab F to Memo, Maj Gen Hayes to CG, ASF, 17 Aug 44, sub: Final Report—Termination of War Department Possession, Control and Operation of Properties and Facilities of the Philadelphia Transportation Company Under Executive Order of the President, August 3, 1944; and PMG Rpts Nos. 6–11; Memo for file by Ohly, 8 Aug 44.

(20) Final Rpt, Maj Gen Hayes to CG, ASF; Three Memos for file by Ohly, 8 and 9 Aug 44, subs: Philadelphia Transportation Company—Miscellaneous Developments, 6 August Through 1000 on 8 August, Philadelphia Transportation Company—Developments, 8 August, and Philadelphia Transportation Strike—Developments; PMG Rpts Nos. 7–15; Telecon, Brig Gen Greenbaum and Maj Gen Hayes, 8 Aug 44, at 1245, sub: Philadelphia Transit Strike; Memo, Louis R. Lautier for Hayes, 5 Aug 44, sub: Report on Activities of Various Organizations To Allay Possible Racial Difficulties in P. T. C. Strike.

(21) Ltr, G. James Fleming, Regional Dir, FEPC, to Lautier, 20 Nov 44.

(22) *New York Times*, 9 and 10 Aug 44; and stories appearing in Philadelphia papers 29 Dec 44, 9 Jan 45, and 14 Mar 1945.

(23) Telecon, Boland, Hebert, and Ohly, n.d.; Ltr, Frederic L. Ballard, attorney for the company, to JAG, 12 Dec 44; *Philadelphia Evening Bulletin*, 8 Dec 44.

CHAPTER 14

The Montgomery Ward and Company Case, December 1944

The Montgomery Ward takeover was unquestionably the most famous of the war, although it was entirely unique and derived its essential characteristics from an unusual set of circumstances that will probably never be duplicated. In the first place the seizure represented only one part of a duration-long struggle over federal labor policies between the government and Sewell L. Avery,[1] the unofficial but widely recognized spokesman of the so-called antilabor element among employers. Avery, who had filled this role since his 1935 defiance of the National Recovery Administration, had served as the chairman of Montgomery Ward and of the U.S. Gypsum Company. Montgomery Ward was the focus of major clashes, primarily because U.S. Gypsum was heavily involved in war production and was subject to legal seizure. Even so, President Roosevelt appealed personally to Avery to secure acceptance of one National War Labor Board (NWLB) order at U.S. Gypsum, and by the end of the war there were noncompliance cases pending at several U.S. Gypsum plants. These struggles grew out of basically divergent philosophies concerning the function and place of labor unions. To Avery it assumed the proportions of a crusade, manifesting itself in nearly uniform nonacceptance of NWLB orders, especially those involving maintenance of membership, checkoff, arbitration of grievances, seniority, automatic wage progression, and other provisions limiting management's authority over business and employment practices. The size and influence of the company and its persistent and militant resistance to federal labor policies demanded a federal response lest it have disastrous effects on the no-strike pledge and on federal agencies erected to maintain labor-management stability. The company was sparing no efforts or funds in its role as the ideological spearhead of management attacks on the NWLB. More than in any other case, operating decisions were of a governmental character and major policies the product of extensive interagency consultation played out in the courts and in the forum of public opinion.

---

[1]Sewell L. Avery (1873–1960) was a Michigan-born businessman educated at the Michigan Military Academy and the University of Michigan Law School. He entered business in 1894 and founded the U.S. Gypsum Company in 1901, staying with that firm until 1951. Avery became the director of U.S. Steel in 1931 and served as chairman of Montgomery Ward from 1935 to 1955. An autocratic business manager and conservative Republican, Avery was a staunch opponent of President Roosevelt and of nearly all New Deal legislation dealing with business affairs and labor-management relations.

A second factor making the case unique was the civilian nature of the business. Montgomery Ward neither produced nor distributed any goods required by the armed forces, and in fact produced very little. Its business was important to the war effort only in that it provided a distribution channel for civilian supplies to the community, many of a nonessential character. In this respect, the company was no different from thousands of other consumer retail businesses, and government efforts to prove the contrary were ineffective.(1) This concept was clearly demonstrated during the Department of Commerce seizure of Montgomery Ward's Chicago properties and in related court proceedings. Company labor difficulties, however, were important because of the potential negative effects they could have on labor relations generally and on other facilities that were critical to the war effort. There were other cases where war interests were small but none where the relationship of the company's business to the war effort was so patently slight. This affected the entire War Department approach and created serious doubts about the government's authority to seize, which in turn led to a third distinguishing feature, the government's lawsuit in support of the takeover. This lawsuit, filed to obtain a judicial declaration of legitimacy, dominated the operation. It was necessary to consider every action for its possible effect on this litigation and to study its propriety and legality under the terms of whatever court order was in force at the particular moment. This suit differed from the one at Ken-Rad because of the serious possibility that ultimately the government could not sustain its position.

A fourth factor distinguishing the case was the knowledge that a seizure would not solve the underlying dispute that caused government intervention. At best, some form of interim arrangement was possible, but this was dependent on a favorable U.S. Supreme Court decision. A potentially expansive government operation, in one form or another, seemed inevitable for the duration. These gloomy prospects influenced War Department and government thinking toward seeking legislative relief.

A final feature of the Montgomery Ward operation was that the War Department possessed only a small portion of the company's large highly integrated business, seizing only twenty of several hundred retail outlets. The War Department did not control purchasing, financing, advertising, or general management services for even those properties—let alone for the entire company. This resulted in two supervisors doing each job, and the inherent difficulties of divided control were increased because the goals of these joint supervisors not only conflicted but were often irreconcilable as each tried to use his power to place the other in a strategically disadvantageous position. In theory, the War Department directly operated the properties it possessed, but as a practical matter it did not do so. What Montgomery Ward always understood, but not the unions or the public, was that the War Department could not directly operate the company unless it seized the entire system—a step of doubtful legality with far-reaching consequences.

There were other distinctions, largely of a quantitative rather than a qualitative nature, including the greater technical intricacy of the case, the large number of labor problems, and unusually militant unions. While this case seemed to consist of one broad general dispute between Montgomery Ward and the government, the War Department discovered many smaller disputes, each with a considerable number of subissues. From an operating standpoint it was not a simple conflict over one point or even over a single NWLB directive order and, to further complicate matters, each union involved had different perspectives, objectives, and needs.(2)

Background of the Seizure

Montgomery Ward and Company was one of the largest retail outlets in the country, with 650 retail stores and mail-order houses and over 200 catalogue offices located in every state and major population center. To support the merchandising outlets, Montgomery Ward owned warehouses and special-purpose facilities and several small manufacturing plants. Net annual sales usually exceeded $500 million and net income exceeded $25 million.

The properties seized by the War Department included three of nine mail-order houses in St. Paul, Chicago, and Portland (Oregon); four retail stores in Detroit and others in St. Paul, Portland, San Rafael (California), Denver, and Jamaica (New York); the Fashion Mail Order House and the Schwinn Warehouse, located in Chicago, which served as central, systemwide purchasing and distribution points for certain merchandise; the Central Printing Department and Display Factory in Chicago; and warehouses and facilities in the above cities. Many Chicago employees not assigned to specific properties, such as the photographic department, telephone exchange, liquidating pool, and maintenance employees, were also covered by NWLB orders enforced by the War Department. The payrolls of these workers and those in the Central Printing Department and the Display Factory were controlled by the Central Payroll Department, located in the Chicago executive offices of Montgomery Ward, which was not initially seized.

Apart from the Schwinn Warehouse and the Fashion House, the War Department lacked control over the buying end of the business, the accounting and advertising offices, and the facilities and personnel who planned purchases or handled the merchandise the War Department distributed through the retail outlets. Similarly, goods bought and distributed by Schwinn and the Fashion House went to retail outlets under Montgomery Ward's control. These facts—the War Department's lack of control over its supplies and Montgomery Ward's dependence on Schwinn and the Fashion House—would, when coupled with regular accounting procedures, create one of the War Department's most difficult problems. Under established procedures a mail-order house or retail store that received an order for a item it did not have accepted the customer's payment and remitted it to the company's central business office. This office forwarded the order to another mail-order house that stocked the item or, as in the case of all fashion items, to Schwinn or the Fashion House. The facility receiving the requisition was given credit on Montgomery Ward's central books—but never any cash. If it could not fill the order, it, and not the collecting mail-order house, was responsible for furnishing a refund check. During the war these refund operations were significant because the scarcity of consumer goods meant that many orders went unfilled. This resulted in the mail-order portion of the business operating at a loss, paid out in large measure through refund checks drawn at Schwinn and the Fashion House. For the year ending 31 January 1945, for example, $105 million was returned to customers on unfilled orders, and as civilian goods became scarcer the volume of these orders increased. The consequences of refunding money through the Fashion House became one of the chief problems of the War Department during the seizure.

In 1941 Montgomery Ward employees were largely unorganized, and the company was noted for its strong opposition to labor unions in general. As time went on, however, several unions made progress, particularly the Retail Clerks International Protective Association (AFofL)[2] in San Rafael; the International Brotherhood of Teamsters, Chauffeurs, Warehousemen, and Helpers of America (AFofL)[3] in the Portland and Detroit warehouses; the United Mail Order, Warehouse, and Retail Employees Union of the United Retail, Wholesale, and Department Store Employees of America (CIO)[4] in Detroit, Denver, Chicago, and Jamaica; the International Longshoremen's and Warehousemen's Union (CIO)[5] in St. Paul; and the Warehouse Employees' Union (AFofL)[6] also in St. Paul.(3) Of these unions, one was eventually certified as the exclusive bargaining agent for employees at each Montgomery Ward outlet, usually after prolonged struggles with the company in the courts or before the National Labor Relations Board (NLRB). Montgomery Ward accepted unionization grudgingly or, more aptly, on its terms. The War Department seizure of Montgomery Ward was an attempt to force compliance with an increasing number of NWLB orders attempting to resolve fundamental labor-management disputes that the company uniformly rejected. Only occasionally, once after a personal plea from President Roosevelt, did Montgomery Ward moderate its extreme position.(4) The company's nationwide advertisements attacking the NWLB and the administration's labor policies became famous, as did its frequent clashes with government agencies. Dealings with the NWLB over a period of two years had convinced Montgomery Ward

that the board is a means by which special privileges are granted to labor unions. The union members of the WLB are men chosen for leadership of the unions, and have actually advanced the interests of the unions. The so-called public members have consistently joined with the union members to support the demands of organized labor. The so-called industry members are committed to a policy of supporting the majority vote of the union

[2]The AFofL-affiliated Retail Clerks International Protective Association was organized in 1890 as the Retail Clerks National Protective Association of America, adopting its present name in 1899. Its 1944 membership was 80,600, and its president between 1926 and 1947 was C. C. Coulter.

[3]The AFofL-affiliated International Brotherhood of Teamsters, Chauffeurs, Warehousemen, and Helpers of America was originally organized in 1899 as the Team Drivers International Union, adopting its present name in 1940. Its 1944 membership, under President Daniel J. Tobin, was 550,500.

[4]The United Mail Order, Warehouse, and Retail Employees Union of the United Retail, Wholesale, and Department Store Employees of America was chartered by the CIO in 1937. Its 1944 membership was 60,000.

[5]The International Longshoremen's and Warehousemen's Union was organized in 1933 as the International Longshoremen's Union, adopting its present name when it joined the CIO in 1937. Its 1944 membership, under President Harry Bridges, was 39,500.

[6]The AFofL-affiliated Warehouse Employees' Union merged with the International Brotherhood of Teamsters, Chauffeurs, Warehousemen, and Helpers of America in 1944.

members and the union-dominated public members. The WLB has always claimed that its orders are law and must be obeyed. It has coerced innumerable employers into acceptance of its orders by threatening the seizure of their businesses. When Ward's brought suit to have the board's order declared illegal, the board asked the courts to dismiss the case. In direct contradiction to its previous claims of power, the board's plea to the court was that its orders were not "legally binding," but were only "advice" which Ward's need not accept. The purpose of this plea was to deny Ward's trial before the courts. The issues raised by Ward's case against the WLB are judicial questions which, under the Constitution, only the courts may decide. The WLB, by asking you to force Ward's to comply with its order while seeking to deprive Ward's of an opportunity for a hearing in the courts, has demonstrated its lack of respect for our Constitution and the fundamental rights which the Constitution guarantees.(5)

The first showdown came in April 1944, when Secretary of Commerce Jesse H. Jones[7] was ordered to seize and operate Montgomery Ward's Chicago properties.(6) The company claimed that the certified union no longer represented a majority of workers and refused to deal with it or to accept an NWLB directive calling for a temporary extension of the collective bargaining agreement until the NLRB could hold a new election. This refusal caused a strike that was ended through a federal takeover that was generally recognized as a fiasco that made the government look ridiculous. It has no counterpart except in the comic operettas of Gilbert and Sullivan for the simple reason that the Commerce Department lacked the War Department's seizure experience.(7) An hour before leaving to direct the takeover, Under Secretary of Commerce Wayne C. Taylor was given a copy of the War Department plant seizure manual and a short briefing from Army experts. The War Department succeeded in shifting its responsibility as the seizing authority to another agency but was still in the unenviable position of having to supply troops to carry out the takeover. The subsequent forcible ejection of Sewell Avery by federal troops from Montgomery Ward's premises while still sitting in his office chair is a part of American folklore, and a photograph of this incident became *Life* magazine's "Picture of the Year."

The public gained the impression, which it never lost, that the Army had seized Montgomery Ward, and this fact, together with the subsequent criticism and ridicule, were important in mounting War Department opinion toward the later seizure and the manner of its conduct.(8) The Commerce Department seizure was terminated in less than two weeks after an NLRB-arranged election reestablished the incumbent union as the bargaining agent at the Chicago properties. The government hastily retreated from the scene, abandoning as moot a variety of legal proceedings instituted when it took possession.(9)

Extensive congressional investigations and reports covering the legal and labor aspects of the operation followed in both houses, with findings split along party lines. During these investigations the War Department seized the Hummer

---

[7]Texas banker and businessman Jesse H. Jones (1874–1966) served as Roosevelt's secretary of commerce (1940–45), having previously served as chairman of the Reconstruction Finance Corporation (1933–39). He was concurrently chairman of the Federal Loan Agency (1939–45).

Secretary of Commerce Jesse H. Jones

properties, which Montgomery Ward did not resist, but this minor government victory had little effect on the larger Montgomery Ward conflict.

Conditions at the Chicago Montgomery Ward did not improve. The recertification of the United Mail Order, Warehouse, and Retail Employees Union was insignificant as the company again refused, for slightly different reasons, to extend the old contract—as the NWLB directed—insisting that a new one be negotiated. Montgomery Ward maintained virtually all the substantive provisions of the old agreement except maintenance of membership, the voluntary checkoff, grievance procedures, and seniority—in effect, all of the provisions of the earlier NWLB order accepted by the company after President Roosevelt's personal appeal. The excepted provisions constituted the principal issues in most of Montgomery Ward's cases.

The situation in Chicago remained tense through the summer and fall, complicated by new problems at other properties in Portland, San Rafael, St. Paul, Denver, Jamaica, and Detroit. By the beginning of December NWLB orders covered several of these locations, but all were rejected by Montgomery Ward.(10) These directives differed from those relevant to Chicago in several respects. In Chicago, except for a small number of employees who received three to five cents per hour increases, employees were committed to the old contract, which merely required Montgomery Ward to reinstate a few rights that from the average employee's viewpoint appeared unimportant. The average employee did not really see any personal benefits from maintenance of membership, the checkoff, a terminal point of arbitration in the grievance procedure, or seniority protection. To the union, however, these rights meant life or death. The orders covering the other properties directed more obvious and tangible benefits—wage increases, retroactive for two years in some cases; equal pay for equal work; holiday pay; and vacation and overtime benefits. They also *inter alia* dealt with such matters as nondiscrimination, restoration of veteran's jobs, health and safety measures, union bulletin boards, stewards committees, free gowns and uniforms, regular positions, company visits of union representatives, and waiting periods before the right to earn commissions accrued. Still another difference between the situation at Chicago and the other locations was a difference in union strength. At Chicago the Retail Employees Union was weak following a long and unsuccessful struggle with the company, and its remaining strength was concentrated at the Schwinn Warehouse. In other cities the certified unions were much stronger.

The Retail Employees Union, among others, pressed for government intervention and received support from many CIO groups that viewed Montgomery Ward's opposition as a union-busting tactic and a threat to the no-strike pledge. Sympathy strikes that threatened war production began in Detroit and Chicago, followed in mid-December by a strike of Montgomery Ward employees in Detroit that caused extensive violence and company court actions. Government officials now concluded that the company's actions jeopardized the entire wartime labor policy and could force a labor vote to end the no-strike pledge. On 20 December the NWLB voted to refer the matter to President Roosevelt.(11)

Preparations for a Takeover

After the third week of December seizure appeared inevitable, for no other technique was available and, in spite of lessons learned in the first Montgomery Ward case, time was too short to permit the enactment of special legislation. The lack of time presented a number of problems including: What agency would conduct the operation? Was the seizure of nonwar-related properties legal under the War Labor Disputes Act or other wartime statutory and constitutional powers of the president, and could it survive a court test? Would the seizure affect the entire business or just properties under NWLB orders?

The Commerce Department's selection in the first Montgomery Ward takeover followed a vigorous fight by the War Department to prevent its own designation as the seizing agency,(12) a task that required Under Secretary Patterson and Secretary Stimson to directly intervene with President Roosevelt and War Mobilization Director Byrnes.(13) Similar efforts were undertaken as soon as a second seizure became imminent, based on the arguments that it was unthinkable for the Army to intrude in civilian economic matters not of its concern and that seizure, at best a dangerous use of executive authority, could seriously damage Army prestige, troop morale, and manpower levels at a critical time considering that the Battle of the Bulge was then in progress.(14) In spite of these arguments the Commerce Department's experience made it difficult for the War Department to suggest a better alternative, and in spite of Stimson's protests Roosevelt concluded that only the Army had the personnel and experience to undertake the operation.

Following Roosevelt's decision, the War Department began to consider the extent of the seizure at an interagency level, a process seriously handicapped by the lack of any real understanding by those outside the War Department of what a takeover entailed. Many thought that a seizure merely required that the War Department place an officer in charge of the properties to give orders to company officials who would explicitly obey. While sheer fantasy, this reasoning was typical of what the War Department encountered. The NWLB, supported by Attorney General Biddle and War Mobilization Director Byrnes,[8] proposed seizing the

---

[8]In December 1944 Byrnes became the director of the Office of War Mobilization and Reconversion (OWMR), created by an Act of Congress on 3 October (58 Stat. 788; 50 U.S.C. 1651) to supersede the Office of War Mobilization, with the additional duties of overseeing the transition to a peacetime economy. John W. Snyder succeeded Byrnes in 1945. For OWMR records, see Record Group 250, NARA.

entire Montgomery Ward system on the practical grounds that doing so avoided a situation of dual control. The War Department understood this reasoning and acknowledged that seizing the whole system might prove necessary, but pointed out that a systemwide takeover was useless if company officials refused cooperation. Control over company books and central offices would not make the business run, and the War Department had to take whatever course appeared most likely to assure the successful operation of any seized properties and the fulfillment of its mission. At the time the Army lacked the personnel to operate a thousand different establishments located all over the country, and its desires prevailed, particularly when the Department of Justice concluded that legal justification for an executive order of broader scope was extremely weak.(15) The Justice Department agreed with the idea of a token operation but encouraged the War Department to make plans for a direct operation.

In addition to discussing the extent of the seizure, the question of timing was also considered. The labor agencies called for the earliest possible date, not realizing the extent of preparation required, the necessity for coast-to-coast personnel movements, the difficulties inherent in obtaining funds, and the desirability of advance Justice Department preparation.(16) The War Department succeeded in postponing seizure for a week, but not until 1 January as desired, a date that would have facilitated the handling of accounting problems. It also considered the question of whether to size Montgomery Ward's affected properties simultaneously or gradually over a period of several days, with the Chicago or Detroit facilities receiving first attention. The first alternative was adopted.(17)

The question of possible court action to support the government takeover was discussed in detail with Attorney General Biddle, who argued that any lawsuit or injunction should wait until such time as Montgomery Ward committed acts interfering with War Department operations. Biddle reasoned that equity relief lacked any basis in advance of overt acts of opposition by Montgomery Ward and was unwilling to risk a case solely on the basis of Sewell Avery's past conduct. The War Department's opposing view ultimately prevailed, however, and it requested that a declaratory judgment suit establishing the seizure's legality be instituted on seizure with ancillary injunctive relief for specific problems coming later if Montgomery Ward took steps in opposition. Taking the initiative would show the government's desire for obtaining a judicial determination concerning the propriety of its action and thus counter the inevitable charges of illegal and arbitrary action. This course of action also enabled the government to choose its forum and type of proceeding and to benefit from the element of surprise.

A further question related to financing the seizure. The War Department had no funds to underwrite the operation of a civilian retail business, but this problem was solved when President Roosevelt allocated $5 million from his emergency fund to the secretary of war. Stimson then deposited these funds with the Defense Supplies Corporation, a wholly owned subsidiary of the Reconstruction Finance Corporation, under an agreement whereby he could obtain on request $750,000 to $1.5 million for the payment of travel, per diem, and other War Department expenses for which no appropriations were available. The balance of the $5 million was to serve as a source for the interest on and as security for advances to the War Department. The latter was not to exceed $50 million and was to meet business expenses to the extent not covered by receipts.(18) The restrictions of this agreement, together with the limiting instructions issued by the War Department budget officer on the use of funds, eventually became great obstacles in carrying out the mission.(19)

Two other interagency discussions centered on whether to exclude Montgomery Ward executives from the properties by force if they refused cooperation and, if so, who would exert this force. The War Department took the solitary position that no useful purpose was served by excluding managers unless they interfered with operations and that a forced removal could produce unfavorable incidents reminiscent of the Commerce Department's takeover. The War Department was equally adamant that if force proved necessary local police, the FBI, or some other civil authority and not federal troops must employ it. The attorney general took precisely the opposite position but grudgingly agreed that troop use was a last resort.(20)

The framing of the executive order raised numerous technical problems that were not novel but did receive more than ordinary attention because of the doubtful legality of the seizure, the intended federal lawsuit, and the War Department's desire for maximum flexibility.(21) The order consequently went through several revisions before an acceptable draft was adopted.

The War Department commenced basic planning as soon as it became clear the seizure was going to be an Army mission,(22) but the discussions that followed were largely a waste of time because higher authorities had not yet made the basic decisions upon which intelligent plans depended.(23)

The War Department plan was a product of the interagency conferences of 20–28 December and simply called for a token seizure accompanied by simultaneous court action. If this token seizure proved ineffective in the first few days, conversion to direct operation by the Army would follow.

Preparation for this mission was difficult because of the large number of problems involved and the many possible contingencies. Moreover, very little was known about the character of the business, the probable reaction to government occupancy by supervisors, the relationship of the seized properties to the entire system, or the feasibility of operating these properties as separate entities. Hundreds of technically qualified persons were alerted for action, and the adjutant general's office made extensive searches to find officers with experience in the retail merchandising business. In addition, each War Department component responsible for a technical phase of plant seizure rapidly augmented groups previously trained for general takeover operations. Fiscal preparations were complicated by questions about the source of funds employed and the possible need for large-scale disbursing activities. Many of these administrative arrangements were managed admirably by the deputy chief of staff for service commands.[9] Maj. Gen.

---

[9]Col. (later Brig. Gen.) Joseph F. Battley (1896–1970) served as the deputy chief of staff for service commands from 6 January 1944 to 15 June 1945. He joined the Virginia National Guard in 1917 and, but for two months of service in France in 1919, served in the United States with the Chemical Warfare Service between
Continued

Brig. Gen. Joseph W. Byron
(Photographed in early 1944)

Joseph W. Byron,[10] chief of the Special Services Division, ASF, was named the War Department representative and participated in the planning stages while acquainting himself with his newly gathered staff.

First Phase: Token Takeover and the Lawsuit

On the morning of 28 December 1944 the seizure of Montgomery Ward's properties (except for the Fashion House, the Schwinn Warehouse, and several minor facilities) took place. Soon after the U.S. attorney in Chicago filed a bill of complaint for a declaratory judgment in the Federal District Court for the Northern District of Illinois. General Byron and his staff were courteously received by Sewell Avery in Chicago, and Byron's deputies were accorded similar treatment by the branch managers in other cities. Byron stated his mission and furnished Avery with documents indicating his authority to take possession. Avery asked for time to consider his company's legal position, indicated clearly that his cooperation was unlikely, declared the seizure illegal, and requested a War Department withdrawal. These statements and requests were repeated at each seized branch. Nowhere, however, was there any resistance, and at the company's Chicago headquarters Avery made office space available for Byron's use as the Army went about its job of posting notices of possession.

At noon, when Avery requested another extension to consider his answer, General Byron demanded that the company furnish additional office space and accounting personnel, convene a meeting of supervisors for the purpose of receiving War Department instructions, inform branch representatives to follow War Department orders and directions, deliver up all books and records of seized facil-

---

1918 and 1932. He also was assigned special duty with the National Recovery Administration and the Works Progress Administration (1933–36), the Office of the Assistant and later Under Secretary of War (1939–41 and 1941–42), the Office of the Quartermaster General (1941), and the Headquarters, Services of Supply (later Army Service Forces) (1942–43). In May 1943 he became the executive officer to the deputy chief of staff, ASF.

[10]Maj. Gen. Joseph W. Byron (1892–1951), a 1914 West Point graduate, left military service in 1919 for private business after serving with the cavalry during World War I. In a civilian capacity he served as an advisor to the National Recovery Administration, the export control administrator, and the War Production Board. He rejoined the Army in July 1942 and was assigned to the Headquarters, Services of Supply, for duty with the Army Exchange Service, becoming chief in August. He took over as the chief of the Special Services Division, ASF, in October 1943.

ities, and refrain from interfering with operations or from giving instructions contravening War Department orders. At 3:00 P.M. Avery told Byron he could not accept any demands or cooperate until a court established the legality of the seizure. When similar demands were ignored elsewhere, it became plain that Montgomery Ward had developed a pre-seizure plan that precluded both physical resistance and any form of cooperation. Avery issued no orders to employees advising cooperation with the War Department, tacitly advocating a course of passive resistance. His actions violated no law, and it seemed clear that he hoped to embarrass the government and make it impossible for the Army to operate the properties.(24)

Second Phase: Direct Operation of Seized Properties

It was obvious that the War Department's mission would remain unfulfilled if Avery's tactics went unchallenged, but the court refused to hear the case prior to 8 January, removing any hope of immediate judicial relief. Under these circumstances, the government was fortunate in having a three-day New Year holiday weekend to conduct a series of interagency planning conferences. It was agreed that the War Department must undertake direct operation of the seized properties on 2 January. The Army planned to ask the managers to cooperate in running their facilities for the War Department and advised them that if they refused, prompt discharge and expulsion from the properties would follow. Should they refuse to leave, local police or FBI agents would attempt to impress them with the seriousness of their actions and gather evidence for prosecution under the War Labor Disputes Act. The Army would then gather other top supervisors and inform them that the manager in question was discharged, that the government was in full possession, and that they must obey government instructions. If they refused to work for the government, they would also face discharge and possible sanctions in the form of War Labor Disputes Act prosecutions, the cancellation of draft deferments, and blacklisting by the War Manpower Commission. The Army further planned to post notices of these sanctions and to take physical custody of the books at each facility and then close them as of the time of seizure. Plans were made to change safe combinations and to ask persons responsible for their contents to turn them over to government representatives. If they refused, the Army representative would take the contents, but only if it was possible to do so without violence. The Army planned to take custody of payroll records and all incoming mail. Finally, War Department representatives would gather small groups of employees and inform them of their new status and ask, but not require, each person to take a loyalty oath to the government. Steps were taken to assemble teams of officers capable of filling top positions vacated by noncooperative executives at each facility. While all this was taking place, the War Department would release a press statement reflecting the vigorous character of the Army's actions. Finally, the Army decided to exercise only limited control of outgoing products and materials at the seized premises to prevent any disruptions that could harm the business.(25)

The War Department plan was developed in a very short time because it was felt that the Army could no longer temporize. As a result, thoroughness was sacrificed for speed and many fundamental problems that later caused difficulties were ignored. Moreover, uncertainty as to company reactions made even the definition of such problems difficult.

The plan was placed in effect at all Montgomery Ward properties at the opening of business on 2 January 1945. The action was announced publicly through the release of a report from General Byron to Secretary Stimson outlining his course of action.(26) The drastic nature of the government's move took Montgomery Ward by complete surprise and for several hours managers and their subordinates were confused and uncertain about what to do. Avery's directions evidently had not contemplated this type of a "blitz." As the day went on, however, a pattern—obviously dictated from the company's Chicago headquarters—became clear: Store managers refused to cooperate and were discharged. Nearly every subordinate indicated a willingness to cooperate, and by nightfall most had accepted appointments as War Department employees. All books and cash, to the extent that they were physically available at premises actually seized, were taken into custody.(27)

These steps placed the War Department in reasonable control of the seized premises but in no way guaranteed effective operation. Montgomery Ward could still cripple Army operations by refusing to supply merchandise, and it was deemed imperative to obtain company cooperation. Many officials clung to the hope that the drastic nature of the government's action might change Avery's attitude. More conferences were arranged, as was a direct appeal to the board of directors.(28) The results were not encouraging. In the belief that company motives for noncooperation were directly tied to its desire to make the best possible court case, the War Department renewed its efforts to change Avery's mind after the court hearing. Montgomery Ward did indicate a willingness to cooperate as long as wage increases did not become effective until the actual court decision, but because of its fear that any agreement might somehow prejudice its position in court, a settlement was impossible.(29) Nevertheless, during further conferences Montgomery Ward again showed the desire to reach informal working agreements on several matters, particularly those of a fiscal nature that required joint action by both Montgomery Ward and the War Department to prevent chaos. Over the next few months a pattern of limited cooperation was established, covering such areas as time payment accounts receivable reflecting transactions occurring prior to War Department seizure, the furnishing of accounting information, the annual inventory, claims against carriers, FHA transactions, and rationing questions.(30)

In spite of the limited agreements obtained by the War Department, its position was still precarious because of the interrelationship of the various units in the Montgomery Ward system. It was easy for Montgomery Ward to intercept cash to which the War Department was entitled, forcing the latter to use its funds for business and operational expenses and causing a cash deficit. This situation was aggravated by the extension of War Department control to the Schwinn Warehouse and the Fashion House in January. These properties, although covered by the executive order and NWLB orders, had not yet been seized but were taken now because War

Department control of such merchandise sources, on which nonseized facilities depended, could enhance the War Department's bargaining power and protect against attempts by Montgomery Ward to cripple operations by refusing to supply merchandise. The step was unquestionably sound at the time but was retracted with embarrassing consequences following a negative court decision.

Subsequent dealings demonstrated the War Department's clear dilemma in not controlling the entire Montgomery Ward system. The company purchased the merchandise that filled the retail shelves, which in turn required that the War Department pay cash to the vendors or risk nondelivery. According to company procedures, revenues from sales at retail outlets were credited to their accounts in the company's central accounting office, which was not under War Department control. The War Department had no access to this money and could not, in view of the doubtful legality of its possession, accept the risks involved in refusing to deliver merchandise to Montgomery Ward's properties. Not only could Montgomery Ward charge that the War Department was disrupting a going business and inconveniencing customers, but it might also retaliate by cutting off the flow of all goods to retail outlets under War Department control. The latter step would either drive the War Department out of business or force the seizure of the entire system. The operation of the Schwinn Warehouse and the Fashion House caused an increasing cash deficit to the government and in effect meant that Montgomery Ward was forcing the War Department to finance company operations with government funds. Moreover, the amount of the deficit was entirely within Montgomery Ward's control as they determined the extent to which inventories were built up at either facility. For all the War Department knew, Montgomery Ward might overpurchase and leave it holding a lot of unsalable goods.(31)

Meanwhile, the labor officers took steps to put applicable NWLB orders into effect. This proved difficult because of the ambiguity and complexity of the orders themselves and because of War Department fears of taking any action that could prejudice or complicate court proceedings or adversely affect public opinion. Nonetheless, the War Department increased employee wages before the court decision—except for workers in Portland and those with the Central Printing Department, Display Factory, and maintenance group in Chicago, where records were not under War Department control or where NWLB orders needed revision. In addition, the War Department announced that several general provisions of the NWLB orders were operative, including those relating to maintenance of membership, grievance procedures, seniority, the checkoff, overtime rates, and holiday and vacation pay. The first three items required the occurrence of a specific case where they could be applied and were not immediately acted on. Similarly, but for different reasons, no decisive steps were taken to make the checkoff operative. An actual checkoff depended on the union submission of employee authorization cards and their verification by a check against the payroll. It also depended on mechanical accounting and disbursing arrangements on the first payday of the month—the day specified by the NWLB's order as the one where deductions were made. Although such a payday occurred within a week after Army occupation, other arrangements were incomplete at that time and when the district court rendered its decision in late January. Failure to implement these provisions, which were published as part of the terms and conditions of employment at most of the properties, was to present serious questions about their status under the later district court rulings.

The company appealed to the public for support at the outset, attacked the NWLB, and accused the War Department of inefficiency, with disruption of its business, and with various illegal actions. While Montgomery Ward's publicity was bitter and highly critical, the War Department limited its publicity to factual statements devoid of recrimination or accusation.

The District Court Decision

Everyone realized that nothing conclusive would occur until the district court rendered a decision. This ruling, depending upon its character, could terminate the seizure or force Montgomery Ward to cooperate. Elaborate plans were necessary for each of four possible eventualities:(32) a decision that War Department possession was legal; a decision that War Department possession was illegal coupled with an order to surrender possession; a decision that War Department possession was illegal, unaccompanied by any order to surrender control; and a decision dismissing the complaint or disposing of the proceeding without a determination of the merits. The War Department expressed its view in letters to President Roosevelt(33) and General Byron(34) that in the case of the second or third instance the War Department should promptly surrender possession unless the court issued an affirmative order permitting continuance of possession pending further court proceedings. The likelihood that any such affirmative order would follow an adverse decision appeared so remote that it was dismissed.

Discussions with other agencies raised serious opposition to War Department plans. Attorney General Biddle felt that relinquishing possession would prejudice the lawsuit and recommended to President Roosevelt that the War Department remain in possession, despite an adverse decision pending interagency consultation. Biddle further suggested that if withdrawal seemed likely, President Roosevelt should issue a statement explaining the situation while indicating that he proposed to seek remedial legislation.(35) The Justice Department argued, however, that any final decision had to await a close examination of the court's decision. The attorney general's objections resulted in more interagency meetings on 26 January, in at which the agencies present took strong exception to the War Department's views and essentially agreed with Biddle's opinion. The War Department replied that it could not accept the onus of further possession under the existing circumstances and would withdraw unless Biddle publicly rendered an opinion affirming the War Department's position.(36)

Meanwhile, with Roosevelt out of the country and therefore unable to break the impasse, the court handed down rulings totally upsetting all plans—in effect creating the one situation both the War Department and Montgomery Ward considered least likely and virtually impossible. The court declared the War

Department's possession illegal(37) but granted a motion for a stay of proceedings after judgment that was hastily submitted by the U.S. attorney.(38) The order simply read: "Ordered that all proceedings after the judgment entered in the above entitled action are hereby stayed until the final determination of appeals by the plaintiff from said judgment." Standing alone this meant absolutely nothing, but a clue to the court's meaning was found in the judge's statement that "the purpose [of the motion of the plaintiff] is very obvious; that they want to be sure in view of my decision and ruling this morning that the situation as it exists there will not be disturbed any more than it has been." This apparently meant the maintenance of the status quo until appealed, but the status quo was not defined and the judge was neither specific in his order nor in his accompanying remarks.

The War Department dilemma was complete, and it was powerless to move. Whatever it did, criticism was sure to follow since the NWLB directives were only partially in place and the unions were dissatisfied at the lack of full enforcement. Montgomery Ward could attack War Department attempts to alter existing labor conditions and might well succeed in upsetting the strange and precarious stay order. The situation at the Schwinn Warehouse and the Fashion House also appeared untenable since there were no wage increases or other similar benefits under the applicable NWLB orders. Possession of these units could bring no material advantages to the union involved, at least not if the stay order precluded enforcement of maintenance of membership and the institution of the checkoff. At the same time, their operation was costing the government hundreds of thousands of dollars each week. Whatever hope there was that a favorable court decision would make possible a successful War Department showdown with Montgomery Ward was gone. It was also obvious, despite the stay order, that Montgomery Ward would repeatedly and publicly capitalize on the court's decision that War Department possession was illegal.(39)

Third Phase: Operations Under the District Court Decision

The War Department had to take four steps to remedy this situation: issue a clear statement from the Justice Department of the legal rights and duties under the court's ruling, plan a course of action regarding labor matters and the Schwinn Warehouse and the Fashion House, renew efforts to reach an operating agreement with Montgomery Ward, and obtain an early and final adjudication of the court case.

General Byron was authorized to negotiate an operating agreement under which receipts from operations he controlled would be given to Montgomery Ward, with the understanding that these monies would be used for business purposes pending disposition of the government's court appeal. The agreement was to guarantee the government's right to an accounting for profits if the court proceedings finally sustained the validity of the executive order and was to make arrangements for the continuance in effect, or placement in escrow, of wage increases previously instituted by the War Department.(40) Byron also addressed a letter to Attorney General Biddle, soliciting his opinion on a number of issues—the legality of War Department possession under the stay order; maintaining previously adopted wage increases, irrespective of whether they were paid from current operating receipts or from government funds; expending government funds for the operating of the Schwinn Warehouse and the Fashion House, even though cash disbursements exceeded and would continue to exceed cash receipts, and recovering this money through litigation of problematical outcome; and the extent and character of any other limitations on War Department powers and rights to carry out the executive order.(41) Simultaneously, the War Department informed the Justice Department of its strong support for an immediate and direct U.S. Supreme Court appeal.

General Byron soon concluded that reaching an operating agreement was impossible because Montgomery Ward would not cooperate after its court victory. Byron did, however, end Army operations at the Schwinn Warehouse and the Fashion House, feeling that the risk of losing further federal funds far outweighed any employee benefits. He conditioned his recommendations on Justice Department decisions that War Department actions did not violate the executive order, did not render the court case moot or prejudice further proceedings, did not impede an early appeal, and did not violate the stay order.(42) An interagency conference endorsed his recommendations provided that discussions were held with the unions.(43) The unions had no objection to nongovernment operation of the Fashion House but did object to similar action at the Schwinn Warehouse, where its membership was strong. Nonetheless, the Army abandoned active operation of both units while retaining nominal possession.

Clarification of labor policies took much more time and was never fully accomplished. At an interagency conference following the court decision certain tentative understandings were reached, but the resulting memorandum was never dispatched because the War Department wanted to remain flexible until Attorney General Biddle rendered his opinion.(44) On 16 February 1945 Biddle stated that the stay order

. . . seems to me to authorize you to continue possession and operation of the plants . . . to the same degree and in the same manner as has been the case since December 28, 1944. In other words . . . the court intended that the status quo . . . should be continued. . . . The duty not to disturb the status quo is the only limitation that I understand the stay imposes upon you pending the final disposition of the case on appeal. We have hitherto informally advised you that the concept of the status quo should be construed with strictness and that you should not attempt to extend your possession or control by taking any steps that differ in kind from those that you have taken prior to January 27, 1945. In other words, I think you should err on the side of caution by staying well within the limits of the action that you have taken prior to January 27, 1945.

He went on to state that wage increases, including those announced through overtime, holiday, and vacation policies, could continue and be paid from federal funds. He closed by confirming the desirability of halting Army operation of the Schwinn Warehouse and the Fashion House.(45)

No specific ruling was requested or given on maintenance of membership or the checkoff since the earlier interagency discussions reached a conclusion not to enforce these provisions. The former was not pressing because the unions were not eager to invoke it, but the same was not true with the checkoff in the case of the United Retail, Wholesale, and Department Store Employees of America. While the other unions were content to enjoy the wage and other material benefits that War Department possession brought without pressing for the checkoff, this organization felt obliged to wage a vigorous fight for such a step. Its membership and funds at Chicago and other locations where it was the bargaining agent were dwindling, and its Chicago members had not received wage or other substantive benefits from the Army's occupation comparable to those elsewhere. The union needed the checkoff to avoid extinction and argued that it did not alter the status quo because the procedure had become effective on its earlier inclusion in the terms and conditions of employment and because the continued effectiveness of the checkoff was not impaired by the failure for mechanical reasons to make an payroll deduction before the court decision. Finally, the union argued, the checkoff was a voluntary matter affecting only those employees who wanted to pay their dues in this fashion, which in no way affected or damaged Montgomery Ward or violated a stay order meant only to protect the company. The union's persistence increased when the U.S. Supreme Court refused to review the district court's decision, making it clear that judicial proceedings and the general stalemate would continue for months.

The issue came to a head in March, when Biddle informed the United Retail, Wholesale, and Department Store Employees of America that he did not object to instituting the checkoff. This placed the War Department representative in an extremely embarrassing situation and led to his recommendation that Biddle put his statement in writing.(46) After some disagreement at headquarters(47) the question was submitted to Biddle,(48) who replied on 12 April that "the stay order does not prevent you from establishing in accordance with Executive Order 9508 the voluntary checkoff as provided by the applicable directive orders of the National War Labor Board."(49) In spite of this ruling the War Department hesitated. Biddle's letter had not stated, as desired, that Secretary of War Stimson was under a specific obligation to place the checkoff in effect. Under Secretary Patterson and General Greenbaum wanted a specific direction given so that the onus of this action was not on the War Department,(50) and they decided to submit the question to Frederick M. Vinson,[11] director of the Office of Economic Stabilization (OES), to ascertain whether Harry S. Truman's 14 April 1945 succession to the presidency had changed the administration's overall policy.(51) Vinson, after unnecessary hesitation and a further conference with impatient union leaders, ordered that the checkoff take effect at the beginning of May.(52) As it was already too late to meet the first May payroll, the Army went ahead, amid bitter union criticism, with the mechanical arrangements necessary to implement it the following month.(53) The unions were asked to submit member authorization cards for a payroll check, but their untimely announcement led to violent public

---

[11]Frederick M. Vinson (1890–1953), a Kentucky native, was a member of Congress (1923–29 and 1931–37), an associate justice of the U.S. Court of Appeals for the District of Columbia (1937–43), director of the Office of Economic Stabilization (1943–45), secretary of the Treasury (1945–46), and chief justice of the U.S. Supreme Court (1946–53).

Frederick M. Vinson

criticism by Montgomery Ward alleging a violation of the stay order. In June the checkoff was again postponed, this time because of a growing feeling that it might prejudice the imminent circuit court decision.

The problem of the checkoff was illustrative of the generally untenable War Department position following the district court's decision. As long as the propriety of War Department possession was doubtful, it was confronted with the dilemma of trying to carry out parts of the executive order, such as the checkoff, while doing practically nothing to enforce the order as a whole. Pursuit of the first mission invariably prompted Montgomery Ward to charge the War Department with illegal and arbitrary actions that might prejudice the latter's case on appeal, while pursuit of the second led to union allegations that the War Department was not carrying out the president's instructions. Such a situation inevitably produced frayed tempers and led to charges and countercharges. Montgomery Ward continued its negative publicity against the Army, and the Retail Employees Union sent a series of increasingly critical letters to the War Department and the administration.

As the spring advanced the War Department increasingly felt that other agencies were forcing the Army to make decisions they were afraid to make.(54) The stalemate led to repeated War Department demands for renewed administration efforts to obtain legislation making NWLB orders enforceable, thus removing the need for continued War Department possession of Montgomery Ward or other companies in noncompliance with government labor policies.(55)

Little progress was made on the major issues after the court decision but many minor questions, including numerous labor problems, were addressed. This necessitated repeated recourse to the NWLB for directive interpretations and to the Justice Department for precise definitions of the scope of Army activities.(56) However, the earlier pattern of informal arrangements with Montgomery Ward for handling specific items continued, which greatly facilitated operations and removed many troublesome fiscal and accounting problems.

The Circuit Court of Appeals Decision

As the date for a U.S. Circuit Court of Appeals decision approached, the War Department asked about what actions it should take in case of each possible ruling. In May it advised the Justice Department that termination should quickly follow an adverse appeals court decision because such a ruling could place it in an impossible position during the interim before the case was heard by the U.S. Supreme Court.(57) At the same time, General Byron was formulating his own ideas. He was basically against the idea of requesting a stay if the court decision were adverse but was for terminating possession at once, with the disbursing officer removing all funds from the State of Illinois to protect them from attachment by Montgomery Ward.(58) He felt that such a course was acceptable to the unions since the United Retail, Wholesale, and Department Store Employees of America considered their position intolerable as long as War Department operations were hamstrung by a stay order.

General Byron devised detailed plans for other contingencies including an adverse decision with no court application for permission to remain in possession; an adverse decision, but with permission granted to remain in possession; an adverse decision, but one granting the War Department permission to remain in possession, but not to continue operation and control; an adverse decision, but with government notice to the court of the intent to file an application to remain in possession; a favorable decision, with the court granting a stay to the company; a favorable decision, but with the court denying a stay to the company; or a favorable decision, but notice by Montgomery Ward to the court that a stay application was intended at some future time.

In response to the War Department plans Attorney General Biddle revealed that any course of action following the court's decision involved policy matters unrelated to the litigation,(59) and at his suggestion the matter was referred to the director of war mobilization.(60) Interagency conferences followed at which several decisions were reached about possible federal responses,(61) and these decisions were sent to Byron together with tentative approval of the detailed programs he had submitted.(62)

On 8 June 1945 the U.S. Circuit Court of Appeals reversed the district court decision and ruled that the War Department possession was legal under the War Labor Disputes Act.(63) Montgomery Ward promptly moved for a stay of mandate until the U.S. Supreme Court decision, hoping to prevent the further implementation of NWLB provisions and the reoccupation of the Schwinn Warehouse and the Fashion House.(64) General Byron immediately requested and received the authority, with qualifications,(65) to proceed with his plans as soon as the court dealt with Montgomery Ward's motion.(66) Three weeks later the court ruled against Montgomery Ward and for the government.

Fourth Phase: Operations Under the Circuit Court Decision

The court's ruling gave the War Department the legal right to take any necessary action to enforce the executive order, but in reality the situation was not that simple. The mere existence of a legal right, itself awaiting a Supreme Court ruling, did not solve War Department problems. Montgomery Ward controlled the bulk of the system, including purchasing, advertising, accounting, distribution, and general business management, and therefore profits, and could yet place obstacles in the way of successful Army operations. By the mere fact of its presence and control the War Department could apply NWLB orders, but it could not insure the necessary profits to continue operations or to pay retroactive wages. Moreover, renewed Army control of the Schwinn Warehouse and the Fashion House threatened again to produce serious cash deficits.

War Department objectives now included the enforcement of NWLB provisions not previously in effect, the prevention of a cash deficit, and the accumulation of sufficient net operating income to pay retroactive wages. These objectives, however, operated at cross-purposes. Full enforcement of the NWLB orders meant resumed control of Schwinn Warehouse and Fashion House operations, which unless accompanied by a radically new approach would cause a cash deficit making the accumulation of income for retroactive wages impossible. To make matters worse, the War Department was advised of a probable future extension of its possession to six other Montgomery Ward facilities where NWLB orders were being ignored.

The denial of Montgomery Ward's motion prompted General Byron to institute the checkoff and apply the NWLB orders. On three points—retroactive wages, extension of control to the Display Factory and other facilities, and resumption of operations at the Schwinn Warehouse and the Fashion House—nothing was done pending a 23 June interagency conference in Washington.(67) The retroactive wage problem was very confused because of doubts about how to compute operating income and whether it was possible, assuming sufficient income was available, to make retroactive payments while this income was in Montgomery Ward's custody.(68) The agency participants(69) conferred and reported all pertinent information to Secretary Stimson, President Truman, and newly appointed OES Director William Davis(70), with the request for further instructions. Due to more pressing events surrounding the end of the war, however, no action was taken.

The conferees wanted to resume operations at the Schwinn Warehouse and the Fashion House, but their desire was dampened by the realization that these operations could cost the War Department $4 million a month unless Montgomery Ward paid for merchandise and services. An agreement appeared remote unless the Army absolutely refused to deliver merchandise and services except on cash payment by Montgomery Ward, and this could result in company reprisals such as refusals to furnish merchandise and services to Army-operated installations. If Montgomery Ward did refuse deliveries, the War Department would face going out of business or would have to develop its own management and purchasing staff, an impractical task requiring many months. Another alternative was to assume control over Montgomery Ward's central offices and perhaps the entire system, also a mammoth undertaking requiring an untold number of Army personnel.(71) The conferees, taking into account these facts plus the doubtful legality of seizing the whole system and of the proposed extension of control to other properties, agreed on a more general course of action. The Retail Employees Union was advised that the War Department would make all NWLB orders effective, including the payment of retroactive wages, as soon profits were available and accounting work was complete, and that Army operation of the Schwinn Warehouse and the Fashion House would not resume until after the Supreme Court decision to avoid the danger of increasing the cash deficit. The War Department believed this explanation, coupled with the disclosure of federal intentions to extend control to new properties where the union had bargaining rights, would suffice, but if dissatisfaction was expressed, the NWLB would work to solicit union acquiescence. Moreover, it renewed efforts to obtain agreements covering the soon-to-be-seized properties, whereby Montgomery Ward would pay for services and merchandise delivered, and it agreed to explore the possibility of extending federal control to the Central Printing Department, Display Factory, and maintenance workers.(72)

The local union violently objected to the government decision and indicated that a strike at Schwinn was inevitable. A subsequent federal investigation indicated that this was no bluff(73) and that only a resumption of War Department control could avert a walkout, despite the fact that a strike under these circumstances violated the War Labor Disputes Act. Meanwhile, conferences with Montgomery Ward revealed that if the company were faced with either paying for goods and services from the Schwinn Warehouse and the Fashion House or not receiving them, they would capitulate. Maj. Gen. David McCoach, Jr., who replaced General Byron in July, recommended resuming control of the Schwinn Warehouse,(74) extending control to other Chicago units such as the Display Factory but not the Fashion House, and forcing a showdown.

On 19 July the War Department acted on General McCoach's recommendations. When Montgomery Ward grudgingly acquiesced,(75) the War Department decided to seize the Fashion House(76) on 1 August. Montgomery Ward was notified of the impending seize,(77) but to the War Department's chagrin refused both its approval and merchandise payments. The Army then refused deliveries, causing Avery to take his case to the public.(78)

This created the kind of crisis the War Department had always feared. If Montgomery Ward remained firm, the Fashion House business would dwindle to nothing, causing a drop in profits and worker layoffs. Moreover, Montgomery Ward might refuse merchandise to other War Department properties, requiring a seizure of the entire system.

The War Department decided to play a waiting game while publicly responding to Avery's attacks(79) and making plans for companywide federal operations.(80) It was still felt that Montgomery Ward could not afford the crippling effects on its business of protracted resistance, but it was further agreed that because the War Department had acted it must remain firm and, if necessary, seize the entire company.(81) This thinking was sound, and within ten days Montgomery Ward capitulated completely.(82) From then on Army operations experienced fewer difficulties.

Extension of War Department possession to the new properties under NWLB orders was delayed because many of these cases were not yet processed, and it was felt that one executive order rather than a series was preferable. War Department plans for the extension were well under way when V–J Day occurred.(83)

Fifth Phase: Operations After V–J Day

The end of the war changed the entire War Department outlook toward the Montgomery Ward operation, because peacetime military control of private facilities in general was indefensible and was even more so when the industries were engaged in nonessential civilian endeavors. The War Department promptly recommended an executive order terminating control at all seized facilities, and on 25 August Executive Order 9603 directed that a general withdrawal take place as soon as possible "as determined in each case by the officer by whom the property . . . is held and operated for the government, with the approval of the Director of Economic Stabilization."(84) The order appeared to clear the way for early termination of possession, and instructions were issued to General McCoach,(85) but serious obstacles developed from the need for the OES director's approval and from union protests.(86) At this point Secretary of Labor Lewis B. Schwellenbach[12] began to argue that he was entitled to the right to attempt settlements in each case before any seized properties were restored, in spite of War Department efforts to explain to him that seizures were the result of the complete failure of every branch of government to accomplish this objective. In particular, Schwellenbach maintained that delaying the return of the Montgomery Ward properties until all possibilities for reaching a settlement were exhausted was vital because of the far-reaching effects the case had on general labor conditions. The labor secretary also supported the NWLB position concerning payment of retroactive wages, feeling that any other course constituted a government breach of faith and that the War Department should remain in possession until net operating income was sufficient to pay the amounts due. The Justice Department finally settled the matter by suggesting that the War Department hold the properties until a final settlement was worked out with Montgomery Ward, and while War Department officials protested and again asked permission to withdraw, two months passed before approval was granted.(87)

The Department of Labor's opposition to termination, based on the hope of a settlement, was short-lived as Schwellenbach was completely unsuccessful in bringing Avery and the unions together. Both the NWLB public members and the director of economic stabilization, himself having endured many trying experiences with Montgomery Ward, also felt such efforts were futile and realized that these labor-management conflicts were best fought out and settled on the economic battlefront.

Retroactive wages were a different question. Everyone, including the War Department, agreed that it was desirable to pay retroactive wages if sufficient funds were available, even after the properties returned to Montgomery Ward's control. On 30 August, however, General McCoach incorrectly reported to his superiors,(88) and eventually to President Truman, that War Department operations to date had not earned sufficient income to pay any part of the retroactive

---

[12]Lewis B. Schwellenbach (1894–1948) was a Wisconsin-born lawyer who served in the U.S. Senate (1935–40) and as a judge for the Eastern District of Washington. He was labor secretary from 1945 until his death.

wages and were unlikely to do so in the near future.(89) This led to discussions about paying the wages from the president's emergency fund following an executive order to that effect, which Truman favored, but the attorney general advised the president that neither emergency funds nor any other monies were available for this purpose.(90)

These delays put the War Department in the impossible position of having to make decisions on how to deal with pressing labor problems and how to operate Montgomery Ward properties effectively and profitably without knowing the duration of government control. The War Department looked more and more ridiculous in the eyes of the employees, while Sewell Avery commenced a new campaign to oust the Army by making public a letter to Secretary Stimson, in which he stated that "this excuse that the war effort

Secretary of Labor Lewis B. Schwellenbach

would be 'unduly impeded or delayed' unless Wards' properties were seized was never justified . . . . The war has ended and even this excuse no longer exists." To make matters worse, the Army was forced to maintain nearly two hundred officers and civilians on duty at Montgomery Ward at a time when demobilization was a major goal.(91)

Nevertheless, the delay did give the War Department an opportunity to seek an interim settlement with Montgomery Ward on many outstanding issues. The War Department, for example, had expended more money than it had collected, because of the company's ability to retain sums entitled to it; however, the company countercharged that it had suffered substantial damages from allegedly illegal War Department actions. The difference between the two claims was several hundred thousands dollars, but neither claim took into account profits to which the War Department was entitled or which Montgomery Ward might have captured nor any right of the company for fair and just compensation for the use of its property. Montgomery Ward agreed to pay the War Department several hundred thousand dollars as part of an interim settlement, and a proposed exchange of letters was prepared fully preserving the rights of both parties.

President Truman finally decided that continued Army operation served no useful purpose and that the question of retroactive wages merited special legislation. Permission was given to withdraw from all Montgomery Ward properties at midnight on 18 October 1945, and General McCoach terminated possession after implementing the agreement with the company and receiving their check.(92)

Termination of possession, however, did not end the case, and many months of work remained to solve the fiscal ramifications, to determine whether net operating income was realized, and to convert the interim agreement into a final settlement,(93) which involved protracted litigation. Audit and verification of the value of the returned properties and of War Department cash expenditures and receipts was necessary. The War Department felt that a final settlement, assuming that no net income was earned, would involve only accounting problems once the U.S. Supreme Court determined the legality of War Department possession and the validity of certain claims of both sides.

Two subsequent events changed the picture. First, the Supreme Court refused to review the circuit court decision because termination made the case moot. This action complicated the final adjustment because some damages claimed by Montgomery Ward were valid only if the court declared the seizure illegal. The second development was more far-reaching. The War Department learned that a profit, perhaps a substantial one, was earned during their possession, and, if so, sufficient income existed to pay some or all of the retroactive wages covered by the executive order. In view of the contrary information provided President Truman and the decisions made by the War Department and other agencies based on the idea that no money existed, the discovery was embarrassing and raised a host of new problems. Such income, to the extent it existed, was now in Avery's hands and no other alternative funding source existed. A new lawsuit against Montgomery Ward to recover the money loomed, together with the prospect of another legal battle reaching to the Supreme Court.(94)[13]

A few fiscal, legal, and labor problems encountered at Montgomery Ward deserve mention because they presented more substantial difficulties here than in any other case. These problems were due to the pervasive, extreme anti-union attitude of key Montgomery Ward supervisors that made providing full-time labor officers for the number of establishments involved nearly impossible. As a result, extensive instructions were developed for the guidance of War Department personnel at each property, as well as rules and procedures for Montgomery Ward personnel employed by the Army.(95) The problem was largely one of policing a broad set of instructions for the company as a whole rather than disposing of individual questions at each property as they arose, although both types of facilities were involved.

In spite of Army instructions many interesting labor questions developed. Montgomery Ward, for example, categorically prohibited all union activity on its property and refused to permit union bulletin boards. Both positions were illegal under the National Labor Relations Act, as the union contended, and NLRB rulings were obtained and promptly placed in effect. As another example, several unions made repeated demands for information concerning individual wage rates paid by Montgomery Ward and related matters dealing with wage inequities. The

---

[13]See Frank M. Kleiler, "The World War II Battles of Montgomery Ward," *Chicago History* 5 (1976): 19–27. Kleiler states that with the end of the seizure Montgomery Ward's case against the government became moot, and the U.S. Supreme Court denied the company's petition for review, never ruling on the merits of the case.

company uniformly refused such information, raising three questions. First, did the National Labor Relations Act require the furnishing of this information? The NLRB said no. Second, would furnishing the information constitute a change in the terms and conditions of employment prevailing at the time of seizure? The Justice Department said no. Finally, would furnishing the information make good industrial relations practices? The NWLB said yes, and Montgomery Ward provided the information.

Another interesting development was the United Retail, Wholesale, and Department Store Employees of America's submission of comprehensive demands for changes in all of the basic terms and conditions of employment prevailing at certain premises akin to the kind normally made in a collective bargaining proceeding. Before any decision on this issue was necessary, however, the operation ended. There were also the usual troubles, more serious in this case than in any other, of applying the applicable NWLB orders. At the Portland facility, for example, the order the Army had to enforce applied to a wage situation that had changed the year before War Department possession. This necessitated the assignment of special NWLB representatives and War Department labor officers to rewrite the order completely and resubmit it for NWLB approval under Section 5 of the War Labor Disputes Act.

An unusual feature of the Montgomery Ward case was the material effect on Army operations of two unrelated strikes. One involved a teamsters strike in Chicago that almost paralyzed Montgomery Ward properties and led Sewell Avery to the conclusion that if his operations were important enough to the war effort to justify seizure, then certainly any outside strike required government intervention under the War Labor Disputes Act as well. The matter was referred to the attorney general with a request to institute any applicable civil or criminal proceedings against the striking teamsters, but no prosecutions resulted. This teamsters strike was a series of secondary boycotts and involved the printing concerns that published the Montgomery Ward catalogue. The stoppage threatened a complete disruption of the operations of the mail-order business and seriously jeopardized the earning of net operating income to pay retroactive wages. Its consequences were so serious that very strong representations for positive, curative action were made to the NWLB. After much irreparable damage was done, the strike was finally terminated and it was possible to complete publication of the catalogue.

Endnotes

(1) Ltr, Biddle to Roosevelt, 22 Apr 44 (reported in *New York Times*, 27 Apr 44, p. 14); Ltr, Davis to Sen Byrd, 29 Apr 44 (reported in *PM*, 2 May 44); *New York Times*, 2 May 44, p. 1; and *PM*, 2 May 44.

(2) Principal source materials available are the daily reports to the provost marshal general; interim and final reports of the War Department representative; headquarters files of the Industrial Personnel Division, the judge advocate general, the fiscal director, and the under secretary of war; recorded telephone conversations between headquarters and the field; and the Chicago records. These sources cover general developments and give detailed accounts of the many technical phases.

(3) Cities bracketed after each union are not meant to indicate that the properties in these cities were the only ones organized by any of these unions. They merely indicate which properties taken by the War Department were represented by each group.

(4) Ltr, Davis to Roosevelt, 13 Apr 44. For a labor view of the company, see *PM*, 24 Apr 44.

(5) From Ltr, Montgomery Ward to Roosevelt, reproduced as a half-page advertisement in most important newspapers on 26 and 27 April 1944 and in the *Washington Evening Star*, 26 Apr 44. This letter was in reply to Telg, Roosevelt to Avery, 23 Apr 44, in which the president asked Montgomery Ward to comply with an NWLB directive order. This exchange immediately preceded the Commerce Department's seizure of the Chicago properties.

(6) EO 9433, 25 Apr 44, 9 F.R. 4459.

(7) Memo for file by Ohly, 29 Apr 44, sub: Montgomery Ward— Miscellaneous Developments.

(8) To verify the popular impression that the Army had taken charge, one need only refer to the daily press of the period. Large banner headlines of 27 April 1944 read: "Troops Seize Montgomery Ward Plant" (*Washington Post*), "Army Bodily Ejects Ward Boss" (*Washington Times Herald*), "Montgomery Ward Seized by Troops" (*PM*), and "Troops Seize Montgomery Ward as It Rejects Roosevelt Order" (*New York Times*).

(9) *New York Times*, 15 Apr–15 May 44.

(10) Ltr, Davis to President, 20 Dec 44, and accompanying Memorandum to the President on the Montgomery Ward Directive Orders Which Have Not Been Complied With, same date (App. V–2).

(11) Ltr, Davis to President, 20 Dec 44 (App. V–2).

(12) Ltr, V. L. Almond, Bureau of the Budget, to Sec War, 13 Apr 44, forwarding for comment proposed executive order entitled "Authorizing the Secretary of War To Take Possession of and Operate the Establishments and Facilities of Montgomery Ward and Company Located in Chicago, Ill."

(13) Memo for file by Ohly, 22 Apr 44, sub: Montgomery Ward and Company; Memo, Under Sec War for War Mobilization Dir, 12 Apr 44, sub: Proposed War Department Seizure of the Chicago Facilities of Montgomery Ward (App. V–3); and Memo, Sec War for War Mobilization Dir, 14 Apr 44 (App. V–4).

(14) Memos, Sec War for War Mobilization Dir, 18 Dec 44 (App. V–5), and 22 Dec 44, sub: Montgomery Ward and Company (App. V–6); Memos for file by Ohly, 20 and 22 Dec 44 and 10 Jan 45, subs: Montgomery Ward—Developments.

(15) Memos for file by Ohly, 20 and 22 Dec 44 and 10 Jan 45.

(16) Memos for file by Ohly, 20 and 22 Dec 44 and 10 Jan 45. See also Memo, Ohly for Brig Gen Greenbaum, 23 Dec 44, sub: Montgomery Ward Timing of Take-Over.

(17) Memo, Ohly for Brig Gen Greenbaum, 23 Dec 44.

(18) Memorandum of Agreement Between the Secretary of War and Defense Supplies Corporation, 28 Dec 44 (App. V–7), and Supplemental Agreement, 19 Mar 45.

(19) Interim Report Covering Army Operation of Certain Plants and Facilities of Montgomery Ward and Company, Inc., Chicago, Ill., 28 Dec 44 Through 24 Mar 45, pp. 23–26 and various apps., esp., 35–42 (hereafter cited as Byron Interim Rpt, 24 Mar 45).

(20) Memo for file by Ohly, 10 Jan 45, pars. 6c and 7b.

(21) Ibid., par. 2.

(22) The Industrial Personnel Division's ideas as to the basic analysis that should be made were incorporated in Memo, n.d., sub: Some Thoughts on the Montgomery Ward Situation (App. V–8).

(23) Plan for the Seizure and Operation by the War Department of the Properties of Montgomery Ward and Company, Inc., 23 Dec 44.

(24) PMG Rpts Nos. 1 and 2, 28 and 30 Dec 44.

(25) Memo for file by Ohly, 10 Jan 45; PMG Rpts Nos. 3 and 4, 31 Dec 44 and 1 Jan 45.

(26) Memo, Maj Gen Byron (thru CG, ASF) for Sec War, 1 Jan 45, sub: Preliminary Report on War Department Operation of Certain Plants and Facilities of Montgomery Ward and Company, Inc. (App. V–9).

(27) PMG Rpt No. 5, 3 Jan 45.

(28) PMG Rpts Nos. 7 and 8, 5 and 6 Jan 45; Memo, Maj Gen Byron for Montgomery Ward Board of Directors, 5 Jan 45, in Byron Interim Rpt, 24 Mar 45, app. 49.

(29) Teletype, Maj Gen Byron to CG, ASF, Attn: Lt Gen Styer, 9 Jan 45 (App. V–10).

(30) Byron Interim Rpt, 24 Mar 45, apps. 30–42; PMG Rpts Nos. 13–15 and 17, respectively 10, 12, 12, and 15 Jan 45.

(31) Memo for file by Ohly, 10 Jan 45, par. 23; Byron Interim Rpt, 24 Mar 45, p. 28.

(32) Memo, Maj Gen Byron for CG, ASF, Attn: Lt Gen Styer, 18 Jan 45, sub: Policy and Planning in the Event of a Court Decision Declaring Government Possession of the Plants and Facilities of Montgomery Ward and Co., Inc., To Be Illegal (App. V–11); Memo, Brig Gen Green for Lt Gen Styer, 20 Jan 45, sub: Conferences With Department of Justice Concerning Action in the Event of an Unfavorable Decision by the U.S. District Court in the Case of U.S. vs. Montgomery Ward and Company; Memo, n.d., sub: Course of Action in Montgomery Ward Case in the Event of a Court Decision Which Does Not Establish the War Department's Right to Possession Affirmatively.

(33) Ltr, Sec War to President, 24 Jan 45 (App. V–12); Memo, Under Sec War for Sec War, 24 Jan 45, sub: Montgomery Ward and Company, Inc.

(34) Memo, Brig Gen Greenbaum for CG, ASF, 25 Jan 45, sub: Policy and Planning in the Event of a Court Decision Declaring Government Possession of the Plants and Facilities of Montgomery Ward and Co., Inc., To Be Illegal; Memo, Maj Gen Byron for Lt Gen Styer, same date and sub. See also Memo, Maj Gen Byron for CG, ASF, 26 Jan 45, sub: Problems and Action Following Favorable Court Decision (App. V–13).

(35) Ltr, Charles Fahy to Roosevelt, 25 Jan 45.

(36) Memo for file by Brig Gen Greenbaum, 26 Jan 45, sub: Montgomery Ward and Company, Inc.; and proposed Memo, Under Sec War for Sec War, same date and sub.

(37) U.S. vs. Montgomery Ward and Company, 58 Fed. Sup. 408 (D.C., N.D., Ill. 1945).

(38) See App. V–14.

(39) Ltr, [Col] Kuhn, [Maj] Sachse, and [Lt Col] Boland to Ohly, 28 Jan 45 (App. V–15).

(40) Memo, Lt Gen Styer for Maj Gen Byron, 29 Jan 45, sub: War Department Operation of Certain Plants and Facilities of Montgomery Ward and Company, Inc.—Additional Instructions.

(41) Ltr, Acting Sec War to Atty Gen, 1 Feb 45 (App. V–15a).

(42) Memo, Maj Gen Byron for CG, ASF, 2 Feb 45, sub: War Department Operation of Certain Facilities of Montgomery Ward and Company, Inc.—Negotiations With the Company Concerning Company Operations and Recommendations Concerning Operation of Non-revenue Producing Properties (Schwinn Warehouse and Fashion Mail Order House) (App. V–16).

(43) Memo, Maj Gen Byron for CG, ASF, 3 Feb 45, sub: Conference of 3 February 1945 in the Office of the Director of Economic Stabilization With Reference to War Department Operation of Certain Non-revenue Producing Facilities of Montgomery Ward and Company, Inc. (Schwinn Warehouse and Fashion Mail Order House) (App. V–17).

(44) Draft Memo for Maj Gen Byron, 28 Jan 45, sub: Instructions on Matters of Labor Policy and Future Action in Conducting the Operation of the Facilities Now in Your Possession (V–17a).

(45) Ltr, Atty Gen to Sec War, 16 Feb 45 (App. V–18).

(46) Memos, Maj Gen Byron for CG, ASF, both 22 Mar 45, subs: Union Request for Check-off of Dues at Montgomery Ward's Properties Being Operated by the War Department; Memo, Acting CofS, ASF, for Under Sec War, 26 Mar 45, sub: Montgomery Ward and Company Union Request for the Institution of the Voluntary Check-off.

(47) Memo, Ohly for Brig Gen Greenbaum, 27 Mar 45, sub: Montgomery Ward Voluntary Check-off.

(48) Ltr, Under Sec War to Atty Gen, 27 Mar 45 (App. V–20).

(49) Ltr, Atty Gen to Sec War, 12 Apr 45 (App. V–23).

(50) Memo, Ohly for Brig Gen Greenbaum, 16 Apr 45, sub: Montgomery Ward Check-off. This memo indicates that there was a sharp division of opinion within the War Department on the matter.

(51) Memo, Brig Gen Greenbaum for Ohly, 23 Apr 45.

(52) Memo, Ohly for Brig Gen Greenbaum, 26 Apr 45, sub: Montgomery Ward Check-off; Memo for file by Ohly, 26 Apr 45, sub: Montgomery Ward Conference With Leo Goodman; Memo for file by Ohly, 30 Apr 45, sub: Montgomery Ward Conference of Under Secretary With Representatives of the United Retail, Mail Order and Wholesale Workers Union [sic]; Memo, Under Sec War for CG, ASF, 30 Apr 45, sub: Montgomery Ward and Company, Inc.—Introduction of Check-off; Telecon, Maj Gen Lutes and Maj Gen Byron, 20 Apr 45, at 1800; Memo, Ohly for Maj Gen Lutes, 1 May 45, sub: Montgomery Ward and Company—Introduction of Check-off.

(53) Memos, Ohly for Brig Gen Greenbaum, 5 Feb and 21 Apr 45, subs: Montgomery Ward, Unfinished Business, and Montgomery Ward, respectively; Memo, Maj Gen Byron for CG, ASF, 23 Apr 45, sub: Urgent Need for Court Action (App. V–25).

(54) Ltr, Irving Abramson to Under Sec War, 10 May 45 (App. V–24), and reply, 22 May 45.

(55) Memo for [Brig] Gen Greenbaum, 7 Apr 45, prepared by the Chicago staff to summarize the situation (App. V–22); Memo, Lt Col Boland for Ohly, 31 Mar 45, sub: Labor Matters Requiring Attention and War Department Action on Montgomery Ward Mission (App. V–21); Memo, Brig Gen Greenbaum for Under Sec War, 20 Apr 45, sub: Montgomery Ward.

(56) Memo, Lt Col Boland for Ohly, 31 Mar 45 (App. V–21).

(57) Ltr, Brig Gen Greenbaum to Hugh Cox, 5 May 45.

(58) Memo, Maj Gen Byron for CG, ASF, 12 May 45, sub: Plan of Action Following Decision by Circuit Court—Hearing (App. V–26a); Memo, Lt Col Boland for Ohly, 14 May 45, sub: Arguments in Favor of Government Policy of Not Attempting To Obtain a Stay Order From the Circuit Court of Appeals.

(59) Memo for file by Ohly, 12 May 45, sub: Montgomery Ward and Company—Action To Be Taken in the Event of Adverse Court Decision.

(60) Ltr, Sec War to War Mobilization Dir, 14 May 45 (App. V–27).

(61) Memo, Brig Gen Greenbaum for Under Sec War, 23 May 45, sub: Montgomery Ward Case—Action After the Court Decision (App. V–28); Memo, Lt Col Myers for Brig Gen Greenbaum, 28 May 45, sub: Report of [Lt.] Col. Sachse Concerning Montgomery Ward Case.

(62) Memo, CofS, ASF, 25 May 45, sub: Plan of Action Following Decision by United States Circuit Court of Appeals—Montgomery Ward and Company Case.

(63) U.S. vs. Montgomery Ward and Co., 150 F(2d) 369 (C.C.A., 7th, 1945).

(64) See App. V–29.

(65) Memo, Col Gow for CG, ASF, 12 Jun 45, sub: Montgomery Ward and Company—Proposed Course of Action.

(66) Memo, Gen Somervell for Maj Gen Byron, 13 Jun 45, sub: Montgomery Ward and Company, Inc.—Future Course of Action.

(67) Memo, Col Gow for CG, ASF, 19 Jun 45, sub: Application of War Labor Board Orders; Memo for file by Ohly, 19 Jun 45, sub: Montgomery Ward—Miscellaneous Developments; Memo, Brig Gen Greenbaum for CG, ASF, 20 Jun 45, sub: Montgomery Ward and Company Check-off; Memos, Gen Somervell for Maj Gen Byron, 19 and 23 Jun 45, subs: Montgomery Ward and Company, Inc.—Application of NWLB Order.

(68) Memo, Maj Gen Byron for CG, ASF, sub: Computation of Net Operating Income Available for Payment of Retroactive Wage Increases—Montgomery Ward and Company, Inc.

(69) Memo, Lt Col Hebert for [Brig] Gen Greenbaum, 25 Jun 45, sub: Conference of 23 June 1945 on Montgomery Ward Matters (App. V–30).

(70) Memo, Maj Gen McCoach for CG, ASF, 11 Jul 45, sub: Payment of Retroactive Wages—Montgomery Ward and Company, Inc.; Ltr, Acting Sec War to President, 25 Jul 45 (App. V–31); Ltr, Sec War to Davis, 25 Jul 45 (App. V–32).

(71) Memo for CG, ASF, 13 Jun 45, sub: Application of Executive Order to Properties Not Now Effectively Controlled by the War Department. See Plan VI, paras. 1, 2, and 3, of Memo, 12 May 45.

(72) Memo, Lt Col Hebert for [Brig] Gen Greenbaum, 25 Jun 45 (App. V–30).

(73) Memo, Lt Col Boland for Maj Gen McCoach, 14 Jul 45, sub: Montgomery Ward and Company, Inc.——Strike at Schwinn Warehouse.

(74) Memo, Maj Gen McCoach for CG, ASF, 13 Jul 45, sub: Resumption of Control——Schwinn Warehouse, Photo Department, Central Printing Department, Display Factory and Maintenance Department, Fashion Mail Order House——Montgomery Ward and Co., Inc., Chicago, Ill. (App. V–33); Telecon, Brig Gen Greenbaum and Davis, 11 Jul 45, at 11:10, on Montgomery Ward Developments; Memo, Lt Gen Lutes for Maj Gen McCoach, 16 Jul 45, sub: Montgomery Ward and Company, Inc.——Resumption of Control of Schwinn Warehouse, Photo Department, Central Printing Department, Display Factory and Maintenance Department, and Fashion Mail Order House.

(75) PMG Special Rpt, 20 Jul 45; PMG Rpt No. 116, 21 Jul 45.

(76) Memo, Maj Gen McCoach for CG, ASF, 24 Jul 45, sub: Montgomery Ward and Company, Inc.——Fashion Mail Order House (App. V–34); Memo, Lt Gen Lutes for Maj Gen McCoach, 26 Jul 45, sub: Extension of War Department Control to Fashion Mail Order House.

(77) Tab A to Memo, Maj Gen McCoach for CG, ASF, 24 Jul 45 (App. V–34).

(78) Ltr, Sewell Avery to Sec War, 2 Aug 45 (App. V–35).

(79) Ltr, Acting Sec War to Avery, 4 Aug 45 (App. V–36).

(80) Memo, Gen Somervell for Maj Gen McCoach, 6 Aug 45, sub: War Department Operation of Certain Properties of Montgomery Ward and Company, Inc.

(81) Ibid.; Memo, Brig Gen Greenbaum for Dir, OES, n.d., sub: War Department Operation of Certain Properties of Montgomery Ward and Company, Inc. (App. V–37); Memo for file by Ohly, 6 Aug 45, sub: War Department Operation of Certain Properties of Montgomery Ward and Company, Inc.

(82) Memos, Montgomery Ward for Maj Gen McCoach, 7 and 9 Aug 45; Memo, Maj Gen McCoach for Montgomery Ward, 9 Aug 45.

(83) Memo, Lt Gen Lutes for Maj Gen McCoach, 22 Jul 45, sub: Montgomery Ward and Company, Inc.——Extension of War Department Possession to New Properties.

(84) See Appendix Y–1 for text of order.

(85) Memo, Gen Somervell for Maj Gen McCoach, n.d., sub: Montgomery Ward and Company, Inc.——Preparations for Terminating Possession (App. V–38); Memo, Maj Gen McCoach for CG, ASF, 27 Aug 45, sub: Action Taken in Preparation for Relinquishment of Possession, Operation and Control of Montgomery Ward and Company, Inc., Facilities.

(86) Memo, Ohly for Under Sec War, 24 Aug 45, sub: Montgomery Ward and Company, Inc.——Meeting With Mr. Abramson.

(87) Ltr, Acting Sec War to Dir, OES,, 28 Aug 45 (App. V–39); Memo for file by Ohly, 11 Sep 45, sub: Termination of Plant Seizures After V–J Day (App. Y–2); Ltr, Sec Labor to Davis, 18 Sep 45.

(88) Memo, Maj Gen McCoach for CG, ASF, 30 Aug 45, sub: Operating Results of War Department Operated Facilities of Montgomery Ward.

(89) Ltr, Sec War to President, 27 Sep 45.

(90) Memo for file by Ohly, 11 Sep 45.

(91) Memos, Ohly for Brig Gen Greenbaum, 12 and 16 Oct 45, subs: Montgomery Ward and Company, Inc.——Termination of War Department Possession.

(92) Memos, Maj Gen McCoach for Montgomery Ward, 18 Oct 45 (Apps. V–40 and V–42); Memo, Avery for Maj Gen McCoach, 18 Oct 45 (App. V–41); Memo, Maj Gen McCoach for CG, ASF, 19 Oct 45, sub: Relinquishment of Possession, Operation and Control of Montgomery Ward and Company, Inc., Facilities.

(93) Memo, Sec War for CG, ASF, n.d., sub: Final Accounting Reports and Recommendations on Accounting Matters——War Department Operation of Certain Plants and Facilities of Montgomery Ward and Company Pursuant to Executive Order No. 9508, dated 27 December 1944 (App. V–43).

(94) Memo, Col Furphy for Dep CG, ASF, n.d., sub: War Department Operation of Montgomery Ward and Company——Unfinished Business (App. V–44); Memo, Maj Gen McCoach for CG, ASF, 16 Nov 45, sub: Progress Report of War Department Representative, Formerly Operating Certain Plants and Facilities of Montgomery Ward and Company, Inc.; Memo, Col Furphy for Dep CG, ASF,

26 Nov 45, sub: War Department Operation of Montgomery Ward and Company, Inc., [With] Comments on Progress Report of the War Department Representative, 16 November 1945.

(95) See Draft Memo for Maj Gen Byron, 28 Jan 45 (App. V–17a) and Teletype, Maj Gen Byron to Dep War Department Reps, 28 Feb 45 (App. V–19).

CHAPTER 15

General Developments, November 1943 to September 1945

During the twelve months following the Salem-Peabody case the most significant developments were taking place in the field, where the number of plant seizures was increasing rapidly. In 1944 there were nineteen takeovers caused by labor difficulties, of which thirteen were assigned to the War Department.(1) Their cumulative effect on the War Department and on the attitudes of federal agencies was marked by continuing discussion as to whether seizures remained a viable response in the face of the growing number of situations requiring extraordinary action. The War Department had halted most efforts to remove itself from the business but still held hopes that other agencies could take on a greater share of the cases and that special legislation would reduce the general seizure load.

Attainment of the first goal was a constant problem, and in each case where it was at all practical the War Department methodically presented reasons for designating some other entity as the seizing agency. Its persistence met with limited success, such as in 1945 when it forced acceptance of the rule that cases involving petroleum should go to Interior Secretary Ickes in his role as the petroleum administrator.(2) The War Department also succeeded in having transportation troubles referred to the Office of Defense Transportation.[1] Important as these successes were, however, the majority of cases were still assigned to the War Department.(3)

The Montgomery Ward case brought the second objective much closer to realization as it was generally recognized that any court decision against the government made some type of special legislation imperative. Public members of the National War Labor Board (NWLB) favored a simple law broadening coverage of the War Labor Disputes Act, to include specific properties used for distribution rather than for production and facilities wholly engaged in civilian as distinguished from war activities,(4) while other agencies favored more fundamental legislation directed towards making NWLB decisions judicially enforceable.(5) Making NWLB orders enforceable through the courts was given strong impetus by President Roosevelt, who directed Attorney General Biddle to prepare such legislation when the Montgomery Ward executive order was signed. This activity was

---

[1]The Office of Defense Transportation (ODT) was established within the Office of Emergency Management by Executive Order 8989, 18 December 1941. It was to assure the maximum utilization of domestic transportation facilities. Its directors were Joseph B. Eastman (1941–44) and Col. John M. Johnson (1944–45). For ODT records, see Record Group 219, NARA.

Attorney General Francis Biddle

spurred on by the later adverse decision of the federal district court.(6) All through the spring a small committee worked intermittently on a draft that finally met everyone's approval by May 1945,(7) just as a rapidly mounting wave of strikes and seizures was taking place. In the first months of 1945 the number of seizures was nearly as large as during all of 1944,(8) and there were indications that industrial unrest would grow at a accelerated pace following V–E Day.(9)

On 5 May 1945 an interagency conference was held to discuss future policy regarding labor disputes,(10) and while many agreements were reached no immediate action was taken. In the meantime, the War Department was forced to undertake three more seizures in which it had no direct interest and in which connections between production and the war effort were remote.(11) By the end of June it was executing twelve separate seizure orders, with an immediate prospect of more to come.(12) Ironically, as the War Department's administrative burden became heavier and heavier the strikes began to drastically interfere with procurement in many critical programs, obliging the War Department to press for prompt administration action. Repeated War Department pleas(13) fell on deaf ears(14), and the favorable court decisions in the Montgomery Ward case killed interest in special legislation. Moreover, it was months before the War Department could get the director of economic stabilization to prepare rules governing the selection of seizing agencies, which caused much confusion, significant delays, and serious damage to the procurement process in June and July 1945 when ten takeovers were necessary.(15) The guidelines finally settled upon were unsatisfactory from the War Department's standpoint.(16)

Plans were made to take up the labor situation directly with President Truman, but the war ended before this was done and all efforts toward seeking special legislation abruptly halted. The War Department shifted its full energies toward the immediate termination of plant seizure missions.

The Termination of All Plant Seizures Following V–J Day

On V–J Day the War Department operated properties under eleven executive orders. Eight cases represented management noncompliance situations where settlements seemed remote,(17) although one case was slated for early settlement because cutbacks had closed the plant.(18) The remaining three cases involved labor intransigence. One involved an emergency railway labor panel recommendation that was rejected because the international union hoped to obtain a industrywide settlement and was uninterested in any ruling applying only to the seized railroad.(19) The other two cases involved interunion disputes, only one of which was close to settlement.(20)

All federal operating agencies were of the opinion that extending any seizure beyond V–J Day was unjustified because the sole justification for takeovers was to further the war effort. With the fighting done the case for prompt restitution was very strong and the agencies involved were eager to relinquish their seizure responsibilities. This was especially true of the rapidly demobilizing War and Navy Departments, which felt that the military had no place in peacetime civilian affairs. Accordingly, within hours of Truman's V–J Day proclamation General Greenbaum began discussing termination of all seizure operations at Army-held properties with the chairman of the NWLB and the director of economic stabilization,(21) who agreed with this course following a delay of several days to allow for the coordination of the government's program with respect to all seizures. The secretaries of war and of the Navy both requested Truman's approval to terminate government control of all plants not later than 31 August 1945.(22)

This flurry of discussion was not immediately followed by definitive action because the president, the NWLB, and the director of economic stabilization had more immediate problems with which to contend. The Department of Justice, however, prepared an executive order to carry out a general termination, and the War Department furnished OES Director Davis with a detailed analysis of the status of its various seizures.(23) Finally, on 22 August 1945 a large interagency conference attended by officials of the War, Navy, Interior, and Justice Departments; the Petroleum Administration for War;[2] the Offices of Defense Transportation, Economic Stabilization, and War Mobilization and Reconversion; and the NWLB studied the entire issue.(24) Ironically, Labor Secretary Schwellenbach was not invited nor informed of the meeting. While the War and Navy Departments reiterated the desire for a prompt general termination, most other conferees preferred a gradual release lasting no longer than 31 August with a case-by-case consideration of possible remedial measures to prevent post-release work stoppages. All of the conferees, with the exception of the Navy, agreed with this proposal. The Justice Department then presented its draft executive order granting each agency head the authority to terminate possession of any plant under his control on determining that it was "practicable" or administratively feasible. The draft order received a general endorsement.

Later that day War Department representatives reviewed their cases with the NWLB public members and eventually reached the conclusion that it was impos-

---

[2]The Petroleum Administration for War (PAW) was established by Executive Order 9276, 2 December 1942. Its purpose was to coordinate and centralize government policies and activities relating to petroleum and to assure adequate supplies for the war effort. See Petroleum Administration for War, *A History of the Petroleum Administration for War, 1941–45*, eds. John W. Frey and H. Chandler (Washington, D.C.: Government Printing Office, 1946). For PAW records, see Record Group 253, NARA.

sible to materially improve labor relations at any Army-controlled property before 31 August. The NWLB, however, did conduct routine checks in two instances through the appropriate regional war labor boards,(25) but these investigations only confirmed the original impressions.

At this point Labor Secretary Schwellenbach forcefully intervened, causing considerable confusion and delay. Appointed only six weeks earlier, Schwellenbach was about to receive all responsibility for maintaining labor peace during the transition period, but without the aid of the soon to be abolished NWLB. He was naturally and understandably anxious to prevent or postpone any kind of labor strife that could accompany the return of seized facilities to private control, and particularly feared that strikes at Montgomery Ward, Goodyear, Gaffney, and U.S. Rubber would kindle disputes in other, currently healthy firms. His concern was exacerbated by labor pressures to continue government operations, particularly by unions in seized plants—the United Retail, Wholesale, and Department Store Employees of America (CIO) at Montgomery Ward; the United Rubber Workers of America (CIO) at U.S. Rubber and Goodyear; and the Textile Workers Union of America (CIO) in the South.

On 25 August special consultant McGrady discussed the problem with Schwellenbach and the secretary's special assistant John W. Gibson,[3] but the secretary refused to voluntarily consent to an Army withdrawal until he had attempted settlements. He insisted on continued possession as a means to guarantee that strikes would not interfere with conciliation efforts and because he believed that settlements were more likely while the War Department maintained the status quo. Although the War Department argued that further attempts along these lines were futile, had proven so in the past, and had prompted the original seizures, Schwellenbach was adamant. The War Department finally agreed to review each case with him, and during the following days he became convinced that further conciliation efforts were useless in all but two cases.

On 25 August President Truman issued the executive order directing agency heads to return properties they controlled to private ownership as soon as practicable "with the approval of the Director of Economic Stabilization."(26) An NWLB procedure was implemented, whereby the War Department would send Davis and Schwellenbach letters detailing the situation at each plant, the extent of compliance with NWLB orders, and the military assessment of whether termination was possible. Davis could then approve or disapprove termination. Letters covering Army-controlled properties were dispatched within forty-eight hours and, following conversations between War Department, OES, and Department of Labor representatives, and after Davis' approval, all but three properties were returned to private ownership by 31 August.(27)

---

[3]John W. Gibson (1910–1976) was an Illinois-born labor leader affiliated with the United Dairy Workers and the United Retail, Wholesale, and Department Store Employees of America. He served on various CIO and state labor councils (1937–41) until appointed to serve in the Michigan Division of the War Production Board, the Office of Price Administration, the War Manpower Commission, and the Michigan Committee for Fair Employment Practice. He became an assistant to the secretary of labor in 1945.

The exceptions were Gaffney Manufacturing, U.S. Rubber, and Montgomery Ward. The delay in the first case resulted from last minute retroactive wage problems and a company request to extend possession so that the Labor Department could attempt a settlement.(28) In the case of U.S. Rubber, Schwellenbach and Davis believed that time could settle the underlying labor difficulties and prevent a post-termination strike.(29) Negotiations at Gaffney collapsed within days, although retroactive wage questions were settled, allowing the Army to withdraw on 8 September.(30) The U.S. Rubber case continued as the War Department restated its desire to leave the property on the grounds that it did not believe that time would heal all wounds and because strikes were threatened that could prove difficult for the Army to control.(31) These fears were unfounded, and the properties remained peaceful after termination on 10 October. With the exception of some minor residual problems at Montgomery Ward, Hughes, and Gaffney, the War Department ended all its plant seizure activities when it left Montgomery Ward on 18 October.(32)

Endnotes

(1) Apps. A–D.

(2) Memo for file by Ohly, 7 Nov 45, sub: Plant Seizure—Cases Involving Plants for Which the PAW Is Responsible (App. W–11). See App. AA–1.

(3) Apps. B, C, and AA–1.

(4) For a summary of the views of the NWLB public members, see Appendix W–4.

(5) May 3d Draft of Administration's Proposed Bill for the Judicial Enforcement of War Labor Board Orders (App. W–1).

(6) See Apps. B and C.

(7) See App. E.

(8) Memo, Brig Gen Greenbaum for Under Sec War, 5 May 45, sub: The Future of Government Policy With Respect to the Enforcement of War Labor Board Orders—Conference With Judge Vinson on Proposed Legislation (App. W–2); Memo for file by Ohly, 5 May 45, sub: Enforcement of War Labor Board Orders (App. W–3).

(9) War Mobilization Director Byrnes in his 1 January and 1 April reports recommended unequivocally that "Congress give the War Labor Board statutory authority to make its decisions enforceable."

(10) The question of sanctions short of seizure was also very thoroughly discussed at earlier interagency meetings in the spring of 1945. Memo, Ohly for [Brig] Gen Greenbaum, 21 Apr 45, sub: Compliance With NWLB Directive Orders (App. W–9).

(11) Gaffney Manufacturing Company, Mary-Leila Cotton Mills, and Cocker Machine and Foundry Company.

(12) Apps. B and C.

(13) On the strike situation, see Ltr, Under Sec War to War Mobilization Dir, 26 Jun 45 (App. W–5); Ltr, Under Sec War to War Mobilization Dir, 4 Jul 45 (App. W–6); and Ltr, Acting Under Sec War to War Mobilization Dir, 27 Jul 45 (App. W–7).

(14) For reply to 4 Jul 45 on the strikes, see Ltr, War Mobilization Dir to Under Sec War, 20 Jul 45 (App. W–8).

(15) Memo, Ohly for Brig Gen Greenbaum, 4 Jul 45, sub: Choice of Take-Over Agency; Ltr, Under Sec War to Davis, 29 Jun 45.

(16) App. W–10.

(17) S. A. Woods Company, Hughes Tool Company, Montgomery Ward and Company, Farrell-Cheek Steel Corporation, Mary-Leila Cotton Mills, Gaffney Manufacturing Company, Cudahy Brothers Company, and Cocker Machine and Foundry Company. In the last two cases there appeared to be some hope for eventual settlement, and at Cudahy a settlement was reached between V–J Day and relinquishment of possession several weeks later.

(18) S. A. Woods Company (App. M–11).

(19) Bingham and Garfield Railway Company. See App. Z–1g.

(20) Ltr, Acting Sec War to Dir, OES, 27 Aug 45, requesting authority to withdraw from the properties of Springfield Plywood Corporation (App. Y–9); Ltr, Acting Sec War to Dir, OES, 28 Aug 45, requesting authority to withdraw from the Detroit properties of the U.S. Rubber Company (App. Y–8).

(21) The terms of each of the eleven executive orders provided, with one exception, that the War Department could only terminate its possession if the secretary determined that the productive efficiency of the facility covered had been restored to the level prevailing prior to seizure. This had been interpreted by the attorney general to mean (a) that production was again back to normal and (b) that upon restoration of the facility to private ownership production would continue as normal and would not be interrupted by a recurrence of the labor disturbance that had led to the takeover (Ltr, Atty Gen to Sec Interior, 14 Jan 44). Since there was only one case in which such a situation clearly existed (Springfield Plywood), relinquishment of possession depended upon further authorization from the president. The one exceptional order was that applicable to S. A. Woods, which specifically provided for prior presidential consent to termination of possession under any circumstances.

(22) Ltr, Acting Sec War to President, 15 Aug 45 (App. Y–3); Ltr, Brig Gen Greenbaum to Davis, 15 Aug 45.

(23) Memo, Col Gow for Dir, OES, n.d. [Aug 45], sub: Properties Now Being Operated by the War Department Pursuant to Executive Orders (App. Y–4).

(24) This conference and the events of the next two weeks are set out in great detail in a Memo for file by Ohly, 11 Sep 45, sub: Termination of Plant Seizures After V–J Day (App. Y–2).

(25) Mary-Leila Cotton Mills and Hughes Tool Company.

(26) EO 9603, 25 Aug 45, 10 F.R. 10960 (App. Y–1).

(27) There were eleven such letters. They serve as an excellent summary of the status of these cases on V–J Day and contain *inter alia* succinct statements of specific reasons why particular properties should no longer be retained. See, for example, Ltr, Acting Sec War to Dir, OES, 27 Aug 45, on Springfield Plywood (App. Y–9); Ltrs, Acting Sec War to Dir, OES, 29 Aug 45, and Brig Gen Greenbaum to Dir, OES, 7 Sep 45, on the Gaffney Manufacturing Company (Apps. Y–6 and Y–7); Ltr, Acting Sec War to Dir, OES, 28 Aug 45, on U.S. Rubber (App. Y–8); Ltr, Acting Sec War to Dir, OES, 28 Aug 45, on Montgomery Ward (App. V–39); and Ltr, Acting Sec War to Dir, OES, 27 Aug 45, on S. A. Woods (App. M–11). See also Apps. Z–3a (Hughes Tool); Z–3b (Farrell-Cheek); Z–3c (Cudahy); Z–3d (Cocker); and Z–3e (Mary-Leila). For special assurances that the War Department would meet any obligations for retroactive wages, to the extent it had the authority to do so, see Ltr, Under Sec War to Dir, OES (App. Y–5); Memos for file by Ohly, 29–31 Aug 45, subs: Status of Plant Seizures as of 0900 on 29 Aug 45, Status of Plant Seizures as of 0900 on 30 Aug 45, and Status of Plant Seizures as of 0900 on 31 Aug 45.

(28) Memo, Ohly for [Brig] Gen Greenbaum, 5 Sep 45, sub: Status of Plant Seizures, par. 1b (App. Y–10); Ltr, Brig Gen Greenbaum to Dir, OES, 7 Sep 45 (App. Y–7).

(29) Memo, Ohly for [Brig] Gen Greenbaum, 5 Sep 45, par. 1a (App. Y–10).

(30) Ltr, Brig Gen Greenbaum to Dir, OES, 7 Sep 45 (App. Y–7).

(31) Memo for file by Ohly, 11 Sep 45, par. 17 (App. Y–2).

(32) Memo, Ohly for [Brig] Gen Greenbaum, 18 Oct 45, sub: Status of Plant Seizures (App. Y–11).

CHAPTER 16

The War Department's Attitude Toward Plant Seizures

The evolution of the War Department's attitude toward involvement in plant seizures grew from three main positions. The War Department believed, first, that some other technique than seizure was needed for keeping industrial peace; second, that some other existing or specially created agency should conduct takeovers; and third, that in some cases, because of the sheer magnitude, urgency, or violent nature of the dispute, the War or Navy Department would have to become involved. The first position was reflected in War Department support for Executive Order 9370, for "work-or-fight orders," and for legislation making National War Labor Board (NWLB) directives judicially enforceable. The second position was evidenced in frequent War Department appeals for relief from its seizure burdens.

The War Department's aversion to seizures was based on practical considerations and on its own interpretation of the proper role of the military in civilian affairs. The practical reasons were obvious. Plant seizures required the diversion of highly skilled Army personnel away from the primary task of fighting a war, as well as the expenditure of valuable time and effort by policymakers who had more important issues to consider.

The conceptual reasons were more fundamental and predominant. Foremost was the belief that the military should not meddle in civilian matters—a reflection of the general principle of American government that control of national affairs was a civilian and not a military responsibility.[1] A second reason was the fear that any mishandling of an operation not properly within the Army's competence or jurisdiction could negatively affect its prestige in the eyes of soldiers at the front and civilians at home. A third reason stemmed from anxieties that any Army involvement in civilian matters could result in accusations of partisanship toward management or labor. The War Department was the guardian of a citizen Army

---

[1] For further reading on the role of the military in labor and civil affairs, see Jerry M. Cooper, *The Army and Civil Disorder: Federal Military Intervention in Labor Disputes, 1877–1900* (Westport, Conn.: Greenwood Press, 1980); Clayton D. Laurie and Ronald H. Cole, *The Role of Federal Military Forces in Domestic Disorders, 1877–1945* (Washington, D.C.: U.S. Army Center of Military History, 1997); and Frederick T. Wilson, *Federal Aid in Domestic Disturbances, 1787–1903* (Washington, D.C.: Government Printing Office, 1903). For legalities, see Robert W. Coakley, *The Role of Federal Military Forces in Domestic Disorders, 1789–1878* (Washington, D.C.: U.S. Army Center of Military History, 1988); and Cassius Dowell, *Military Aid to the Civil Power* (Ft. Leavenworth, Kans.: General Service Schools Press, 1925).

comprised of all classes and elements of the population responsible in part for prosecuting the war. Under such circumstances it could not afford accusations of partisanship or the reputation of being antilabor or antimanagement. This danger was real and was in constant evidence, especially in takeover cases where there was deep-rooted and intense bitterness. Each party watched for any move it could construe as disadvantageous, and each was willing to employ any means to fashion the seizure to its own advantage. In spite of its efforts at neutrality, the War Department was often charged with partisanship, prejudice, and unfairness.(1)

Nearly all of the top military and civilian leaders in the War Department held these views and constantly advanced them to higher authority. However, while others in the government also recognized these concerns, they did not deem them serious enough to disqualify the Army from participation in the seizure process. In addition, most federal agencies were unwilling to experiment with alternative techniques and persisted in the belief, until practically V–E Day, that the military was the best qualified organization for undertaking seizure activities.(2)

Corollary Policies

These attitudes led to the formulation of corollary policies, designed to reduce the possibility of a labor dispute causing a seizure. The policies were first and foremost intended to discourage any labor-management beliefs that a War Department takeover was the result of an actual or threatened strike or that it would benefit either party. This was necessary because many unions tended to press or encourage a seizure in the belief that it was a panacea—that a takeover would help "crack" a tough employer, destroy a rival union, result in a quicker settlement, produce more rapid action by the NWLB, or simply hurt management. Sometimes unions deluded themselves into thinking that the War Department would undertake conciliation or the disposition of outstanding disputes in a more satisfactory manner than the NWLB. Employers too often wanted a takeover when they were harassed by an unruly union, plagued by a jurisdictional dispute, or unable to handle personnel problems. The presence of the Army guaranteed production and profits, and intervention was often welcomed as a face-saving device by all parties. Such attitudes were often strengthened by public calls for an Army "crackdown" or by unauthorized statements from federal officials threatening a seizure if a dispute was not ended. The War Department, however, counteracted these impressions by always keeping the contending parties guessing as to if and when a seizure might take place, and whenever the occasion presented itself it was emphasized that any takeover would purposely be prevented from benefiting the party whose actions forced its use.(3) In this manner the War Department hoped that disputing parties would seek to avoid seizures rather than cause them, but this objective was never fully attained.

Attitude Toward Seizure in Particular Disputes

In spite of its aversion to plant takeovers, the War Department realized that its participation was necessary in disputes involving war procurement or in situations where other remedies were not available or immediately forthcoming. Seizure was the most effective method for restoring or maintaining production when other measures were exhausted, and in a crisis the main question was how to get production going, not the wisdom of basic government policy. Consequently, the War Department frequently sought the right to take over companies, especially towards the end of the war when labor disputes had an increasingly negative impact on military procurement.

Recognition of the practical inevitability of government seizure resulted in the development of four unwritten but well-defined policies governing the War Department's position as the seizing agency. The first applied to operations that were not essential to Army programs. In such cases the War Department objected to being designated the seizing agency and used every possible argument to force the selection of some other department.(4) The second policy applied to threatened operations that were essential to Army programs but where another agency had supervisory responsibility. In these cases the War Department opposed its designation and recommended the selection of another agency,(5) such as the Petroleum Administration for War, the Office of Defense Transportation, the War Production Board, the Solid Fuels Administration for War,[2] the Department of Agriculture, or the War Food Administration.[3] This policy was fundamentally sound but had one practical difficulty in that many agencies were mere policymaking bodies, totally unequipped in terms of personnel, facilities, and experience to conduct complicated plant operations. Such was the case with the War Communications Board and the Federal Communications Commission, which were small policymaking bodies, composed exclusively of high-level representatives of several agencies, that had quasi-judicial functions but lacked the physical ability to operate a city or statewide telephone system. Similarly, there were no other qualified federal agencies with the necessary organization or personnel to step in to handle these problems. As a result, the War Department often ended up as the designee.

The third policy applied where the War Department and some other body had a joint interest and responsibility. In this situation the War Department would oppose its own designation and press for selection of another agency(6) on the grounds that its interests were less urgent and that its seizure load was such that some other less-burdened agency should undertake the new case. The fourth policy applied to situations directly affecting essential military operations where it was impractical to designate another agency. The War Department then either urged or acquiesced in its own selection. This position was subject to the qualification that all other remedies were exhausted prior to seizure, but as a practical

---

[2] The Solid Fuels Administration for War was a part of the Department of the Interior, with Secretary Harold L. Ickes serving as the solid fuels administrator. For records, see Record Group 245, NARA.

[3] The War Food Administration was established within the Department of Agriculture by Executive Order 9322, 26 March 1943. Its powers were extended by Executive Order 9334, 19 April 1943. Its purpose was to determine military and civilian food requirements, allocate the country's farm resources, assign priorities, make allocations of food for all uses, and insure efficient and proper distribution of food supplies. When the agency was abolished by Executive Order 9577, 29 June 1945, functions were transferred to the secretary of agriculture. The first director was Chester C. Davis (1943), followed by Marvin Jones (1944–45). For records, see Record Group 224, NARA.

matter this was usually not possible. In many cases the War Department urged seizure before other remedies were exhausted against NWLB wishes. The NWLB invariably accepted any War Department statement that a given seizure had to take place, and an analysis of War Department seizures shows that the majority fell in this category.

Intelligent application of these policies required accurate information at headquarters on the extent of War Department interests at a facility and the exact time Army interests were so adversely affected that seizure was necessary. Early in the war headquarters was often handicapped by a lack of such information but as time went on a more satisfactory system developed. Information was gathered at the outset of any dispute that might lead to a seizure, with the technical services and top AAF and ASF production personnel being impressed with the need for providing reliable facts.

Armed with such information the War Department followed well-defined procedures to avoid being selected for cases not in its immediate interests, often informally meeting with the NWLB before a dispute reached a critical stage. These efforts produced some favorable results as the NWLB was sympathetic to the War Department's position, recognized the Army's burden, and cooperated in attempts to assign other agencies a fair share of the load. There were many cases, however, where the NWLB thought that the War Department alone could undertake the job. In such situations, once a case was referred by the NWLB to the president, the War Department would state its position in a letter to the Bureau of the Budget and could urge an interagency conference. A more likely course, however, was for the secretary of war or General Greenbaum to carry the War Department's case directly to the director of economic stabilization or of war mobilization. In several cases, none of which involved war production, the War Department's protests were taken—without success—directly to the president.

An analysis of cases where the War Department would have become the seizing agency if takeovers had resulted shows how successful these policies were. Such analysis also shows the extent to which the Army went to urge seizure to protect its own procurement. Of the twenty-nine War Department takeovers, nineteen were requested with NWLB concurrence. Sixteen of these involved strikes already interfering with procurement, while the other three threatened to do so. In most cases the threat was direct because it involved the production of essential products for the Army, although in four cases the threat was more indirect because it involved a service industry, such as a utility or railroad. Of the ten situations in which the War Department unsuccessfully opposed designation, seven were cases in which it had no material interest. In the other three cases the War Department claimed a vital interest but asserted that production responsibility was vested in another civilian agency.

Of the thirty-odd cases in which other agencies were finally selected as the seizing agent, the War Department was initially considered for designation in fourteen and took a position on the selection of an alternate agency in twenty-five. In eight seizure cases the War Department-recommended agency was named as the seizing agent without serious opposition. There were seventeen situations where the War Department sought authority for seizing vital war plants that were on strike or were being threatened by stoppages. In the eight other situations the War Department was opposed to becoming involved. In four of these cases the War Department succeeded in its efforts to avoid involvement, whereas in one involving telephone systems it lost. In the remaining three cases the issue was never resolved.

The War Department considered seizures an effective means of maintaining production in cases of labor-management disputes. Whatever its view on the desirability of finding a substitute technique or of creating agencies to handle takeovers, it made frequent use of plant takeovers to support procurement programs. This is well illustrated by War Department actions after March 1945: On fifteen occasions—on average once every two weeks—the War Department initiated a seizure action.

Endnotes

(1) For the dangers of embroilment in civilian controversies, see Draft Ltr, Under Sec War to Byrnes, n.d. (App. AA–7). This letter was never dispatched but the views expressed were conveyed orally and reiterated at a meeting with Wayne Morse (NWLB), Oscar Cox (Justice), and Ben Cohen (OES) at this time. See also Ltr, Brig Gen Greenbaum to Dir, Bureau of the Budget, 24 Mar 45 (App. AA–2), and App. AA–1.

(2) Memo, Col O'Connell for Chiefs of All Technical Services and CGs of All Service Commands, 21 Jan 44, sub: Instructions Regarding Labor Disputes (App. AA–5); Memo, Ohly for [Brig] Gen Greenbaum, 8 Feb 45, sub: Plant Seizure (App. AA–3); Memo, Col Gow for CG, First Service Command, 15 Jan 45, sub: Plant Seizure—Effect of Plant Seizure on Settlement of Issues in New Bedford Case (App. AA–4).

(3) See App. AA–1. Actual War Department seizures falling under this category included Salem-Peabody leather manufacturing plants, Fall River textile mills, Hummer Manufacturing Division of Montgomery Ward and Company, Gaffney Manufacturing Company, and Mary-Leila Cotton Mills. Seizures assigned to other agencies that fall within this category included Jenkins Brothers (Navy) and Scranton Transit Company (ODT). Illustrative cases that did not develop into seizures but in which the War Department took this position included the Western Foundry case.

(4) See App. AA–1. Actual War Department seizures falling in this category included Philadelphia Transportation Company, Cudahy Brothers Company, and Cocker Machine and Foundry Company. Seizures finally assigned to other agencies that fall within this category included Midwest Motor Carrier Systems (ODT), Toledo, Peoria, and Western Railroad (ODT), Humble Oil and Refining Company (PAW), Pure Oil Company (PAW), Texas Company (PAW), and Sinclair Rubber (PAW). Illustrative cases that did not develop into seizures but in which the War Department took this position included Chicago North Shore belt line (ODT), Tide Water Gulf (PAW), Dayton, Ohio, to Washington, D.C., regional telephone systems (FCC or War Communications Board), Capital Transit Company (ODT), and Minnesota R.R. and Warehouse Commission (Agriculture).

(5) See App. AA–1. War Department seizures falling in this category were undertaken, although in many cases there was an important but minor interest of some other agency. Seizures assigned to other agencies that fall within this category included Atlantic Basin Iron Works (War Shipping Administration), United Engineering Company (Navy), Goodyear Tire and Rubber Company (Navy), and General Cable Corporation (Navy). Cases that did not develop into seizures but in which the War Department took this position included the Firestone Company (Navy) case.

(6) Memo, Col O'Connell for Chiefs of All Technical Services, 2 Feb 44, sub: Certification of Work Stoppage Which Interferes Substantially With Attaining a Procurement Goal (App. AA–6). See also Memo, Col O'Connell for Chiefs of All Technical Services, and CGs of All Service Commands, 21 Jan 44 (App. AA–5).

CHAPTER 17

The Administrative Steps of a Plant Seizure

The Labor Branch, Industrial Personnel Division, kept a close check on all labor disputes that could or did affect War Department production, as well as other controversies that could require later government action.(1) Through such information the Labor Branch could generally predict situations requiring federal attention and keep the commanding generals and Production Divisions of the Army Service Forces (ASF) and Army Air Forces (AAF) and the under secretary of war apprised.(2)

These situations were of two types. The first comprised cases where a technical service or the Production Divisions of the ASF and AAF advised the Labor Branch that an existing strike or a threatened stoppage continuing beyond a certain date could seriously affect procurement. The other class involved cases where an employer was in noncompliance with National War Labor Board (NWLB) orders but War Department interests were insignificant or nonexistent. In cases of the first type the Labor Branch advised the NWLB of the War Department's position and urged referral of the matter to the president so a seizure could take place before the specified deadline. In the second type of case the procedure was reversed, with the NWLB advising the War Department that it was referring a dispute to the president and recommending it as the seizing agency. In the first instance the War Department, as the sponsoring agency, would address a letter to the director of the Bureau of the Budget, Harold D. Smith, or to the director of economic stabilization, setting forth its position and requesting executive arrangements to facilitate seizure.(3) Simultaneously, the NWLB would advise the president of its concurrence. In the second situation the NWLB was the initiating agency but everyone knew that unless Executive Order 9370 was employed there was only one possible remedy——Army intervention. The War Department customarily objected to its designation through letters prepared in the Labor Branch for the Office of the Under Secretary of War. Decisions were considered matters of policy requiring Under Secretary Patterson's input, although the actual decision was usually made by the Labor Branch after field meetings. Frequently, in management noncompliance cases a series of conferences regarding the possible use of Executive Order 9370 would ensue before seizure was seriously discussed.

Although not always true at the outset, the NWLB usually prepared an executive order that was drafted according to a standard form agreed upon by the

NWLB, the War Department, and the Department of Justice. Working relations among these agencies became so close that the War and Justice Departments normally accepted any proposed NWLB order without comment, and any differences were settled informally at a low staff level. Exceptions occurred in complicated cases like Montgomery Ward, where the time schedule mandated War Department draftsmanship, and in cases where the NWLB lacked jurisdiction.

Preparations Within the War Department

As soon as a seizure became likely, the Labor Branch conferred with the NWLB and alerted Army technical components responsible for seizure team personnel, the deputy chief of staff for service commands, and the interested procurement unit.(4) The Production Division, either ASF or AAF, was then asked to select an individual to serve as the War Department representative.(5) Meanwhile, the pertinent service command labor branch and technical service labor branch were asked to assemble all pertinent information on the plant's production and its labor problems.

As the time for takeover approached, the Labor Branch briefed the seizure team members and their superiors. In early operations, before procedures and policies were crystallized, these conferences were conducted by the ASF chief of staff and were attended by ranking officials of Army components that were interested in the takeover or were furnishing personnel to the seizure team. Later, the inclusion of these higher officials was dispensed with except in the most critical cases, and the conferences were shifted to the ASF's Office of the Deputy Chief of Staff (*Chart 3*). Here, the Labor Branch representative gave a summary of the case and suggested the best possible approach. A general discussion followed while a representative of the ASF deputy chief of staff arranged for various administrative details—travel orders, transportation, posters, hotel accommodations—all the steps necessary for moving the team to the plant site and assuring local service command assistance.(6) Although necessary, this was a thankless and dull job, but the deputy chief's efficiency contributed tremendously to the smoothness of subsequent missions.

At these conferences War Department representatives were furnished with copies of all pertinent papers—principally, three documents known as delegations of authority and instructions. They consisted of a memorandum from the secretary of war to the appropriate commanding general, a similar memorandum from the latter to the War Department representative, and a memorandum of instructions covering plant operations. The documents, which the Labor Branch prepared, varied from case to case in only the smallest particulars.(7)

Following this general conference the team met, and each technician spent some time informing the War Department representative of the specific steps the team was required to take. General indoctrination was always done by the judge advocate, who provided all necessary legal documents including a proposed operating contract for execution by the company, notices to insurers and to vendors and vendees, and copies of the executive order and plant seizure manual.(8)

CHART 3—ORGANIZATION OF THE ARMY SERVICE FORCES, NOVEMBER 1943

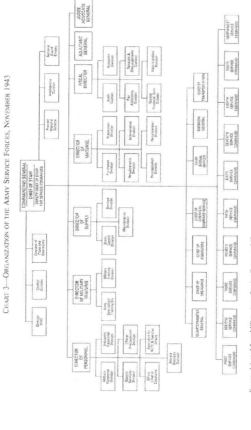

Source: Adapted from Millett, Army Service Forces, p. 342

Other team members received materials relating to their own particular phase of the operation.

Departure from Washington, normally by air, depended on the time of seizure, and when time permitted an attempt was made to meet one day in advance of the actual takeover. The team was met by representatives of the local service command, including the person serving as the liaison officer. A conference with the local service command officials followed where useful and late-breaking local information was supplied, particularly information on the physical location and characteristics of the plant.(9) Arrangements were worked out to cover administrative services supplied by the service commander including arrangements for occupation officers, troops, secretaries, transportation, phone installations, posters, flags, recording machines, dictaphones, typewriters, other office equipment, and hotel accommodations.(10) Service command additions to the staff were then assimilated into the team and indoctrinated in their duties. Final detailed plans were perfected, occupation officers were assigned, and liaison with other federal agencies was established. The team was now ready for action.

Processing the Executive Order

While the seizure team prepared, the executive order was processed, conferences took place, and last minute War Department and NWLB efforts to avert a crisis were made. Meanwhile, the Labor Branch obtained signatures on the original delegations of authority and memorandum of instructions, which were then placed in escrow undated.(11) Whenever possible, the War Department sought to have a seizure team ready well before the event, and there were numerous cases where teams were already on the scene when the need for seizure was removed or when some other agency was designated.

Once the need for a War Department seizure was established, General Greenbaum or the Labor Branch made arrangements with the White House or the director of war mobilization concerning the best time to publicly release the executive order. Official views were expressed after obtaining the recommendation of the War Department representative on the scene, and these suggestions were invariably taken except when the president's unavailability required a postponement. These arrangements required precision since the White House objected to seizures before executive orders were issued and because it was advantageous to act with great speed once the White House announcement was made. It was customary, after confirming the release of the executive order, for the seizure to take place from five to fifteen minutes after simultaneous White House and War Department announcements. The time schedule often varied if the distance from the rendezvous point to the plant was great because last-minute telephone instructions were always given by the Labor Branch to the War Department representative. The announcements themselves were usually perfunctory and limited to a simple recitation of the president's seizure order and the naming of the War Department representative. In a difficult case a back-to-work order, veiled threats as to the consequences of a strike, or some other information of general public interest might be included.(12) More detailed announcements were left to the War Department representative.(13) Such releases to the press or over the radio were carefully drafted to best crystallize public opinion in support of the government's action and toward obtaining the maximum effect on workers or management.

Actual Seizure

On orders from Washington the seizure team traveled to the seizure site. On arrival the representative sought out the highest-ranking company official, explained his mission, and furnished him with copies of the executive order, a notice of possession, and instruments of authority. The War Department representative normally did not divulge the details of his instructions so as not to tip his hand in the ensuing negotiations, but would ask for the company's cooperation and, with the judge advocate, seek company acquiescence through an operating agreement. Meanwhile, occupation officers raised the American flag and posted notices of possession and sometimes a poster describing Section 6 of the War Labor Disputes Act. A labor officer immediately contacted union officials to seek their assistance in obtaining a return to work if a strike was in progress or otherwise to gain their cooperation, while fiscal and disbursing officers examined company books. Notices to insurers and designation of a plant manager followed. The fact of seizure was reported by the War Department representative to the Labor Branch, together with a summary of significant facts.(14)

Establishment of Relations With Other Agencies

As soon as seizure preparations were under way, the War Department established liaison with other agencies, including the NWLB, Justice Department, Selective Service System, War Manpower Commission, and interested procurement agencies. Although securing FBI aid often proved difficult, relations with the Justice Department were generally good because of the need for opinions from the attorney general and the likelihood of lawsuits. Liaison with the Selective Service System was necessary when the Army sought the cancellation of occupational deferments, and while the Army wanted to draft strikers on several occasions, the Selective Service lacked the legal authority to take this step. The War Department called upon the War Manpower Commission in cases where a blacklist was considered for intimidating strikers or, in a more positive way, when the commission was needed to help fill labor shortages at seized plants. Relations with procurement agencies were usually amicable, but on occasion, as in the case of the Navy, difficult problems arose. The need to place operations on as firm a basis as possible prompted many pre-seizure efforts to obtain the cooperation of procurement agencies. The Army's seizure team usually contacted local procurement representatives before the takeover, if time permitted, and notified the state governor, the mayor of the community, and any interested representatives of state and federal labor agencies as soon as possession was taken. These contacts were usually mere courtesy calls, but they often served the War Department well in a prolonged seizure where local cooperation and support was vital. To the same end, the public relations officers always sought close contacts with local media representatives.

Reports

The War Department representative's orders required the submission of a daily report to the provost marshal general. These reports varied in length as circumstances required and were often dispensed with or placed on a weekly basis in the case of a prolonged operation. It was also customary for the representative to submit formal preliminary, interim, and final reports to the commanding general of the service command, with copies of formal documents and a summary of all actions taken to fulfill the mission outlined in the memorandum of instructions. In addition, detailed reports by fiscal, disbursing, production, public relations, and labor relations officers were attached when appropriate, as were copies of press statements and photostats of newspaper clippings. A log was customarily kept, and in some cases a final narrative history was prepared, along with special reports to the Labor Branch on important aspects of the operation and notices describing items needing further attention.

Activities With Respect to Termination

When the War Department decided to terminate an operation, all of the initial steps were reversed. The War Department representative advised company officials of the withdrawal and made legal arrangements with the judge advocate connected with a release. Other staff members informed labor groups of the decision; removed notices of possession and American flags; arranged for the transport of Army equipment; and drafted messages to the workers, thanking them for their cooperation and emphasizing the need for continued production. Press releases briefly recited the facts of the termination, thanked various groups for their cooperation, and contained a statement of hope for future labor peace, all designed on the theory that the War Department wanted everybody to forget the incident. Officials of federal, state, and local governments and agencies were advised of the War Department's plans, and labor-management conferences were held, separately or together, to provide suggestions for fostering future industrial peace. With these arrangements completed, the seizure team returned to Washington to prepare the final report.(15)

Endnotes

(1) The plant seizure manual, especially paragraph 9, gives many additional details.

(2) Labor Branch files date from December 1940 and are very complete. In February 1941 the branch began to widely circulate (both within and outside the War Department) a daily report in the form of a mimeographed memo to the under secretary of war (later to the commanding general, ASF), that summarized each dispute in some detail, both as to current status and as to War Department interest. These reports continued until V–J Day. In addition, major cases were the subject of special recurrent memoranda, which were distributed to all interested parties. The primary uses of information so gathered were to enable the War Department to take appropriate steps in each labor dispute, to apprise other agencies of the character and urgency of War Department interest in all current disputes, and to keep production and purchasing people fully advised of the effects that labor conditions generally or in particular plants were likely to have on their procurement. For the type of information gathered, see Appendixes AA–5 and AA–6.

(3) Ltr, Under Sec War to Dir, Bureau of the Budget, 16 Jun 45 (App. BB–9).

(4) Cases involving railroads or a municipality are illustrative of those where the NWLB had no jurisdiction. Legal problems incident to the preparation of an executive order have not been covered in this history except as they have related to a few special situations, such as that at Ken-Rad or Montgomery Ward. The plant seizure manual discusses the question only briefly (par. 6). Appendix X contains copies of executive orders in eight cases. A study of these will give a fairly good picture of the changes through which the form of these orders went.

(5) Memo, Col Gow for CG (All Service Commands), n.d., sub: Labor Officers for Plant Seizures (App. BB–6). For a list of some of the key personnel participating in various War Department plant seizures, see Appendix BB–16.

(6) Memo, Dep CofS for Service Commands for CofS, ASF, 18 Sep 44, sub: War Department Representatives (App. BB–4); Memo, Col Gow for Dir of Personnel, ASF, 14 Dec 44, sub: Choice of War Department Representatives for Plant Take-Overs (App. BB–5).

(7) See App. BB–1.

(8) Copies of these three memoranda, as prepared in the U.S. Rubber Company case, are included as Appendixes BB–10a, BB–10b, and BB–10c. See also plant seizure manual, sec. 8 and app. I, pts. 3, 4, and 5.

(9) See plant seizure manual, app. I, particularly forms 6 (Notice of Possession), 7 (Notice to Insurers), 8 (Orders Appointing Plant Manager), 9 (Form of Contract), 10 (Notice to Suppliers), 11 (Notice to Customers), 12 (Form of Payroll Certificate), 13 (Form of Finding by Secretary of War Extending Government Possession to Subsidiary Plants), 14–18 (Papers Relating to Termination).

(10) Late in the war some service commands began the practice in every case of compiling a very elaborate strike manual, which might run to thirty pages. This would have attached as exhibits every conceivable paper that might be useful; lists of the names, addresses, and phone numbers of all persons whom the team might wish to contact; and ground plans of the properties involved. See, for example, the Kelsey-Hayes Wheel Company, Chrysler Corporation, and Chicago Motor Cartage manuals or intelligence surveys prepared by the Sixth Service Command.

(11) See App. BB–1.

(12) Occasionally, these documents would be turned over in escrow to the judge advocate on the mission before the team departed. Distribution of the original and copies was later made in accordance with Ltr, Under Sec War to Dir, Bureau of the Budget, 16 Jun 45 (App. BB–9).

(13) For examples of the types of releases used in the more unusual cases, see Appendixes BB–13 (S. A. Woods) and BB–14 (Farrell-Cheek).

(14) For examples of typical initial statements of War Department representatives, see Appendixes BB–11, BB–12, and BB–14.

(15) See Ltr, Acting Sec War to Dir, Selective Service, 23 Dec 43 (App. BB–18); Ltr, Acting Sec War to Chairman, National War Manpower Commission, 23 Dec 43 (Apps. BB–17 and AA–1); Memo for file by Ohly, 12 Feb 45, sub: Plant Seizure—Liaison With Navy (App. BB–2), and Memo,

Capt G. M. Keller (USN) for Rear Adm F. G. Crisp, 2 Feb 45, sub: Liaison Procedure Between Field Representatives of SECP and War Department Representatives in Charge of Seized Plants (App. BB–3). As to further details on termination, see plant seizure manual, pt. IX and app. I, forms 14–18.

CHAPTER 18

The Labor Phases of a Plant Seizure

It is essential when discussing plant seizures to keep in mind the two basic elements of the government's wartime labor policy—the no-strike pledge and the acceptance of National War Labor Board (NWLB) decisions. Although neither policy was legally binding, employers and employees often felt a patriotic compulsion to accept and comply with both. This distinction is important because in the terminology of seizure words like *decisions*, *order*, *right*, *duty*, and *obligation* were used in a moral rather than a legal sense because strikes and lockouts were not illegal, nor was the failure to comply with an NWLB order.

Plant seizures were resorted to when vital production was directly affected or threatened or, in some cases, even when the production was not important to the war effort. The rationale in the latter situation revolved around the idea that inaction was a fatal mistake and that a prolonged strike or extended noncompliance with NWLB orders in a large firm, particularly in an important industrial center, bred other strikes and noncompliance cases, threatening overall war production.

In some cases plant seizures were merely techniques for enforcing NWLB orders. Nearly all War Department seizures involved some form of vital production, and enforcing NWLB orders was merely a part of the mechanism used to assure continuous production. The takeovers were not intended as punishments, and when a seizure did injure one party it was usually the result of the company's refusal to cooperate. Inevitably, the very fact that the Army could effectively operate private facilities constituted pressure on noncompliant parties to accept conditions the government said were fair. While measures were often taken to persuade or force labor or management acceptance of government conditions, the War Department was careful to insure that these steps were also in the interests of efficient operations.

Significance of the Labor Factor

All wartime seizures were undertaken to secure the resumption or maintenance of operations at plants where actual or threatened labor or management difficulties interfered with production. Takeovers constituted the principal measure used by the government to keep people working or to bring them back to work when their actions were inconsistent with the need for continued production. While no two cases were the same, the broad outlines of every seizure were calculated to attain this objective, and all operational phases were planned with this fundamental purpose in mind. This applied to the handling of public relations, the disposition of procurement and production problems, determinations about using troops, and the treatment of fiscal matters.(1)

Three Basic Types of Labor Problems

Three broad types of labor problems were usually present during all wartime plant seizures. Resuming or continuing production was always the first labor problem encountered, and its solution was often closely tied to efforts to maintain or implement the terms and conditions of employment the government said should prevail during operations. The War Department deemed it essential that any return to or continuation of work was on its terms, without compromise or concession, even though these terms were often offensive to the disputing parties. This problem was basically psychological, determining what steps under what circumstances were most likely to produce a return to or continuation of work. Solutions were simple when labor was united in wanting terms and conditions of employment that management simply refused to grant but were difficult when labor was divided with different factions each having their own demands. These difficulties were especially great when demands were unrealistic or impossible to grant except after a long waiting period.

The War Department dealt with only three takeovers where all the employees did not return to work: at the Western Electric Company, the Philadelphia Transportation Company, and the Fall River textile mills. The Navy, the Office of Defense Transportation, and the Department of the Interior encountered similar difficulties during seizures of the San Francisco machine shops, the Cartage Exchange of Chicago, and the nationwide coal companies, respectively.

After production was restored or assured by War Department seizure, the next objective was to insure continued production without government control—an obvious prerequisite to termination. Solutions included trying to force or persuade the warring factions to voluntarily reach a mutually acceptable settlement or to change their attitudes toward government policies and decisions or toward existing arbitration agencies and procedures.

A second problem in all but a few cases involved securing the unequivocal acceptance of a settlement derived from a law or pre-seizure government action by the noncompliant party whose prior rejection had prompted seizure. If a solution was not found before seizure, post-takeover steps included the resort to such steps as collective bargaining and implementation of NWLB orders in an effort to obtain acceptance by all parties of whatever solution was reached or to obtain the defaulting party's agreement to follow orderly procedures in good faith and abide by the results irrespective of their character.

When the War Department operated a facility, it assumed full responsibility for seeing that daily labor problems were resolved in an appropriate manner. In many cases, it delegated these problems to the former plant managers, but it could never disregard its ultimate responsibility for what went on in the eyes of labor, management, and the public. On other occasions, however, delegating problems elsewhere was not feasible, and the War Department had to deal with these difficulties while taking into consideration any overriding federal policies, the transitory character of the takeover, and the effect its actions might have on efforts to dispose of the underlying labor dispute and to restore the plant to private control.

Analysis of Labor Situations That Gave Rise to Plant Seizures

All wartime seizures involved either management or labor noncompliance with federal labor policies or the decisions of various government agencies. There were twelve takeover cases dealing with management noncompliance and seventeen dealing with labor.(2) Seizures by other agencies showed labor more often at fault,(3) but a careful analysis discloses that the underlying conditions were often the fault of both management and labor. The twelve cases of management noncompliance followed no particular geographical or industrial patterns and were spread over eleven states,(4) although towards V–J Day there was some concentration of cases in the southeastern textile industry (*see Map*). Similarly, these seizures involved eleven different industries,(5) with no discernable relationship between particular management noncompliance cases and a specific union or unions. Coincidental exceptions existed in the case of the United Electrical Radio and Machine Workers of America (CIO) and the Textile Workers Union of America (CIO), which were parties in two and three cases, respectively, but two of these situations involved nonrelated union organization struggles in the South.

In spite of the lack of similarities in these areas, there were other features where the uniformity was striking. With the exception of Montgomery Ward, Hughes, and Ken-Rad, every seized firm employed fewer than 1,000 people and at two, Cocker Machine and Foundry and Twentieth Century Brass, there were only 125 and 43 workers, respectively. No industrial giants were seized.

Secondly, these companies were usually owned and dominated by a very few people. At Air Associates a small group of absentee owners entrusted policy to a single man, while at S. A. Woods three people controlled most of the stock and company policy. Ownership was wider at Ken-Rad but one member of one family controlled the largest interest in a fashion similar to that of the Cocker Machine and Foundry, which was also a family firm. Three families owned 70 percent of Mary-Leila Cotton Mills stock and filled all principal corporate posts, while at the Twentieth Century Brass and Farrell-Cheek policies were dictated by father-and-son teams. By contrast, Montgomery Ward and Hummer had many stockholders, but Sewell Avery exercised unquestioned authority to make decisions regarding labor at both companies. The control of the Gaffney Manufacturing Company was more indirect, with a few individuals at Deering-Milliken dominating the firm. At Hughes the owner, Howard Hughes, was the chief stockholder, but he left company policies to a small clique of local people.

In the third place, most of these firms exercised a paternalistic management style and had experienced a long period of bad labor relations. More striking, however, was the fact that union security was involved in eleven of twelve cases, the

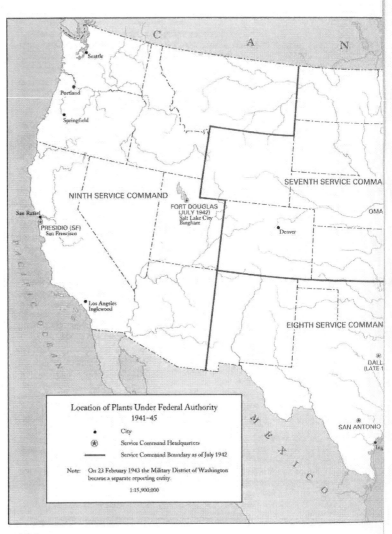

MAP

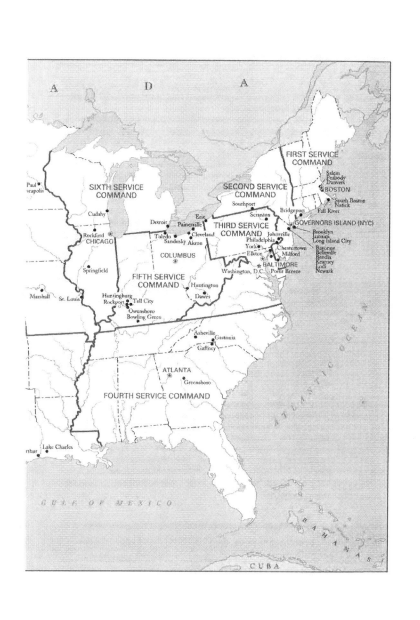

exception being Air Associates.[1] Union security was the key factor in at least six cases(6) and, along with arbitration of grievances, seniority, and retroactive wages, was the major obstacle in four others.(7)

Analysis of the labor noncompliance cases shows that the great majority were jurisdictional disputes—the product of interunion fights or internal control struggles. The strikes at Salem-Peabody, Fall River textile mills, International Nickel Company, Springfield Plywood Corporation, U.S. Rubber, and Fairport, Painesville, and Eastern Railroad were notable examples. Even in cases where clear union demands on management existed, closer examination reveals that one group was using the larger dispute to further its interests against those of a rival. At Western Electric the racial issue was injected by the independent union to refute National Labor Relations Board (NLRB) charges that it was company-dominated and to augment its membership in preparation for rival organization drives. Similarly, at Philadelphia Transportation a defeated union raised the racial issue as a device to strengthen membership and regain control. At North American Aviation a recently victorious CIO union felt compelled to force a showdown, demonstrate its strength, and consolidate its triumph over the AFofL by obtaining promised benefits. The significance here lies in the fact that in most instances there was no government machinery to bring about a quick solution to these interunion or internal union struggles, which caused bitter feelings at the plant level. There were only a few cases where normal collective bargaining issues were involved, and many were of a special nature. In three cases rather unusual collective bargaining limitations existed. At American Enka Corporation a duration-long agreement was in place that allowed no room for any union-favored adjustments. The contract at Diamond Alkali, also lasting for the duration, contained an escalator clause providing cost-of-living increases, but the federal wage stabilization program forbade this and effectively vitiated the premises on which the contract was drawn. The fact that workers at the Department of Water and Power of the City of Los Angeles were municipal employees deterred collective bargaining there.

Another significant feature of labor noncompliance cases was union culpability. The nation's two largest associations of unions, the AFofL and CIO, were responsible for only seven of seventeen cases—a CIO union in four, an AFofL union in two, and affiliates of both in one. Neither the AFofL or the CIO international was concerned with more than one case. The Railroad Brotherhoods, the United Mine Workers of America, and the Mechanics Educational Society of America (MESA)[2] were each involved in two seizures, while four seizures involved unaffiliated unions.(8)

---

[1] See Nelson Lichtenstein, "Ambiguous Legacy: The Union Security Problem During World War II," Labor History 18 (1977): 214–38.

[2] The Mechanics Educational Society of America was formed in Detroit in 1933 by tool and die makers employed in the automobile industry. MESA was originally intended as a nonmilitant self-help and educational association representing skilled workers rather than production-line laborers. The association adopted a standard union charter in 1934 and accepted both skilled and unskilled workers as members following passage of the National Labor Relations Act of 1935. It maintained its independent status until 1955, when it joined the AFL-CIO. MESA's 1939 membership of 5,500 grew to 36,400 by 1945.

Most labor defiance cases were the result of long periods of labor-management problems, which in turn made wartime seizures inevitable. These difficulties fit two categories—management noncompliance cases and those involving actual or threatened employee strikes due to unmet demands. In the first category were situations where employers refused compliance with federal agency decisions, usually those of the NWLB. In such cases workers often halted or threatened to halt production as a last resort to force compliance with orders granting benefits, while the company used the situation to serve notice to the government that the no-strike and no-lockout policies were not legally binding. Whether a strike was actually in progress or only imminent, production in these cases was readily restored or maintained because the reason for a strike was usually eliminated through the mere act of government seizure and subsequent enforcement of any unmet order. Consequently, the real problem did not lie in ending the threat to production but in securing management acceptance of the decision or some variation agreeable to both parties and the original responsible agency.

At least twelve War Department takeovers fell into this class. In the first eight cases a strike was in progress at the time of seizure, but the employees returned to work within hours. In four others a strike was threatened but not in progress at the time of seizure. In all but one case the War Department promptly implemented federal orders with limited exceptions,(9) but delayed enforcement in any situation where such action might adversely affect production. In the Montgomery Ward case the district court intervened before many provisions were implemented or made effective. There was often a temporary delay in implementing NWLB orders because of a need for clarification and further interpretation, but this never constituted a threat to production.(10)

The second general category involved situations in which employees of a facility struck or threatened to strike for reasons not related to management noncompliance. These situations involved three types of cases: a federal order failed to meet employee demands or employees found suggested procedures unsatisfactory; employees made demands beyond wartime labor dispute settlement procedures or wanted to pressure the responsible agency; and workers were expressing sympathy with other strikers.

Those cases in the first category were the direct opposite of management noncompliance cases, and the War Department's job was primarily one of getting men back to work and keeping them at work under conditions they did not want to accept and had no possibility of altering. In the six cases where these problems occurred, the War Department insisted on and obtained a return to work under the conditions specified in the decisions.(11) This type of situation was in many respects the most difficult because the workers had no further avenue of appeal from the ruling to which they objected.

Another difficulty in such cases was discovering and taking effective measures to provide a safe return of the facility to private operation. There was the danger that the workers, devoid of any hope of relief, might take the position that, although they would work for the government under the conditions directed, they would not work for private management under the same circumstances.

In the second group of labor-initiated disputes, particularly cases where employees struck or threatened to strike to obtain demands contrary to established wartime labor dispute settlement procedures, relief depended upon the nature and the adequacy of the procedures available. The many possible variations are well illustrated in the War Department takeovers, such as North American Aviation where employees stuck while their demands were pending before the National Defense Mediation Board (NDMB). The strike was called in order to pressure the NDMB into a quick and favorable decision. Once the seizure had occurred and the men had returned to work, it was possible for the NDMB to continue consideration of the case without pressure and to hand down a decision. Other cases that were variations of this type included the American Railroad Company, Cleveland Electric Illuminating Company, Salem-Peabody, Fall River textile mills, Springfield Plywood, U.S. Rubber, and Fairport, Painesville, and Eastern Railroad.

The International Nickel case was a special variation. It involved a strike ostensibly caused by a company failure to dispose of outstanding grievances. In spite of the existence of these unremediated grievances, the union had not attempted their disposition through contract procedures, choosing instead to use the issues as part of a subterfuge for other purposes, in this case a bitter intraunion fight. Recently elected union officers were attempting to coerce the support of members for the election of their candidate as district representative of the parent international union. The incumbent belonged to another faction and had considerable support within the plant. The strike was intended to discredit this incumbent and to gain support for the newly elected officers. The situation was so out of hand before the War Department intervened that the international union had suspended the local officers. This was a case in which, although an adequate procedure for the solution of the ostensible issue existed, it was convenient for certain individuals to use the issue as a pretext for striking for different purposes. The problem in such cases was several fold: to dispose of the grievances through available procedures, thus eliminating any excuse for a strike; to prompt the international union to restore local discipline and responsibility; and to instill an understanding in the union that the selection of officers and the conduct of union business had to come under the framework of the union's charter.

The Department of Water and Power of the City of Los Angeles presented a unique problem because it was municipally owned. A union seeking to organize employees struck to obtain recognition and wage increases, but because government bodies are inherently restricted in relations with employees and because of city charter limitations it was impossible to grant these demands. Furthermore, no independent federal agency existed to handle the dispute, leaving the task to the employer. This was a case where established procedures were wholly unsatisfactory to the workers but where no alternative course for redress existed. The War Department took over, obtained a rapid return to work, and withdrew when the city worked out a satisfactory agreement.

A sympathy strike by employees with no demands of their own was the third sort of case, best illustrated by the MESA strike in Toledo and Detroit. The root of the trouble was a fight between the CIO-affiliated United Automobile Workers of

America (UAW) and MESA for control of production workers in the Toledo Electric Auto-Lite Company. MESA was the certified agent for toolroom and other skilled employees, while the UAW represented production workers. To stop MESA activities among the latter, the UAW invoked its maintenance of membership privileges to suspend several production workers who belonged to both groups and who actively supported the latter. MESA insisted that the suspended men return to work while the NWLB considered the suspension, but the UAW maintained that the dispute was an internal union matter. The MESA workers then struck, hoping that this would force UAW members out of work; but when the strike faltered, MESA called a sympathy strike at twenty-six plants, including those in Toledo and Detroit. MESA knew the strike would focus federal attention on the case and throw tens of thousands of UAW members out of work, placing heavy pressure on the UAW to back down in Toledo. Considerable prestige was at stake, and neither side was willing to back down without some face-saving measure, although both sides knew that the entire sympathy strike would collapse if the original controversy were settled. Adequate procedures for securing a settlement were present, and the War Department seized only six plants that were critical to its own procurement, not including the plant where the trouble started. This action undermined MESA's position, for the seizure forced thousands of UAW members back to work but left substantial pressure on the UAW to settle the original dispute. Within twenty-four hours the War Department returned the six plants to private control after working out the basic dispute to the agreement of the UAW and MESA and thereby removing the reason for a continued sympathy strike.

Basic Laws, Policies, and Other Considerations Governing the Treatment of Labor Factors

After passage of the War Labor Disputes Act the character and scope of War Department seizure activities was circumscribed by laws, executive orders, federal policies, and other considerations. Earlier the situation was different, but significant features of policies adopted later had been understood. Not all of these policies were always rigidly adhered to, but neither major policies nor the laws were ever compromised for the sake of convenience, and the instances of deviation were few and far between.

Section 9 of the Selective Training and Service Act of 1940 provided that existing state or federal laws relating to the health, safety, security, and employment standards of the employees of any seized facility remained in place and in force during government operations. This provision was designed, in the words of its sponsor Senator Robert F. Wagner,[3] to prevent affected employees from losing

---

[3] Robert F. Wagner (1877–1953) was a Democratic senator from New York State who served twenty-three years in Congress. Born in Germany, Wagner was educated in law at New York City College. He practiced law before entering state politics in 1904. Wagner left the New York State Senate in 1918 for the New York Supreme Court, where he stayed for eight years before gaining election to the U.S. Senate. Wagner was an avid supporter of the New Deal and of Roosevelt's foreign policies. He sponsored a great deal of social welfare, civil rights, and labor legislation, of which the National Labor Relations Act and Social Security Act of 1935 are perhaps the most famous.

Senator Robert F. Wagner

"all their rights to social security, old age pensions, unemployment benefits, workmen's compensation, rights under the Walsh-Healy Act, the National Labor Relations Act, and other laws which are not in existence." Insofar as state and federal labor laws were concerned, a seized plant was operated just as if it were still privately controlled.

The most useful piece of legislation facilitating War Department seizures was the War Labor Disputes Act. Section 4 provided that where possession was taken of a facility pursuant to the authority contained in Section 9 of the Selective Training and Service Act, the facility was to be operated under the wages and other terms and conditions of employment in effect at the time possession was taken. Section 5 provided that the NWLB might, on application by the federal agency in possession or by a majority of employees or their representatives, and after hearings and investigations, order any changes in wages or other terms and conditions it deemed fair and reasonable that did not conflict with any act of Congress or executive order. Section 5 further made compliance with these orders mandatory on the part of the seizing agency but did not require the president's approval except where the agency objected to the NWLB order or requested it for other reasons.(12)

The executive order directing seizure, in addition to instructing the agency head involved to take all necessary steps to operate the facility, included provisions dealing with labor problems. The first included the authorization to employ or continue to employ any and all persons the secretary deemed necessary. Second, the seizing agency was directed to observe the terms and conditions of employment at the time of seizure, reiterating the requirements of the War Labor Disputes Act. Frequently, these orders were appended with a more specific direction "to observe" some or all of the terms of a prior NWLB order not yet fully accepted by one or both parties or specific limitations on the extent of the order and how it was to be carried out. The Department of Justice held that NWLB orders were part of the conditions of employment at the time of seizure and approved numerous executive orders containing such instructions for the president.(13) Third, the secretary of war was directed to take all steps necessary to protect employees or those seeking employment in the affected plant who feared physical violence. Fourth, other agencies, such as the War Manpower Commission, the Selective Service System, or the Justice Department, were ordered to render general or specified assistance to the operating agency. Occasionally, as at Jenkins Brothers and Ken-Rad, the president or the director of war mobilization issued instructions on specific labor problems not fully covered by the executive order.

One fundamental War Department policy in all seizures was the absolute refusal to make promises or concessions on issues in dispute to the party whose noncompliance prompted the takeover. Neither the return to or the continuance at work of employees nor the cooperation of management was ever conditional on a government quid pro quo. If either party wanted relief from a wrong done by the other party or by the government, such relief was possible only through orderly collective bargaining processes or federally established procedures. Neither employers nor employees were to reap any benefits from a wrongful strike or noncompliance with federal orders because the War Department believed concessions would invite others to disregard wartime labor procedures. It was made abundantly plain at the outset of all seizures that employees were obligated to return to work under conditions as they existed, even though temptations to seek compromises were often great and the pressures compelling. Nonetheless, the War Department adhered to a policy of neutrality with rare exceptions.(14)

The second major policy was never to force the nonguilty party to make concessions to the party responsible for the seizure. If employee and employer rights in a dispute were not specifically spelled out by an NWLB order—which they usually were—the procedure for the establishment or clarification of such rights were made available. These rights, both substantive and procedural, while of a moral rather than a legal character, were entitled to protection if employers and employees were expected to observe the no-strike, no-lockout pledge. Government intervention was not intended as an occasion for forcing any party to waive, surrender, or modify their rights.(15)

As a third basic policy the War Department usually acquiesced if the disputing parties, free from federal pressure and economic pressure from either party, worked out an agreement that was at variance with or modified the rights one party might already have, provided that this agreement conformed with applicable laws and executive policies.

The War Department never sought to conciliate, mediate, or arbitrate disputes that led to seizures, nor did it participate in negotiations between parties. This fourth basic policy clarified its position that unresolved labor issues were the domain of the involved parties and the federal civilian agencies established to aid them in settling disputes. The War Department had no interest in the merits of any controversy and made this plain to all concerned. Any other position than one of strict neutrality could have drawn the War Department into the field of industrial relations, where it lacked expertise and where charges of partisanship could irreparably damage its prestige and basic plant seizure mission. It did, however, encourage and provide opportunities for contending parties to meet and work out their differences and sought assistance whenever possible from other federal agencies. This particular policy was frequently bent, if not broken, but nearly always in a way that avoided charges of partisanship. Army labor officers, in fact, came very close to conciliating in some cases because realism demanded it.

A fifth and final War Department policy was to maintain the status quo on all basic issues until contrary instructions were obtained from another agency. This policy went beyond the provisions of Section 4 of the War Labor Disputes Act that required the War Department to continue the terms and conditions of employment existing at the time of seizure. Sections 4 and 5 were often inapplicable in cases involving a transportation system or a municipal or state facility, and other situations sometimes revolved around disputed questions unrelated to the terms and conditions of employment as ordinarily understood. For example, several cases involved questions of representation or grew out of disputes about the employment status of an individual or group. The same general principle of maintaining the status quo was followed under these circumstances because any change without recourse to established government procedures constituted a concession to the guilty party.(16) This did not mean that the War Department avoided the everyday labor problems incident to plant operations, particularly if the operation was an extended one. The department could and did—either itself or through management—make and put into effect decisions necessary for efficient plant operation, provided they did not constitute concessions.

Considerable publicity, which became the subject of careful scrutiny by both management and labor, accompanied every takeover. Consequently, the War Department's actions were very likely to influence the extent to which labor and management attempted to avoid future seizures. If a seizure brought a victory to the guilty party, it constituted an invitation for other groups to urge seizure for gaining similar and otherwise unobtainable advantages. If such a psychology had developed, it inevitably would have destroyed the roots of the government's no-strike policy and increased the War Department's takeover burden to intolerable levels. It is essential in wartime that the Army have the public's confidence, respect, and support. Failures, irrespective of their relationship to the major mission of winning the war, affected the Army's public standing, and the opportunity for failures during plant seizures were high. The War Department had to maintain or restore production quickly, without compromising government policies, and uphold its reputation for impartiality while retaining the confidence and respect of labor, management, and the public. The difficulties of accomplishing this are apparent. Plant seizures were only required in extreme cases where militant positions were taken or where feelings ran high. Significant political implications were often involved on the local level in the sense that one or more of the disputing parties was supported by political, racial, national, or social elements, so that the community itself became involved or felt strongly about the dispute. In other cases the implications were national in scope because the questions involved partisan political debates. The intervention of the federal government in the affairs of a state or municipality, for example, could raise delicate issues concerning federal-state relationships, while questions of union security, arbitration of grievances, and retroactive wages often involved intense conflict between rival economic and philosophical groups. The War Department sought to avoid any involvement in the politics or merits of such situations even when the strongest pressures were exerted, including those from other federal agencies, and when the most subtle devices were tried to force the War Department on to one side or the other.

The War Department's effectiveness in a plant takeover tended to wane over time as the novelty of its presence wore off and its ability to materially influence the situation eroded. Operations tended to settle into a rut, making the Army's withdrawal difficult, while latent issues between parties presented new problems that necessitated further federal action. Similarly, the parties often sought to use the Army's presence to their own advantage, making it more difficult to avoid taking sides. The War Department quickly learned that it was advantageous to work toward the swift conclusion of any seizure mission.

The War Department's primary mission in any plant seizure was to restore or maintain production, but the kind of production or services involved and the length of time that could elapse before an interruption seriously affected the war effort varied from case to case. The degree of urgency materially influenced the techniques used, especially if operations were interrupted by a strike when seizure occurred. The relative order in which various sanctions were employed and the time schedule for their use had in some measure to turn upon the need of the War Department to get operations under way. If needs were desperate, the War Department immediately and simultaneously invoked every available technique irrespective of whether such actions might result in both a longer dispute and prolonged takeover. In cases where products or services were less vital it was possible to move with more caution and to allow more time for the development of detailed plans of action.

Techniques Designed To Restore or To Maintain Production During Government Possession

Restoring or maintaining production was only a problem in seizure situations resulting from labor defiance. In the typical management noncompliance case workers usually returned to work immediately when the government assured them that NWLB orders would be implemented, thus removing any incentive to strike. The only exception occurred at the Schwinn Warehouse of Montgomery Ward, resulting from the government's protracted inability—because of court-imposed restrictions—to provide certain workers benefits to which they were entitled.

Cases of labor noncompliance provided a wide variety of conditions. The cause of the outbreak, the likelihood of settling underlying issues through orderly decisions, the relative degree of bitterness, the existence and attitudes of any international unions, and the views of the workers and their leaders concerning the effect of seizure upon their own interests all varied. They materially affected the techniques adopted in each case and the character and degree of firmness of any sanctions employed.

In the average case the War Department depended upon simple appeals to worker patriotism, believing that such appeals coupled with the knowledge that they were returning to work for the government rather than for a private concern was sufficient. While this was usually true, there were instances where intense per-

260 INDUSTRIALISTS IN OLIVE DRAB

sonal feelings required application of more than these ordinary measures. In these cases the War Department operated on the basic premise that production depended on getting the strikers back to work because under wartime labor market conditions it was impossible to recruit other civilians as replacements. While supplementing the existing work force was feasible at times, it was possible only on an extremely limited and relatively insignificant scale.(17)

Assuming this premise, there were three possible courses of action, none of them mutually exclusive. The first course involved measures to eliminate any fear of violence or intimidation held by those wanting to return to work, including the provision of physical protection. In such cases as Philadelphia Transportation the War Department went further and began to remove possible sources of violence by threatening to invoke the War Labor Disputes Act or to initiate FBI investigations. The question of picket lines arose in this connection. This issue first surfaced at North American Aviation, where peaceful picketing was allowed if it presented no threat to workers entering or leaving the plant. The decision to prohibit any such picketing within a mile of the plant, however, in reality constituted a ban on such activities. The issue did not reappear until after passage of the War Labor Disputes Act, which made picketing a government-seized plant a criminal offense. In all later cases, when the government took the position that picketing was illegal, officials invariably had no difficulty in securing immediate withdrawal by merely sending word to the picket captain or to local union leaders.

With the exception of North American Aviation there were few instances where any violence or intimidation occurred away from the plant. In cases where such danger did exist, the War Department representative customarily offered protection to workers going to and from work or in their homes, as well as to their families.

The second possible course of action sought to eliminate any influences keeping workers on strike. Measures here were designed to discredit strike leaders or to convince them that their own best interests lay in encouraging a return to work. There were too few cases where strikers did not promptly return to work at the time of seizure to establish any patterns of response. At North American Aviation and at Philadelphia Transportation the general policy of discrediting strike leaders was adopted, coupled with their removal from the scene by discharge or the application of sanctions under the War Labor Disputes Act, the use of a blacklist, or the removal of deferments under the Selective Training and Service Act. In the Western Electric and Fall River textile mills cases a policy of winning over the responsible leaders was followed, based in part on the virtual impossibility of discrediting them. It was possible in some cases, and this was particularly true at Philadelphia Transportation, to undermine the strikers' platform and remove misconceptions that the average worker had about the issues of the strike or the likelihood that striking would lead to satisfaction of their demands.

The third and most important line of approach sought to create a positive desire to return to work in one of several ways. It was preferable, if possible, to make the workers feel that it was their patriotic duty to work through the use of a wide variety of techniques familiar to any advertising man. There was often a profound lack of knowledge on the part of workers concerning the significance of their work to the war effort and of the grave military consequences likely to result from a strike. The War Department believed that once the worker truly understood the negative ramifications of his actions to the war effort he would readily resume his labors. This practice was not entirely foolproof, however, especially in such places as Salem-Peabody and some of the Fall River textile mills, where it was widely known that the plants produced only civilian goods.

If relying on worker patriotism failed to effect a return to work, other techniques—such as shaming those who stayed away from the job or attaching a social stigma to those who shirked their job—were tried. Newspapers and the radio were effectively used toward these ends against both workers and trade union leaders. The benefits of returning to work in terms of the employee's personal economic well being were emphasized, and it was frequently made clear that continued idleness, however prolonged, would never further the workers' goals. In many cases local and international labor officials who had decided to cooperate with the War Department were able to place the full weight of trade union appeal and discipline behind the termination of a strike. Unfortunately, most of the really serious cases were ones where labor leaders were weak, had lost control, or were beyond persuasion. Finally, as a last resort, the War Department could invoke measures intended to make employees afraid to stay away from their jobs, such as criminal prosecution under the War Labor Disputes Act, the elimination of draft deferments, the establishment of a blacklist, the denial of unemployment benefits, and/or permanent discharge of those failing to report to work.

Since seizure was meant to restore production rather than merely to punish, penalties were usually not invoked against individuals.(18) The only exceptions occurred at North American Aviation and at Philadelphia Transportation, where circumstances led to active measures being taken against strike ringleaders. Any other policy would have meant that NWLB orders and the no-strike pledge were essentially unenforceable.

One problem connected with securing a full return to work that often appeared in prolonged strikes was that employees found more attractive employment elsewhere. The War Department always took the position that these individuals should report to the seized plant, but it was powerless to enforce its stance. Nearly every case like this was one where management was in noncompliance with an NWLB order and where the individuals who found other work did so in good faith. While it was possible to use wartime manpower controls to force workers to return to their former employers, this policy was deemed unwise. A more practical and effective solution was to ask union leaders to persuade former employees to return. A somewhat different problem arose when employers replaced striking workers.(19) The War Department, after consulating the NLRB and NWLB, often directed the immediate reemployment of displaced workers even if it meant discharging more recent hires.(20)

Another fundamental principle relating to the return to work was that any return was on government conditions. This was originally only a matter of policy but became the law after the enactment of the War Labor Disputes Act. The War

Department consequently followed the practice of making it clear to all workers that they must return to work under the terms and conditions of employment that existed on seizure and that no changes would occur during the takeover except those obtained through recognized and orderly procedures. This uncompromising policy unquestionably made the problem of securing a return to work more difficult,(21) but the War Department had to operate under certain rules even when they complicated operations.

Operating Labor Problems

The War Department was often unable to avoid dealing with common day-to-day labor problems of a type that were always present no matter who controlled an industrial facility. The solution to the most common problems usually involved one to three steps, depending upon the circumstances of a given case: a determination of the terms and conditions of employment being followed at the time of seizure; the amendment or supplementation of these terms and conditions to comply with any NWLB orders; and the embodiment of these terms and conditions as amended or supplemented in a published statement.

The first step was always necessary to some degree as it was essential to have a point of reference for use in dealing with labor problems that might exist or could arise. Moreover, by law the War Department was obligated to see that previously existing conditions continued. The difficulty of making the necessary determination depended on the extent to which the terms of employment were embodied in a collective bargaining agreement or were so fixed by custom that little labor-management disagreement existed as to what had gone on before. Solutions were complicated if these terms and conditions of employment comprised part of the underlying controversy or if one or both parties were reluctant or unable to furnish the War Department with information. The question of what constituted terms and conditions of employment under the War Labor Disputes Act was frequently an involved process. On the one hand, it was clear that both the provisions of a collective bargaining agreement and some established practices of the type ordinarily included in a collective bargaining agreement came within the definition. It was less clear whether many personnel practices, some forms of plant rules, and certain physical plant conditions were included. It never proved possible to establish an inflexible line of demarcation, and to the very end of the war questions continually arose about what type of practice fell within the scope of the law's requirements. NWLB opinions, generally accepted in government circles as fair interpretations of the law, provided much clarification.(22) Questions were submitted to the attorney general or to the NWLB for answers, and on at least one occasion the NWLB was actually asked to investigate and determine what were the terms of employment.

The second step in establishing terms and conditions of employment was necessary only in cases in which the War Department was directed to implement the provisions of an outstanding NWLB order. This was often a difficult task due to the ambiguities that often characterized NWLB directives, which were normally framed with the expectation of good faith acceptance by both parties. The NWLB assumed that people who understood the problems involved and who had intimate experience in the particular plant could take the orders, iron out ambiguities, and agree on its adaptation to specific plant conditions. The NWLB's staggering case load and the fact that the board's members were strangers to most controversies prevented the rendering of precise, detailed decisions conducive to exact application by a third party, such as a War Department representative with no prior knowledge of the background of the dispute. When one party refused acceptance of an order and seizure became necessary, the situation changed considerably. In the first place, weeks and sometimes months or even years might elapse before seizure. Frequently, changes occurred in the very conditions toward which the order was directed, and it was difficult to adapt the order to these new circumstances. In the second place, the War Department often found itself attempting to apply an order without the benefit of the background and experience that the NWLB assumed would be utilized by the parties in making the order effective. Finally, an order often contained provisions requiring further collective bargaining negotiations between the participants. With one of the participants removed from the scene through noncompliance, the possibility of executing this phase of the order was gone. For these reasons it was often necessary for the War Department to solicit further NWLB instructions and interpretations. A general procedure was gradually developed to handle such situations whereby a memorandum raising and fully discussing a particular question was transmitted by the War Department representative to the Labor Branch, Industrial Personnel Division, which in turn submitted the question by formal letter to the NWLB. The latter developed efficient administrative procedures for processing these matters and responding promptly. In making these references to the NWLB, the War Department always maintained strict neutrality,(23) even in those cases where one interpretation was more advantageous to its carrying out its obligations as a seizing agency.

The third step was the embodiment of the terms and conditions in a single published document for the guidance of all concerned.(24) In most seizures resulting from labor fault, where there was usually no complicated, substantive NWLB order to apply, publication was ordinarily dispensed with.

There were a few exceptions to the rule that the terms and conditions of employment that existed at the time of seizure would continue in effect during government operation. These exceptions concerned contract provisions or practices that seriously limited production, that authorized strikes under certain conditions, or that were contrary to an executive order, such as that relating to premium pay (No. 9240), or to discrimination (No. 8802), or to a federal wage stabilization law.(25)

There was also one other situation where the War Department considered deviating from the rule in lieu of presidential direction. For the Hughes takeover, it was instructed to enforce an NWLB order directing maintenance of membership.(26) At the time of the seizure a large number of highly skilled and irreplaceable craftsmen at the plant were covered by this provision and were delinquent in their dues, having recently attempted to resign from the certified union

(United Steel Workers Association) for membership in another group. It was feared that applying maintenance of membership would result in their termination, which was unthinkable in a vital war plant, and that it would trigger an uncontrollable strike of all Hughes workers. In anticipation of a CIO discharge request, a plan was developed under which the War Department would inform the union that because of urgent production requirements the discharges would not take place unless replacements were supplied or higher authority so directed.(27) The plan also called for referring the dispute to the president for the clarification of War Department alternatives: either carrying out that part of the executive order directing the continuation of full production or the enforcement of NWLB provisions on maintenance of membership. The plan stated that simultaneous execution of both provisions appeared impossible. To avert a crisis, the problem was discussed informally, frankly, and at great length with the international officers of the CIO, who fully appreciated the War Department's dilemma and suggested a compromise solution obviating the problems posed by invocation of maintenance of membership. The union would apply to the NWLB for a change in the terms and conditions of employment, pursuant to Section 5 of the War Labor Disputes Act, to make the involuntary checkoff applicable to all of those persons previously covered by the maintenance of membership provision. Such a change would enable the union to collect its future dues without recourse to the threat of discharge. Involuntary deduction of dues could precipitate labor trouble in the plant or lead to resignations on the part of those who had left the CIO fold, but it was far less likely to do so than enforcement of maintenance of membership. The union filed its application with the NWLB, and the application was granted and received presidential approval. The War Department submitted a statement of pertinent facts without taking a specific position.(28) With much trepidation as to the possible consequences, it then made involuntary checkoff effective after a series of conferences with individuals and groups who were bound to resent the action. There were no serious incidents.

It was imperative for the War Department to maintain a position of impartiality, not only with respect to unsettled matters in the underlying substantive dispute but also with respect to other controversial matters. It could insist that the employees return and stay at work and observe the existing terms and conditions of employment, including applicable NWLB orders, but the War Department was merely carrying out policies expressed by law or by civilian agencies that had the responsibility for formulating such policies. Maintaining this position was not always easy or even possible under the circumstances, but the War Department did successfully escape being used by the parties in furtherance of their own ends. The danger of being used in this fashion was great. Management often saw seizures as opportunities to take steps under the cloak of the War Department that were impossible under ordinary circumstances—an opportunity to get rid of alleged troublemakers, to punish strike leaders, to exercise management prerogatives, to introduce new plant rules, to tighten discipline, to eliminate union-imposed limitations on production, or even to undermine unions. Labor tended to view takeovers as a chance to pin management's ears back, to get rid of unfriendly supervisors, to obtain information relative to production and wages previously denied them, to shake off restrictions, to secure greater union rights on company property, to dispose of long-accumulated grievances by direct appeal to the War Department, or to obtain major collective bargaining concessions. Moreover, even in cases where it was noncompliant, labor attempted to do everything possible to turn the seizure into a victory. The War Department had to resist all of these efforts, often pressed vigorously and with great cunning and subtlety, because they were not fully justified under the applicable terms and conditions of employment. Neither party was to receive incidental benefits from the seizure.(29)

Who performed what functions was easy to define in a situation where direct government operation was necessary or where, as at S. A. Woods, another going concern operated as an independent contractor. In the former case the government could not escape responsibility for personnel and industrial relations decisions, but in the latter instance the contractor had virtually full responsibility. The division of functions was far less clear; the company became the agent of the War Department in operating its own properties subject to the latter's direction and control. This was the situation in the majority of plant seizures. The problem was always troublesome, and no clear-cut demarcation was ever worked out. Certain general observations and conclusions are possible, however.

The War Department unquestionably was the top management in any plant it seized, and it could not entirely escape this fact by delegating labor relations responsibilities to the company. The government was ostensibly running the properties, and while it could not expect to reform industrial relations, it also could not permit just any type of labor practice to persist nor ignore grievances or other conditions normally dealt with by top management. In addition, the War Department could not avoid responsibility for the terms and conditions of employment that were top management prerogatives, nor disregard deviations by either side from the terms and conditions of employment or violations of applicable laws in the conduct of a seizure. On the other hand, it was desirable to avoid involvement in any decisions that might decrease the Army's influence or prestige or that might lead to charges of partisanship or make management or labor conclude that a takeover was desirable. With these various factors in mind the War Department adopted general policies that included: insisting upon strict compliance by all parties with all terms and conditions of employment; referring to civilian agencies all questions concerning the interpretation or application of such terms, conditions, and laws; becoming involved in the merits of a controversy only where the Army, as top management, had an inescapable duty to act; providing, to the extent possible and in cases where its involvement was inescapable, procedures that assured equitable results and that shifted the onus of decisions to other agencies; refusing to sponsor any changes except where such changes were of a noncontroversial nature or were jointly agreed to by management and labor; and refusing to favor or disapprove changes proposed by unions under Section 5 of the War Labor Disputes Act. The War Department insisted that it was the company's responsibility to handle labor relations, with the distinct understanding that the Army reserved the right to intervene where necessary to assure compliance with the terms and conditions of employment or where the terms themselves required it.

Major deviations from this pattern were unusual except as part of a general plan to provide for a return of the properties to private ownership, and they ordinarily took the form of very informal suggestions rather than orders. Such informal suggestions were common in cases where a better understanding between the parties was a principal key to a peaceful return to private ownership. Thus, at American Enka, Philadelphia Transportation, Western Electric, Los Angeles Department of Water and Power, International Nickel, Cleveland Graphite Bronze Company, and Cocker Machine and Foundry, the War Department made suggestions for reforms in personnel policies, the hiring of a skilled industrial relations director, the alteration of physical facilities, and the institution of educational programs. These suggestions were usually well received and more often than not were acted on favorably.

For the most part the War Department's job in relation to day-to-day labor problems was that of making certain that management was following procedures embodied in the terms and conditions of employment, the law, and executive orders, and correcting any actions that did not conform. This proved a sizeable task in cases of management noncompliance where a history of antiunion activity or of unintelligent and or unenlightened industrial relations existed.

The War Department's relation to the grievance procedure in cases where there was a management operating contract was one of the most difficult problems. Policy consisted of five fundamental parts. First, where the existing grievance procedure ended in mandatory arbitration, the War Department left to the top company management the responsibility for sitting in as the its representative in the last stage of the procedure before arbitration. There existed under the procedure itself a means by which the employees were assured an impartial result. Second, where the grievance procedure provided that a dispute might be submitted to voluntary arbitration upon consent of management or upon consent of both parties, the War Department would not participate in the grievance procedure but directed in every instance that the company as its agent consent to voluntary arbitration in the event that top company representatives were unable to reach an agreement with the union in the last preceding step of the procedure. Again, there was left open to the union the opportunity to obtain an impartial decision.(30) Third, where the grievance procedure had no provision for arbitration, the War Department participated in the final stage of the grievance procedure in its capacity as top management, but endeavored to escape responsibility for the basic decision by seeking and following the recommendations of some impartial entity selected by an outside civilian agency. Fourth, where there was no grievance procedure as part of the terms and conditions of employment that it inherited, the War Department established a simple interim grievance procedure for use until a permanent procedure was developed by the parties and its approval was secured under Section 5 of the War Labor Disputes Act.(31) Fifth and finally, in the case of every grievance procedure, the War Department insisted that the company and the union scrupulously observe its provisions, particularly those as to time limitations, and did everything possible to convince the parties to settle any grievance at the lowest possible level.

Both parties in a case were made to realize that they could not circumvent the grievance procedure by coming directly to the War Department or by attempting to otherwise deviate from its prescribed terms. While there were exceptions to the rules before the War Labor Disputes Act, this was due to inexperience.(32) It was believed that good industrial relations required continuity in the disposition of grievances and that those arising prior to government possession could not be brushed aside.(33)

Disciplinary action against employees was likely in the tense atmosphere that often prevailed at the start of a seizure, and it became necessary in some cases for the War Department to deviate from the previously stated policy of nonintervention in labor matters at the shop level by requiring that any proposed disciplinary action of a serious nature receive prior approval. This precautionary measure proved effective as a restraining influence on managers who were eager to punish persons for having struck or to get rid of employees whom they did not like during a seizure.(34) While the assumption of this role did occasionally involve the War Department in substantive labor matters, on the whole it was able to avoid serious criticisms. In the ordinary case, particularly after the initial emotional tensions were removed, the War Department representative either abandoned this rule or uniformly accepted management's recommendations as to disciplinary action, leaving to the employee affected the right to test its propriety in the normal fashion through the grievance procedure.

The War Labor Disputes Act prohibited any changes in the terms and conditions of employment existing at the time of takeover except upon an order entered by the NWLB after application by either the government operating agency or the employees or their representatives. The War Department was never eager to initiate changes. To do so might result in criticism from the company or union, would require substantive decisions on labor matters, and might place the War Department in a position where either party could seek to use the seizure for its own benefit. The War Department, therefore, refrained from making applications except when the company and union agreed that a change was desirable, when the company desired a change and the employees were unorganized, when production factors necessitated a change, or when a change was noncontroversial. When a union requested a change, the War Department always took the position that the matter was not one for it to decide and that the union had an adequate remedy through an application to the NWLB. Moreover, whenever such a union application was filed, the War Department limited its comments to a statement of the pertinent facts and expressed no official opinion.(35) If a particular NWLB order under Section 5 seemed controversial or the likely subject of later litigation, it requested that such orders receive presidential approval.(36) Procedures for handling these applications and the optional submission of resulting orders to the president were worked out in great detail between the War Department and the NWLB.

Reference has been made to that portion of Section 9 of the Selective Training and Service Act that required that federal, state, and local labor laws applicable before seizure remain in force during possession. While the employees of a seized plant were probably government employees, they continued to have all the rights and privileges previously held and the government inherited the legal obligations of the former management. By congressional fiat workers in these plants had a special status, which was of great assistance to the War Department in providing continuity and an operating framework. It removed the difficulties experienced at S. A. Woods and Air Associates with such laws as the Social Security Act and workmen's compensation statutes. The applicable laws served as a definite guide, and when the War Department was in doubt as to their application or meaning, it could always obtain an opinion from the responsible federal, state, or local agency. It continued to apply social security, workmen's compensation, and other similar laws as though private control still existed. It followed those deferment procedures under the Selective Training and Service Act that were prescribed for private employees rather than those special ones developed for use in case of government employment. It insisted on conformity with the letter and spirit of the National Labor Relations Act and with state laws concerning labor standards and exacted compliance with executive orders that would have been applicable had the properties remained under private control.

The principal issue that arose under this policy concerned the National Labor Relations Act. At Montgomery Ward, for example, practices were in effect when the War Department took over that the union claimed constituted unfair labor practices. The War Department submitted the question to the NLRB for an opinion and on its receipt promptly placed it in effect. Prior to the Hughes Tool seizure the NLRB had issued an order against the company requiring it to cease and desist from certain practices, to post notices, and to bargain in good faith with the certified union. Hughes had refused to comply with this decision, as it was permitted to do under the act, and the NLRB had instituted prescribed statutory proceedings in the circuit court of appeals to obtain an order directing compliance. The War Department took the position that the decision was enforceable until the court ruled otherwise, although the matter was still in the courts, and the company, as a private concern, was not required to accept the decision until so ordered. Its reasoning was that it was obligated to comply with the law, and in doing so it should follow the then best obtainable opinion of an authorized agency as to what such compliance required. At the moment of possession the best obtainable opinion was that of the NLRB. When the court later modified the NLRB order, the War Department accordingly modified its own instructions to Hughes.(37)

In at least two types of situations it sometimes proved necessary for a War Department representative to issue operating instructions on labor matters. The first sort involved cases where company managers or supervisors needed further guidance in applying the terms and conditions of employment or in making their practices conform to the requirements of the National Labor Relations Act or to some other law or in carrying out their obligations as War Department operating agents.(38) The other situations embraced cases of multiple seizure where in the interests of uniformity, or because it was impossible to assign labor officers to each plant, or where the labor officers were inexperienced, some form of general operating rules seemed desirable. These included cases in which War Department representatives were likely to encounter problems with company supervisors.(39) The War Department never had the problem faced by several other federal agencies of operating a whole industry under circumstances where it was impossible to assign a government representative to each facility and where there was serious danger of local troubles unless careful guidance was given to company managers. However, well after the close of the war the War Department, at the request of the Department of Agriculture, prepared a series of documents to cover this kind of situation as it cropped up in the meat packing industry. These documents represent the final crystallization of War Department thinking on labor problems.(40)

Endnotes

(1) Examples of this type of approach are found in the following documents: Memo, Ohly to Col Furphy, 22 Jan 46, sub: Steel Strikes—Notes Concerning Factors Involved in Any Proposal for Army Seizure of the Steel Mills (App. CC–1); unsigned Memo, prepared in Labor Branch, IPD, ca. 2 Aug 44, sub: Approach to Philadelphia Transportation Seizure (App. CC–4); Apps. K–3, K–4, K–6, and K–7, all relating to plans for the seizure of the coal mines; App. Q–1, relating to plans for the seizure of the American railroads.

(2) Cases classified as being management noncompliance included: Air Associates; S. A. Woods Machine Company; Ken-Rad Tube and Lamp Corporation; Hummer Manufacturing Division; Hughes Tool Company; Twentieth Century Brass Company; Farrell-Cheek Steel Corporation; Cudahy Brothers Company; Montgomery Ward and Company; Gaffney Manufacturing Company; Mary-Leila Cotton Mills; and Cocker Machine and Foundry Company. Cases classified as being labor defiance included: North American Aviation; Salem-Peabody leather manufacturing plants; Fairport, Painesville, and Eastern Railroad; Western Electric Company; American railroads; Fall River textile mills; Department of Water and Power of the City of Los Angeles; Philadelphia Transportation Company; International Nickel Company; Cleveland Graphite Bronze Company; Toledo MESA strike; Cleveland Electric Illuminating Company; Bingham and Garfield Railway Company; American Enka Corporation; Diamond Alkali Company; Springfield Plywood Corporation; and U.S. Rubber Company.

(3) See Apps. B and C.

(4) Massachusetts, New Jersey, Illinois, Kentucky, Texas, Minnesota, Ohio, Wisconsin, North Carolina, South Carolina, and Georgia. In making this statement only the principal situs of the seizure has been taken into account. Two seizures occurred in Illinois involving Montgomery Ward, although properties in Minnesota, California, Oregon, Colorado, Michigan, and New York were also involved. Ken-Rad has been classified as a Kentucky seizure and Air Associates as a New Jersey seizure.

(5) The basic company business included cotton textiles and textile machinery, retail merchandising, meat processing, steel castings, bushings, radio tubes, oil drilling equipment, farm equipment, aircraft parts, and woodworking machinery.

(6) S. A. Woods, Hughes Tool Company, Farrell-Cheek Steel Corporation, Cudahy Brothers Company, Gaffney Manufacturing Company, and Mary-Leila Cotton Mills.

(7) Hummer Manufacturing Division, Montgomery Ward and Company, Twentieth Century Brass Company, and Cocker Machine and Foundry Company.

(8) Seizures involving CIO unions were North American Aviation (United Automobile Workers); International Nickel Company (United Steel Workers Association), although later evidence disclosed that the United Mine Workers was behind it; Cleveland Electric Illuminating Company (Utility Workers Organizing Committee); and U.S. Rubber Company (United Rubber Workers), although the case equally might be assigned to MESA. Seizures involving AFofL unions included the Department of Water and Power of the City of Los Angeles (International Brotherhood of Electrical Workers), and American Enka Corporation (United Textile Workers of America). The Springfield Plywood Corporation seizure involved both the AFofL and CIO (International Brotherhood of Carpenters and the CIO's International Woodworkers of America). Seizures caused by the Railroad Brotherhoods included the American railroads (Brotherhood of Locomotive Firemen and Enginemen, Order of Railway Conductors, Switchmen's Union) and the Bingham and Garfield Railway (Brotherhood of Locomotive Firemen and Enginemen). Seizures involving the United Mine Workers included the Fairport, Painesville, and Eastern Railroad and the Diamond Alkali Company. MESA seizures included the Cleveland Graphite Bronze Company and the Toledo strike. Seizures induced by unaffiliated unions included Salem-Peabody tanneries (National Leather Workers Association), which affiliated with the AFofL after the seizure; Western Electric (Point Breeze Employees Association); Fall River textile mills (three small independent guild unions); and Philadelphia Transportation Company (Philadelphia Rapid Transit Employees Union).

(9) The twelve cases are Air Associates, Hummer Manufacturing Division, Twentieth Century Brass, Farrell-Cheek Steel Corporation, Montgomery Ward, Cocker Machine and Foundry

Company, Gaffney Manufacturing Company, Mary-Leila Cotton Mills, S. A. Woods, Hughes Tool Company, Ken-Rad Tube and Lamp Corporation, and Cudahy Brothers.

(10) This presented no problem in cases following the War Labor Disputes Act.

(11) The six cases were Western Electric, Philadelphia Transportation, Bingham and Garfield Railway, Diamond Alkali, Cleveland Graphite Bronze, and American Enka.

(12) See Opinion to the NWLB on Interpretation and Coverage of Sections 4 and 5 of the War Labor Disputes Act, 22 Aug 44, prepared by Jesse Freidin, General Counsel, NWLB (App. CC–3).

(13) See Ltr, Under Sec War to Dir, Bureau of the Budget, n.d. (App. S–9).

(14) Ltr, Philip Murray to Under Sec War, 15 Feb 44 (App. CC–5a), and reply, 18 Feb 44 (App. CC–5b); Ltr, Emil Rieve to Murray, 24 Feb 44 (App. CC–5c); Memo, Maj Boland for Ohly, 3 Apr 44, sub: Suggestions and Recommendations Resulting From Fall River Textile Mills Seizure and Operation (App. CC–6).

(15) Memo, Maj Boland for Ohly, 3 Apr 44; Memo, Under Sec War for CG, AAF, n.d., sub: War Department Operation of Certain Plants and Facilities of the Hughes Tool Company, Located in and Around Houston, Texas—Proposed Letter of the Company to the United Steel Workers of America (CIO) (App. CC–7). See Apps. P–1, P–2, and P–5.

(16) For early arguments in favor of a contrary policy see Memo, Maj Boland for Ohly, 3 Apr 44 (App. CC–6).

(17) See Apps. CC–1, CC–4, K–3, K–4, K–6, and Q–1.

(18) See Memo for file by Ohly, 27 Oct 44, sub: Cleveland Graphite Bronze Company—Report of Meeting With Company Officials and Analysis Thereof, par. 4a (App. CC–8); Memo for file by Ohly, 4 Oct 44, sub: International Nickel Company—Developments (App. CC–9).

(19) See Memo for file by Ohly, 10 Jan 45, sub: Montgomery Ward, par. 5b. The precedent was followed by Cocker Machine and Foundry Company. See Memo for file by Ohly, 23 May 45, sub: Cocker Machine and Foundry Company—Developments, par. 1.

(20) Apps. CC–1, CC–4, K–3, K–4, K–6, K–7, and Q–1.

(21) Compare, however, action taken in the Fall River textile mills case, as described in Appendix CC–5.

(22) App. CC–3; Memo, Col Gow for Col Hastings, 21 May 45, sub: Bingham and Garfield Railroad—Suspension of Engineer Wilford Nielsen (App. CC–10), discusses one situation involving this question.

(23) Ltr, Brig Gen Greenbaum to W. H. Davis, 19 Apr 44, relating to Ken-Rad (App. CC–11).

(24) App. CC–12.

(25) A good example of the last situation is to be found in the Hughes Tool Company case, where several practices in effect had been held by the NLRB to be unfair labor practices and therefore illegal. See Memo, Brig Gen Greenbaum for CG, AAF, n.d., sub: Instructions for War Department Representative Operating Certain Plants of the Hughes Tool Company, Houston, Texas, in View of Recent Decision of the Fifth Circuit Court of Appeals in the Matter of Hughes Tool Company Petitioner vs. National Labor Relations Board Respondent (App. CC–20); and Ltr, Under Sec War to Tom M. Davis, Esq., n.d. (App. CC–21).

(26) The Hughes case is contained in Memo, Col Gow for Under Sec War, 29 Sep 44, sub: Hughes Tool Company—Problem Requiring Consideration (App. CC–13).

(27) Memo, CG, AAF, for Col Cawthon, 23 Oct 44, sub: War Department Possession and Operation of Certain Plants and Facilities of the Hughes Tool Company Located in and Around Houston, Texas—Instructions Regarding Maintenance of Membership (App. CC–14).

(28) Ltr, Under Sec War to W. H. Davis, 27 Nov 44 (App. CC–15).

(29) For examples of management's expectations in these cases and the War Department's attitude, see Appendixes CC–8 and CC–9.

(30) Memo, Col Gow for CG, AAF, Attn: Brig Gen A. E. Jones, 21 Feb 45 (App. C–16).

(31) For an example of an interim grievance procedure, see Appendix CC–17, taken from Hummer terms and conditions of employment.

(32) As an illustration of the conflict in thinking on this subject, see excerpts from Memo for file by Ohly, 1 Sep 44, sub: International Nickel Company—Developments (App. CC–18). See also Decisions as to Handling of Grievances (App. CC–19), being the decision finally reached at

International Nickel. Note should be made of paragraph d of the latter. At a later date the trend of thought was toward viewing the results of any such arbitration as binding.

(33) This was true at Cleveland Graphite Bronze and International Nickel.

(34) Memos for file by Ohly, 4 and 27 Oct 44 (Apps. CC–8 and CC–9).

(35) Ltr, Under Sec War to W. H. Davis, 27 Nov 44 (App. CC–15).

(36) Hughes Tool Company, Gaffney Manufacturing Company, and Montgomery Ward were among the cases where this was done.

(37) See Apps. CC–20 and CC–21. See also Ltr, Under Sec War to the U.S. Circuit Court of Appeals for the Fifth Circuit, 10 Oct 44 (App. CC–22) and later letter (n.d.) between the same parties (App. CC–23).

(38) See Memo, War Department Representative Operating Hummer for All Supervisory Employees, n.d. (App. CC–24).

(39) See the two series of instructions issued in the Montgomery Ward case, included as Appendixes V–19 and V–26. See also proposed Instructions to Labor Officers (App. CC–25).

(40) Memo, designed to be sent to the manager of each company involved in the meat packing seizure by the government representative, sub: Conduct of Industrial Relations—Bulletin No. 1 (App. CC–26); Proposed Industrial Relations Organization (App. CC–27); Memo by Ohly, n.d., sub: Memorandum on Labor Phases of Department of Agriculture Operation of Meat Packing Plants (App. CC–28); Memo, Ohly for Armstrong, n.d., sub: Industrial Relations Problems Incident to Government Operation of Meat Packing Plants (App. CC–29). For the steps leading to termination, see Memo, Lt Col Boland for Ohly, 23 Aug 45, sub: Matters To Be Handled by the Labor Officer at Time of Army Withdrawal From a Seized Plant (App. CC–30).

CHAPTER 19

The War Department's Participation in Seizures by Other Agencies

The War Department assisted other agencies in the conduct of takeovers pursuant to a general clause or to one of two types of specific clauses frequently included in executive orders, quoted here in the forms in which they were normally cast.(1) A general clause read:

In carrying out this order, the Secretary of Interior shall act through or with the aid of such public or private instrumentalities or persons as he may designate. All Federal agencies, including, but not limited to, the War Manpower Commission, the National Selective Service System, the War Department, and the Department of Justice, are directed to cooperate with the Secretary of the Interior to the fullest extent possible in carrying out the purposes of this order.(2)

Specific clauses were either discretionary or mandatory in nature. An example of the former, such as one requiring the Army to provide protection, stated:

The Secretary of the Interior shall . . . provide protection to all employees working at such mines and to persons seeking employment so far as they may be needed; and upon the request of the Secretary of Interior, the Secretary of War shall take such action, if any, as he may deem necessary or desirable to provide protection to all such persons and mines.(3)

The following is an example of a mandatory clause:

The Petroleum Administrator is authorized to take such action, if any, as he may deem necessary or desirable to provide protection for the plants and all persons employed or seeking employment therein, and upon request of the Petroleum Administration, or such person as may be designated to act for him, the Secretary of War shall take such action as may be necessary to provide such protection to such persons and property.(4)

The following is an example of a clause requiring the Army to furnish personnel, equipment, and other forms of assistance, in addition to protection:

The Director of the Office of Defense Transportation may request the Secretary of War to furnish protection for persons employed or seeking employment in the plants, facilities or transportation systems of which possession is taken and to furnish protection for such plants, facilities and transportation systems, and may request the Secretary of War to furnish equipment, manpower, and other facilities or services deemed necessary by the Director to carry out the provisions and purposes of this order; and the Secretary of War is authorized and directed upon such request to take such action as he deems necessary to furnish such protection, equipment, manpower, or other facilities or services.(5)

Apart from furnishing informal advice or the occasional loan of a technician, active assistance was requested and given in only three cases—to the Department of Commerce in its 1944 seizure of Montgomery Ward, to the petroleum administrator at Cities Service Refining Company, and to the Office of Defense Transportation (ODT) in connection with its operation of the Cartage Exchange of Chicago. Each involved a different form of aid.

The War Department had succeeded in not being designated as the seizing agency during the Commerce Department's troubles with Montgomery Ward, but Under Secretary Patterson could not prevent its inclusion in the broad language of the order that read(6) "Upon request of the Secretary of Commerce, the Secretary of War shall take any action that may be necessary to enable the Secretary of Commerce to carry out the provisions and purposes of this order."(7) His opposition was based on the belief that the War Department had no business in purely civilian matters and would look thoroughly ridiculous. He concluded that any assistance must be kept to the minimum and must be furnished only as a last resort.(8) Brig. Gen. John F. Davis, chief of staff of the Sixth Service Command,[1] was tasked to furnish any aid required, but only after receipt of a written request from the under secretary of commerce, the government's representative, and a specific clearance from headquarters.(9)

Commerce Department representatives entered the properties on 26 April 1944 intent upon serving notices of seizure and gaining actual possession of the properties, apparently thinking this meant the eviction of Sewell Avery from the premises. Avery was in no mood to cooperate, and someone came up with the idea that a show of force was needed. Under Secretary Patterson was initially successful in persuading the commerce secretary to use U.S. marshals to serve these papers and to conduct Avery from the premises.(10) When they failed, a request for War Department assistance was repeated,(11) asking specifically for military personnel to accompany Commerce Department representatives during the seizure and to furnish guards to protect property and maintain order. After a certain amount of sparring, Davis was ordered to comply with the request(12) but to keep military participation to a minimum, to effect a withdrawal as soon as possible, and to check out any unusual situation with headquarters. Specific authority was given, however, for Davis to physically conduct Avery from the premises.

A military police platoon, consisting of thirty-nine enlisted men, three noncommissioned officers, and one lieutenant, immediately entered company offices

---

[1]The Sixth Service Command, with headquarters in Chicago, consisted of Illinois, Michigan, and Wisconsin.

without incident. The notices were served and Avery left his office voluntarily, although perhaps only because it was his normal hour for leaving work. The platoon began standing guard inside the building.(13) Up to this point everything had gone well, with the exception that the Commerce Department and the attorney general were indignant that a lieutenant rather than high-ranking officer was given this mission(14) and that the under secretary of commerce had issued a press statement specifically stating that the Army lieutenant was "now in charge of the plant" and was "to maintain possession in the name of the United States." The latter was serious because it implied that the Army had seized Montgomery Ward and was now running the properties. Events of the following day imprinted this impression indelibly on the public,(15) leading to a sharp protest from Patterson to the commerce secretary since the Army was still anxious to disassociate itself completely from the mission.(16)

The following morning Avery returned to his office and told the Attorney General Biddle that the government was bluffing and that he refused any form of cooperation. When he failed to leave the premises on request, Biddle ordered the lieutenant to remove him forcibly, and Avery, sitting comfortably with his hands folded across his stomach, rode out of the main entrance in the arms of two military policemen. The event was the news of the day, and the resulting photograph became the *Life* magazine picture of the year.(17)

The remainder of the mission was uneventful from an Army standpoint. Avery did not reenter the premises except to attend several authorized meetings, and instructions were issued to the Army to bar him if he attempted to do so. After repeated efforts, the Army succeeded in obtaining permission to withdraw and did so by noon on 29 April.(18)

The situation at the Cities Service Refinery Company at Lake Charles, Louisiana, was very different, and in this case the call for assistance was willingly met. In April 1945 production at this refinery, a key source of high-octane aviation fuel, was interrupted as a result of a dispute over rent levels at a nearby independent housing project, where some of the refinery's employees resided. The tenants claimed that the rents, approved by both the Office of Price Administration and the National Housing Agency,[2] were disproportionate and more than they could afford. Employees went on strike in protest. The issue became a community affair, accompanied by a certain amount of civil disorder. The latter included the erection of roadblocks on highways leading to the plant, the molestation of persons approaching the plant, and threats of sabotage to refinery equipment, a valuable government investment. These threats were so serious that the War Department was called prior to seizure, upon the failure of local authorities to act, and furnished military police to maintain a guard in the refinery. The purpose of this action was purely the protection of government property, and it did not extend to the dispersal of pickets or the handling of civil disorders outside the plant.(19)

---

[2] The National Housing Agency (NHA) was created by the First War Powers Act and Executive Order 9070, 24 January 1942, to coordinate the seventeen federal agencies concerned with private, public, and military housing. John B. Blandford, Jr., was its director. For NHA records, see Record Group 207, NARA.

When Petroleum Administrator Ickes took over the operation of the properties, he immediately exercised his rights under the mandatory protection clauses in the executive order by requesting military aid.(20) Maj. Gen. Richard Donovan,[3] commanding the Eighth Service Command,[4] was ordered to carry out the request,(21) and he supplemented military personnel already on duty. Although guarding the properties continued for a number of days and motor patrols were placed on the principal access roads to prevent picketing and any other obstructions, these precautionary measures proved unnecessary. The rent strike was immediately called off, the pickets disappeared, and the strikers went back to work. There were no incidents of any kind.(22)

The third case, that of the Cartage Exchange of Chicago, was entirely different. The takeover grew out of a wage dispute, complicated by serious jurisdictional issues between the AFofL and an independent union of approximately 9,500 of Chicago's 11,000 local teamsters. This strike tied up virtually all local freight transportation, complicated truck movements in and out of the city, and congested railway terminals to such an extent that freight embargoes were considered. There was a large amount of violence, and emotions were running very high. War production was seriously crippled.(23) There was a unique conflict within the War Department as to whether it should seize or whether it should insist on seizure by ODT, with the former designated to furnish assistance under a broad assistance clause in the executive order. Proponents of the former course argued that the men would not return to work for ODT, whereas they probably would for the War Department. Consequently, if ODT conducted the seizure, then the Army would be requested to give extensive assistance. If such assistance was necessary on a large scale, it was preferable for the War Department to have total control over the operation rather than ODT.(24) Those who favored the latter course were fearful that the War Department would become involved and permanently saddled with the known financial difficulties of some of the cartage concerns. Although it was pointed out that such a situation need not develop from a properly administered seizure, this latter view nevertheless prevailed.

The teamsters did not return to work at the request of the ODT representatives, who then proceeded on the theory that they had the whole Army to call upon.(25) The first request for assistance was for 4,000 troops within forty-eight hours, 3,000 for protective purposes and 1,000 to drive trucks. Within a few hours the estimate of needs rose to include 15,000 drivers. The War Department under the terms of the executive order had no alternative but to comply. The responsibility for assistance was vested in General McCoach, now commanding the Sixth Service Command,

---

[3]Maj. Gen. Richard Donovan (1885–1949) was born in Paducah, Kentucky, and was educated at West Point (Class of 1908). He held various peacetime command positions with the Coast Artillery in the United States, the Philippines, France, and the Panama Canal Zone before being assigned as the assistant chief of staff, G–4, in the Eighth Corps Area. He became the commander of the Eighth Corps Area (later Eighth Service Command) in October 1940. Donovan was promoted to the rank of major general in 1941 and in May 1945 became deputy chief of staff to the ASF commanding general. He retired in 1947.

[4]The Eighth Service Command, with headquarters in Dallas, consisted of Texas, New Mexico, Oklahoma, Arkansas, and Louisiana.

under the most carefully prepared instructions.(26) The actual demands for aid exceeded in some respects even the estimates, and at the peak of the operation troop strength was in excess of 16,000 men. The assistance provided took many forms and included sending guards to protect civilian drivers, providing Army drivers with MP guards to operate civilian trucks under governmental control, deploying truck convoy guards for "over the road" operators, dispatching Army vehicles with military drivers and guards, and protecting civilian operators in carbarns, terminals, and warehouses, though this was left generally to local police. The number of soldiers assigned varied with the progress and character of the strike. For example, the number of guards for civilian drivers increased from 415 on 20 June to a peak of 6,341 on 26 June as teamsters began to return to work and then dropped

Maj. Gen. Richard Donovan

sharply to 600 on 27 June as the strike and the likelihood of widespread violence ended. An early peak of almost 2,500 Army drivers dropped sharply as civilians resumed their jobs with military escorts. The operation was in fact a War Department operation, complicated by ODT control.(27)

The case was a real object lesson for the War Department. It demonstrated, as predicted, that there were situations in which it was preferable for the War Department to handle the entire operation rather than to assist another agency. This was especially true in cases entailing large-scale Army assistance extending beyond mere protection. Divided control or a subordinate role did not work well.(28)

In other cases, where assistance could have been requested but was not, liaison was established between the War Department and the operating agency. In some cases, particularly those involving the coal mines, elaborate plans for the furnishing of assistance were drafted. Responsibility was normally delegated to the commanding general of the service command area within which the facility was located, and a liaison officer was assigned to keep in close touch with the government representative in charge of the seizure. Instructions issued, such as for the use of troops for protective purposes, customarily followed the lines employed in the Chicago Cartage case(29) and grew out of a basic document prepared in the Labor Branch, Industrial Personnel Division, during the 1943 coal crisis.(30) A standard operating plan for these missions was never reduced to writing during the war, but during the reconversion period when War Department assistance clauses in executive orders became frequent such a plan was published.(31)

Three other minor comments are desirable for purposes of completeness, two relating to the furnishing of protection and the other to the use by other agencies in their seizure operations of uniformed Army personnel. The War Department attempted to adhere to the policy of insisting upon the prior exhaustion of efforts by federal, state, and local civil authorities before furnishing troops. This effort was consistent with its general belief that troops should not intervene in civil affairs except as a last resort, and during the war it generally maintained this position. The War Department, however, was advised by higher authority that its obligations under the executive orders upon receipt of a request were not dependent on whether civil authority was adequate. It always endeavored to have the assistance clause in an executive order phrased in such a fashion that any decision to use troops and all determinations as to their numbers and the method of their use were vested in the secretary of war and that all discretion was left in military hands. The problem as to the use of uniformed military personnel by other agencies came about largely because many soldiers were assigned to civilian agencies temporarily. The latter, faced with a takeover, often concluded that the presence of the Army at the site of the operation had a salutary effect and gave the impression that the Army was participating in the seizure. The War Department was anxious to prevent such an impression(32) and the flat rule was adopted that, except where the assistance clause so required, uniformed personnel—whether or not assigned temporarily to a civilian seizing agency—might not participate at the scene. Assistance was restricted to advice at headquarters.

Endnotes

(1) The following executive orders either specifically or by implication directed the War Department to furnish protection and/or other forms of assistance if called upon to do so by the operating agency: EO 9340 (1943, 8 F.R. 5695), EOs 9469, 9474, 9476, 9478, 9481, 9482, 9483 (1944, 9 F.R. 10343, 10815, 10817, 11045, 11387, 11459, and 11601), and EOs 9536 and 9548 (1945, 10 F.R. 3939 and 5025)—all relating to coal mines; EO 9341 (1943, 8 F.R. 6323), American Railroad Company of Puerto Rico; EO 9438 (1944, 9 F.R. 4459), Montgomery Ward and Company; EO 9554 (1945, 10 F.R. 5981), Cartage Exchange of Chicago; EO 9540 (1945, 10 F.R. 4193), Cities Service Refining Company; EO 9462 (1944, 9 F.R. 10071), Midwest Motor Carrier Systems; EO 9570 (1945, 10 F.R. 7235), Scranton Transit Company; EO 9564 (1945, 10 F.R. 6791), Humble Oil and Refining Company; EO 9565 (1945, 10 F.R. 6792), Pure Oil Company; EO 9589a (1945, 10 F.R. 8949), Sinclair Rubber, Inc.; EO 9577a (1945, 10 F.R. 8090), Texas Company; EO 9602 (1945, 10 F.R. 10957), Illinois Central Railroad Company; and EO 9658 (1945, 10 F.R. 14351), Capital Transit Company.

(2) EO 9469, 23 Aug 44 (9 F.R. 10343), coal mines, par. 3.

(3) EO 9548, 3 May 45 (10 F.R. 5025), coal mines, par. 5.

(4) EO 9564, 5 Jun 45 (10 F.R. 6792), Humble Oil Company, par. 3.

(5) EO 9554, 23 May 45 (10 F.R. 5981), Cartage Exchange of Chicago, par. 6.

(6) Memo for file by Ohly, 22 Apr 44, sub: Montgomery Ward and Company; Memo, Brig Gen Greenbaum for Patterson, 22 Apr 44, sub: Montgomery Ward.

(7) EO 9438, 25 May 44 (9 F.R. 4459), Montgomery Ward and Company, par. 4.

(8) Memo, Brig Gen Greenbaum for Lt Gen Somervell, 26 Apr 44, sub: Montgomery Ward and Company.

(9) Telecon, Maj Gen Styer and Brig Gen Davis, 26 Apr 44, at 1525.

(10) Memo, Brig Gen Greenbaum for Patterson, 26 Apr 44, sub: Montgomery Ward; and Telecon, Maj Gen Styer and Brig Gen Greenbaum, 26 Apr 44, at 1707.

(11) Telecons, Maj Gen Styer and Atty Gen, 26 Apr 44, at 1530, and Brig Gen Davis, 26 Apr 44, at 1555, 1800, and 1830.

(12) Teletype, Lt Gen Somervell to CG, Sixth Service Command, 26 Apr 44.

(13) Memo, Capt Jacobs for Maj Gen Styer, 26 Apr 44, sub: Report From Col Meyers of Occurrences at Montgomery Ward Plant; Teletype, Brig Gen Davis to Lt Gen Somervell, 26 Apr 44.

(14) Telecon, Maj Gen Styer and Brig Gen Davis, 27 Apr 44, at 1220.

(15) See Chapter 14 for the extent to which the popular impression was created that the Army was in charge.

(16) Ltr, Under Sec War to Sec Commerce, 27 Apr 44 (App. DD–5).

(17) Telecon, Maj Gen Styer and Brig Gen Davis, 27 Apr 44, at 1515, as well as daily newspapers of that date and of 28 April, which carried detailed stories and contained pictures of the whole procedure.

(18) Telecons, Maj Gen Styer and Brig Gen Davis, 27 Apr 44, at 1620, 1715, and 1750; 28 Apr 44, at 1125; and 29 Apr 44, at 1200. See also Telecon, Brig Gen Davis and Col Nash, 29 Apr 44, at 1245.

(19) Memo, Under Sec War for War Mobilization Dir, ca. 14 Apr 45, sub: Interruption of Production at the Cities Service Oil [sic] Company Refinery at Lake Charles, La.—Effect on 120 Octane Gasoline; and Ltr, Under Sec War to Dir, Bureau of the Budget, 16 Apr 45, same sub.

(20) Ltr, Ralph K. Davies to Sec War, ca. 17 Apr 45.

(21) Memo, Dep CofS for Service Commands for CG, Eighth Service Command, 18 Apr 45, sub: Plan for Action in Possession and operation by Petroleum Administrator of Cities Service Refining Corporation [sic], Lake Charles, La.

(22) Daily Rpts, Eighth Service Command, to PMG, 20–30 Apr 45.

(23) Memo, Ohly for [Maj] Gen Lutes, n.d., sub: Chicago Teamsters Strike—1600 on 19 May 45 (App. DD–7). See also Rpt, Lt Col F. A. Calvert, Jr., Ch, Intel Br, Security and Intel Div, Sixth Service Command, 18 May 45, sub: Survey of the Chicago Trucking Situation, and Rpt, Labor

Branch, Sixth Service Command, 30 May 45, sub: The Strike of Truck Drivers, Chauffeurs, and Helpers Union of Chicago and Vicinity, Local No. 705, Independent, 16–24 May 45.

(24) Memo, Ohly for [Maj] Gen Lutes, 19 May 45 (App. DD–7).

(25) Ltrs, Ellis T. Longenecker, Federal Manager, to Sec War, both 14 Jun 45.

(26) Memo, Sec War for CG, ASF, 15 Jun 45, sub: ODT Operation of Chicago Motor Carriers—Instructions Relative to War Department Assistance Under Executive Order 9554 (App. DD–1), and Memo, Gen Somervell for CG, Sixth Service Command, same date and sub (App. DD–2).

(27) Operations are reported in great detail in Daily Rpts, Sixth Service Command to PMG, 20–27 Jun 45, subs: Chicago Trucking Strike, and in Rpt, Labor Branch, Sixth Service Command, 30 Jun 45, sub: Summary of Labor Events Transpiring Before, During, and at Termination of Chicago Truck Drivers' Strike From 16–26 June 1945.

(28) Memo, Ohly for [Brig] Gen Greenbaum, 19 Jun 45, sub: Chicago Teamsters Strike—Lessons To Be Learned (App. DD–8); Unsigned and unaddressed Memo, 30 Jun 45, sub: General Comments Pertaining to Chicago Truck Drivers' Strike From 16–26 June 1945 (App. DD–9), prepared by Labor Branch, Sixth Service Command.

(29) Apps. DD–1 and DD–2.

(30) Unsigned and unaddressed Memo, 3 May 43, sub: Memorandum on Labor Relations Factors Involved in the Discharge by the War Department of Its Responsibilities in the Coal Strike (App. DD–4). This memo was in turn the product of a less formal document, prepared in the Labor Branch, IPD, on the extent to which troops should be used in the proposed Army seizure of the captive mines in 1941.

(31) Memo, Maj Gen S. L. Scott for CofS, ASF, 25 Feb 46, sub: War Department Assistance in Government Seizure and Operation of Plants, to which is attached the "Guide for Preparation of Directives for War Department Assistance in Government Seizure and Operation of Plants and Facilities by Agencies Other than the War Department" and proposed standard documents for use in connection therewith (App. DD–3).

(32) Memo, Ohly for [Brig] Gen Greenbaum, 23 Apr 45, sub: Plant Seizure—Use of Uniformed Personnel by Other Agencies Engaged in Plant Seizures (App. DD–6).

Conclusion

It is not the purpose of this section to draw a large number of specific conclusions from the wartime plant seizure experience of the War Department. Many such conclusions have been intimated in previous chapters. For example, the advantages and disadvantages of using seizures in serious labor disputes and more particularly of designating the War Department as a seizing agency have been discussed. Similarly, possible improvements in organization and in approach have been indicated, and the great desirability of studying alternative techniques for maintaining wartime labor peace has been repeatedly suggested. There are other conclusions that are beyond the scope of this history, either because factual data was not obtained to support them or because they should properly come from some other agency. These might include the question of the direct financial cost to the government of undertaking these operations and should of course include an evaluation of the extent to which plant seizures were an effective force in maintaining the no-strike pledge generally and in contributing to the success of wartime labor policies. Some thought should also certainly be given to the long-range effects of using this technique upon labor-management relations and collective bargaining and upon the role of the government in such matters. However, in spite of all these reservations, certain relevant and very important observations seem appropriate at this point.

First, plant seizures by the War Department were uniformly effective in restoring or maintaining production or services at a facility where a strike was in progress or threatened. Only in three out of the twenty-some cases in which strikes were in progress at the time of seizure was there any delay in effecting an immediate return to work, and in all three of these the delay was substantially overcome in a matter of two days to a week.(1) Furthermore, in five other cases strikes that most certainly would have occurred otherwise were averted completely. Production or service, with the three exceptions noted, was promptly restored to normal—in fact just as rapidly as technical production problems resulting from the strike could be solved. These problems were often solved in record time. Moreover—and this is highly significant—in virtually every case where operations were put under the War Department's control production soared to unprecedented heights. It was not merely restored or maintained at normal levels—it rose, often very substantially. It would, of course, be unfair to attribute all of such increases or all of any individual increase to affirmative activities of the Army, although these were often an important contributing cause. Nevertheless, the fact stands out indisputably that War Department possession almost invariably meant higher production.(2) Since much of this production was of an extremely critical nature (3) the benefits derived are obvious.

Second, termination of a War Department seizure was almost always the beginning of an extended period of at least nominal labor-management peace. It is believed that at every facility at which the War Department had a chance to complete its mission—that is, to restore the facility to private management before V–J Day—no strike of any significance occurred for the balance of the war. This meant that Army occupation, designed to keep labor peace by force at first, was effective in establishing a basis for or in creating the relationships and attitudes that later enabled the parties to maintain that peace themselves. Moreover, even the return to private control after V–J Day of facilities where the underlying disputes had not been fully solved was not followed in most cases by strikes.

Third, in spite of the widespread criticism that seizure was unfair or unwise, particularly in management circles, the fact was that management and labor at a particular plant affected not uniformly, but certainly usually, praised the seizure upon its completion. These attitudes could perhaps be attributed to the increase in profits and to the improved industrial relations usually resulting from seizures. Some of the many reasons set forth in chapters on specific cases as to why management or labor actively sought takeovers will supply further answers. Moreover, with a few early exceptions,(4) management or labor at a plant seemed to harbor no ill will toward the Army as such or toward the War Department representatives. Relations were almost always cordial. Whatever resentment individuals might have against the government for the seizure and accompanying sanctions, it was not usually personalized in expressed antagonism toward local Army officials. This does not mean that both sides did not seek to use the War Department or sometimes to resort to public criticism, although this was rare, but it does mean that there was generally an absence of any ill will at the plant level.

Fourth, seizures as handled by the War Department never caused a real economic hardship on either management or labor, except at S. A. Woods or in the very unusual case where management forced direct government operations or refused to cooperate. In fact, both management and labor usually benefited from seizure and said so. Thus, frequent statements in newspaper editorials and by management associations that it was unfair to penalize management by using plant seizure in cases of labor fault must be considered to be the products of either uninformed or intentionally deceptive persons. In only one instance of a takeover resulting from labor defiance did a management spokesman indicate resentment or displeasure at the arrival of the Army. The exception did not spring from any fear of untoward consequences to production or profits, but rather from a distaste of having his plant unfairly branded as one where industrial relations were so poor as to warrant government seizure.(5)

Fifth, the success of plant seizure as carried on by the War Department during wartime should not be taken as any indication that plant seizure in the same form, whether by the Army or some other government instrumentality, can be used successfully in peacetime or that if it could be it should be. Many of the elements that contributed to its great effectiveness were either the product of war or were peculiarly related to institutions and conditions that the war made possible or created.

Finally, War Department plant seizures were an important factor in furthering vital military procurement in a sizeable number of situations where no other means of doing so were immediately available. In this fashion, these seizures materially contributed to the conduct of the war.(6)

Endnotes

(1) Fall River textile mills, Western Electric Company, and Philadelphia Transportation Company.

(2) The facts upon which these conclusions are based are set forth in Appendix EE.

(3) See App. AA–1.

(4) The Fall River textile mills, Air Associates, and S. A. Woods cases are examples.

(5) The plant was Willys-Overland in Toledo, which was one of a series taken over in the Toledo MESA seizure. The strike was a sympathy strike and one in which the company's labor relations—which were very good—were not at fault. Because of this, everything possible was done to deny publicly the implication that this company was at fault.

(6) See App. AA–1.

List of Appendixes

J–3   Letter, F. Leroy Hill to the Acting Secretary of War, dated 3 November 1941, protesting the seizure and demanding action to protect the branch plants

J–4   Memorandum for file by Ohly, dated 8 November 1941, subject: Air Associates—Conference of Nov 2nd, 1941

J–5   Letter, Acting Secretary of War to the President, dated 3 November 1941, relative to extending possession to the branch plants

J–6   Letter, Under Secretary of War to Col. Roy M. Jones, dated 4 November 1941, being instructions relative to the extension of possession to the branch plants

J–7   Memorandum, Under Secretary of War for Lt. Col. Charles E. Branshaw, dated 5 November 1941, subject: Possession of Branch Plants of Air Associates, Incorporated, being a sample of instructions issued to officers detailed to take actual possession of the branch plants

J–8   Memorandum for file by Ohly, dated 22 December 1941, subject: Air Associates—Developments

J–9   Memorandum, Col. Roy M. Jones for the Secretary of War, dated 9 November 1941, subject: Report of Developments Touching Termination of Government Possession

J–10   Memorandum, Arthur F. Tripp, Jr., and Joseph W. Bishop, Jr., for Julius H. Amberg, dated 4 November 1941, subject: Outline of Contractual Relations Between the Government and Corporation Operating the Plant of Air Associates, Inc.

J–11   Memorandum, Julius H. Amberg for the Under Secretary of War, dated 6 November 1941, subject: Air Associates, Incorporated, commenting on difficulties of direct operation and suggesting the operation of the plant through a corporation

J–12   Supplemental contract between Air Associates, two banks, and the United States relative to the operation and the financing of the operation, dated 22 November 1941

J–12a   War Department press release, dated 26 November 1941, in answer to charges against it by F. Leroy Hill, President of Air Associates

J–13   Letter, Under Secretary of War to Air Associates, dated 29 December 1941, relative to termination of possession

J–14   Letter, Air Associates to the Secretary of War, dated 29 December 1941, relative to termination of possession

J–15   Letter, Under Secretary of War to the President, dated 26 December 1941, requesting the latter's concurrence in a War Department proposal to terminate the operation

O–1   Memorandum, Under Secretary of War for the Attorney General, dated 13 May 1941, subject: Proposed Regulations Under Sections 9 and 10 of the Selective [Training and] Service Act

O–2   Memorandum, Attorney General for the Under Secretary of War, dated 20 May 1941, subject: Proposed Regulations Under Sections 9 and 10 of the Selective [Training and] Service Act

O–3   Draft of proposed amendment to Section 9 of the Selective Training and Service Act of 1940, prepared by the Navy Department in March 1941.

O–4   Memorandum, Julius H. Amberg for Thom and Ohly, dated 20 March 1941, relative to the Navy Department's proposal for the amendment of Section 9 of the Selective Training and Service Act of 1940

O–5   Draft of proposed amendment to the Selective Training and Service Act of 1940, of undetermined source

O–6   Section 9 of the Selective Training and Service Act of 1940 (Public No. 783, 76th Congress)

O–7   Memorandum, Julius H. Amberg for Wayne Coy, dated 16 July 1941, subject: Connally Amendment

O–8   Statement of War Department Views on H.R. 6058 and H.R. 6070

O–9   Draft Letter, Secretary of War to Mary T. Norton, Chairman, House Labor Committee, commenting on proposed bill H.R. 2027

O–10   Letters, War, Navy, and Labor Departments, the Maritime Commission, the National Labor Relations Board, the National War Labor Board Public Members, and the War Production Board to Honorable Sam Rayburn, Speaker of the House, to Majority Leader McCormack, and to Chairman May of the House Military Affairs Committee, each dated 17 May 1943, setting forth the joint views of these agencies on S. 796 as amended by the House Committee on Military Affairs

O–11   Statement proposed for delivery by John J. McCloy to the House Committee on Military Affairs relative to S. 796 as amended by that committee

O–12   Summary prepared for McCloy on the War Department position on S. 796 as amended by the House Committee on Military Affairs

O–13   Letter, Secretaries of War and the Navy to the Director, Bureau of the Budget, dated 17 June 1943, urging the President to approve the Smith-Connally Act

O–14   Excerpts from the Smith-Connally Act (Sections 3, 4, 5, and 6)

O–15 Proposed memorandum, Brig. Gen. Edward S. Greenbaum for the Under Secretary of War, no date, subject: Procedure in Handling the Seizure and Operation of Private Industrial Facilities

O–16 Memorandum, Under Secretary of War for the Commanding Generals, Army Air Forces and Army Service Forces, dated 9 August 1943, subject: Procedure for War Department Operation of Industrial Facilities Under Executive Orders

O–17 Memorandum, Capt. John P. Chapman for Ohly, dated 16 July 1945, subject: Emergency Operations of Industrial Facilities by the War Department, being a critique of existing procedures and policies

O–18 Executive Order 9370, dated 16 August 1943, which authorized the economic stabilization director to take certain action in connection with the enforcement of directives of the National War Labor Board

O–19 List of Executive Order 9370 cases referred to the War Department for comment

O–20 Letter, Brig. Gen. Edward S. Greenbaum to George W. Taylor, Chairman, National War Labor Board, dated 24 March 1945, relating to Executive Order 9523

Appendix P Papers relating to the Salem-Peabody leather manufacturers case and problems discussed in connection therewith

P–1 Memorandum for file by Ohly, dated 2 December 1943, subject: Plant Seizure of Massachusetts Tanneries—Telephone Conversation Between Ohly and Colonel Pratt, 1700, 1 December 1943, being a summary of Colonel Pratt's proposed course of action

P–2 Memorandum for file by Ohly, dated 2 December 1943, subject: Analysis of Colonel Pratt's Proposed Recommendations Concerning the Handling of Labor Problems in the Tanneries Strike

P–3 Memorandum, Col. Curtis G. Pratt for the Commanding General, Army Service Forces, dated 8 December 1943, subject: Termination of Government Possession—War Department Operation of Thirteen Leather Manufacturing Plants in Area of Salem-Peabody, Massachusetts, Under Executive Order of the President

P–4 Memorandum, Col. Curtis G. Pratt for Maj. Gen. W. D. Styer, Chief of Staff, Army Service Forces, no date, subject: Suggestions for Consideration in Connection With Army Operation of Plants or Other Industrial Facilities Under Executive Order of the President

Appendix T   Papers relating to the Hummer seizure and similar cases and
             problems discussed in connection therewith

    T–1   Letter, Lt. Col. Nelson S. Talbott to Montgomery Ward and
             Company, Inc., dated 23 May 1944, setting forth the basis of the
             proposed agreement for the company to operate the properties

    T–2   Letter, Harold L. Pearson, Vice President and Treasurer,
             Montgomery Ward, to Lt. Col. Nelson S. Talbott, dated 25 May
             1944, in response to Talbott's letter of 23 May

    T–3   Letter, Lt. Col. Nelson S. Talbott to Montgomery Ward and Co.,
             dated 26 May 1944, in response to Pearson's letter of 25 May

    T–4   Memorandum, Maj. Daniel L. Boland for [Lt.] Col. Nelson S.
             Talbott, dated 28 July 1944, subject: Supplemental Report on
             Labor Matters

    T–5   Memorandum, Lt. Col. Daniel L. Boland for Ohly, dated 13
             December 1944, subject: Hummer Manufacturing Company [*sic*]

    T–6   Memorandum for file by Ohly, dated 5 March 1945, subject:
             Hummer Manufacturing Division of Montgomery Ward—
             Analysis of Situation

    T–7   Letter, Sewall [*sic*] Avery to the Secretary of War, dated 31 May
             1945, protesting against continued War Department operation

    T–8   Letter, Secretary of War to the Attorney General, dated 28 June
             1945, outlining proposed procedure for terminating possession

    T–9   Letter, Attorney General to the Secretary of War, dated 29 June
             1945, in reply to the secretary's letter of 28 June

    T–10a   Memorandum, Col. Ralph F. Gow for Lt. Col. T. N. Gearreald,
             dated 20 December 1944, subject: War Department Possession
             and Operation of the Plants and Facilities of Cudahy Brothers
             Company located in and Around Cudahy, Wisconsin—Request
             for Recommendations on Termination of War Department
             Operation

    T–10b   First indorsement, Lt. Col. T. N. Gearreald to Commanding
             General, Army Service Forces

    T–10c   Memorandum, Ohly for [Brig.] Gen. Greenbaum, dated 2
             January 1945, subject: Cudahy Bros. Co.—Steps Required in
             Order To Bring About Termination of War Department
             Operation

    T–10d   Memorandum, Ohly for [Brig.] Gen. Greenbaum, dated 12
             January 1945, subject: Cudahy Brothers Co.—Proposed Course
             of Action

    T–10e   Memorandum, Ohly for [Lt.] Gen. Styer, dated 18 January 1945,
             subject: Cudahy Brothers Co.—Notes for Conference

V–22   Unsigned and untitled memorandum for [Brig.] Gen.
       Greenbaum, dated 7 April 1945, prepared by Chicago staff sum-
       marizing situation

V–23   Letter, Attorney General to the Secretary of War, dated 12 April
       1945, giving an opinion on the question of checkoff raised in the
       latter's letter of 27 March 1945

V–24   Letter, Irving Abramson, National Director, Montgomery Ward
       Organizing Committee, to the Under Secretary of War, dated 10
       May 1945

V–25   Memorandum, Maj. Gen. Joseph W. Byron for the Commanding
       General, ASF, dated 23 April 1945, subject: Urgent Need for
       Court Action

V–26   Memorandum, Lt. Col. Daniel L. Boland for All Labor Officers,
       dated 2 March 1945, subject: General Labor Policies and Practices

V–26a Memorandum, Maj. Gen. Joseph W. Byron for the Commanding
       General, ASF, dated 12 May 1945, subject: Plan of Action
       Following Decision by Circuit Court—Hearing

V–27   Letter, Secretary of War to the Director of War Mobilization,
       dated 14 May 1945, setting forth the proposed course of action
       of the War Department after a decision by the Circuit Court

V–28   Memorandum, Brig. Gen. Edward S. Greenbaum for the Under
       Secretary of War, dated 23 May 1945, subject: Montgomery
       Ward Case—Action After the Court Decision

V–29   Motion for Stay of Mandate

V–30   Memorandum, Lt. Col. Paul M. Hebert for [Brig.] Gen.
       Greenbaum, dated 25 June 1945, subject: Conference of 23 June
       1945 on Montgomery Ward Matters

V–31   Letter, Acting Secretary of War to the President, dated 25 July
       1945, reporting on the situation with respect to retroactive wages

V–32   Letter, Secretary of War to William H. Davis, dated 25 July
       1945, relative to retroactive wages

V–33   Memorandum, Maj. Gen. D. McCoach, Jr., for the Commanding
       General, Army Service Forces, dated 13 July 1945, subject:
       Resumption of Control—Schwinn Warehouse, Photo
       Department, Central Printing Department, Display Factory and
       Maintenance Department, Fashion Mail Order House—
       Montgomery Ward and Co., Inc., Chicago, Ill.

V–34   Memorandum, Maj. Gen. D. McCoach, Jr., for the Commanding
       General, Army Service Forces, dated 24 July 1945, subject:
       Montgomery Ward and Company, Inc.—Fashion Mail Order
       House

W–2   Memorandum, Brig. Gen. Edward S. Greenbaum for the Under
      Secretary of War, dated 5 May 1945, subject: The Future
      Government Policy With Respect to the Enforcement of War
      Labor Board Orders—Conference With Judge Vinson and
      Proposed Legislation

W–3   Memorandum for file by Ohly, dated 5 May 1945, subject:
      Enforcement of War Labor Board Orders

W–4   Summary of views expressed by Garrison, Taylor and Davis on
      the enforcement of NWLB orders

W–5   Letter, Under Secretary of War for the Director of War
      Mobilization, dated 26 June 1945, relative to strike situation

W–6   Letter, Under Secretary of War to the Director of War
      Mobilization, dated 4 July 1945, relative to strike situation

W–7   Letter, Acting Secretary of War to the Director of War
      Mobilization, dated 27 July 1945, relative to strike situation

W–8   Letter, Director of War Mobilization to the Under Secretary of
      War, dated 20 July 1945, in answer to the latter's letter of 4 July
      on strikes

W–9   Memorandum, Ohly for [Brig.] Gen. Greenbaum, dated 21 April
      1945, subject: Compliance With NWLB Directive Orders

W–10 Proposed interagency procedure for processing seizure cases

W–11 Memorandum for file by Ohly, dated 7 November 1944, subject:
      Plant Seizure—Cases Involving Plants for Which PAW Is
      Responsible

Appendix X   Typical executive orders used at different stages of the war

X–1   8773, dated 9 June 1941, 6 F.R. 2777–78 (North American
      Aviation Co.)

X–2   8928, dated 30 October 1941, 6 F.R. 5559–60 (Air Associates,
      Inc.)

X–3   9225, dated 19 August 1942, 7 F.R. 6627 (S. A. Woods Machine
      Co.)

X–4   9408, dated 19 December 1943, 8 F.R. 16958 (Western Electric
      Co.)

X–5   9412, dated 27 December 1943, 8 F.R. 17395 (American
      Railroads)

X–6   9549, dated 3 August 1944, 9 F.R. 9878 (Philadelphia
      Transportation Co.)

X–7   9508, dated 27 December 1944, 9 F.R. 15079 (Montgomery
      Ward and Co.)

X–8   9595, dated 30 July 1945, 10 F.R. 9571 (U.S. Rubber Co.)

Z–1b   Fall River Textile Mills—Summary Prepared by Judge Advocate
        General's Department

Z–1c   International Nickel Company—Summary Prepared by Judge
        Advocate General's Department

Z–1d   Cleveland Graphite Bronze Company—Summary Prepared by
        Judge Advocate General's Department

Z–1e   Toledo MESA Strike—Summary Prepared by Judge Advocate
        General's Department

Z–1f   Cleveland Electric Illuminating Company—Summary Prepared
        by Judge Advocate General's Department

Z–1g   Bingham and Garfield Railway Company—Summary Prepared
        by Judge Advocate General's Department

Z–1h   American Enka Corporation—Summary Prepared by Judge
        Advocate General's Department

Z–2   Cases involving management noncompliance in which manage-
        ment refused to cooperate

Z–2a   Twentieth Century Brass Works, Inc.—Summary Prepared by
        Judge Advocate General's Department

Z–3   Cases involving management noncompliance in which manage-
        ment cooperated in operation

Z–3a   Hughes Tool Company—Summary Prepared by Judge Advocate
        General's Department, covering the period up to about 1 March
        (the period of real activity); and Letter, Acting Secretary of War
        to the Director, Office of Economic Stabilization, dated 27
        August 1945

Z–3b   Farrell-Cheek Steel Company—Summary Prepared by Judge
        Advocate General's Department, covering the period up to about
        1 March (the period of real activity); and Letter, Acting
        Secretary of War to the Director, Office of Economic
        Stabilization, dated 27 August 1945

Z–3c   Cudahy Brothers Company—Summary Prepared by the Judge
        Advocate General's Department, covering the period up to about
        1 March (the period of real activity); and Letter, Acting
        Secretary of War to the Director, Office of Economic
        Stabilization, dated 29 August 1945

Z–3d   Cocker Machine and Foundry Company—Letter, Acting
        Secretary of War to the Director, Office of Economic
        Stabilization, dated 28 August 1945

Z–3e   Mary-Leila Cotton Mills, Inc.—Letter, Acting Secretary of War
        to the Director, Office of Economic Stabilization, dated 28
        August 1945

Appendix AA   Papers relating to the attitude of the War Department on plant seizures

     AA–1   Chart showing the position of the War Department in every case in which it was proposed as a possible seizing agency, together with pertinent facts concerning the war importance of the case, the interests of other agencies, and the disposition finally made

     AA–2   Letter, Brig. Gen. Edward S. Greenbaum to the Director, Bureau of the Budget, dated 24 March 1945, being a letter protesting the proposed designation of the War Department as seizing agency in the case of Western Foundry Company and containing a good exposition of the War Department's basic position

     AA–3   Memorandum, Ohly for [Brig.] Gen. Greenbaum, dated 8 February 1945, subject: Plant Seizure, being an exposition of the reasons why parties to a labor dispute should not be told that a seizure might result from their failure to settle their differences peacefully

     AA–4   Memorandum, Col. Ralph F. Gow for the Commanding General, First Service Command, dated 15 January 1945, subject: Plant Seizure—Effect of Plant Seizure on Settlement of Issues in the New Bedford Case, being a statement of the reasons why a takeover might be disadvantageous to a party who was seeking it

     AA–5   Memorandum, Col. James T. O'Connell for the Chiefs of All Technical Services and the Commanding Generals of All Service Commands, dated 21 January 1944, subject: Instructions Regarding Labor Disputes, being an injunction against any action that might serve as an intimation to any party to a labor dispute that the War Department might invoke plant seizure

     AA–6   Memorandum, Col. James T. O'Connell for the Chiefs of All Technical Services, dated 2 February 1944, subject: Certification of Work Stoppage Which Interferes Substantially With Attaining a Procurement Goal

     AA–7   Draft Letter, Under Secretary of War to the Chairman, Economic Stabilization Board, no date, being an exposition of the serious consequences which may flow from injecting the War Department into labor-management controversies such as those involved in plant seizures

Appendix BB   Papers relating to the general administration and operation of a takeover

     BB–1   Plant Seizure Procedure—being the procedure of the Office of the Deputy Chief of Staff for Service Commands in the seizure of facilities, with accompanying forms and charts

BB–2   Memorandum for file by Ohly, dated 12 February 1945, subject: Plant Seizure—Liaison With Navy

BB–3   Memorandum, Capt. G. M. Keller (USN) for Rear Admiral F. G. Crisp, dated 2 February 1945, subject: Liaison Procedures Between Field Representatives of SECP and War Department Representatives in Charge of Seized Plants

BB–4   Memorandum, Deputy Chief of Staff for Service Commands for the Chief of Staff, Army Service Forces, dated 18 September 1944, subject: War Department Representatives

BB–5   Memorandum, Col. Ralph F. Gow for the Director of Personnel, ASF, dated 14 December 1944, subject: Choice of War Department Representatives for Plant Takeovers

BB–6   Memorandum, Col. Ralph F. Gow for the Commanding General (All Service Commands), no date, subject: Labor Officers for Plant Seizures

BB–7   Letter, Brig. Gen. E. S. Greenbaum to the Chairman, National War Labor Board, dated 3 August 1945, requesting greater care in the framing of War Labor Board orders

BB–8   Unsigned and unaddressed memorandum, no date, subject: Distribution of Documents in Plant Seizure, showing persons to whom original and copies of the delegations of authority, instructions to the War Department representative, and executive order should be sent

BB–9   Letter, Under Secretary of War to the Director, Bureau of the Budget, dated 16 June 1945, relative to the necessity for seizing the facilities of Diamond Alkali and illustrating the kind of letter used by the War Department in initiating a seizure

BB–10   Documents Relating to the Delegation of Authority

BB–10a Memorandum, Acting Secretary of War for the Commanding General, Army Air Forces, dated 30 July 1945, subject: War Department Operation of Certain Properties of the United States Rubber Company Located in or Around Detroit, Michigan, being illustrative of the statement issued by the War Department representatives at outset of a typical seizure involving labor defiance

BB–10b Delegation of Authority, Brig. Gen. A. E. Jones (for the Deputy Commander, Army Air Forces) to Lt. Col. Hervey Humlong, dated 30 July 1945, subject: War Department Operation of Certain Properties of the United States Rubber Company Located in or Around Detroit, Michigan, illustrating a typical delegation from a commanding general to a War Department representative

forms and conditions of employment under Section 5 of the War Labor Disputes Act were to be submitted for presidential approval; and reply of W. Willard Wirtz, dated 9 August 1945, agreeing to War Department proposal

CC–3   Opinion to the National War Labor Board on the Interpretation and Coverage of Sections 4 and 5 of the War Labor Disputes Act, dated 22 August 1944, prepared by Jesse Freidin, General Counsel

CC–4   Unsigned memorandum, prepared in Labor Branch, IPD, circa 2 August 1944, subject: Approach to Philadelphia Transportation Seizure

CC–5   Exchange of letters relating to the Fall River Case and showing the dangers of War Department deviation from the policy of not making concessions to the party at fault as a condition to obtaining a return to work

CC–5a   Letter, Philip Murray to the Under Secretary of War, dated 15 February 1944

CC–5b   Letter, Under Secretary of War to Philip Murray, dated 18 February 1944

CC–5c   Letter, Emil Rieve to Philip Murray, dated 24 February 1944

CC–6   Memorandum, Maj. Daniel L. Boland for Ohly, dated 3 April 1944, subject: Suggestions and Recommendations Resulting From Fall River Textile Mills Seizure and Operation

CC–7   Memorandum, Under Secretary of War for the Commanding General, Army Air Forces, no date, subject: War Department Operation of Certain Plants and Facilities of the Hughes Tool Company, Located in and Around Houston, Texas—Proposed Letter of the Company to the United Steel Workers of America (CIO)

CC–8   Memorandum for file by Ohly, dated 27 October 1944, subject: Cleveland Graphite Bronze Company—Report of Meeting With Company Officials and Analysis Thereof

CC–9   Memorandum for file by Ohly, dated 4 October 1944, subject: International Nickel Company—Developments

CC–10   Memorandum, Col. Ralph F. Gow for Col. Wallace N. [sic] Hastings, War Department Representative, dated 21 May 1945, subject: Bingham and Garfield Railroad—Suspension of Engineer Wilford Neilsen

CC–11   Letter, Brig. Gen. Edward S. Greenbaum to William H. Davis, dated 19 April 1944, relating to Ken-Rad and illustrating the type of letter sent to the War Labor Board in seeking interpretations of board orders

CC–12 Typical statement of terms and conditions of employment for all employees

CC–13 Memorandum, Col. Ralph F. Gow for Under Secretary of War, dated 29 September 1944, subject: Hughes Tool Company—Problem Requiring Consideration

CC–14 Memorandum, Commanding General, AAF, for Col. Frank W. Cawthon, dated 23 October 1944, subject: War Department Possession and Operation of Certain Plants and Facilities of the Hughes Tool Company Located in and Around Houston, Texas—Instructions Regarding Maintenance of Membership

CC–15 Letter, Under Secretary of War to William H. Davis, dated 27 November 1944, relative to the CIO proposed amendment of the terms and conditions of employment at Hughes Tool Company to include maintenance of membership

CC–16 Memorandum, Col. Ralph F. Gow for the Commanding General, AAF, Attn.: Brig. Gen. A. E. Jones, dated 21 February 1945, relative to grievance procedures at Hughes Tool Company

CC–17 Article VIII, Settlement of Grievances (Extract from terms and conditions of employment published at Hummer Manufacturing Division)

CC–18 Excerpts from Memorandum for file by Ohly, dated 1 September 1944, subject: International Nickel Company—Developments

CC–19 Decisions as to Handling of Grievances, being decision reached in International Nickel Company case

CC–20 Memorandum, Brig. Gen. Edward S. Greenbaum for the Commanding General, Army Air Forces, no date, subject: Instructions for War Department Representative Operating Certain Plants and Facilities of the Hughes Tool Company, Houston, Texas, in View of Recent Decision of the Fifth Circuit Court of Appeals in the Matter of Hughes Tool Company Petitioner vs. National Labor Relations Board Respondent

CC–21 Letter, Under Secretary of War to Tom M. Davis, Esq., no date., relating to Hughes Tool Company

CC–22 Letter, Under Secretary of War to the U.S. Circuit Court of Appeals for the Fifth Circuit, dated 10 October 1944

CC–23 Letter, Under Secretary of War to the U.S. Circuit Court of Appeals of the Fifth Circuit, no date

CC–24 Memorandum, War Department Representative Operating Hummer for All Supervisory Employees, no date

CC–25 Proposed Instructions to Labor Officers

APPENDIX A

War Department Plant Takeovers

Company and Location	Approximate Number of Employees Affected	Duration of Takeover	Executive Order References
North American Aviation Inglewood, Calif.	11,000	9 Jun–2 Jul 41	8773, 6 F.R. 2777 8814, 6 F.R. 3253
Air Associates Bendix, Belleville, and Lodi, N.J.; Chicago and Rockford, Ill.; Dallas, Tex.; Marshall, Mo.; Los Angeles, Calif.	900	30 Oct–29 Dec 41	9828, 6 F.R. 5559
S. A. Woods Machine Co. South Boston and Natick, Mass.	900	19 Aug–22 Oct 42 (another operator as of 31 Aug 45)	9225, 7 F.R. 6627 9603, 10 F.R. 10960
Fairport, Painesville, and Eastern Railroad Painesville, Ohio	80	7–10 Nov 42	None
13 Leather Manufacturing Plants Salem, Peabody, and Danvers, Mass.	3,500	24 Nov–13 Dec 43	9395B, 8 F.R. 16957 9403, 8 F.R. 16957
Western Electric Co. Point Breeze, Md.	9,000	19 Dec 43–23 Mar 44	9408, 8 F.R. 16958
565 Railroads	1,800,000	27 Dec 43–18 Jan 44	9412, 8 F.R. 17395
7 Textile Mills Fall River, Mass.	7,400	7–28 Feb 44	9420, 9 F.R. 1563
Department of Water and Power of the City of Los Angeles Los Angeles, Calif.	6,000	23–29 Feb 44	9426, 9 F.R. 2113

Company and Location	Approximate Number of Employees Affected	Duration of Takeover	Executive Order References
Ken-Rad Tube and Lamp Corp. Owensboro and Bowling Green, Ky.; Tell City, Huntingburg and Rockport, Ind.	3,125	14 Apr–25 May 44	9436, 9 F.R. 4063
Hummer Manufacturing Div., Montgomery Ward and Co. Springfield, Ill.	500	21 May 44–2 Jul 45	9443, 9 F.R. 5395
Philadelphia Transportation Corp. Philadelphia, Pa.	11,000	3–17 Aug 44	9459, 9 F.R. 9878
International Nickel Co. Huntington, W.Va.	1,666	29 Aug–14 Oct 44	9473, 9 F.R. 10613
Cleveland Graphite Bronze Co. Cleveland, Ohio	6,000	5 Sep–8 Nov 44	9477, 9 F.R. 10941
Hughes Tool Co. Houston, Tex.	6,700	6 Sep 44–29 Aug 45	9475A, 9 F.R. 10943 9603, 10 F.R. 10960
Twentieth Century Brass Co. Minneapolis, Minn.	43	9 Sep 44–17 Feb 45	9480, 9 F.R. 11143
Farrell-Cheek Steel Co. Sandusky, Ohio	700	25 Sep 44–28 Aug 45	9484, 9 F.R. 11731 9603, 10 F.R. 10960
MESA Strike (8 companies) Toledo, Ohio	16,000	4–6 Nov 44	9496, 9 F.R. 13187
Cudahy Brothers Co. Cudahy, Wisc.	966	8 Dec 44–31 Aug 45	9505, 9 F.R. 14473 9603, 10 F.R. 10960
Montgomery Ward and Co. Chicago, Ill.; Detroit, Mich.; Portland, Oreg.; Denver, Colo.; Jamaica, N.Y.; San Raphael, Calif.; St. Paul, Minn.	12,000	28 Dec 44–18 Oct 45	9508, 9 F.R. 15079 9603, 10F.R. 10960

Company and Location	Approximate Number of Employees Affected	Duration of Takeover	Executive Order References
Cleveland Electric Illuminating Co. Cleveland, Ohio	3,300	13–15 Jan 45	9511, 10 F.R. 549
Bingham and Garfield Railway Co. Bingham, Utah	285	25 Jan–29 Aug 45	9516, 10 F.R. 1313 9603, 10 F.R.10960
American Enka Corp. Asheville, N.C.	3,600	18 Feb–6 Jun 45	9523, 10 F.R. 2133
Cocker Machine and Foundry Co. Gastonia, N.C.	100	19 May–31 Aug 45	9552, 10 F.R. 5757 9603, 10 F.R. 10960
Gaffney Manufacturing Co. Gaffney, S.C.	800	28 May–9 Sep 45	9559, 10 F.R. 6287 9603, 10 F.R. 10960
Mary-Leila Cotton Mills Greensboro, Ga.	200	31 May–30 Aug 45	9560, 10 F.R. 6547 9603, 10 F.R. 10960
Diamond Alkali Co. Painesville, Ohio	2,700	19 Jun–19 Jul 45	9574, 10 F.R. 7435
Springfield Plywood Corp. Springfield, Oreg.	200	25 Jul–30 Aug 45	9593, 10 F.R. 9379 9603, 10 F.R. 10960
U.S. Rubber Co. Detroit, Mich.	6,500	30 Jul–10 Oct 45	9595, 10 F.R. 9571 9603, 10 F.R. 10960

Appendix B

Takeovers by Agencies Other Than the War Department

Year	Agency	Plant and Location	Executive Orders	Cause[1]
1941	Navy	Federal Shipbuilding and Drydock Co. Kearney, N.J.	8868, 6 F.R. 4349 9012, 7 F.R. 145	Labor dispute/ management fault
1941	Maritime Commission	Three Ships	None	Labor dispute/ labor fault
1942	Navy	Brewster Aeronautical Corp. Long Island City, N.Y.; Newark, N.J.; and Johnsville, Pa.	9141, 7 F.R. 2961 9169, 7 F.R. 3841	Inefficient management and virtual insolvency
1942	Navy	General Cable Corp. Bayonne, N.J.	9220, 7 F.R. 6413 9229, 7 F.R. 6630	Labor dispute/ labor fault
1942	Navy	Triumph Explosives Elkton and Chestertown, Md.; Milford, Del.	9254, 7 F.R. 8333 9306, 8 F.R. 2519 9386, 8 F.R. 7517	Management inefficiency
1942	ODT	Toledo, Peoria, and Western Railroad Co. Chicago, Ill.	9225, 7 F.R. 2201 9320, 10 F.R. 7315 9603, 10 F.R. 10960	Labor dispute/ management fault
1943	Interior	Coal mines	9340, 8 F.R. 5695 9393, 8 F.R. 14877	Labor dispute/ labor fault
1943	ODT	American Railroad Co. of Puerto Rico Puerto Rico	9341, 8 F.R. 6323	Labor dispute/ labor fault

Year	Agency	Plant and Location	Executive Orders	Cause[1]
1943	Navy	Howarth Pivoted Bearings Co. Philadelphia, Pa.	9351, 8 F.R. 8097 9603, 10 F.R. 10960	Management inefficiency
1943	Navy	Los Angeles Shipbuilding and Drydock Corp. Los Angeles, Calif.	9400, 8 F.R. 16641 9603, 10 F.R. 10960	Failure to perform satisfactory work under contracts
1943	Navy	Remington Rand Southport, N.Y.	9399, 8 F.R. 16269 9485, 9 F.R. 11987	Management inefficiency
1943	War Shipping Administration	Atlantic Basin Iron Works Brooklyn, N.Y.	9375, 8 F.R. 12253 9377, 8 F.R. 12963	Labor dispute/ management fault
1944	Commerce	Montgomery Ward and Co. Chicago, Ill.	9438, 9 F.R. 4459	Labor dispute/ management fault
1944	ODT	Midwest Motor Carrier Systems	9462, 9 F.R. 10071 9603, 10 F.R. 10960	Labor dispute/ management fault
1944	Interior	Mines and Collieries of Philadelphia and Reading Coal and Iron Co.	9469, 9 F.R. 10343	Labor dispute
1944	Interior	Miscellaneous coal mines	9474, 9476, 9478, 9481, 9482, 9483; 9 F.R. 10815, 10817, 11045, 11387, 11459, 11601	Labor dispute/ labor fault
1944	Navy	Jenkins Brothers Bridgeport, Conn.	9435, 9 F.R. 4063	Labor dispute/ management fault

Year	Agency	Plant and Location	Executive Orders	Cause[1]
1944	Navy	Lord Manufacturing Co. Erie, Pa.	9493, 9 F.R. 12860 9603, 10 F.R. 10960	Refusal to sell at fair price
1944	Navy	York Safe and Lock Co. York, Pa.	9416, 9 F.R. 936 9527, 10 F.R. 2424	Management inefficiency
1944	Navy	San Francisco machine shops San Francisco, Calif.	9463, 9 F.R. 9879 9466, 9 F.R. 10139 9603, 10 F.R. 10960	Labor dispute/ labor fault
1945	ODT	Cartage Exchange of Chicago Chicago, Ill.	9554, 10 F.R. 5981	Labor dispute/ labor fault
1945	ODT	Scranton Transit Co. Scranton, Pa.	9570, 10 F.R. 7235	Labor dispute/ labor fault
1945	Interior	Bituminous coal mines	9536, 10 F.R. 3939	Labor dispute/ labor fault
1945	Interior	Anthracite coal mines	9548, 10 F.R. 5025	Labor dispute/ labor fault
1945	Navy	United Engineering Co. San Francisco, Calif.	9542, 10 F.R. 4591 9603, 10 F.R. 10960	Labor dispute/ labor fault
1945	Navy	Goodyear Tire and Rubber Co. Akron, Ohio	9585, 10 F.R. 8335 9603, 10 F.R. 10960	Labor dispute/ labor fault
1945	PAW	Cities Service Refining Co. Lake Charles, La.	9540, 10 F.R. 4193 9603, 10 F.R. 10960	Rent dispute

Year	Agency	Plant and Location	Executive Orders	Cause[1]
1945	PAW	Humble Oil and Refining Co. Ingleside, Tex.	9564, 10 F.R. 6791 9603, 10 F.R. 10960	Labor dispute/ management fault
1945	PAW	Pure Oil Co. (Cabin Creek Oil Field) Dawes, W.Va.	9565, 10 F.R. 6792 9603, 10 F.R. 10960	Labor dispute/ management fault
1945	PAW	Sinclair Rubber Houston, Tex.	9589a, 10 F.R. 8949 9603, 10 F.R. 10960	Labor dispute/ labor fault
1945	PAW	Texas Co. Port Arthur, Tex.	9577a, 10 F.R. 8090 9603, 10 F.R. 10960	Labor dispute/ labor fault
1945[2]	ODT	Illinois Central Railroad	9602, 10 F.R. 10957	
1945[2]	ODT	Capital Transit Co. Washington, D.C.	9658, 10 F.R. 14351	
1945[2]	ODT	Great Lakes Towing Co.	9661 10 F.R. 14591	
1945[2]	Navy	Oil companies	9639, 10 F.R. 12592	

[1] In cases where a labor dispute caused the seizure, fault is ascribed to management or labor on the basis of which party failed to follow the orderly wartime procedures of government or to comply with the decisions or recommendations of the appropriate government agencies and not on the basis of who was right or wrong on the issue in dispute. Cases following V–J Day have not been so classified because the no-strike pledge lapsed and the War Labor Board ceased to make "decisions."

[2] Post–V–J Day.

APPENDIX C

Schedule Showing Number of Seizures by Year, by Agency, and by Type

Year	Cause	Army	Navy	ODT	Commerce	WSA	Interior	PAW	Maritime Com	Total
1941	Labor	2	1						1	4
	Nonlabor									
1942	Labor	2	1	1						4
	Nonlabor		2							2
1943	Labor	3		1		1	1			6
	Nonlabor		3							3
1944	Labor	13	2	1	1		2			19
	Nonlabor		2							2
1945	Labor	9	2	2			2	5		20
	Nonlabor									
Total[a]	Labor	29	6	5	1	1	5	5	1	53
	Nonlabor		7							7
1945	Labor		1	3						4
	Nonlabor									
Grand Total[b]	Labor	29	7	8	1	1	5	5	1	57
	Nonlabor		7							7

[a] Up to V-J Day.
[b] After V-J Day.

APPENDIX D–2

Cause and Duration of Plant Seizures

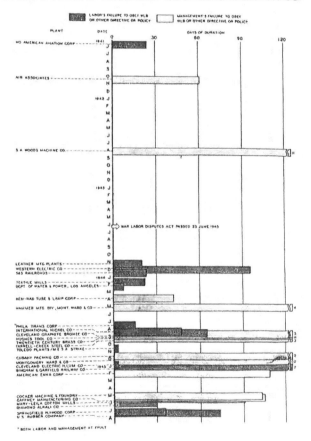

Number of Employees Affected During Plant Seizures

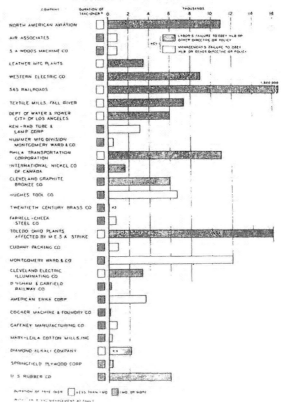

APPENDIX E–1

Number of New Plants Taken Over and Number of All
Plants Being Operated by the War Department During
Any Part of Each Quarter, 1941 Through 1945

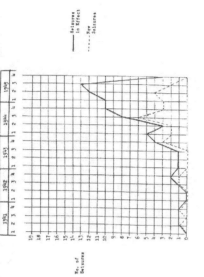

Number of Strikes and Man-Days Lost Through Strikes Affecting War Department Procurement for the Years 1941–July 1945[a]

Month	1941 Strikes/Man-Days	1942 Strikes/Man-Days	1943 Strikes/Man-Days	1944[b] Strikes/Man-Days	1945[b] Strikes/Man-Days
January	35/101,000	13/7,945	39/203,385	87/445,865	45/75,000
February	63/429,900	25/35,360	43/25,285	86/305,405	63/200,000
March	71/668,000	24/91,100	60/64,520	69/126,005	99/463,000
April	44/305,000	39/91,215	98/105,040	112/226,485	124/880,000[c]
May	81/507,000	56/49,975	128/469,075	121/809,940	101/600,245
June	79/534,000	97/132,110	98/175,210	80/244,270	134/1,135,000[d]
July	88/300,000	91/143,780	95/105,195	88/243,615	139/896,000
August	88/497,000	81/79,010	70/76,425	122/549,340	
September	78/287,000	79/128,380	62/45,210	103/221,245	
October	83/365,000	51/63,340	83/99,620	92/372,905	
November	59/267,000	41/50,650	113/187,245	98/492,750	
December	23/19,000	43/41,310	104/468,115	72/109,040	
Total	4,279,000	913,975	2,024,325	4,146,865	4,249,245

[a] Computations of man-days lost exclude Sundays and Christmas Day. Those for 1941 also exclude Saturdays.

[b] Many strikes that in earlier years would have been included in the figures have been omitted because, even though they were in plants producing for the War Department, their effect on our procurement was insignificant.

[c] Included 150,000 of the 1,320,000 man-days lost in the coal strike. The figure is a rough approximation of time lost in basic steel production, in which the War Department is indirectly interested.

[d] Includes 240,000 (Goodyear), 192,750 (Packard), and 39,000 (Mack).

APPENDIX E-3

Number of Strikes, by Months, 1942, 1943, and 1944

Man-Days Lost Due to Strikes
1942, 1943, and 1944

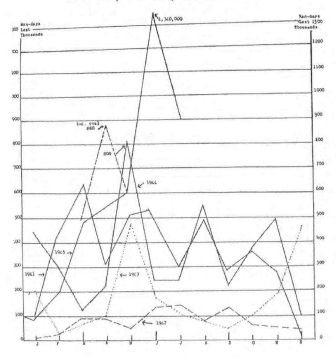

Appendix X–1

Executive Order No. 8773

WHEREAS, on the 27th day of May 1941, a Presidential proclamation was issued,[1] declaring an unlimited national emergency and calling upon all loyal citizens in production for defense to give precedence to the needs of the Nation to the end that a system of government which makes private enterprise possible may survive; and calling upon all our loyal workmen as well as employers to merge their lesser differences in the larger effort to insure the survival of the only kind of government which recognizes the rights of labor or of capital, and calling upon all loyal citizens to place the Nation's needs first in mind and in action to the end that we may mobilize and have ready for instant defensive use, all of the physical powers, all of the moral strength and all of the material resources of the Nation; and

WHEREAS North American Aviation, Inc., at its Inglewood plant in the City of Los Angeles, State of California, has contracts with the United States for manufacture of military aircraft and other material and articles vital to the defense of the United States; and the United States owns aircraft in the course of production, raw material, machinery, and other property situated in the said Company's plant; and

WHEREAS a controversy arose at said plant over terms and conditions of employment between the company and the workers which they have been unable to adjust by collective bargaining; and whereas the controversy was duly certified to the National Defense Mediation Board, established by the Executive Order of March 19, 1941;[2] and whereas before the negotiations had been concluded before the said Board, and in violation of an agreement between the bargaining representatives of the company and the workers authorized to appear before the Board and conduct the negotiations, production at said plant of said aircraft and other articles and materials vital to the defense of the United States was interrupted by a strike which still continues; and

WHEREAS the objectives of said proclamation of May 27, 1941, are jeopardized and the ability of the United States to obtain aircraft essential to its armed forces and to the national defense is seriously impaired by said cessation of production; and

---

[1] 6 F.R. 2617
[2] 6 F.R. 1532

WHEREAS for the time being and under the circumstances hereinabove set forth it is essential in order that such operations be assured and safeguarded that the plant be operated by the United States;

NOW, THEREFORE, I, Franklin D. Roosevelt, pursuant to the powers vested in me by the Constitution and laws of the United States, as President of the United States of America and Commander in Chief of the Army and Navy of the United States, hereby authorize and direct that the Secretary of War immediately take possession of and operate the said plant of North American Aviation, Inc., through such person or persons as he may designate, to produce the aircraft and other articles and material called for by its contracts, with the United States or otherwise, and to do all things necessary or incidental thereto. Such necessary or appropriate adjustments shall be made with respect to existing and future contracts and with respect to compensation to the company, as further orders hereafter issued by the Secretary of War shall provide. The Secretary of War shall employ or authorize the employment of such employees, including a competent civilian advisor on industrial relations, as are necessary to carry out the provisions of this order. And I hereby direct the Secretary of War to take such measures as may be necessary to protect workers returning to the plant.

Possession and operation hereunder shall be terminated by the President as soon as he determines that the plant will be privately operated in a manner consistent with the needs of the national defense.

FRANKLIN D. ROOSEVELT

THE WHITE HOUSE
   June 9, 1941, 10:40 a.m., E.S.T.

[No. 8773]

[F.R. Doc. 41–4120; Filed, June 9, 1941, 12:21 p.m.]

6 F.R. 2777–78

Appendix X–2

Executive Order No. 8928

WHEREAS, on the 27th day of May, 1941,[1] a Presidential proclamation was issued, declaring an unlimited national emergency and calling upon all loyal citizens in production for defense to give precedence to the needs of the Nation to the end that a system of government which makes private enterprise possible may survive; and calling upon our loyal workmen and employers to merge their lesser differences in the larger effort to insure the survival of the only kind of government which recognizes the rights of labor or of capital, and calling upon all loyal citizens to place the Nation's needs first in mind and in action to the end that we may mobilize and have ready for instant defensive use, all of the physical powers, all of the moral strength and all of the material resources of the Nation; and

WHEREAS, Air Associates, Incorporated, has contracted to furnish the United States and its contractors with parts and equipment necessary for the production of military aircraft vital to the defense of the United States and such parts and equipment have been in the course of manufacture at the Bendix, New Jersey, plants of said company, and the United States owns facilities there situated; and

WHEREAS, a controversy arose concerning the terms and conditions of employment between said company and its workers which they have been unable to adjust by collective bargaining and the controversy was duly certified to the National Defense Mediation Board established by Executive Order of March 19, 1941;[2] and whereas production was interrupted at said plants during the course of mediation before said Board by a strike and the Board, pending further mediation, recommended that the workers call off the strike and the company return all strikers upon application to their former jobs without discrimination, and whereas the workers affected, through their representatives, have accepted but the company has failed to carry out the Board's recommendation; and

WHEREAS, due to such failure on the part of the Company, production has now been impaired and complete cessation of production is now imminent at said plants and the objectives of said proclamation of May 27, 1941, are thereby jeopardized and it is essential to the defense of the United States that normal production be assured and cessation averted; and

[1] 6 F.R. 2617
[2] 6 F.R. 1532

WHEREAS, for the time being and under the circumstances set forth, it is essential in order that full production at said plants be assured, that the plants be operated by or for the United States in such manner as may be expedient;

NOW, THEREFORE, I, FRANKLIN D. ROOSEVELT, pursuant to the powers vested in me by the Constitution and laws of the United States, as President of the United States and Commander-in-Chief of the Army and Navy of the United States, hereby authorize and direct the Secretary of War immediately, in so far as may be necessary or desirable, to take possession of and operate the Bendix, New Jersey, plants of Air Associates, Incorporated, through and with the aid of such person or persons or instrumentality as he may designate, and to produce the military airplane parts and equipment called for by the company's contracts or as may be otherwise required for the national defense, and do all things necessary or incidental to that end. The Secretary of War shall employ or authorize the employment of such employees, including a competent civilian advisor on industrial relations, as are necessary to carry out the provisions of this order, and, in furtherance of the purposes of this order, the Secretary of War may exercise any existing contractual or other rights of said company, or take such other steps as may be necessary or desirable including the use of troops.

Possession and operation hereunder shall be terminated by the President as soon as he determines that such possession and operation are no longer required in the interests of national defense.

FRANKLIN D. ROOSEVELT

THE WHITE HOUSE,
    October 30, 1941

[No. 8928]

[F.R. Doc. 41–805; Filed, October 31, 1941; 12:35 p.m.]

6 F.R. 5559–60

Appendix X–3

Executive Order No. 9225

AUTHORIZING THE SECRETARY OF WAR TO TAKE POSSESSION OF AND OPERATE THE PLANT OF THE S. A. WOODS MACHINE COMPANY AT SOUTH BOSTON, MASSACHUSETTS.

By the virtue of the power and authority vested in me by the Constitution and laws of the United States, as President of the United States and Commander in Chief of the Army and Navy of the United States, it is hereby ordered and directed as follows:

The Secretary of War is authorized and directed immediately to take possession of and operate the plant of the S. A. Woods Machine Company located at South Boston, Massachusetts, through and with the aid of such person or persons or instrumentality as he may designate, and, in so far as may be necessary or desirable, to produce the war materials called for by the Company's contracts with the United States, its departments and agencies, or as may be otherwise required for the war effort, and do all things necessary or incidental to that end. The Secretary of War shall employ such employees, including a competent civilian advisor on industrial relations, as are necessary to carry out the provisions of this order and the purposes of the directive order of the War Labor Board of August 1, 1942, in the matter of S. A. Woods Machine Company et al., and, in furtherance of the purpose of this order, the Secretary of War may exercise any existing contractual or other rights of said Company, or take such steps as may be necessary or desirable.

Possession and operation hereunder shall be terminated by the President as soon as he determines that the plant of the S. A. Woods Machine Company at South Boston, Massachusetts, will be privately operated in a manner consistent with the war effort.

FRANKLIN D. ROOSEVELT

THE WHITE HOUSE,
    August 19, 1942, 10:40 A.M. E.W.T.

[F.R. Doc. 42–8144; Filed, August 20, 1942; 2:11 p.m.]

7 F.R. 6627

Executive Order No. 9412

POSSESSION AND OPERATION OF RAILROADS

WHEREAS the continuous operation of transportation service in the Nation is necessary for the movement of troops, materials of war, necessary passenger traffic, and supplies and food for the armed forces and the civilian population, and is otherwise essential to the successful prosecution of the war; and

WHEREAS the continuous operation of some transportation systems is threatened by strikes called to commence on December 30, 1943.

NOW, THEREFORE, by virtue of the authority vested in me by the Constitution and laws of the United States, including the Act of August 29, 1916, 30 Stat. 646, and as President of the United States and Commander in Chief of the Army and Navy, I hereby order:

1. Possession and control of all common carriers by railroad, express companies, terminal companies and associations, sleeping, parlor and railroad-owned or controlled private car companies (all hereinafter referred to as carriers) located in the continental United States, together with any and all appurtenances and facilities used in connection therewith, are hereby taken and assumed, through the Secretary of War, as of seven o'clock p.m., on the twenty-seventh day of December, 1943. Carriers taken over under this order shall not include, because not now deemed necessary, street electric passenger railways, including railways commonly called interurbans, or local public transit systems whether or not the same be owned or controlled by any of the systems of transportation taken hereunder; but if and when the Secretary finds it necessary or appropriate to carry out the purposes of this order, he may, by subsequent order, take and assume possession, control and operation of all or any part of any transportation system, including subways and tunnels, and any transportation system so taken shall be deemed a carrier for the purposes of this order.

2. The Secretary of War is directed to manage and operate or arrange for the management and operation of the carriers taken under this order in such manner as he deems necessary to assure to the fullest possible extent continuous and uninterrupted transportation service.

3. In carrying out this order the Secretary may act through or with the aid of such public or private instrumentalities or persons as he may designate, and may

delegate such of his authority as he may deem necessary or desirable, with power of successive redelegation. The Secretary may issue such general and special orders, rules and regulations as may be necessary or appropriate for carrying out the purposes of this order. All Federal agencies shall comply with the directives of the Secretary hereunder and shall cooperate to the fullest extent of their authority with the Secretary in carrying out the purposes of this order.

4. The Secretary shall permit the management of carriers taken under this order to continue their respective managerial functions to the maximum degree possible consistent with the purposes of this order. Except so far as the Secretary shall from time to time otherwise provide by appropriate order or regulation, the board of directors, trustees, receivers, officers, and employees of such carriers shall continue the operation of the carriers, including the collection and disbursement of funds thereof, in the usual and ordinary course of the business of the carriers, in the names of their respective companies, and by means of any agencies, associations or other instrumentalities now utilized by the carriers.

5. Except so far as the Secretary shall from time to time otherwise determine and provide by appropriate orders or regulations, existing contracts and agreements to which carriers taken hereunder are parties shall remain in full force and effect. Nothing in this order shall have the effect of suspending or releasing any obligation owed to any carrier affected hereby, and all payments shall be made by the persons obligated to the carrier to which they are or may become due. Except as the Secretary may otherwise direct, dividends on stock and sinking fund, principal, interest and other distributions upon bonds, debentures and other obligations may be paid in due course, and expenditures for other ordinary corporate purposes may be made.

6. The Secretary shall provide protection for all persons employed or seeking employment. The Secretary is authorized to prescribe the compensation to be received by such employees subject to any approval which may be required by applicable statutes, Executive orders and regulations related to economic stabilization. To the extent deemed practical by him, he may maintain the working conditions which are specified in existing contracts between the carriers and their employees. He shall recognize the right of the workers to continue their membership in labor organizations, to bargain collectively through representatives of their own choosing with the representatives of the owners of the carriers, subject to the provisions of applicable statutes and Executive orders, as to matters pertaining to wages to be paid or conditions to prevail after termination of possession, control and operation under this order; and to engage in concerted activities for the purpose of such collective bargaining or for other mutual aid or protection, provided that in his opinion such concerted activities do not interfere with the operation of the carriers.

7. Except as this order otherwise provides and except as the Secretary otherwise directs, the operation of carriers hereunder shall be in conformity with the

Interstate Commerce Act, as amended, the Railway Labor Act, the Safety Appliance Acts, the Employers' Liability Acts, and other applicable Federal and State laws, Executive orders, local ordinances and rules and regulations issued pursuant to such laws, Executive orders and ordinances.

8. Except with the prior written consent of the Secretary, no receivership, reorganization or similar proceeding affecting any carrier taken hereunder shall be instituted, and no attachment by mesne process, garnishment, execution or otherwise shall be levied on or against any of the real or personal property or other assets of any such carrier, provided that nothing herein shall prevent or require approval by the Secretary of any action authorized or required by any interlocutory or final decree of any United States court in reorganization proceedings now pending under the Bankruptcy Act or in equity receivership cases now pending.

9. From and after seven o'clock P.M. on the said twenty-seventh day of December, 1943, all properties taken under this order shall be conclusively deemed to be within the possession and control of the United States without further act or notice.

10. Possession, control and operation of any carrier or carriers, or parts thereof, taken under this order shall be terminated by the Secretary as soon as he determines that such possession, control and operation are no longer required to prevent interruption of transportation service.

FRANKLIN D. ROOSEVELT

THE WHITE HOUSE,
    December 27, 1943, 6 P.M., E.W.T.

[F.R. Doc. 43–20547; Filed, December 28, 1943; 10:58 a.m.]

8 F.R. 17395

Executive Order No. 9549

By virtue of the authority vested in me by the Constitution and laws of the United States including the Act of August 29, 1916, 39 Stat. 645, the First War Powers Act 1941, and Section 9 of the Selective Training and Service Act of 1940, as amended, as President of the United States and Commander in Chief of the Army and Navy, I hereby authorize the Secretary of War to take possession and assume control of the transportation systems of the Philadelphia Transportation Company, including all real and personal property and other assets, wherever situated, used or useful in connection with the operation of said systems and I authorize him to utilize such systems for such purposes connected with the war emergency as he may deem needful or desirable and to terminate the possession and control of such systems when he determines that such possession and control are no longer necessary for purposes connected with the war emergency.

August 3, 1944

(9 F.R. 9878)

Executive Order No. 9508

AUTHORIZING THE SECRETARY OF WAR TO TAKE POSSESSION OF AND TO OPERATE CERTAIN PLANTS AND FACILITIES OF MONT-GOMERY WARD & CO INCORPORATED

WHEREAS the National War Labor Board has found and reported to me that labor disturbances involving nearly 12,000 workers now exist in the plants and facilities of Montgomery Ward & Co., Incorporated in Jamaica, New York; Detroit, Dearborn and Royal Oak, Michigan; Chicago, Illinois; St. Paul, Minnesota; Denver, Colorado; San Rafael, California; and Portland, Oregon; that in the exercise of the authority conferred upon it by the War Labor Disputes Act, the National War Labor Board has issued directive orders deciding the labor disputes that gave rise to the said disturbances; that the said directive orders provide terms and conditions, of a kind customarily included in collective bargaining agreements, to govern the relations between the parties to such disputes; that the terms and conditions provided for by the said directive orders are fair and equitable to employer and employee under all the circumstances of the cases; that Montgomery Ward & Co., Incorporated has refused to put into effect the terms and conditions contained in these directive orders; that as a result of the refusal of Montgomery Ward & Co., Incorporated to put into effect the terms and conditions contained in the directive orders issued by the National War Labor Board in the dispute in the plants and facilities of Montgomery Ward & Co., Incorporated in Detroit, Michigan, a serious strike involving approximately 1,800 employees is now in progress in that city; that there is a present danger that the strike now existing in the plants and facilities of Montgomery Ward & Co., Incorporated in Detroit, Michigan, will spread to plants and facilities of Montgomery Ward & Co., Incorporated located in other cities and will adversely affect the operation of other plants and facilities, located in the Detroit area and elsewhere, that are engaged in the production of materials used in the prosecution of the war; and

WHEREAS the National War Labor Board has also found and reported to me that Montgomery Ward & Co., Incorporated, employs approximately 70,000 workers, and serves approximately 30 million customers; that an interruption of the Company's activities would unduly delay and impede the war effort; that the preservation of the war-time structure of labor relations and the prevention of interruptions of war production depend upon the peaceful settlement of labor disputes by the National War Labor Board in the manner provided for by the Congress; that the preservation of the national stabilization program requires peaceful settlement of wage disputes during the war by the procedure provided for by the Congress; that the persistent refusal of Montgomery Ward & Co., Incorporated, to put into effect the terms and conditions contained in directive orders issued by the National War Labor Board, pursuant to the War Labor Disputes Act, threatens to destroy both the wartime structure of labor relations and the procedure established by the Congress for the peaceful settlement of wage disputes during the war, and unduly impedes and delays the war effort; and

WHEREAS after investigation I find and proclaim that the plants and facilities of Montgomery Ward & Co., Incorporated, located in Jamaica, New York; Detroit, Dearborn and Royal Oak, Michigan; Chicago, Illinois; St. Paul, Minnesota; Denver, Colorado; San Rafael, California; and Portland, Oregon, are plants and facilities that are equipped for the production of articles or materials which may be required for the war effort or which may be useful in connection therewith, within the meaning of the War Labor Disputes Act; that Montgomery Ward & Co., Incorporated, is engaged in the distribution of articles and materials that are essential to the maintenance of the war economy; that as a result of labor disturbances there are existing and threatened interruptions of the operations of the said plants and facilities of Montgomery Ward & Co., Incorporated; that the war effort will be unduly impeded or delayed by these interruptions; that the operation of other plants and facilities essential to the war effort is threatened by the labor disturbances at the plants and facilities of Montgomery Ward & Co., Incorporated; and that the exercise as hereinafter specified of the powers and authority vested in me is necessary to insure, in the interest of the war effort, the operation of these plants and facilities, and of other plants and facilities that are threatened to be affected by the said labor disturbances; and

WHEREAS, after investigation I also find and proclaim that these existing and threatened interruptions result from the failure of Montgomery Ward & Co., Incorporated, to adjust labor disputes of long standing with respect to the terms and conditions of employment at the Company's plants and facilities; that the National War Labor Board has considered these disputes and issued directive orders determining and providing methods for their adjustment; that the labor unions involved have expressed their willingness to adjust the disputes in accordance with the directive orders of the National War Labor Board, but Montgomery Ward & Co., Incorporated, has persistently refused to accept the provisions of the directive orders as a basis for the adjustment of such disputes; and that this refusal unduly impedes and delays the successful prosecution of the war;

NOW, THEREFORE, by virtue of the power and authority vested in me by the Constitution and laws of the United States, including the War Labor Disputes Act (57 Stat. 163) and section 9 of the Selective Training and Service Act of 1940 (54 Stat. 892) as amended by the War Labor Disputes Act, as President of the United States and Commander in Chief of the Army and Navy of the United States, it is hereby ordered as follows:

1. The Secretary of War is hereby authorized and directed, through and with the aid of any persons or instrumentalities that he may designate, to take possession of the plants and facilities of Montgomery Ward & Co., Incorporated that are located in Jamaica, New York; Detroit, Dearborn and Royal Oak, Michigan; Chicago, Illinois; St. Paul, Minnesota, Denver, Colorado; San Rafael, California; and Portland, Oregon, and any real or personal property or other assets used or useful in connection with the operation of such plants and facilities, and to operate or to arrange for the operation of such plants and facilities in any manner that he deems essential for the successful prosecution of the war. The Secretary of War is also authorized to exercise any contractual or other rights of Montgomery Ward & Co., Incorporated; to continue the employment of, or to employ, any persons; to do any other thing that he may deem necessary for the operation of the said plants and facilities, including the production, sale, and distribution of the articles and materials customarily produced in or sold or distributed from the said plants and facilities; and to take any other steps that he deems necessary to carry out the provisions and purposes of this order.

2. The Secretary of War shall operate the said plants and facilities under the terms and conditions of employment that are in effect at the time possession of the said plants and facilities is taken, and during his operation of the plants and facilities shall observe the terms and conditions of the directive orders of the National War Labor Board, including those dated June 6 and 16, 1944, and December 14 and 15, 1944, provided that the Secretary of War is authorized to pay the wage increases specified in said directive orders, from the effective dates specified in said directive orders to the date possession of said plants and facilities is taken under this order, only out of the net operating income of said plants and facilities during the period of their operation by the Secretary of War. In the event that it appears to the Secretary of War that the net operating income of said plants and facilities will be insufficient to pay the aforesaid accrued wage increases, the Secretary shall make a report to the President with respect thereto.

3. All federal agencies, including, but not limited to, the War Manpower Commission, the National Selective Service, the Department of Justice, and the Reconstruction Finance Corporation, are directed to cooperate with the Secretary of War to the fullest extent possible in carrying out the purposes of this order. The Secretary of War may request other federal agencies, including those mentioned above, to assign personnel to assist him in the performance of his duties hereunder.

4. Possession, control, and operation of any plant or facility, taken under this order shall be terminated by the Secretary of War within sixty days after he determines that the productive efficiency of the plant or facility prevailing prior to the existing and threatened interruptions of operations, referred to in the recitals of this order, has been restored.

5. The words "plants and facilities of Montgomery Ward & Co., Incorporated," whenever used in this order, shall be deemed to include, without limitation, any mail order house, warehouse, office, retail store, factory, or production or assembly unit, owned or operated by Montgomery Ward & Co., Incorporated, in the areas specified in this order.

/s/ FRANKLIN D. ROOSEVELT

THE WHITE HOUSE

December 27, 1944.

(9 F.R. 15079)

Appendix Y–1

Executive Order No. 9603

TERMINATION OF POSSESSION OF CERTAIN PROPERTY TAKEN BY THE GOVERNMENT

By virtue of the authority vested in me by the Constitution and the laws of the United States, including section 9 of the Selective Training and Service Act of 1940 (54 Stat. 892) as amended by the War Labor Disputes Act (57 Stat. 163), it is hereby ordered as follows:

All plants, mines, facilities, and all other property of whatever kind seized or taken by the United States under and pursuant to the following-described Executive Orders, or amendments thereof, shall be returned to the owners thereof as soon as practicable, as determined in each case by the officer by whom the property in question is held and operated for the government, with the approval of the Director of Economic Stabilization:

No. 9103 of Mar. 21, 1942	No. 9536 of Apr. 10, 1945
No. 9225 of Aug. 19, 1942	No. 9540 of Apr. 17, 1945
No. 9351 of June 14, 1943	No. 9542 of Apr. 23, 1945
No. 9400 of Dec. 3, 1943	No. 9552 of May 19, 1945
No. 9462 of Aug. 11, 1944	No. 9559 of May 28, 1945
No. 9463 of Aug. 12, 1944	No. 9560 of June 1, 1945
No. 9466 of Aug. 19, 1944	No. 9564 of June 5, 1945
No. 9475A of Sept. 2, 1944	No. 9565 of June 5, 1945
No. 9484 of Sept. 23, 1944	No. 9577A of July 1, 1945
No. 9493 of Oct. 24, 1944	No. 9585 of July 4, 1945
No. 9505 of Dec. 6, 1944	No. 9589A of July 19, 1945
No. 9508 of Dec. 27, 1944	No. 9593 of July 25, 1945
No. 9516 of Jan. 24, 1945	No. 9595 of July 30, 1945

Any of the above-listed orders in conflict with this order is hereby amended to the extent of such conflict.

HARRY S. TRUMAN

THE WHITE HOUSE

August 25, 1945

List of Some of the Key Personnel Participating in War Department Plant Seizures

North American Aviation

War Department Representative:
    Lt. Col. Charles E. Branshaw, Western Procurement District, AAF

Advisor:
    Lt. Col. Edward S. Greenbaum, OUSW

Civilian Labor Advisor:
    Eric Nicols, loaned by OPM

Air Associates

War Department Representative:
    Col. Roy M. Jones, Chief, Eastern Procurement District, AAF

Deputy War Department Representative and Production Director:
    Maj. Peter Beasley, AAF

Judge Advocate:
    Maj. Karl R. Bendetson, JAGD

Assistant Judge Advocate:
    Maj. Charles Burnett, JAGD

Labor Officer (for first two days):
    Lt. Donald Ipson, Labor Branch, OUSW

Civilian Labor Advisor:
    Robert F. Gaffney, Consultant

Public Relations Officer:
    Maj. Robert S. Pickens, BPR

S. A. Woods Machine Company

War Department Representative:
    Maj. Ralph F. Gow, Boston Ordnance District

Judge Advocate:
    Maj. Charles Burnett, JAGD

Assistant Judge Advocate:
    Capt. Frank Hammond, OUSW

Civilian Labor Advisor:
    Joseph Miller, Consultant

Fairport, Painesville, and Eastern Railroad

War Department Representative:
    Col. Daley, Fifth Service Command (a direct military operation, with Daley
    having no technical staff)

Salem-Peabody Leather Manufacturing Plants

War Department Representative:
    Col. Curtis G. Pratt, Readjustment Division, ASF

Judge Advocate:
    Lt. Col. Paul M. Hebert, JAGD

Assistant Judge Advocates:
    Maj. Victor Sachse, JAGD
    Maj. Edward F. Gallagher, JAGD

Fiscal Advisor:
    Harold A. Wythes, Office of the Fiscal Director, ASF

Labor Officer:
    Maj. Dale Hill, Labor Branch, IPD

Public Relations Officer:
    Lt. O. Harrelson, Industrial Services Division, BPR

Western Electric Company

War Department Representative:
    Brig. Gen. Archie A. Farmer, Philadelphia Signal Depot

Judge Advocate:
    Lt. Col. Paul M. Hebert , JAGD

Assistant Judge Advocates:
    Lt. Col. William Thurman, JAGD
    Maj. Balfour S. Jeffrey, JAGD

Labor Officer:
    Maj. Ira B. Cross, Labor Branch, IPD

Assistant Labor Officers:
  Maj. James T. Rhudy, Signal Corps labor office, Philadelphia
  Lt. Col. John H. Long, Chief, Labor Branch, Third Service Command

Public Relations Officer:
  Lt. O. Harrelson, Industrial Services Division, BPR

American Railroads

(Only a few of the field technicians are included.)

War Department Representative:
  Maj. Gen. Charles P. Gross, Chief of Transportation

Labor Officers:
  Maj. Charles Ballon, Chief, Labor Branch, Second Service Command
  Maj. John H. Long, Chief, Labor Branch, Third Service Command
  Maj. Arthur Krim, Labor Branch, IPD
  Maj. Daniel L. Boland, Labor Branch, IPD
  Maj. Ira B. Cross, Labor Branch, IPD
  Lt. Col. Harry Branner, Chief, Labor Branch, Sixth Service Command
  Lt. Col. Gerald Coxe, Chief, Labor Branch, First Service Command
  Col. W. H. Nelson, Chief, Labor Branch, Eighth Service Command

Judge Advocates:
  Lt. Col. Abe Goff, JAGD
  Maj. George Bickford, JAGD
  Lt. Col. Howard Brundage, JAGD
  Maj. Randolph Kerr, JAGD
  Maj. Joseph V. Hodgson, JAGD
  Capt. John F. Cotter, JAGD
  Maj. Thomas F. Mount, JAGD
  Capt. Lynn K. Twinem, JAGD
  Maj. Thomas D. Carney, JAGD
  Maj. Everett A. Bogne, JAGD
  Maj. George W. Tackabury, JAGD
  Capt. Paul A. Rose, JAGD
  Maj. Edward F. Gallagher, JAGD
  Capt. Edgar A. Donahue, JAGD

Fall River Textile Mills

War Department Representative:
  Col. Curtis G. Pratt, Readjustment Division, ASF

Labor Officer:
  Maj. Daniel L. Boland, Labor Branch, IPD

Assistant Labor Officer:
  Capt. Frederick E. Winchester, Corps of Engineers labor office, New
    England Region

Judge Advocate:
  Lt. Col. Paul M. Hebert, JAGD

Assistant Judge Advocates:
  Maj. Victor Sachse, JAGD
  Maj. Albert Kulp, JAGD

Fiscal Advisor:
  Harold A. Wythes, Office of the Fiscal Director, ASF

Department of Water and Power of the City of Los Angeles

War Department Representative:
  Col. Rufus W. Putnam, District Engineer, Los Angeles, Calif.

Advisor:
  Brig. Gen. Theodore Weaver, Production Division, ASF

Judge Advocate:
  Lt. Col. Paul M. Hebert, JAGD

Assistant Judge Advocate:
  Maj. Harold L. Holland, JAGD, Western Procurement District, AAF

Fiscal Officer:
  Capt. R. C. Gross, Los Angeles finance office

Labor Officer:
  Maj. Walter Burroughs, Chief, Labor Branch, San Francisco Ordnance
    District

Assistant Labor Officer:
  Maj. Thomas Shea, Labor Branch, Ninth Service Command

Public Relations Officer:
  Maj. Howard H. Adams, Western Procurement District, AAF

Ken-Rad Tube and Lamp Corporation

War Department Representative:
  Col. Carroll Badeau, Chief, Lexington Signal Depot

Judge Advocate:
  Lt. Col. Paul M. Hebert, JAGD

Assistant Judge Advocate:
  Maj. Victor Sachse, JAGD

Labor Officer:
Maj. Daniel L. Boland, Labor Branch, IPD

Assistant Labor Officers:
Lt. Col. Kenneth Johnson, Chief, Labor Branch, Signal Corps
Capt. Seymour Peyser, Labor Branch, IPD

Fiscal Advisor:
Harold A. Wythes, Office of the Fiscal Director, ASF

Production Director:
Lt. Col. O'Shea, Production Division, Signal Corps

Disbursing Officer:
Maj. David S. Combs, Office of the Fiscal Director, ASF

Assistant Disbursing Officers:
Capt. Henry F. Gillie, Office of the Fiscal Director, ASF
Maj. I. M. Greller
Lt. F. W. Hill

Hummer Manufacturing Division

War Department Representative:
Lt. Col. Nelson S. Talbott, Chief, Central Procurement District, AAF

Labor Officer:
Lt. Col. Daniel L. Boland, Labor Branch, IPD

Assistant Labor Officers:
Capt. J. K. Gerdell, Labor Branch, Central Procurement District, AAF
Capt. Joseph A. Walsh, Labor Branch, IPD
Lt. Lawrence M. Kearns, Labor Branch, IPD

Judge Advocate:
Lt. Col. Paul M. Hebert, AGD

Assistant Judge Advocate:
Maj. George W. Tackabury, JAGD

Public Relations Officer:
Maj. A. H. Raskin, Industrial Services Division, BPR

Assistant Public Relations Officer:
Lt. O. Harrelson, Industrial Services Division, BPR

Fiscal Advisor:
Harold A. Wythes, Office of the Fiscal Director, ASF

Disbursing Officer:
Maj. David S. Combs, Office of the Fiscal Director, ASF

Philadelphia Transportation Company

War Department Representative:
Maj. Gen. Philip Hayes, CG, Third Service Command

Judge Advocate:
Lt. Col. Paul M. Hebert, JAGD

Assistant Judge Advocate:
Maj. Victor Sachse, JAGD

Labor Officer:
Lt. Col. Daniel L. Boland, Labor Branch, IPD

Assistant Labor Officer:
Lt. Lawrence M. Kearns, Labor Branch, IPD

Fiscal Advisor:
Harold A. Wythes, Office of the Fiscal Director, ASF

Public Relations Officer:
Maj. A. H. Raskin, Industrial Services Division, BPR

International Nickel Company

War Department Representative:
Lt. Col. George Woods, Production Division, ASF

Fiscal Advisor:
Maj. Frederick W. Braun, Office of the Fiscal Director, ASF

Judge Advocate:
Lt. Col. Paul M. Hebert, JAGD

Labor Officer:
Lt. Col. Daniel L. Boland, Labor Branch, IPD

Cleveland Graphite Bronze Company

War Department Representative:
Lt. Col. George D. Lynn, Deputy Director, Cleveland Ordnance District

Judge Advocate:
Lt. Col. William Thurman, JAGD

Labor Officer:
Lt. Col. John H. Long, Chief, Labor Branch, Third Service Command

Hughes Tool Company

War Department Representatives:
  Col. Frank W. Cawthon, Deputy Director, Midwestern Procurement
  District, AAF (Sep 44–Feb 45)
  Col. Ora M. Baldinger, AAF (Feb–Aug 45)

Deputy War Department Representative:
  Maj. James A. Bell, AAF, Kansas City

Labor Officers:
  Maj. John A. Coover, Labor Branch, IPD, Kansas City (Sep 44)
  Maj. Thomas Shea, Labor Branch, Ninth Service Command (Sep 45–Aug 46)

Assistant Labor Officers:
  Capt. Karl A. Ziegler, AAF, Kansas City
  Capt. Frederick C. Manning, Labor Branch, Eighth Service Command

Fiscal Officer:
  Lt. Col. John H. Savage, Jr., Office of the Fiscal Director, ASF

Accounting Officer:
  Lt. Col. William T. Chumney, AAF, Wichita

Judge Advocate:
  Maj. Victor Sachse, JAGD

Assistant Judge Advocates:
  Capt. E. A. Klierver, Jr., JAGD
  Capt. Terrence Slattery, JAGD, AAF, Wichita

Public Relations Officer:
  Lt. O. Harrelson, Industrial Services Division, BPR

Twentieth Century Brass Company

War Department Representative:
  Col. Lynn C. Barnes, District Engineer, Minneapolis, Minn.

Labor Officer:
  Lt. Lawrence M. Kearns, Labor Branch, IPD

Judge Advocate:
  Maj. George W. Tackabury, JAGD

Assistant Judge Advocate:
  Capt. John J. McKasy, JAGD

Disbursing Officer:
  Maj. David S. Combs, Office of the Fiscal Director, ASF

Assistant in Charge of Production:
    1st Lt. Royce H. Huss

Fiscal Advisor:
    Capt. Johnson, Office of the Fiscal Director, ASF

Assistant Disbursing and Fiscal Officer:
    2d Lt. J. E. Libaw, Ordnance Department

Public Relations Officer:
    Capt. Edward J. Dudley, Industrial Services Division, BPR

Purchasing Officer:
    Capt. S. W. Kovalick

Farrell-Cheek Steel Corporation

War Department Representative:
    Lt. Col. Norman J. Riebe, District Engineer, Buffalo, N.Y.

Executive Officer:
    Maj. Ernest A. Schlender

Labor Officer:
    Lt. Col. Daniel L. Boland, Labor Branch, IPD

Assistant Labor Officer:
    Maj. Frederick E. Winchester, Labor Branch, IPD

Judge Advocate:
    Lt. Col. Paul M. Hebert, JAGD

Assistant Judge Advocate:
    Capt. Hugh B. Archer, JAGD

Toledo MESA Strike

War Department Representative:
    Col. Philip Faymonville, ASF

Labor Officer:
    Maj. Daniel L. Boland, Labor Branch, IPD

Assistant Labor Officers:
    Capt. J. B. McLure, Labor Branch, Sixth Service Command
    Lt. Lawrence M. Kearns, Labor Branch, IPD

Judge Advocate:
    Lt. Col. Paul M. Hebert, JAGD

Assistant Judge Advocate:
    Lt. Col. Thomas F. Mount, JAGD

Public Relations Officer:
    Capt. Edward J. Dudley, Industrial Services Division, BPR

Assistant Public Relations Officer:
    Lt. O. Harrelson, Industrial Services Division, BPR

Fiscal Advisor:
    Maj. F. W. Brann, Office of the Fiscal Director, ASF

Production Advisors:
    Col. George Woods, Production Division, ASF
    Maj. Charles Conley, AAF, Detroit

Cudahy Brothers Company

War Department Representative:
    Lt. Col. T. N. Gearreald, Meat Division, OQMG, New York

Deputy War Department Representative:
    Lt. Marshall N. Norseng, JAGD, Sixth Service Command

Labor Officer:
    Lt. Col. Daniel L. Boland, Labor Branch, IPD

Assistant Labor Officer:
    Maj. Frederick E. Winchester, Labor Branch, IPD

Judge Advocate:
    Maj. Thomas F. Mount, JAGD

Assistant Judge Advocate:
    Lt. Marshall N. Norseng, JAGD, Sixth Service Command

Fiscal Officer:
    Maj. Harry H. Hart, Office of the Fiscal Director, ASF

Disbursing Officer:
    Maj. David S. Combs, Office of the Fiscal Director, ASF

Public Relations Officer:
    Lt. O. Harrelson, Industrial Services Division, BPR

Montgomery Ward and Company

(Only some of the key personnel are given.)

War Department Representatives:
    Maj. Gen. Joseph W. Byron, Chief, Special Services Division, ASF
    (Dec 44–Jul 45)
    Maj. Gen. David McCoach, Jr., CG, Sixth Service Command (Jul–Oct 45)

Deputy War Department Representatives:
　　Lt. Col. Donald J. Anderson
　　Col. R. P. Kuhn

Deputy War Department Representative for Finance:
　　Col. D. H. Tyson, Office of the Fiscal Director, ASF

Disbursing Officers:
　　Lt. Col. John H. Savage, Jr., Office of the Fiscal Director, ASF
　　Capt. Robert Jacob, Office of the Fiscal Director, ASF
　　Capt. Henry F. Gillie, Office of the Fiscal Director, ASF

Judge Advocates:
　　Lt. Col. Paul M. Hebert, JAGD
　　Maj. Victor Sachse, JAGD
　　Lt. Harold F. Rouin, JAGD

Labor Officers:
　　Lt. Col. Daniel L. Boland, Labor Branch, IPD
　　Maj. V. J. O'Connell, Labor Branch, IPD
　　Lt. Joseph A. Walsh, Labor Branch, IPD
　　Lt. Frederick C. Manning, Labor Branch, Eighth Service Command
　　Maj. Frederick E. Winchester, Labor Branch, IPD
　　Lt. Col. John H. Long, Chief, Labor Branch, Third Service Command
　　Lt. Col. Victor H. Kuschel, Labor Branch, Ninth Service Command
　　Maj. David E. Ring, Labor Branch, Ninth Service Command
　　Lt. Henry Jaffe, Labor Branch, IPD

Cleveland Electric Illuminating Company

War Department Representative:
　　Col. E. A. Lynn, Chief, Cleveland Ordnance District

Judge Advocate:
　　Maj. Victor Sachse, JAGD

Labor Officer:
　　Lt. Col. James Perley, Chief, Labor Branch, Fifth Service Command

Assistant Labor Officer:
　　Capt. Irving Segal, Labor Branch, Fifth Service Command

Bingham and Garfield Railway Company

War Department Representatives:
　　Col. Wallace H. Hastings, Transportation Officer, Ninth Zone (Jan–Aug 45)
　　Lt. Col. E. J. Dryer, Jr., Transportation Corps (2–29 Aug 45)

Labor Officer:
    Maj. Clifford Ferguson, Regional Industrial Relations Officer, Ninth Zone

Judge Advocate:
    Lt. Col. Thomas F. Mount, JAGD

Assistant Judge Advocates:
    Maj. R. O. Hillis
    Capt. Charles F. Welch

Fiscal Officer:
    Capt. James R. Duffy

Public Relations Officer:
    1st Lt. T. B. Sherwin

American Enka Corporation

War Department Representative:
    Col. Curtis G. Pratt

Labor Officer:
    Capt. Lawrence M. Kearns, Labor Branch, IPD

Assistant Labor Officers:
    Lt. John Chapman, Labor Branch, IPD
    Lt. Arthur R. Donovan, AAF

Judge Advocate:
    Lt. Col. Thomas F. Mount, JAGD

Assistant Judge Advocate:
    Capt. John J. McKasy, JAGD

Public Relations Officer:
    Capt. Louis P. Ade, Industrial Services Division, BPR

Cocker Machine and Foundry Company

War Department Representative:
    Capt. Benjamin P. Anderson, Priority Division, OQMG

Labor Officer:
    Capt. John Chapman, Labor Branch, IPD

Assistant Labor Officers:
    Lt. Eugene McClaskey, Labor Branch, IPD
    Lt. Theodore Smoot, Labor Branch, IPD

Judge Advocate:
    Maj. George W. Tackabury, JAGD

Assistant Judge Advocate:
Capt. James A. Bistline, JAGD

Public Relations Officer:
Capt. Louis P. Ade, Industrial Services Division, BPR

Fiscal Officer:
Maj. Harry H. Hart, Office of the Fiscal Director, ASF

Assistant Fiscal Officer:
Lt. S. S. Zamos, Office of the Fiscal Director, ASF

Disbursing Officer:
Capt. Emanuel G. Manteuffel, Office of the Fiscal Director, ASF

Gaffney Manufacturing Company

War Department Representative:
Capt. Halpert M. Jones, Renegotiation Division, OQMG, Greenville, S.C.

Deputy War Department Representative:
Capt. Robert L. Cole, OQMG

Judge Advocate:
Lt. Col. George W. Tackabury, JAGD

Assistant Judge Advocates:
Capt. James A. Bistline, JAGD
Lt. William A. Lowe, JAGD

Labor Officer:
Lt. Theodore Smoot, Labor Branch, IPD

Public Relations Officer:
Capt. Louis P. Ade, Industrial Services Division, BPR

Purchasing and Contracting Officer:
Capt. Clarence L. McCoy, Jr., 707th Bombardment Squadron, AAF

Fiscal Advisor:
Maj. Harry H. Hart, Office of the Fiscal Director, ASF

Assistant Fiscal Advisor:
George Hogshead

Disbursing Advisor:
Maj. David S. Combs, Office of the Fiscal Director, ASF

Disbursing Officer:
Capt. Julius M. Green

Diamond Alkali Company

War Department Representative:
    Lt. Col. John Sargent, Production Division, ASF

Labor Officer:
    Lt. Col. Charles Ballon, Chief, Labor Branch, Second Service Command

Assistant Labor Officer:
    Maj. John O'Donnell, Labor Branch, IPD

Judge Advocate:
    Maj. John J. McKasy, JAGD

Fiscal Officer:
    Maj. Harry H. Hart, Office of Fiscal Director, ASF

Public Relations Officer:
    Capt. Louis P. Ade, Industrial Services Division, BPR

Mary-Leila Cotton Mills

War Department Representative:
    Capt. James D. Hammett, Readjustment Divison, ASF

Labor Officer:
    Lt. Joseph A. Walsh, Labor Branch, IPD

Assistant Labor Officer:
    Lt. George Kopolow, Labor Branch, IPD

Judge Advocate:
    Maj. George W. Tackabury, JAGD

Public Relations Officer:
    Capt. Louis P. Ade, Industrial Services Division, BPR

Fiscal Advisor:
    Capt. Robert B. Brown, Office of the Fiscal Director, ASF

Disbursing Officer:
    Capt. Emanuel G. Manteuffel, Office of the Fiscal Director, ASF

Springfield Plywood Corporation

War Department Representative:
    Lt. Col. Leroy G. Burns

Labor Officer:
    Capt. Lawrence M. Kearns, Labor Branch, IPD

Judge Advocate:
    Maj. George W. Tackabury, JAGD

Public Relations Officer:
    Capt. Frederick B. Wilmar, AAF

U.S. Rubber Company

War Department Representative:
    Lt. Col. Hervey Humlong, AAF

Labor Officer:
    Maj. John O'Donnell, Labor Branch, IPD

Executive:
    Maj. Theodore Taube, AAF

Judge Advocate:
    Lt. Col. Paul M. Hebert, JAGD

Assistant Judge Advocate:
    Lt. William A. Lowe, JAGD

Fiscal Advisor:
    Maj. Harry H. Hart, Office of the Fiscal Director, ASF

Public Relations Officer:
    Capt. Louis P. Ade, Industrial Services Division, BPR

Assistant Public Relations Officer:
    Capt. H. C. Pearson, AAF

Summary of Effect on Production or Operations in War Department Plant Seizures

(The information supplied below is based upon a brief examination of headquarters files and of the final reports of War Department representatives in the various cases. Study of the field files would furnish further supporting data.)

1. *North American Aviation*

   (token operation - labor at fault - strike in effect - duration: twenty-three days)

   Production was restored to normal after about a week. No specific data discovered on subject.

2. *Air Associates*

   (direct operation - management at fault - strike in effect - duration: two months)

   Production was quickly restored to normal and then built up to levels unprecedented in the company's history. At the end of the period production was up 30 percent and sales had materially increased. In the second month of operation net income exceeded that of the best previous month. Moreover, seizure probably prevented receivership and resulted in placing the company on a much sounder financial basis. In addition the whole organization of production and operations was materially improved. Company directors and customers were laudatory in their praise.

3. *S. A. Woods Machine Company*

   (direct operations, later changed to operation by outside company - management at fault - no strike in progress - duration: three years)

   Pertinent data not found. However, production sufficient to meet war requirements at particular moments was obtained. Some technical problems in the manufacture of shells were encountered at later dates. Varying requirements caused fluctuations in the quantity of production.

4. *Salem-Peabody Leather Manufacturing Plants*

(token operation - labor at fault - strike in progress - duration: nineteen days)

Production generally was restored to normal at all plants within ten days, and to virtually normal within several days. Delays were of a technical character growing out of damages caused by the earlier stoppage of work. See par. 3 of memorandum from Colonel Pratt to the Commanding General, ASF, dated 4 December 1943, subject: Restoration of Normal Production—War Department Possession and Operation of Thirteen Leather Manufacturing Plants in Salem-Peabody Area, in which reports of plant managers are set forth. Delays were of a technical character growing out of damages caused by earlier stoppage of work. No data on whether subsequently production rose higher than previously.

5. *Western Electric Company*

(token operation - labor at fault - strike in progress - duration: three months plus)

After a difficult two weeks in which problems were encountered in getting all the employees back to work and overcoming technical problems created by the previous stoppage of production, production was restored to normal. Subsequently, production of many items exceeded the highest monthly forecasts or exceeded the highest monthly production for many months. This was true of some of the items, particularly special wires and cables, which were most needed by the Army. See daily and weekly reports of the War Department representative to the provost marshal general. No data on general production levels of the plant over the whole period were found.

6. *American Railroads*

(token operation - labor at fault - no strike in progress - duration: three weeks)

Operations were maintained at normal levels.

7. *Fall River Textile Mills*

(token operation - labor at fault - strike in progress - duration: three weeks)

Difficulties were encountered in the first two weeks due to the problem of getting striking technicians back to work and undoing extensive damage caused by the strike, including handling of machinery by unskilled replacements. Shortly before termination of possession production varied between 86 and 100 percent of normal according to the various plant managers. See tab B of memorandum from Colonel Pratt to the Commanding General, ASF, dated 19 February 1944, subject: Termination of Government Possession—War Department Operation of Ten Textile Plants in and About Area of Fall River, Massachusetts, Under the Executive Order of the President dated 7 February 1944. At the time of termination production was virtually normal.

8. *Department of Water and Power of the City of Los Angeles*

(token operation - labor at fault - strike in progress - duration: one week)

Normal service to all war plants was restored in twenty-four hours, and to balance of city in forty-eight hours, this in spite of extensive flood storm damage requiring repairs.

9. *Ken-Rad Tube and Lamp Corporation*

(direct operation - management at fault - no strike in progress - duration: six weeks)

In spite of the refusal of key management officials to cooperate, production was raised from 1,641,896 finished acceptable tubes during the two-week period immediately preceding seizure to 1,765,763 units respectively for the next two two-week periods. See letter from the under secretary of war to Senator Chandler. Plant conditions were also generally improved.

10. *Hummer Manufacturing Division*

(token operation - management at fault - strike in progress - duration: one year and six weeks)

Production restored to normal in forty-eight hours. No further data found.

11. *Philadelphia Transportation Company*

(token operations - labor at fault - strike in progress - duration: ten days)

After two days of inability to restore transportation services, except on a very partial basis for short periods, the War Department succeeded not only in fully restoring such services but in raising them above normal levels. Absenteeism was held at an all-time low and more equipment was rolling than at any time during the previous four months.

12. *International Nickel Company*

(token operation - labor at fault - strike in progress - duration: five weeks)

No data except to the effect that production was restored to normal. See final report of Colonel Woods, War Department representative, dated 12 October 1944.

13. *Cleveland Graphite Bronze Company*

(token operation - labor at fault - strike in progress - duration: two months)

Within two days production reached pre-strike levels. No data on subsequent developments, although production was believed to have remained at about normal.

14. *Hughes Tool Company*

(token operation - management at fault - no strike in progress - duration: almost a year)

Production went decidedly upward under Army control. Although it should not be concluded that the increase was by any means entirely the result of the Army's activities, much of it was. Unrest was lessened, and the Army worked hard to recruit badly needed personnel. In the period from September 1944 to February 1945 employment increased from 7,369 to 9,123, reversing a serious downward trend. While this high level dropped slightly after V–E Day, it again rose in the summer of 1945. Production was similarly on a downward trend at the time of takeover, and this trend was also reversed, reaching the highest peak in the company's history during the period of Army occupation. See History of Operation, pp. 20–21. This was confirmed in a letter from the company to the secretary of war, dated 3 April 1945. This is also illustrated in the supplemental report of Colonel Cawthon, dated 15 February 1945, and more particularly by tab VV thereof which contains the following comparative figures on units produced or repaired:

	June 1944*	January 1945
Rockbits	16,632	20,344
Tool joints	10,188	18,618
C.B. crowns	1,847	2,270
C.B. heads	1,683	1,762
Valves	293	347
Drill collars	23	42
Flash welds	5,011	7,617

*Before intermittent strikes affected production.

15. *Twentieth Century Brass Company*

  (direct operation - management at fault - strike in progress - duration:
  five months plus)

In spite of the fact of the prior protracted strike that had resulted in the dispersal of many key employees, production was quickly restored to normal and then raised to unprecedented levels. This can be illustrated by a few graphic figures. The company's average monthly shipment for the two years preceding the strike was approximately 141,000 units, and the highest monthly shipment that it had ever attained was 170,000 units. The average War Department's monthly shipment exceeded this peak, reaching 173,000 units (in spite of above difficulties at the outset), and in one month rose to 196,000 units. The increase amounted to about 140 percent. Moreover, in spite of concentrating almost exclusively on high priority war business rather than on some of the more profitable nonessential items that the company had also produced, average monthly net income during War Department possession rose from the prior two-year average of $36,000 to $38,200. Rejection rates were better, backlogs were reduced or eliminated, deliveries were met on time, and more high priority war goods were delivered.

16. *Farrell-Cheek Steel Corporation*

  (token operation - management at fault - strike in progress - duration:
  eleven months)

Within less than a week production was normal or better than normal. See preliminary report of Colonel Riebe, War Department representative, dated 3 October 1944. Within thirty days a serious order backlog had been eliminated. Thereafter, production climbed from the company's all-time maximum monthly production of 1,270 tons to monthly production in February of 1,324.5 tons, with 25 percent (159) fewer employees. All schedules were maintained, and productive capacity was developed that exceeded the work available. New war business was sought, and virtually the entire operation was placed on high priority war work. Scrap records showed an efficiency above, and scrap experience on efficiency below, the normal average for the industry as a whole. In general, efficiency of operations was increased, and many commendatory letters were received from purchasers. See final report of Colonel Riebe, dated 23 September 1945.

17. *Fairport, Painesville, and Eastern Railroad*

  (direct military intervention - labor at fault - strike in progress - duration:
  three days)

Service fully restored in a few hours.

18. *Toledo MESA Strike*

(token operation - labor at fault - strike in progress - duration: two days)

Strike promptly terminated and production restored fully as soon as men returned to work.

19. *Cudahy Brothers Company*

(token operation - management at fault - no strike in progress - duration: nine and a half months)

Production was raised to higher levels than normal and shipments of produce went to higher priorities. Shipments to the armed forces increased over prior years. A set-aside deficit of 2,600,000 pounds was changed to a total of 500,000 pounds in excess. Quotas were exceeded in boneless beef. In the boneless beef department productivity went from 76 percent of standard to 126 percent and production per man-hour from 136 pounds to 224 pounds. In the fresh pork processing department the comparable figures were 70 percent to 149 percent and 87 pounds to 281 pounds; and in the processed ham department, 88 percent to 121 percent and 72 pounds to 117 pounds. These changes could not, of course, by any means be entirely attributed to the Army, but a substantial part was due to Army control. One responsible factor was the introduction of an incentive system that both management and the union stated could not and would not have been successfully placed in effect without the presence and extensive assistance of the Army. See par. 5 of final report by Col. Gearreald, dated 31 August 1945. Production reached peak of company's history. See Ohly for file, dated 30 January 1945, subject: Cudahy.

20. *Montgomery Ward and Company*

(direct operation of a sort - management at fault - strike inprogress at a few properties - duration: ten and a half months)

Operations were promptly restored to normal. No reliable data has been located, although such data is known to be available, showing comparative sales and income figures. It is known that business at the seized properties increased over that for previous years. This was, of course, largely the product of business conditions, although increased sales at some of the properties, particularly those in Detroit, have been in part reliably attributed to the fact of the Army's presence.

21. *Cleveland Electric Illuminating Company*

(token operation - labor at fault - strike in progress - duration: two days minus)

Service restored to normal in a few hours. See final report of Colonel Lynn, dated 15 January 1945.

22. *Bingham and Garfield Railway Company*

(token operation - labor at fault - strike in progress - duration: seven months plus)

Service immediately restored to normal and maintained at that level. See final report of Colonel Dryer, dated 29 November 1945.

23. *American Enka Corporation*

(token operation - labor at fault - strike in progress - duration: three and a half months)

Production was restored to normal as soon as the long and arduous task of cleaning out continuous-process machinery affected by the strike could be completed. This task was completed in record time. Thereafter production was maintained at about 100 percent of capacity. See par. 4 of part I of supplemental and final report of Colonel Pratt, dated 14 June 1945.

24. *Cocker Machine and Foundry Company*

(token operation - management at fault - strike in progress - duration: three months plus)

Production was restored and was raised to higher than normal levels and was directed to higher priorities. Outstanding job done in expediting the production of three high-priority high-tenacity rayon manufacturing machines for American Viscose Company. Delivery schedules that could not have been met by a two-month's margin under company operations were beaten. See par. 2b of final report of Captain Anderson, dated 31 August 1945.

25. *Gaffney Manufacturing Company*

(direct operation - management at fault - strike in progress - duration: three months plus)

Production was quickly restored to the level preceding the strike. Then the sharp downward trend of production under company management was halted, and substantial increases were registered. Average weekly production under company management had dropped from 186,855 pounds and 1,044,532 yards of cloth in January 1944 to 125,971 pounds and 710,345 yards in May 1945. Under the Army it rose again to a weekly production of 170,751 pounds and 983,561 yards for the week of 26 August 1945, or more than 25 percent. This was the highest weekly production since March 1944. It would have exceeded the previous company maximum had operations continued a few weeks more. All this was accomplished while equaling the loom efficiency and percentage of first quality cloth of the company during the previous six months. See par. 18 of interim report of Captain Jones, dated 25 July 1945, and par. 2a of supplemental report, dated 17 September 1945.

26. *Mary-Leila Cotton Mills*

(token operation - management at fault - strike in progress - duration: two months)

Production was rapidly restored to normal. Production during War Department possession was 98.2 percent of the normal preceding the strike in terms of yardage and 98.7 percent in terms of pounds. The slightly lower rate is to be accounted for by the normal summer slack in this plant and in the particular industry. See supplemental and final report of Captain Hammett, dated 30 August 1945.

27. *Diamond Alkali Company*

(token operation - labor at fault - strike in progress - duration: one month)

As soon as damage caused by the cessation of operations to continuous-process machinery could be repaired, operations went to normal or above normal. See Exhibit K to final report of Colonel Sargent, dated August 1945.

28. *Springfield Plywood Corporation*

(token operation - labor at fault - strike in progress - duration: one month plus)

Production was quickly restored to nearly normal. Average hourly production for the entire period and the average output per man was slightly lower under Army control than was normal immediately prior to the strike, but this was due to a change in the type of production to increase "exterior's production" in response to war needs. In several 24-hour periods, particularly toward the end, production was greater (even on this changed basis) than at any time in the company's previous history. See par. 7 and tabs L–1 and L–2 of interim and final report of Colonel Burns, dated 25 September 1945.

29. *U.S. Rubber Company*

(token operation - labor at fault - strike in progress - duration: two and a half months)

Production was restored to, and generally maintained at or above, normal. However, holidays surrounding V–J Day, temporary adjustments because of cutbacks, and reconversion changes affected production adversely in late August and early September 1945. From then on production increased and reached 24-hour peaks that exceeded any since Pearl Harbor. See tab B of final report of Colonel Humlong, dated 12 October 1945.

Bibliographical Note

John Ohly's work on War Department plant seizures remains the definitive history of the subject. Except for a study by political scientist John L. Blackman entitled *Presidential Seizures in Labor Disputes* (Cambridge, Mass.: Harvard University Press, 1967), a comprehensive work on the legal aspects of all federal seizures of private businesses and industries, nothing has been written on the topic since World War II. With the expansion of the study of labor and military history in the last three decades, however, a number of pertinent books and journal articles dealing with general aspects of wartime civil-military and labor-industrial relations have been published. Collectively, they provide a useful historical context for this study. Furthermore, a larger number of older works on various aspects of labor relations of the period and on the activities of various wartime government agencies still remain important.

The National Archives and Records Administration in Washington, D.C., has in its custody pertinent documents belonging to both federal civilian and military organizations involved in the emergency operation of plants under federal authority. For those individuals interested in doing further research from these primary sources, I have included their locations in my explanatory footnotes in the appropriate chapters.

The documents used by Ohly in preparing this volume are now held by the Modern Military Reference Branch of the National Archives. Researchers will find that Entries 169–79, especially Entry 177, Industrial Personnel Division and Service Command Reports, Record Group 160, Records of Headquarters, Army Service Forces, contain the bulk of surviving materials. The records of the Industrial Personnel Division are arranged by case and consolidate relevant documents from many federal civilian and military agencies. In the same record group Entries 81–83 and 89–90 hold the documents belonging to the Control Division, ASF, with Entry 95 covering the seizures on a case-by-case basis. Although most of the documents used by Ohly were transferred to the Army Service Forces before the end of the war, many of the records concerning specific plant seizures remain in Under Secretary Patterson's correspondence and papers, particularly in Entries 141–45 in Record Group 107, Records of the Office of the Secretary of War. In this same record group are the papers and correspondence of several of Ohly's colleagues, including Brig. Gen. Edward S. Greenbaum (Entry 151), Julius H. Amberg (Entries 153–55), and Edward F. McGrady (Entry 157), as well as records dealing exclusively with the S. A. Woods seizure (Entries 172–73).

Ohly's manuscript, with appendixes consisting of over one thousand pages of documents, is available for research purposes from the Historical Records Branch of the U.S. Army Center of Military History in Washington, D.C. Researchers interested in other aspects of Ohly's twenty-eight years of government service should consult his papers, part of the permanent collection of the Harry S. Truman Presidential Library in Independence, Missouri.

For those seeking secondary sources relevant to the events described in this volume, many germane works exist. On the attitudes of American business see Howell Harris' *The Right To Manage: Industrial Relations Policies of American Business in the 1940s* (Madison: University of Wisconsin Press, 1982). On labor relations in the United States between the wars a good starting point would be two works by Irving Bernstein entitled *The Lean Years: A History of the American Worker* (Boston: Houghton Mifflin, 1960), dealing with the period 1920–33, and *The Turbulent Years: A History of the American Worker, 1933–1941* (Boston: Houghton Mifflin, 1970), followed by Walter Galenson's *The CIO Challenge to the AFL: A History of the American Labor Movement, 1935–1941* (Cambridge, Mass.: Harvard University Press, 1960). A collection of essays entitled *Labor and the New Deal*, ed. David E. Cronon (Chicago: Rand McNally, 1963), combined with the above works, provides a background on the state of labor organization before the war and on President Roosevelt's labor policies, as does another entitled *The New Deal*, ed. John Braeman, Robert H. Bremner, and David Brody, 2 vols. (Columbus: Ohio State University Press, 1975), vol. 1, *The National Level* (1975). David Brody's essay in this collection, "The New Deal and World War II," is especially useful.

These general works and essays complement earlier publications, such as Joseph Rosenfarb's *The National Labor Policy and How It Works* (New York: Harper and Row, 1940), Harold W. Metz's *The Labor Policy of the Federal Government* (Washington, D.C.: Brookings Institution, 1945), Howard S. Kaltenborn's *Government Adjustment of Labor Disputes* (Chicago: Foundation Press, 1943), and an official statement of federal labor policy for American workers by the U.S. Office of Education entitled *The Worker, His Job, and His Government: An Introduction to Federal Labor Law* (Washington, D.C.: Government Printing Office, 1942). Several other studies are useful, including Milton Derber and Edwin Young's *Labor and the New Deal* (Madison: University of Wisconsin Press, 1957), Derber's *The American Ideal of Industrial Democracy, 1865–1965* (Champaign-Urbana: University of Illinois Press, 1970), and Harry A. Millis and Emily Brown Clark's *From the Wagner Act to Taft-Hartley: A Study of National Labor Policy and Relations* (Chicago: University of Chicago Press, 1950). Newer works include: James R. Green's *The World of the Worker: Labor in Twentieth Century America* (New York: Hill and Wang, 1980), David Brody's *Workers in Industrial America: Essays on the Twentieth Century Struggle* (New York: Oxford University Press, 1980), Mike Davis' *Prisoners of the American Dream* (London: Verso, 1993), and Sally M. Miller and Daniel A. Cornford, eds., *American Labor in the Era of World War II* (Wesport, Conn.: Greenwood, 1995).

The war years witnessed an unprecedented growth of organized labor, coupled with a corresponding increase in labor militancy. For the extent of labor unrest at this time see P. K. Edwards' *Strikes in the United States, 1881–1974* (Oxford: Oxford University Press, 1981), and Rosa L. Swafford's *Wartime Record of Strikes and Lockouts, 1940–1945* (Washington, D.C.: Government Printing Office, 1946). For a general overview of wartime organized labor see James B. Atleson's *Labor and the Wartime State: Labor Relations During World War II* (Urbana: University of Illinois Press, 1998); Steve Rosswurm, ed., *The CIO's Left-Led Unions* (New Brunswick, N.J.: Rutgers University Press, 1992); Joshua Freedman's "Delivering the Goods: Industrial Unionism During World War II," *Labor History* 19 (1978): 570–93; and Joel Seidman's older but still useful *American Labor From Defense to Reconversion* (Chicago: University of Chicago Press, 1953). Robert H. Ziegar's book *American Workers, American Unions, 1920–1985* (Baltimore: Johns Hopkins University Press, 1988) provides a more recent account of organized labor. Martin Glaberman's *Wartime Strikes: The Struggle Against the No-Strike Pledge in the UAW During World War II* (Detroit: Berwick Press, 1980) and Nelson Lichtenstein's *Labor's War at Home: The CIO in World War II* (Cambridge, Mass.: Harvard University Press, 1982) are histories of specific labor groups during the war, the latter being the published version of Lichtenstein's Ph.D. dissertation "Industrial Unionism Under the No-Strike Pledge: A Study of the CIO During the Second World War" (University of California–Berkeley, 1974). Lichtenstein also has examined other aspects of the American labor movement during the war years in "Ambiguous Legacy: The Union Security Problem During World War II," *Labor History* 18 (1977): 214–38; "Defending the No-Strike Pledge: CIO Politics During World War II," *Radical America* 9 (1975): 49–76; and "Auto Worker Militancy and the Structure of Factory Life, 1937–1955," *Journal of American History* 67 (1980): 335–53. For a further view of labor's assertiveness during the period see James R. Green's "Fighting on Two Fronts: Working Class Militancy in the 1940s," *Radical America* 9 (1975): 7–48.

For information on the War Department's relations with American industry and the problems associated with manpower and economic and industrial mobilization, see Byron Fairchild and Jonathan Grossman's *The Army and Industrial Manpower* (Washington, D.C.: Office of the Chief of Military History, 1959), Marvin A. Kreidberg and Henry G. Merton's *History of Military Mobilization in the United States Army, 1775–1945* (1955; reprint ed., Washington, D.C.: U.S. Army Center of Military History, 1984), and R. Elberton Smith's *The Army and Economic Mobilization* (Washington, D.C.: Office of the Chief of Military History, 1959). These official histories are the most comprehensive studies on the above-mentioned topics. In particular, Fairchild and Grossman discuss many of the cases examined by Ohly within the larger context of military-labor relations during the war.

Other official histories offer more specific information about the relationships between the various Army branches and industries. For the aircraft industry and the Army Air Forces see Irving Brinton Holley, Jr.'s "The Management of Technological Change: Aircraft Production in the United States During World War II," *Aerospace Historian* 22 (Winter/December 1975): 161–65, and his *Buying Aircraft: Materiel Procurement for the Army Air Forces* (Washington, D.C.: Office of the Chief of Military History, 1964), which is the standard work on the subject. For the official Army view concerning labor-industrial relations and procurement experiences of Army ordnance, quartermaster, and transportation personnel see portions of Harry C. Thomson and Lida Mayo's *The Ordnance Department: Procurement and Supply* (Washington, D.C.: Office of the Chief of Military History, 1960), Erna Risch's *The Quartermaster Corps: Organization, Supply, and Services*, vol. 1 (Washington, D.C.: Office of the Chief of Military History, 1953), and Chester Wardlow's *The Transportation Corps: Responsibilities, Organization, and Operations* (Washington, D.C.: Office of the Chief of Military History, 1951). John D. Millett's *The Organization and Role of the Army Service Forces* (Washington, D.C.: Office of the Chief of Military History, 1954) remains the most comprehensive work describing the organization and functioning of the Army Service Forces and its predecessor organization, the Services of Supply. It provides a different viewpoint to many of the cases covered by Ohly, offers key indicators as to the locations of additional documents on plant seizure cases, and includes material on the labor branches of the Office of the Under Secretary of War and the Civilian (later Industrial) Personnel Division, SOS (later ASF), where Ohly worked. Although rare, the War Department manuals used by the CPD and IPD members when conducting seizures are valuable sources on actual procedures and processes followed. Several editions were produced, none of which is available in published form. The version by the War Department, Judge Advocate General's Department, entitled "Emergency Operation of Industrial Facilities," ASF-EOIF-44, 23 September 1944, is available at the U.S. Army Center of Military History in Washington, D.C., and at the U.S. Army Military History Institute in Carlisle Barracks, Pennsylvania.

For other works on civil-military-industrial relations from the First World War period through the Second World War see the works of Paul A. C. Koistinen, which include: *The Hammer and the Sword: Labor, the Military, and Industrial Mobilization, 1920–1945* (New York: Arno Press, 1979), the published version of his Ph.D. dissertation; "The Industrial-Military Complex in Historical Perspective: World War I," *Business History Review* 41 (1967): 378–403; "The 'Industrial-Military Complex' in Historical Perspective: The InterWar Years," *Journal of American History* 56 (1970): 819–39; and "Mobilizing the World War II Economy: Labor and the Industrial-Military Alliance," *Pacific Historical Review* 42 (1973): 443–78. Useful information on the wartime American aircraft industry may be found in Wesley F. Craven and James L. Cates, eds., *Army Air Forces in World War II*, 7 vols. (Chicago: University of Chicago Press, 1948–58), especially vol. 6, *Men and Planes* (1955); John B. Rae's *Climb to Greatness: The American Aircraft Industry, 1920–1960* (Cambridge: MIT Press, 1968); and Allen A. P. and Betty V. H. Schneider's *Industrial Relations in the California Aircraft Industry* (Berkeley: University of California Press, 1956).

I found *The Biographical Dictionary of American Labor* and *Who's Who in Labor* very helpful for preparing biographical sketches of labor leaders prominent a half century ago, while Leo Troy's *Trade Union Membership, 1897–1962* (New York: National Bureau of Economic Research, Columbia University Press, 1965) provided vital information and statistics on the strength of organized labor during the war years.

Of inestimable value in determining the authority and functions of the many wartime government agencies were *The Greenwood Encyclopedia of American Institutions: Government Agencies* and, for the years 1941–45, *The United States Government Manual*. Produced on a regular basis, often biannually, by the Bureau of the Budget's Division of Public Inquiries, the manuals show the changing nature of the government during wartime.

Among the many useful works on the emergency and regulatory agencies created by the Executive Branch to administer the war effort are U.S. Civilian Production Administration's *Industrial Mobilization for War: History of the War Production Board and Predecessor Agencies, 1940–1945* (Washington, D.C.: Government Printing Office, 1947), U.S. Office of Defense Transportation's *Civilian War Transport: A Record of the Control of Domestic Traffic Operations by the Office of Defense Transportation, 1941–1946* (Washington, D.C.: Government Printing Office, 1946), U.S. Department of Labor, Bureau of Labor Statistics' *Report on the Work of the National Defense Mediation Board* (Washington, D.C.: Government Printing Office, 1942), Richard J. Purcell's *Labor Policies of the National Defense Advisory Commission and the Office of Production Management, May 1940 to April 1942* (Washington, D.C.: Government Printing Office, 1946), Herman M. Somers' *Presidential Agency, OWMR: The Office of War Mobilization and Reconversion* (Cambridge, Mass.: Harvard University Press, 1950), James A. Gross' *The Making of the National Labor Relations Board* (Albany: State University of New York Press, 1974) and *The Reshaping of the National Labor Relations Board* (Albany: State University of New York Press, 1981), and Fred Witney's older work *Wartime Experiences of the National Labor Relations Board, 1941–1945* (Urbana: University of Illinois Press, 1949).

List of Abbreviations

AAF	Army Air Forces
AFofL	American Federation of Labor
AGF	Army Ground Forces
App(s)	Appendix(es)
ASF	Army Service Forces
Asst	Assistant
Atty	Attorney
BPR	Bureau of Public Relations
Br	Branch
Bros.	Brothers
BRT	Brotherhood of Railroad Trainmen
CG	Commanding general
CIO	Congress of Industrial Organizations
Co.	Company
CO	Commanding officer
Comdr	Commander
CofOrd	Chief of Ordnance
Corp.	Corporation
CPD	Civilian Personnel Division
CofS	Chief of Staff
Dep	Deputy
Dir	Director
Dist	District
Div	Division
DPC	Defense Plant Corporation
Encl(s)	Enclosure(s)
EO	Executive Order
EST	Eastern Standard Time

FBI	Federal Bureau of Investigation
FEPC	Fair Employment Practice, Committee on
FHA	Federal Housing Authority
GAO	General Accounting Office
Gen	General
GO	General Order
IBEW	International Brotherhood of Electrical Workers
IFLWU	International Fur and Leather Workers Union
IFWU	International Fur Workers Union
Intel	Intelligence
IPD	Industrial Personnel Division
JAG	Judge advocate general
JAGD	Judge Advocate General's Department
Ltr(s)	Letter(s)
Memo(s)	Memorandum(a)
MESA	Mechanics Educational Society of America
Mil	Military
NARA	National Archives and Records Administration
n.d.	no date
NDMB	National Defense Mediation Board
NHA	National Housing Agency
NLRB	National Labor Relations Board
NWLB	National War Labor Board
ODT	Office of Defense Transportation
Off	Officer, Office
OEM	Office of Emergency Management
OES	Office of Economic Stabilization
OPM	Office of Production Management
Opns	Operations
Ord	Ordnance
OQMG	Office of the Quartermaster General

OPA	Office of Price Administration
ORC	Order of Railway Conductors
OSD	Office of the Secretary of Defense
OUSW	Office of the Under Secretary of War
OWMR	Office of War Mobilization and Reconversion
PAW	Petroleum Administration for War
PMG	Provost marshal general
Prelim	Preliminary
Rep.	Representative
Req.	Requisition
RFC	Reconstruction Finance Corporation
Rpt(s)	Report(s)
Sec	Secretary, Section
Sen	Senator
SOS	Services of Supply
Telecon(s)	Telephone conversation(s)
Telg	Telegram
Treas	Treasurer
UAW	United Automobile Workers of America
UMW	United Mine Workers of America
USACMH	U.S. Army Center of Military History
USWA	United Steel Workers Association
WMC	War Manpower Commission
WPB	War Production Board
WSA	War Shipping Administration

Index

PIN : 075901–000

Made in the USA
Middletown, DE
02 March 2025

72092451R00225